Medicine and Justice

CW01064708

This monograph makes a major new contribution to the historiography of criminal justice in England and Wales by focusing on the intersection of the history of law and crime with medical history. It does this through the lens provided by one group of historical actors, medical professionals who gave evidence in criminal proceedings. They are the means of illuminating the developing methods and personnel associated with investigating and prosecuting crime in the eighteenth and nineteenth centuries, when two linchpins of modern society, centralised policing and the adversarial criminal trial, emerged and matured. The book is devoted to two central questions: what did medical practitioners contribute to the investigation of serious violent crime in the period 1700 to 1914, and what impact did this have on the process of criminal justice? Drawing on the details of 2,600 cases of infanticide, murder and rape which occurred in central England, Wales and London, the book offers a comparative long-term perspective on medico-legal practice – that is, what doctors actually did when they were faced with a body that had become the object of a criminal investigation. It argues that medico-legal work developed in tandem with and was shaped by the needs of two evolving processes: pre-trial investigative procedures dominated successively by coroners, magistrates and the police; and criminal trials in which lawyers moved from the periphery to the centre of courtroom proceedings. In bringing together for the first time four groups of specialists – doctors, coroners, lawyers and police officers – this study offers a new interpretation of the processes that shaped the modern criminal justice system.

Katherine D. Watson is a Reader in History at Oxford Brookes University and a Fellow of the Royal Historical Society. Her research interests focus on areas where medicine, crime and the law intersect, including the history of infanticide and crimes against children, forensic medicine and science, and an unusual form of assault known as vitriol throwing. She is the author of *Poisoned Lives: English Poisoners and their Victims* (2004) and *Forensic Medicine in Western Society: A History* (2011).

Routledge Studies in the History of Science, Technology and Medicine

Urban Histories of Science
Making Knowledge in the City, 1820–1940
Edited by Oliver Hochadel and Agustí Nieto-Galan

Pioneering Health in London, 1935–2000
The Peckham Experiment
David Kuchenbuch

Soviet Science and Engineering in the Shadow of the Cold War
Hiroshi Ichikawa

Cold Science
Environmental Knowledge in the North American Arctic During the Cold War
Stephen Bocking and Daniel Heidt

Medical Memories and Experiences in Postwar East Germany
Treatments of the Past
Markus Wahl

Politics, Statistics and Weather Forecasting, 1840–1910
Taming the Weather
Aitor Anduaga

Social Class and Mental Illness in Northern Europe
Edited by Petteri Pietikäinen and Jesper Vaczy Kragh

Medicine and Justice
Medico-Legal Practice in England and Wales, 1700–1914
Katherine D. Watson

For the full list of titles in the series, please visit: www.routledge.com/Routledge-Studies-in-the-History-of-Science-Technology-and-Medicine/book-series/HISTSCI

Medicine and Justice

Medico-Legal Practice in England
and Wales, 1700–1914

Katherine D. Watson

Routledge
Taylor & Francis Group

LONDON AND NEW YORK

First published 2020
by Routledge
2 Park Square, Milton Park, Abingdon, Oxon OX14 4RN

and by Routledge
605 Third Avenue, New York, NY 10017

First issued in paperback 2021

Routledge is an imprint of the Taylor & Francis Group, an informa business

British Library Cataloguing-in-Publication Data
A catalogue record for this book is available from the British Library

Library of Congress Cataloging-in-Publication Data
A catalog record for this book has been requested

ISBN 13: 978-1-03-208257-8 (pbk)
ISBN 13: 978-1-4724-5412-6 (hbk)

Typeset in Bembo
by Apex CoVantage, LLC

MIX
Paper from
responsible sources
FSC
www.fsc.org
FSC® C013985

Printed in the United Kingdom
by Henry Ling Limited

Contents

List of figures   ix

List of tables   xi

List of abbreviations   xiii

Currency   xv

Dates   xvii

Preface and acknowledgments   xix

1   Introduction: the medico-legal landscape   1

Medico-legal history: the story so far 5
Criminal justice: process and procedure 7
Aims, methods and sources 12
Argument and structure 18

2   Medical education and forensic medicine   33

Teaching and learning forensic medicine: an overview 34
The late eighteenth century 39
London 1836–1837 42
Leeds c.1869–1888 47
Edinburgh 1900 54
Conclusion 63

3   Locating patterns of medico-legal provision   73

The criminal offences: number and location 74
    The coroner's officer 81
Medical evidence in criminal trials: statistical overview 85
Medical witnesses 94
    Police surgeons 100
    Medical coroners 103
    Female medical witnesses 106

Homicide in medico-legal practice: statistical overview 110
   Cause of death 111
   Medicalised testimony by lay witnesses 118
   Specialist evidence and expert witnesses 121
Explaining patterns: crime, medicine and policing in 1881 130
Conclusion 132

4   **Infant murder in medico-legal practice**   143

   Characteristics of infant murderers 145
   Forensic characteristics of infant murder 154
      The (crime) scene 157
      The mother 158
      The infant 163
   The case against Jane Williams, Montgomeryshire, 1734 173
      Lay women and medical men 174
   The trial of Martha John, Pembrokeshire, 1808 175
      The judge's perspective 179
   The importance of plain speaking: the trial of Hannah Mottram,
      Cheshire, 1833 183
      The jury's perspective 185
   Conclusion 188

5   **Crime (scene) investigation: expertise in action**   199

   Examining and documenting murder scenes 202
      The murder of Francis Longuet, 1817 206
      Medical investigator: Regina v. John Isaac Jones, 1859 208
      Diagnosing murder? The Kidwelly tragedy, Carmarthenshire,
         1881 209
      A modern investigation: the Herefordshire murder, 1885 211
      "The position of Mrs Griffiths as I found her": Regina v.
         Thomas Henry Bevan, 1887 212
   Scientific aids to investigation 215
   Expertise and expert status: fees and costs 221
   Sufficient charge for the services rendered 226
   Conclusion 232

6   **Conclusion: medicine and justice**   243

   Appendix 1: Chronology of events and statutes affecting medical
      and legal practice   249
   Appendix 2: Medical practitioners in Wales, 1783   267

Appendix 3: Introduction of the new police into London, Wales and
  the counties of the Oxford Circuit   271

    Rural policing, 1855 273
    Police strength, Counties and Boroughs, 1899 274

Appendix 4: Coroners trained as surgeons or physicians   275
Appendix 5: Glossary of medical and legal terms   279
Bibliography   285
Index   307

Figures

1.1 Stages in the process of criminal justice, from crime discovery to trial 8

1.2 Map of England and Wales, showing the 22 counties included in this study 14

2.1 The chest cavity of a stillborn child 44

2.2 Changes in the volume and situation of infant lungs caused by the admission of air 45

2.3 Extract from student notes on rape, University of Edinburgh, 16 June 1900 61

3.1 Use of medical evidence in homicide cases, 1699–1914 88

3.2 Unknown or non-use of medical evidence in homicide cases, 1699–1914 89

3.3 Use of selective medical evidence in homicide cases, 1699–1914 116

4.1 Use of the hydrostatic lung test by circuit, 1720–1912 165

4.2 Use of the hydrostatic lung test as a proportion of all infant murder cases, 1701–1912 166

5.1 Drawing of wounds inflicted on Francis Longuet, 1817 206

5.2 Plan of the scene of the murder at Kidwelly, 1881 210

5.3 Scene of the murder at 37 Henry Street, Church Coppenhall, drawn in April 1887 213

First published 2020
by Routledge
2 Park Square, Milton Park, Abingdon, Oxon OX14 4RN

and by Routledge
605 Third Avenue, New York, NY 10017

First issued in paperback 2021

Routledge is an imprint of the Taylor & Francis Group, an informa business

Publisher's Note
The publisher has gone to great lengths to ensure the quality of this
reprint but points out that some imperfections in the original copies may
be apparent.

British Library Cataloguing-in-Publication Data
A catalogue record for this book is available from the British Library

Library of Congress Cataloging-in-Publication Data
A catalog record for this book has been requested

ISBN: 978-1-4724-5412-6 (hbk)
ISBN: 978-1-003-00980-1 (ebk)

Typeset in Bembo
by Apex CoVantage, LLC

ISBN 13: 978-1-03-209885-2 (pbk)
ISBN 13: 978-1-4724-1552-3 (hbk)

Tables

3.1	Number of cases by Assize Circuit	74
3.2	Location of offences, by county	76
3.3	Wales – number of cases before and after the abolition of the Court of Great Sessions	77
3.4	Principal location of offences, by town	77
3.5	Type of offence, by circuit	79
3.6	Context in which criminal offences occurred	80
3.7	Relationship of prosecutor to victim, by circuit	82
3.8	The use of medical evidence, by type of offence	86
3.9	Proportional use of medical evidence in homicide cases, by circuit	87
3.10	Specialist practitioners, by circuit	95
3.11	Surgeons involved in four or more forensic cases	96
3.12	Midwives as medico-legal witnesses	107
3.13	Main cause of death in cases of homicide	112
3.14	Main cause of death in cases of homicide, by circuit	113
3.15	Cause of death – percentage by age of homicide victim	114
3.16	Use of selective medical evidence in homicide cases, 1831–1914	117
3.17	Medicalised testimony by lay witnesses per circuit, 1699–1914	119
3.18	Proportion of medicalised testimony by lay witnesses, 1699–1914	120
3.19	Use of a formal medical defence of insanity in homicide trials, by circuit	122
3.20	Use of a medical defence, by circuit and offence	124
3.21	Proportion of medical defences, 1699–1914	125
3.22	The presence of expert witnesses in criminal cases over time	127
3.23	Specialist tests, by circuit	128
3.24	Use of multiple specialist tests, by circuit	129
3.25	Number of police, medical practitioners, and homicide indictments in 1881, in order of decreasing population	131

3.26	Murders reported by the police in England and Wales, 1880–1881	132
4.1	Perpetrators of infant murder	147
4.2	The context for cases of infant murder	147
4.3	The context for cases of infant murder: perpetrator's sex and relationship to victim	148
4.4	Trial verdicts in cases of infant murder	149
4.5	Trial verdicts according to the defendant's relationship to the victim	150
4.6	Trial verdicts according to the victim's age	152
4.7	Questions and indicative signs in the medico-legal investigation of infant murder	155
4.8	Midwives and surgeons in trials for infant murder, 1699–1914	159
4.9	Insanity in trials for infant murder, 1699–1914	161
4.10	Verdicts in trials of insane mothers for infant murder	162
4.11	Medical evidence derived from the examination of infant lungs	168
4.12	Cause of death in cases of infant murder	171
4.13	Trial verdicts according to the main causes of death in cases of newborn child murder	172
5.1	Regina v. J. I. Jones, important points proved by William Griffin, 1859	209

Abbreviations

ASSI	assize records at TNA
BMJ	*British Medical Journal*
c.	a chapter in a statute
d.	pence
fols.	folios
GMC	General Medical Council (General Council of Medical Education and Registration of the United Kingdom)
GP	general practitioner
GS	Great Sessions
HMP	Her/His Majesty's Prison
JP	justice of the peace
LSA	Licentiate of The Society of Apothecaries
MO	medical officer
MOH	Medical Officer of Health
MRCP	Member of the Royal College of Physicians
MRCS	Member of the Royal College of Surgeons
MRCSE	Member of the Royal College of Surgeons of Edinburgh
n.d.	no date
NLW	The National Library of Wales, Aberystwyth
OBP	Old Bailey Proceedings
r.	recto
s.	section
s.	shillings
Sgt	Sergeant
ss.	sections
st.	statute
TNA	The National Archives, Kew
v.	verso; versus

Currency

$12d. = 1s.$
$20s. = £1$
$21s. = 1$ guinea

Dates

Months have been abbreviated: Jan; Feb; Mar; Apr; May; Jun; Jul; Aug; Sep; Oct; Nov; Dec. Dates in the old style have been corrected so that the New Year begins on January 1.

Preface and acknowledgments

Life and death are objects too important to be sported with in the manner they are sometimes: nor should the valuable connections of our fellow-citizens be ever sacrificed to the ignorance of the faculty, the caprice of a court, or the artifices of revenge and disappointment.

Samuel Farr, *Elements of Medical Jurisprudence* (London: T. Becket, 1788), p. vi

This project has had a long gestation, and along the way its focus has shifted from medicine to law and from medical practices to legal processes; it has expanded to encompass not only doctors but coroners, lawyers and police officers in order to arrive at a central point of clarity. In essence, what I discovered in researching and writing this book – what I should have yet somehow did not recognise when I first set out – is that the history of medico-legal practice is not simply a story of doctors in the service of the law, nor even purely a history of medicine and its relationship with the law. It is more than a history of forensic medicine (or science) as a developing academic discipline. Rather, it is an integral part of criminal justice history, and thus more complicated, challenging and exciting, albeit frequently more mundane, than a history of the professional development of the law, medicine or policing, or of a concept such as 'expertise'.[1] What this book sets out to demonstrate is that since the early eighteenth century, medical, legal and policing practices have been inextricably intertwined in the common law procedures that govern the investigation of serious violent crime. Initially led by coroners and magistrates, these procedures came increasingly under the control of the police, but doctors were always part of the process. Furthermore, the connections between medicine, law and crime investigation in England and Wales before the First World War were more extensive and better developed than the historiography of individual areas of study has previously acknowledged. Medico-legal work was one facet of eighteenth- and nineteenth-century medical practice – not quotidian, to be sure, but not unusual or exclusive.

Many of the issues raised by the medical contribution to crime investigation suggest that this is an area of academic study with a promising future, not least because the archival foundation for such scholarship is so rich. The records created by the legal system, albeit skewed to a central purpose – prosecution – offer a still largely untapped window into the lives of real people who lived and died in communities large and small throughout England and Wales. Despite a certain amount of 'legalese', the depositions created by coroners and magistrates deliver a palpable appreciation of deponents' emotions and experiences – from shock, to annoyance, anger, fear, sadness, bravery, intellectual curiosity, professionalism, confusion, indignation, resignation and, just occasionally, the downright bizarre. I hope, therefore, that this book will stimulate further scholarly research on the relationship between medicine, law and crime and on other aspects of history that legal records can illuminate.

This book would not have come to fruition without the support of a number of people and institutions. I would like to acknowledge with gratitude The Wellcome Trust, whose financial support in the early years of the project (grant reference 082207/Z/07) was an invaluable stimulus not just to this research but also to my academic career, subsequently fostered by Oxford Brookes University and our brilliant History team. The Cambridge Group for the History of Population and Social Structure provided the data that I used to create the map in the Introduction. I wish especially to thank the staff of The National Archives at Kew and The National Library of Wales in Aberystwyth, where I spent many exciting hours in the Map Room and the South Reading Room, respectively.

Visits to Aber would not have been the same without Richard and Eirlys Huws, whose hospitality and enthusiasm for Welsh history made my research trips more like mini holidays; special thanks go to Richard for attempting to teach me some Welsh and for furnishing translations upon request. Thanks are also due to Valerie Johnston and Carmen Bonnell, who provided invaluable research assistance; Daniel Grey, for sharing his unpublished research; Chris Milroy, for answering questions about pathology; Fraser Joyce, for tracking down a hard-to-find publication; and to Angela Buckley, whose doctoral research in Liverpool yielded a gem that appears in Chapter 5. I am very grateful for the patient support of my editors at Routledge, Rob Langham and Dana Moss – thank you both.

Permission to reproduce the images in Chapter 5 was provided by The National Archives and is recognised with thanks. Figure 1.3 is reproduced with permission from the WS Society in Edinburgh. I wish to record my gratitude to James Hamilton of The Signet Library, for his hospitality and wealth of knowledge; my work at the Library helped to bring this project to fruition and planted the seeds of the next. Thanks are also due to the Brotherton Library, University of Leeds, for making publically available the images of Thomas Scattergood's notebooks. Quotations from Crown copyright documents held in The National Archives and The National Library of Wales are duly acknowledged.

I am above all indebted to the friends who have read and commented on various drafts of the book chapters: their professional expertise, perceptive observations and helpful suggestions have been an invaluable means of strengthening the book's content, structure and clarity. Very special thanks are owed to Anne-Marie Kilday for seeing through to the core of the argument and helping me to make it more clearly; and to Sara Butler, Krista Kesselring and Haia

Shpayer-Makov, for their guidance at various points in this process. You are all fantastic historians and wonderful friends – thank you.

At the heart of this history lie the lives and deaths, words and deeds of real people faced with real life-and-death situations in difficult circumstances that presented limited options. It is the victims of violent crime who provide the foundation on which this study rests, and I hope that by returning their stories to the public eye this book will serve in some small way to honour their memory. For every victim, however, there was a group of professionals and laymen on whom the state relied to ensure the efficient functioning of the English legal system, so that justice was done, and was seen to be done. It is to these individuals – most especially the doctors, but also the police officers, coroners, lawyers, magistrates, lay witnesses, judges and jurors – that I dedicate this book.

Note

1 I have deliberately avoided using the term 'expert witness' to describe all medical witnesses for reasons explained in Chapters 1, 3 and 5.

1 Introduction

The medico-legal landscape

> In delivering his opinion, or explaining the cause of death, the surgeon's narrative should be simple and candid; let him use as few technical terms as possible, both for the better information of the jury, and to avoid giving a lawyer an opportunity of embarrassing him.
>
> William Dease, *Remarks on Medical Jurisprudence; Intended for the General Information of Juries and Young Surgeons* (Dublin: James Reilly, 1793), p. 22

In a scenario replayed countless times in modern fiction, a hapless doctor sits transfixed in a courtroom witness box, pinned like a bug to a board by the questioning of a just-barely-civil defence barrister determined to undermine their credibility, weaken their evidence and ensure the client's acquittal. This, it seems, was a state of affairs not unknown to the medical profession of the late eighteenth century, as the warning issued by the Irish surgeon William Dease (c.1752–1798) attests. Though he was speaking of the practices he had witnessed at first hand in Dublin, there was little difference to the English courts of the day, as noted by the Somerset-based physician Samuel Farr (1741–1795) in his earlier textbook: "it is to be hoped, that this little treatise will meet the attention of judges and lawyers . . . and that they will be enabled to correct the errors of coroners, or ignorant surgeons, who may have been misled in the depositions they give in."[1] But what do we really know about the encounters between medicine and law, doctors and lawyers, in the criminal courts of the past? How and why did medical professionals enter the courtroom; what did they do to get there and what reception did they receive? This book will situate doctors in their rightful place as contributors to the investigation of crime, as part of a criminal justice system that evolved over the course of the eighteenth and nineteenth centuries to create the regularised policing and legal structures so familiar today.

The book is conceived primarily as a contribution to the historiography of criminal justice in England and Wales. As such, it is broadly concerned with the history of the formal systems of practice directed at deterring, detecting and punishing crime.[2] But it engages this far-reaching field of study by focusing on the intersection of the social history of law and crime with medical history. Legal historians examine the common law and legal process, in order to understand how and why these embodiments of the state-controlled administration of justice adapt and evolve in response to internal and external stimuli.[3] Crime historians adopt a complementary perspective, taking as their main focus of study the individuals who engaged with the criminal justice system and the terms on which they did so to explain how people in the past understood crime and criminality and either engaged in criminal conduct or attempted to manage it.[4] The present study examines the history of crime and legal process through the lens provided by one group of historical actors: medical professionals who gave evidence in criminal proceedings. They are the means of illuminating the developing methods and personnel associated with investigating and prosecuting crime in eighteenth- and nineteenth-century England and Wales, when two linchpins of modern society, centralised policing and the adversarial criminal trial, emerged and matured.[5] It is devoted to two central questions: what did medical practitioners contribute to the investigation of serious violent crime in the period 1700 to 1914, and what impact did this have on the process of criminal justice?

Criminal justice historians – a term used here to include all scholars who study law and crime in historical context – are interested in specific groups of actors and particular practices. Thus, the scholarship of the past 30 years has shed considerable light on offenders and victims; juries; law officers such as police, magistrates, lawyers, judges and coroners; criminal trials and punishment, including execution, transportation and imprisonment. Key themes that serve to unite these broad areas of study have emerged, including the relationship between gender, law and crime, examined most often through women's experience of the criminal justice system;[6] and the changing attitudes to violence revealed through criminal justice proceedings. Probably no form of criminal behaviour has been subject to more scrutiny than homicide (a term used here to denote three species of fatal interpersonal violence: murder, manslaughter and infanticide), as historians have sought to identify the incidence and characteristics of violence in the past.[7] Similarly, the history of rape is integral to understanding contemporary beliefs about sexual assault.[8] The prosecution of homicide and rape, as crimes against the person, involved some estimation of physical harm done to a victim, yet medical professionals have for the most part been excluded from British criminal justice historiography. This represents a significant omission given the observation with which this chapter began. By the late eighteenth century, the medical contribution to the prosecution of serious crimes against the person had become so common as to merit both publications on the subject and Dease's note of caution to young practitioners who might be called into court: they must be wary of lawyers but considerate of jurors.[9]

A great deal of scholarly attention has concentrated on England in the eighteenth and nineteenth centuries, when "legal, procedural and cultural changes crystallized modern attitudes" to violence and crime,[10] stimulated the adoption of professionalised methods of policing and prosecution,[11] encouraged more reliance on lawyers in criminal trials and inspired the development of evidentiary rules.[12] Legal historian Lindsay Farmer has noted that as a result of these innovations, trials became longer and more contentious, began to rely more on expert evidence, and allowed more influence to accrue to "the personalities of the law-yers, detectives and scientific experts that came to dominate" legal proceedings.[13] The same might be said of the coroner's inquest, the other jurisdiction where the evidence of a medical practitioner was most likely to be required.

Historical interest in the inquest as a legal process began in the late 1950s,[14] but doctors and the evidence they provided have escaped thorough scrutiny despite the fact that the inquest's primary function was the investigation of sud-den death – which by definition created a decision-making process to establish cause and manner of death: natural, accident, suicide or homicide.[15] Detailed research on inquisitions, the formal records of inquest findings, led to the con-clusion that medical determination of cause of death, as opposed to lay assess-ment, was relatively under-developed in relation to continental practices, though it was becoming more usual by the early nineteenth century.[16] A later series of important books on medico-scientific expertise considered medical evidence in both inquests and the criminal courts, but focused on public accountability and scientific objectivity rather than matters of routine practice.[17] Thus, despite the pioneering work of Catherine Crawford and Jennifer Ward on the institutional development of forensic medicine,[18] few academic studies have examined medi-cal practitioners as ordinary actors in the criminal justice system.[19]

The fact that forensic practices are embedded in socio-legal context was highlighted by an important collection of essays, *Legal Medicine in History*, which emphasised the "formative influence of legal systems on medico-legal knowl-edge and practice" through a series of case studies.[20] Crawford's seminal chapter presented a persuasive interpretation of the slow development of "medico-legal science" in early modern England as a product of the framework created by the common law tradition of jury trial and oral evidence. Unlike the procedures created by the Roman-canon legal system, there was no requirement for the testimony of experts, written or otherwise, and hence no ready-made point of entry for medical practitioners to the English courtroom. Crawford noted that medical testimony *was* often sought by "English coroners, magistrates and trial participants" before 1800, but dated the beginnings of legal acceptance of medi-cal expertise to the nineteenth century, thereby explaining the late development of forensic medicine as a learned science.[21] In Crawford's interpretation, the law led and medico-legal practice followed. Although subsequent studies by Julia Rudolph and Carol Loar have dispelled the assumption that early modern death investigations placed little reliance on medical evidence,[22] there has, to date, been no study of medico-legal practice across precisely the period that historians of crime have identified as crucial to the development of English criminal proce-dure, the eighteenth and nineteenth centuries.

Crawford's research firmly linked legal history to the social history of medicine, a third area of study directly relevant to this book. Engaged in what is now a flourishing historical sub-discipline, social historians of medicine examine all aspects of health, illness and medical practice from a range of per-spectives including the political, socio-economic and cultural; important areas of focus include health, disease, institutions, patients and the development of the various professions involved in medicine.[23] The concept of the 'medical marketplace', used to describe the variety of medical provision available to sick people in the past, is particularly interesting, as historians have identified eighteenth-century changes brought about by a burgeoning consumer society as factors that expanded both the demand for and supply of medical services. The very diversity of the available provision suggests, however, that "historians should . . . think of the *markets* for medical goods and services rather than a generalized image of the medical market or marketplace."[24] While the medical market has been used by historians in relation to health care, the historiography of this important concept has largely overlooked a very different yet parallel market for medical services: the market created by the needs of the English legal system. The service offered was not health care but crime investigation; the consumers were not sick people but legal officials; there were no patients, only victims. This relationship evolved, like the traditional medical market, on the basis of supply and demand, but, in a departure from the customary model of medical care, the 'commercialising' marketplace in which medical practitioners were located was that defined by the requirements of criminal justice administration.

It is therefore important to recognise a distinction between academic scholarship and what the average practitioner actually did. The former is best described as the body of systematic knowledge known as forensic medicine: during the course of the nineteenth century an international group of university lecturers wrote textbooks that came to define and establish the intellectual standards for this emerging medical specialism.[25] The terms 'legal medicine' and 'medical jurisprudence' were often used interchangeably to signify the same scholarly field: the application of medical science to legal problems. But the hands-on forensic activities that medical practitioners actually undertook are more accurately understood as 'medico-legal work', a term that embraces all possible applications of medical knowledge for legal purposes but which in criminal cases most often involved some form of body examination, of the living or the dead or, less frequently, an assessment of mental capacity. Both terms are informed by the presumption that forensic medicine and its practical mechanisms – that is, forensic practices – exemplify the use of medical evidence to establish facts in aid of legal decision-making processes.

Medico-legal work in England and Wales pre-dates the academic discipline of forensic medicine. Thus, one of the main tasks of this book will be to identify its form and scope and to show how embedded in and responsive to wider patterns in crime and criminal justice administration it was. Essentially, medico-legal work developed in tandem with and was shaped by the needs of two evolving processes: pre-trial investigative procedures dominated successively by coroners, magistrates and the police; and criminal trials in which lawyers moved from the periphery to the centre of courtroom proceedings. In bringing together for the first time four groups of specialists – doctors, coroners, lawyers and police officers – this study offers a new interpretation of the processes that shaped the modern criminal justice system.

Medico-legal history: the story so far

The important role played by medicine in legal settings since the medieval period has been clearly established by a range of medical and legal historians who, since the early studies of T. R. Forbes, have used inquisitions, legal manuals and criminal trial accounts to consider issues of civic concern – chiefly death investigation, the most common focus of medico-legal practice. Sara Butler has demonstrated the importance of medical evidence in medieval inquests;[26] a larger body of work has examined the early modern period to show that medico-legal practice, albeit sporadic, occurred in sixteenth- and seventeenth-century death investigations;[27] and Orna Alyagon Darr has published a novel study of medical testimony in English witch trials.[28] It is clear that the principles of forensic medicine were visible in some parts of England by the middle of the eighteenth century:[29] from around 1750 uncertainties in medical testimony gave English courts a justifiable reason to acquit women accused of newborn child murder,[30] and medical witnesses on insanity began to venture into the courtroom.[31] Institutional progress occurred in the first third of the nineteenth century, when forensic medicine offered medical reformers a particularly useful means by which to demonstrate the power of scientific medicine, giving the profession a more public importance and authority. The first substantial English-language textbooks were published and a periodical literature appeared, the Society of Apothecaries made training in forensic medicine a condition of medical qualification from 1 January 1831 and Guy's Hospital established a lectureship in the subject (to which the soon-to-be famed toxicologist Alfred Swaine Taylor [1806–1880] was appointed), and in 1836 the government introduced statutory fees for medical testimony at inquests.[32]

Poisoning and suicide became increasingly important subjects of medico-legal consideration as the incidence of both rose during the nineteenth century;[33] and so did child sexual abuse, although the medical contribution had a rather less positive impact on trial outcomes.[34] The mental and physical characteristics of newborn child murder, or infanticide, became one of the most frequent issues on which medical evidence was sought, but both were medically and legally contentious.[35] Toxicology and psychiatry emerged as key areas of potential collaboration but also of conflict between doctors and lawyers, who did not necessarily share a common conception of certainty, proof or free will.[36] It is perhaps unsurprising, then, that these were the areas of medical practice most closely associated with the rise of the expert witness, a figure that appeared in the late eighteenth century as a uniquely qualified individual permitted to give evidence about both fact and opinion on the basis of professional experience. This figure, linked closely to the notion of 'expertise' and seen as a potentially partisan advocate within the adversarial criminal trial structure rather than an impartial purveyor of accurate information,[37] is typically distinguished from more usual medical witnesses in the historiography. The expert witness relies on specialised knowledge developed during the course of a professional career and can thus be called to give evidence about matters that they have not witnessed directly in order to offer opinions about causation. Other medical witnesses, by contrast, testify only to their direct observations and the interpretations they draw from them.[38]

The most dramatic evidence of the status and knowledge claims of forensic medicine and medical witnesses was apparent in criminal trials. Anne Crowther and Brenda White noted that in England and Scotland "a small group with special experience, usually drawn from the hospitals, universities, or police surgeons, provided an unofficial cadre of forensic experts. By the end of the century, although general practitioners still performed autopsies, particularly in remote areas, most courts preferred a specialist."[39] So, after 1900, a smaller group of 'experts' concerned themselves with the criminal aspects of forensic medicine.[40] At the same time, government support turned to the application of science (physics, chemistry and biology) to crime detection as part of a central reorganisation of policing.[41] The emerging historiographical consensus was thus that forensic medicine in England advanced from informal early modern origins through a period of expansion and consolidation in the early nineteenth century, only to become the poor relation of forensic science a century later.

New scholarship has begun to explore scientific policing and the twentieth-century separation of forensic science from forensic medicine,[42] but there has as yet been no systematic investigation of the way in which forensic medicine came to rely on a small group of 'experts' (who have themselves featured disproportionately in the historiography) or, indeed, of the individuals engaged in routine forensic practice in any period. The medico-legal history of the British Isles remains inadequate and under-developed because, quite apart from the intellectual focus on toxicology, insanity and infanticide to the near exclusion of more typical cases (most victims of homicide were adults who died from head injuries or stabbing),[43] the geographical spotlight has tended to rest upon London and trials held at its central criminal court, the Old Bailey. This (one suspects) is at least partly because of the attention that crime historians level on London as a result of its vast archival riches. Less astonishing perhaps is the fact that forensic practice is almost completely unexplored in the historiography of crime in Wales which, though less extensive than that of England or Scotland, is beginning to grow.[44] Social historians of medicine, meanwhile, have largely been interested in health care in the Principality;[45] legal historians in the law in Wales.[46] But given that England and Wales have been united under a common administrative and legal system since the mid-sixteenth century, yet have very separate socio-cultural identities, the investigation of medico-legal practice in Wales is merited both in its own right and as a foundation for future comparative work. Furthermore, such a study opens up to exploration essential questions suggested by Peter King, who has warned against the assumption that central initiatives were simply applied nationwide *in toto*. Instead, he asks historians to consider the ways in which law and the practice of justice "can be explored by contrasting the central and the marginal and by analysing the relationship between them," since it is likely that in many respects "the operation of justice was remade as much from the bottom up as from the centre down."[47]

A new generation of historians has adopted the regional approach advocated by King: in the past decade more doctoral theses exploiting records produced outside London to examine medico-legal topics have appeared than at any previous time. Fisher's work on the office of coroner provided a truly national perspective,[48] while Daniel Grey and Victoria Bates compared London with regions in the west of England in their work on infanticide and child sexual assault, respectively.[49] Further afield, Elaine Farrell's study of infanticide in Ireland focused in part on medical evidence in coroners' courts;[50] and forensic practices in Scotland were examined by Nicholas Duvall and Tim Siddons, who carefully acknowledged the wider institutional, investigative and geographical networks in which Scottish medico-legal work was ensconced.[51] These studies have developed their arguments with a close attention to and regard for legal practices, embracing an interdisciplinary approach that draws on the sources and methods of the history of medicine, law and crime. In so doing, they have helped to bring historical forensic practices into criminal justice decision-making structures, siting medico-legal work within an integrated investigative process.[52] The present study contributes to the strands of analysis developed by these scholars, and extends them. In adopting a wider regional comparison across a significantly longer period of time, this book will identify the contribution made by medical practitioners to the investigation of serious violent crime and establish its transformative impact on the process of criminal justice.

Criminal justice: process and procedure

The process of organising a criminal case began when a violent crime was identified, involving the collaboration of doctors, coroners, lawyers and the police in the service of the principal branches of eighteenth- and nineteenth-century criminal justice: law enforcement and the court system. A large supporting cast of lay witnesses, magistrates, jurors and judges were also essential contributors to this system. Historians of law and crime have long been interested in the development of criminal investigation and court procedures,[53] but have directed little attention to doctors even in relation to the coroner's inquest.[54] Histories of the office of coroner, by contrast, tend not to examine criminal justice procedure as a fundamental attribute of the developing importance of medical knowledge at inquests.[55] For this book, however, it is important to recognise the intersecting roles played by these disparate groups as a foundation for the analysis presented in later chapters. Figure 1.1 demonstrates this relationship as a series of separate yet linked processes that proceeded in a forward direction, from pre-trial hearing by a coroner and/or magistrate to a criminal trial presided over by a judge and jury. Eyewitnesses and jurors were essential to crime investigation, prosecution and trial throughout the period, but their contribution became progressively more passive as professionals assumed a greater responsibility in the practices of criminal justice. The holders of ancient office – judges, magistrates and coroners (of whom until the nineteenth century only the judges could be defined as professionals) – were joined by doctors, lawyers

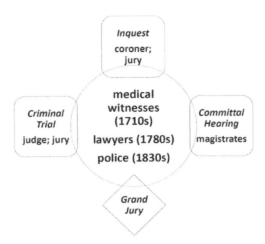

Figure 1.1 Stages in the process of criminal justice, from crime discovery to trial

and finally the uniformed police, thereby establishing the modern system of criminal investigation.

The investigation of a crime was initially reactive: a criminal case began when a lay witness gave information or made a formal complaint to a coroner, magistrate (also known as a justice of the peace or JP) or parish constable. A system largely unaltered for centuries began to change rapidly in the nineteenth century when the 'new police',[56] organised at county or borough level, replaced parish constables and in larger towns police courts staffed by stipendiary magistrates superseded amateur JPs. Although the new police were primarily a preventive force, they swiftly took on a central role in investigating serious crimes against the person: victims and witnesses turned to the police as the appropriate authority and logical first step in the process of criminal justice. However, the police shared that position with another group: it was entirely typical for members of the public to send for the police *and* a doctor following the discovery of a crime such as homicide. Early police methods in such cases perhaps differed little from those of "the more conscientious and determined of their predecessors," in that they relied largely on information gathering, circulation and storage techniques pioneered in mid-eighteenth-century London by the Bow Street magistrates.[57] However, the new police joined coroners and magistrates as an important source of demand for medico-legal knowledge, and part of what this book will do is demonstrate how that relationship worked. To that end, Appendix 3 provides a chronological summary of the introduction of the new police in the areas relevant to the project (see the next section, Aims, Methods and Sources).

Coroners were under no legal imperative to seek medical evidence at inquests, although clearly some did so, before a more systematic practice began to develop in the eighteenth century under the stimulus of published manuals designed to establish clear protocols. In 1761 the senior coroner for Middlesex, lawyer Edward Umfreville (c.1702–1786), advised coroners to have a surgeon present in all cases of suspected homicide. If the parish surgeon refused to attend without payment, as had been known to happen, then the churchwardens and overseers could be directed to send a surgeon to attend the inquest, to open and inspect the body and give evidence for the crown.[58] In cases of homicide, the inquest verdict recorded in an inquisition had the status of an indictment: any named individual had to stand trial. At the same time, numerous manuals devoted to the duties of JPs instructed magistrates on the different categories of homicide; but JPs were similarly under no legal obligation to obtain medical evidence, merely "the best evidence that may be had."[59] Common sense dictates that suspected murder made the need for medical evidence obvious; and the cases examined here demonstrate that it did indeed become a regular component of homicide trials early in the eighteenth century. There was no reason *not* to call upon a doctor's skill in a potentially capital case: coroners and magistrates had the power to compel witnesses to testify in criminal cases by entering them into recognizances, usually about £20 at mid-century but nearer £40 by 1800. If the witness failed to appear in court, the money was forfeit and few individuals could afford such a penalty. If doctors wanted to avoid getting involved in a case, therefore, they had to do so before an inquest or committal hearing commenced.

The coroner's main obligation ended with the inquest, but if there was no complainant it was his duty to prosecute the suspected party.[60] Magistrates never acted as prosecutors, but could depose additional witnesses until the court was due to convene in an effort to strengthen a case. Although the evidence taken at inquest or before a magistrate in the same case was normally the same, there was a crucial distinction: inquests inquired into the facts of a death and therefore heard evidence for and against a suspect, but committal hearings inquired only into the evidence needed to prove the felony.[61] Information flowed informally between the two, however, in the form of the eyewitnesses, doctors and constables. Following the introduction of the new police, the senior investigating officer generally appeared at both proceedings where, increasingly, the accused made use of the services of a solicitor. When an individual was committed for trial the depositions from both hearings were sent to the assize court and there used by the prosecutor to construct a narrative designed to guide a jury to convict.

Before a case got to court, however, a grand jury comprising 23 magistrates heard the prosecution evidence from the mouths of the prosecutor and witnesses. If the presumptive evidence against the accused was sufficiently convincing, they deemed the indictment a true bill; in the contrary case, no bill. Suspects who had also been committed by a coroner were tried first upon indictment or, if no bill was found, solely upon the inquisition.[62] The actual trial took place before a judge and jury of 12 men. Judges took notes of the oral evidence, sometimes put questions to witnesses (for their own elucidation or to aid a prisoner undefended by counsel), and finally summed up the evidence for the jury, noting any particularly relevant points of fact or law. In 1822, these procedures were summarised by Charles Cottu (1778–1849), a French observer, who raised two additional points of interest: surgeons tended to give their evidence just before the defence witnesses; and prisoners and prosecutors often had a barrister to speak for them at trial, although this was more common in the provinces than in London.[63]

Legal historians studying the development of the criminal trial have concentrated on the emerging law of evidence, the privilege against self-incrimination, the adversary system, and the relationship between judge and jury. John Langbein and others have concluded that many of the most important changes identified took place during the eighteenth century, stimulated by the increasing presence of defence counsel.[64] This became more regular in the 1730s as judges presiding over criminal trials attempted to correct the imbalance between the unaided accused and prosecutions progressively more reliant upon solicitors and thief-takers,[65] but the key turning point came in the 1780s, "when there was a spurt in the reported use of defence counsel."[66] T. P. Gallanis has put forward the most convincing explanation for the timing of this development: the decisive factor was the cessation of transportation to America in 1775. The principal punishments short of death then became "disease-ridden prisons or transportation to the fledgling and dangerous colony in Australia" – unpleasant prospects that defendants sought to avoid by employing defence counsel.[67] Furthermore, the 1780s was a decade of unprecedented concern about crime manifested in expanded use of the death penalty.[68] The value of defence counsel lay in their ability to cross-examine witnesses: the defendant avoided making dangerous admissions during the course of trying to do so himself; also, a vigorous cross-examination could lead to a directed verdict, so that the accused did not have to say anything at all.[69]

Although lawyers were slow to acknowledge it, doctors had a vital role to play in prosecuting crimes against the person: the prosecution had to specify and prove all the facts and circumstances that constituted the offence alleged, including the medical facts that supported a charge of homicide or rape. As successive treatises on criminal law defined crimes ever more carefully, the importance of medical evidence became increasingly overt in the works of the most highly respected and widely cited legal authors of the eighteenth and nineteenth centuries. This is most apparent in treatises on the law of evidence. In English law, an act became a crime when two conditions were satisfied: there was, firstly, a will to do harm and, secondly, an unlawful act consequent upon it.[70] Medical evidence gained a recognised status as one of several complementary forms of necessary proof of these two conditions. Doctors could testify to the mental competency of the accused, to establish that they were of "sound discretion" and capable of forming a vicious intent; but they more frequently gave evidence about the nature of the injuries sustained by the victim to help establish the act alleged.

As stated by Brian Levack, the law of evidence in England is "essentially a law of jury control" created by judicial management of courtroom procedure, including decisions about what types of testimony to allow and the instructions given to juries.[71] The modern law of evidence began to develop during the eighteenth century and was, according to Langbein, clearly in place by the mid-nineteenth century, driven by the increasing presence of lawyers in criminal trials. Judges had to control the oral evidence given by witnesses, the questions put to them by prosecution and defence counsel, and the inferences that juries were to draw from the evidence they heard. While the rapid development of adversary criminal procedure in the last quarter of the eighteenth century made the law of evidence possible,[72] nothing in Langbein's analysis suggests the impact that medical witnesses might have had on this process. Gallanis reached a similar conclusion about the origins of modern evidence law, but dated its creation to the somewhat narrower period bounded by the texts of Sir Geoffrey Gilbert (1754) and Thomas Starkie (1824),[73] both of whom employed medicine-related examples. Prompted by courtroom dilemmas caused by the 1624 Infanticide Act, which inferred murder from the fact of concealing the birth and death of an illegitimate infant, Gilbert cited the statute in relation to "the elements of a civil action or criminal charge, the defenses available under it, and the proof necessary to sustain it."[74] Starkie discussed a number of issues that Gilbert ignored, including expert evidence, witnesses allowed to refresh their memory with notes made at the time of the events in question, and the role of lawyers in examining witnesses.[75] These, as we will see, were all points of relevance to medical witnesses.

The first formal statement about the role of what we now designate the expert witness was made in Capel Lofft's 1791 edition of Gilbert's *Law of Evidence*, noting that "in proportion as experience and science advocates, the uncertainty and danger from this kind of proof diminishes."[76] Using poisoning and infanticide as examples, Lofft put into words what had by then become typical practice in cases of felonious assault: "when testimonies of professional men of just estimation are affirmative, they may be safely credited; but when negative, they do not amount to a disproof of a charge otherwise established by strong, various, and independent circumstances."[77] Thirty years later one of the most prolific writers of legal treatises and digests of the nineteenth century, barrister J. F. Archbold, was less ambiguous about what doctors contributed to criminal trials: it was their professional opinion on "the probable result of or consequence from certain facts already proved."[78] This was a unique role, because most witnesses may testify only to what they experienced at first hand, and so it necessitated certain protocols. Medical witnesses could not read their evidence, but they could refresh their memory from books or notes seen or made at the time. If however a doctor knew a fact only from seeing it in a book or paper, that publication had to become evidence.[79] By 1922, when Archbold's text had expanded to over three times its original length, all of these points appeared in very similar language, but the term used to denote this special witness category was "experts."[80]

From the early eighteenth century, medical men provided their opinions about the relevance of the facts that lay within their own "knowledge and recollection" – that is, the facts they had seen for themselves and, in so doing, implicitly guided the court in its decision-making responsibility. In order to demonstrate this, we must examine archival records to get a clear picture of actual practice.

Aims, methods and sources

As should by now be evident, the history of medico-legal practice sits at the intersection of three hitherto rather separate areas of scholarship, and this project seeks to bridge some of the gaps by examining medico-legal work as a contributing factor in the investigation of violent felonies,[81] particularly homicide (murder, manslaughter and infanticide) and, to a lesser extent, rape. Although these were by no means common offences, they provide a systematic indicator of local efforts to apply medico-legal principles in the courts of assize where felonies were tried, and at pre-trial stage in inquests and magistrates' committal hearings. To provide a comparative, nationally representative analysis, medico-legal experience and practice will be examined in three distinct regions: London, the eight counties of the Oxford Assize Circuit stretching from Berkshire to the Welsh border and Wales and its neighbouring English county, Cheshire. In order to take in the important socio-legal changes that affected medico-legal practice, the analysis covers the period between about 1700 and the First World War. The temporal focus reflects the parallel developments in the history of law, crime and medicine that together acted to shape medico-legal work, ensuring the inclusion of vital transitions in legal practices and policing systems, as well as important institutional, intellectual and educational developments in medicine. Appendix 1 sets out the socio-legal framework by listing the key pieces of legislation relevant to the themes of the book, together with related historical and professional milestones, in an annotated chronology intended to provide a summative overview of the context within which medico-legal practice occurred. By 1914 the growing demarcation between forensic medicine and forensic science, soon to be compounded by the effects of war, marked the start of a new chapter in the history of crime investigation and thus a natural ending point for this study. Emphasis throughout is placed on the contributions made by medical practitioners to criminal inquiries, to assess the intrinsic content of the medico-legal work undertaken and its impact on the vital processes of investigation, prosecution and trial. The aim, then, is to study medico-legal work within the framework of the totality of actions carried out to achieve the effective administration of justice.

A series of sub-questions shape the research:

1 What was the nature and extent of medico-legal practice across England and Wales, and how did this change during the period 1700–1914?
2 Who provided medico-legal testimony, and how/why did they come to the attention of officers of the criminal justice system?
3 How important were institutions such as hospitals, medical schools, workhouses, colleges and asylums as factors shaping the local availability of forensic knowledge and practice?
4 What was the extent of scientific forensic practice prior to 1914, and what was its relationship to local medico-legal provision?
5 How was medico-legal evidence deployed and received in the criminal courts and what impact did this have on the professional development of medico-legal witnesses?

To address these questions, I have adopted a methodology common to the social history of crime:[82] a regional, quantitative and qualitative study based principally on the records created by the criminal justice system. The regions to be studied have been selected to facilitate direct comparison between London, which was at once the most populous city in the country, "the heart of legal England" and a centre of medical education;[83] the provincial regions of England; and Wales. The specific counties under study create a fully contiguous area that, by the early nineteenth century, encompassed some of the most heavily populated and economically diverse parts of England as well as a significant agricultural hinterland. Staffordshire was part of a broad western spine of urbanisation, and the border counties of Cheshire, Shropshire and Monmouthshire were uniquely situated between England and Wales.

Figure 1.2 shows the geographical relationship of the selected counties. (There is a small gap between Berkshire and Middlesex occupied by Surrey and Buckinghamshire, but at 2.92 km it is small enough to be considered negligible.) The wide geographical scope is important for four reasons. Firstly, it allows cross-border investigative practices to be identified, whereby magistrates or the police from different counties worked cooperatively to solve a case, a medical practitioner from one county was called in to examine a body found in a neighbouring one, or samples were sent from one county to an expert in another. Secondly, this approach facilitates consideration of the extent to which this medical expertise was peripatetic or local.[84] Thirdly, the conclusions reached will reflect typical practices associated with particular patterns of reported criminality, in the context of medical and policing provisions, and so will be more widely portable to other parts of the country than a study based solely on London or a single county. Finally, as a culturally separate but legally, medically and politically integrated part of Great Britain, Wales provides a self-contained case study and a contrast to England which suggests the possible importance of the concept of the periphery.[85] Three peripheries are discernible: all the areas of England outside London, Wales in relation to England and rural areas located on the periphery of English and Welsh towns. What impact did being 'on the periphery' have on medico-legal practice?

The analysis is based on five main types of sources: records created by the criminal justice system, chiefly pre-trial depositions taken by coroners and magistrates but also inquisitions, recognizances, bills and indictments; trial reports published in newspapers, pamphlets and the *Proceedings* of the Old Bailey; police and government memoranda; professional literature such as legal and medical texts; other manuscript and printed sources including diaries, journals, letters, trade directories and obituaries. The *Proceedings* and depositions were used to construct a dataset of 2,615 cases of rape and especially homicide that occurred across the 22 counties studied (see Tables 3.1–3.4 in Chapter 3). Thousands of individual documents were consulted so as to provide full details for each separate criminal case; and further research was done on hundreds of individual doctors named in the files in order to develop a detailed picture of their medico-legal careers. All cases in the dataset were tried before the highest criminal courts

Figure 1.2 Map of England and Wales, showing the 22 counties included in this study

in the country: the English assizes, periodic courts held around six circuits (each comprising five to eight counties) of which the Oxford Circuit remained unchanged throughout the period of study; the Welsh Court of Great Sessions, which was established in 1543 and organised into four circuits; and the Court of Great Sessions of the palatinate of Chester (Cheshire). In 1830 Cheshire and the Welsh counties were absorbed into the English assize system and two new circuits were created: North Wales, including Cheshire, and South Wales. Middlesex was not on any circuit: until 1834 crimes committed in the county or in the City of London were tried at the Old Bailey, or Sessions House, which was then renamed the Central Criminal Court and its jurisdiction extended to parts of Essex, Kent and Surrey. The Old Bailey thus became the assize court for these areas; it also gained jurisdiction over offences committed on the high seas or elsewhere abroad previously tried by the Admiralty.

The records created by these courts are exceptionally rich, but a number of caveats should be noted. The nature of the surviving material means that direct quantitative and to some extent qualitative comparison between the years before and after 1830 is unfeasible. The criminal records of the Court of Great Sessions "are more comprehensive than their English assize counterparts,"[86] but they do not include Monmouthshire, which was culturally part of Wales but administratively part of the Oxford Circuit, for which the surviving pre-1830 depositions are limited. Files for the 12 counties of the Welsh Great Sessions cover all known criminal cases up to 1830, catalogued from 1730 in an online database which includes trial outcomes. All of the assize and Great Sessions records were sampled. For the former, entire years of criminal depositions were read, including all surviving files to 1845, and from 23 of the following 69 years; for the latter, selections were made on the basis that the case file included depositions. The surviving criminal files for the palatinate of Chester are as voluminous as the Great Sessions material but are not catalogued or sorted; I therefore sampled 20 years between 1756 and 1824. For London and Middlesex, the digitised *Proceedings* of the Old Bailey provide the main source of data: the transcripts of thousands of trials held in the period 1674 to 1913 (the year *before* my coverage for the other counties ends).[87] Using the offence categories assigned by the project creators, all murder and manslaughter trials for London and Middlesex from 1700 to 1749 were included in order to provide insight into medico-legal practice prior to and just after the important decade of the 1730s which, as we saw previously, heralded the regular presence of medical witnesses and defence counsel.[88] All trials for infanticide were analysed for the years 1700 to 1913, but its nineteenth-century allied offence, concealment of birth, was excluded because such trials were not fully reported. A broad sampling technique for murder trials after 1749 included the 1780s and then groups of years set apart by successively smaller intervals, taking in the crucial 1830s and similarly excluding trials that did not include actual testimony.[89] All rape trials held at the Old Bailey after 1739 were examined, but only those that recorded testimony – rather than a brief account of the verdict or legal arguments – were entered into the database; the last substantive entry is for a trial held in 1797 and only three cases after 1800 could be included.

After 1830 the records for all parts of the country except London and Middlesex are incomplete: almost no cases of rape survive among the extant depositions; homicide files survive well but not in their entirety. Depositions in cases of rape-murder record medical evidence of both crimes, but my dataset is comprised mainly of homicides, with a small group of Georgian rape cases from London and Wales. Textbooks can fill some gaps from the perspective of professional literature, but it is not possible to study medico-legal practice in Victorian rape trials with the depth possible for homicide, a problem compounded by journalistic prudery: from 1796 a self-imposed censorship restricted the reporting of Old Bailey rape trials,[90] and Victorian newspapers often claimed that the details of such cases were unfit for publication. But for homicide trials newspaper reports provide a vital source of information: they record, often verbatim, what people said in court. This includes the judge's charge to the grand jury and summing up, barristers' opening and closing arguments, witness testimony and cross examination, jurors' questions, and any statements made by the accused. Using newspapers, it is possible to examine the reception of medico-legal evidence in the assize courts to supplement the information provided by depositions and the Old Bailey *Proceedings* (the latter usually exclude the statements made by judges and lawyers). The provincial press delivers a voluminous source of crime news,[91] particularly since the advent of online resource *The British Newspaper Archive* in 2011,[92] and it is reliable. According to Judith Rowbotham and Kim Stevenson, the Victorian press can be used as a source of fact, information about legal roles and public perceptions of crime and criminal justice. Legal professionals produced most of the court reporting: their detailed explanations were intended to reinforce a positive public awareness of the mechanics of criminal justice because "a legal system works effectively only when its operations have a firm basis in public consent."[93] Methodologically, nineteenth-century newspaper reportage offers precisely the detail needed to gauge the reception and impact of medico-legal evidence in the criminal courts, though some points may well have been left out or downplayed. Systematic searches were made for each case of murder and infanticide in two principal online repositories, *Welsh Newspapers Online* and *The British Newspaper Archive*, as well as general searches to identify individuals such as coroners and police surgeons.

While the newspapers themselves may contain accurate trial reports, their use by historians is not without risk. Tim Hitchcock has suggested that, due to the problems associated with digitisation and optical character recognition, searches of online historical resources can be neither fully systematic nor entirely complete.[94] Certainly it became evident that some online titles produce more legible search results than others, as do newspapers published after about 1890. Similarly, what might seem to be minor transcription errors in the Old Bailey *Proceedings* could be problematic because medical terms and doctors' names were important pieces of information that were not always transcribed correctly. But in both scenarios the original documents were also available online and so all factual details were checked and newspaper reports of the same trial could be cross-checked. Trial accounts produced from shorthand notes for commercial purposes were also used, particularly when more than one edition was available for comparison.[95] I would argue that the brevity with which medical evidence was sometimes reported suggests the extent to which it was considered an unexceptional part of the criminal justice process, as for example in this account of the trial of John Griffiths, who was executed in 1811 for wife murder: "Dr Howell and the former witness proved satisfactorily that the deceased was poisoned."[96]

The reliance on records related to a formal criminal charge suggests that the data has been shaped by two influences: the fact that a crime was reported and investigated as such by the authorities, and the use of medical evidence obtained on behalf of the prosecution by officers of the state, who generally had more resource advantages than the accused had. As social historians of crime have long acknowledged, assumptions about class and social status pervaded the justice system,[97] while qualifications about the 'dark figure' of unknown or unreported crime are usually applicable,[98] even in relation to homicide.[99] However, my intention is not to calculate crime rates, which clearly are affected by the dark figure, but rather to identify medico-legal practice in the two types of crimes where we might expect it most frequently to be found and, given their capital nature, have the greatest potential impact on trial outcomes.[100] Of course coroners held more inquests on people who died by accident or suicide than homicide, and the use of post-mortem examinations has been documented in such cases; but the findings suggest considerable regional variation, as well as a marked reluctance to resort to medico-legal examination in cases of presumed suicide.[101] Indeed, under the terms of the Criminal Justice Act 1826 there was no requirement for coroners to take written evidence unless a charge of murder or manslaughter was likely to ensue,[102] leading Pamela Fisher to note that "witness depositions rarely exist, other than for cases that went before the assize courts."[103] Meaningful results can therefore be obtained by comparing extant criminal cases: while the selected files reflect medico-legal work undertaken in a minority of *all* recorded crime,[104] they relate to the most serious types of violence and so are a *significant* minority, typical of the routine use of forensic knowledge in felony trials.

The inherent class biases of the past are less easy to dismiss: members of the working or labouring class far outnumber the middle or upper classes in the extant criminal records, with the exception of a few notable *causes célèbres*. It is entirely possible that, in the absence of a statutory duty to notify the coroner of cases within his jurisdiction,[105] criminal deaths in respectable families went unnoticed or unreported. Coroners could order an inquest on a deceased person only after notification by a member of the public, and evidently used a selection process to separate the potentially criminal from the mundane cases. But to all intents and purposes selection began at the local level, with the family, friends, neighbours, doctors and constables who provided notification: they decided that a case was one for the coroner, based on obvious signs of violence, community suspicion or even financial imperative. As we cannot study the records of the cases never subject to inquest or for which no witness statements exist, depositions in prosecuted cases offer the most consistent source of information on medico-legal work and the medical practitioners who carried it out. They afford a further analytical prospect, moreover, because barristers were usually instructed just before the assizes began and so sometimes annotated the witness statements, providing a summary of the main points of the prosecution and an indication of where the medical evidence was seen to fit. Additionally, the increasing presence of attorneys at inquests and committal hearings, questioning and cross-examining witnesses, sheds light on the issues that ignited disagreement or attracted the attention of defence counsel seeking to undermine the prosecution case.[106]

One further methodological point must be borne in mind. Throughout the period under study, the criminal courts in Wales were in theory no different in operation than the English assizes, with the major exception of language. Office holders had to be bilingual, but in 1800 perhaps 70 per cent of the people spoke only Welsh;[107] by 1900 this figure had dropped to about 15 per cent.[108] The use of translators in court was commonplace, albeit their presence was not recorded systematically;[109] so depositions have been doubly mediated, first by the process of translation and then by transcribing practices. Admittedly, this process remains largely hidden, but where revealed in depositions and trial accounts legal officials had evidently taken care to ensure that there was an accurate record of what Welsh deponents and defendants actually said.[110] Not only was this a legal requirement,[111] but the speed at which legal proceedings occurred left little time for coroners, clerks or magistrates to put words in the mouths of witnesses.[112] Deletions and insertions also suggest that depositions give an accurate account of pre-trial testimony, the purpose of which was to establish the facts of a case: surprises at trial were unwelcome and witnesses normally repeated the evidence contained in their deposition.

Argument and structure

Local influences on medico-legal practice, and therefore on the emergence of forensic expertise, were crucial and included the investigations undertaken by coroners, magistrates and (after the mid-nineteenth century) the police. The competence and zeal of local medical practitioners were also important. At the same time, local reactions took place in relation to national trends in the processes of criminal justice. This is why, for example, there was more variety of medico-legal experience in Glamorgan than in any other Welsh county: it was one of the few places in nineteenth-century Wales where the number of reported homicides might permit a doctor and the police to develop a degree of forensic experience, a growing population necessitated an extensive medical infrastructure and the rising crime rates led to the appointment of stipendiary magistrates. These sorts of demographic and structural issues help to explain the public dominance of London-based experts: London was where most of the institutions which tended to employ such professionals were located earliest and in the largest numbers, teaching hospitals and the Metropolitan Police being important innovators. Since there was no formal system for employing forensic practitioners and no way to become an 'expert' prior to the creation of specialist posts, legal officials consulted those who were close at hand. Expertise of the type we associate with modern forensic activity developed from hands-on practice that, for a small group, was combined with teaching or a hospital post; for others, it evolved from their role as a police surgeon. But this group of experts were the exception, not the rule.

Medico-legal testimony in homicide cases was normally provided by local surgeons, who carried out some form of body inspection at the explicit request of a coroner or magistrate. This changed during the period of study, from simple external examination and wound measurement, to a more selective anatomisation (opening only the evidently injured part of the body), to a full post-mortem in which both the body and brain were examined in order to identify a specific cause of death as well as the manner of death.[113] Medical practitioners began to adopt a formal forensic language: by the 1830s references to 'opening' the body had largely given way to the term 'post-mortem'. However, causes of death remained surprisingly vague and it is not clear that what practitioners claimed was a post-mortem was in fact the full procedure implied by the term. The lack of a precise cause of death was especially problematic in cases of newborn child murder, when indeterminate medical evidence made deliberate killing impossible to prove.[114] In most cases, forensic evidence was not the main form of proof: circumstantial and eyewitness evidence was equally if not more important.[115] As late as 1886, for example, a Glamorgan man was convicted and executed for murder even though no post-mortem had been conducted. Given that the deceased child was drowned and the killer caught within minutes this is perhaps understandable; but in an example of the locally contingent practices that this study seeks to uncover, the medico-legal work of the workhouse surgeon, appearing in at least his seventh homicide case, seems incomplete by the standards evident elsewhere at the time.[116]

Few cases of homicide, even in the early eighteenth century, involved no medical witness at all; most towns and villages had a local surgeon or surgeon-apothecary, often more than one. Physicians were fewer in number and much less visible in the extant legal records: their focus on internal medicine rather than the external body-centred practice of the surgeon meant they were rarely the obvious practitioner for coroners or magistrates to turn to in cases of inter-personal violence. This began to change in the nineteenth century, most clearly in relation to questions of criminal responsibility, as psychiatrists sought to establish themselves as experts on mental derangement. They were preceded into the courtroom by the man-midwife, another area of medical specialism that found a ready entrée to the legal realm, displacing female midwives in the process. During the first half of the eighteenth century women had acted as medico-legal witnesses in cases of rape and infanticide, but over the next 25 years midwives were replaced by male surgeons, only some of whom were also man-midwives.[117] The evidence drawn from two centuries of medico-legal practice shows that members of the medical profession supplied knowledge required by the criminal justice system; the following chapters investigate the nature of the exchange.

Chapter 2 examines the place of forensic medicine in English medical education, to trace its gradual adoption into the curriculum: by 1831 it had become a compulsory subject for all would-be general practitioners. To identify what students were taught and could reasonably be expected to know if they were called upon in a medico-legal capacity, the chapter then uses textbooks and three sets of lecture notes to provide a detailed overview of the course content at four particular points in time. These include 1788, when Samuel Farr published the first English-language textbook of forensic medicine; 1836, when William Cummin delivered a course of lectures in London; 1869, based on lecture notes assembled by Thomas Scattergood at the Leeds School of Medicine; and 1900, when a medical student at the University of Edinburgh compiled a set of notes during his attendance at a two-month course taught by Professor Henry Littlejohn. Collectively, these sources support two arguments. Firstly, following the reforms of the early 1830s, the average British-trained general practitioner had access to a basic knowledge of forensic medicine and medico-legal practice, and was therefore not wholly unprepared to be called upon in a criminal case. Secondly, the somewhat disproportionate stress on infanticide suggests that the effort to control this offence was particularly relevant to the development of forensic medicine and the refinement of medico-legal practice.

Chapter 3 presents a quantitative overview of the criminal cases on which the book is based, and in so doing identifies the different channels through which medico-legal testimony was obtained. The content and impact of such testimony, and how it changed over time, is examined using homicide cases to explain how surgeons met the needs of the criminal justice system as it evolved over the course of the eighteenth and nineteenth centuries. The focus lies on post-mortem examination of the dead: the main causes of death were head wounds, body blows, and stab wounds – injuries frequently inflicted in so-called fair fights or by domestic violence; crime historians have shown that popular beliefs about acceptable levels of violence helped to shape trial outcomes.[118] Most of these cases were uncontroversial, however, at least in respect to the medical evidence: the cause of death was straightforward to identify and so expert witnesses were rarely needed. The chapter will also consider the role of insanity as a defence to homicide: prison medical officers emerged as recognised authorities on mental illness and crime in the 1870s as a result of changes in criminal procedure initiated by government. Chapter 3 therefore tackles questions of typicality in medico-legal practice by considering the dataset in its entirety. The links between medicine, location and crime are also explored, via illustrative case studies of selected medical professionals who through their role as coroners or authorities played a greater than average role in criminal investigations. This chapter considers the development of institutions and offices as sources of medical expertise, particularly the medical officers to workhouses, prisons, asylums and hospitals; and police surgeons. It also seeks signs of recognised expertise through the use of cross-border consultation. In Wales, for example, this may have been related to geography but was more likely because the staff of the growing number of hospitals, medical colleges and universities were located mainly in England. For example, in 1876 magistrates in Flintshire sent a liver to be examined by the resident surgeon at the Royal Infirmary in Liverpool.[119] Similarly, specialists located in larger regional cities like Birmingham were consulted by magistrates in Staffordshire and Shropshire.[120]

Chapter 4 examines medico-legal practice in cases of infant murder. Mark Jackson has shown that the provisions of the statute of 1624, which presumed that a single woman who gave birth in secret to an infant later found dead was guilty of murder, made it increasingly likely that juries would expect to hear medical testimony "as to the cause of death and the possibility of still-birth."[121] This, combined with a growing interest in the body as a source of knowledge, meant that the inquest became "the major form of pre-trial inquiry into suspicious infant deaths."[122] The historiography tends to focus on the medically tricky task of establishing live birth and separate existence,[123] or the social context of infanticide as a woman's crime frequently brought to light by other women,[124] but recently Elaine Farrell and Tim Siddons have pointed out the important yet under-researched role of the police in nineteenth-century infanticide investigations.[125] The chapter combines elements of all three historiographical strands, to consider the medico-legal approach to infant murder within the context of the whole investigation. Thus, although doctors were primarily interested in the victim's body, the focus of their interest varied depending on the infant's age: different forensic approaches were needed for newborns and older babies, and laymen accordingly had different roles in revealing the crime. Moreover, many doctors took on investigative but value-laden and sometimes antagonistic roles in dealing with reputed mothers, using intrusive physical examinations to establish recent delivery,[126] or reaching conclusions about sanity based on lay perceptions, often in relation to assumptions about unmarried women and always at the behest of the police, coroner or magistrate. The chapter therefore looks carefully at the changing content of medical evidence in cases of infant murder, as well as the medically inflected comments of lay witnesses and the accused women themselves, and then turns to consider the presentation and reception of medical evidence in court. The trial notebooks of Samuel Heywood (1753–1828), chief justice of the Carmarthen Circuit in South Wales from 1807 to 1828, are used as a source of information about the structure and content of criminal trials, the judge's prior preparation and attention to detail and, most crucially, the evidence presented and its interpretation. Many scholars have noted that doctors were reluctant to make statements that might lead to conviction, or were simply embarrassed by their ignorance in the witness box; but there were numerous instances where local surgeons were fully prepared to state that an infant had been murdered, particularly when the body showed signs of violence. It was up to the jury to make of that what they would, guided by the judge – who frequently pointed out that the pre-trial evidence was too weak to sustain a conviction. This chapter therefore uses medicine as a way to examine the history of criminal procedure revealed by judicial control of the jury.

The final chapter considers the active role of medical practitioners in crime scene investigation as a means of examining two related themes: the position and status of the expert witness; and the relationship between forensic medicine and forensic science. The distinction between them can best be expressed in relation to their principal concern or focus of interest: in forensic medicine, it is the body; in forensic science, it is things (which may be in, on or near a body). The modern expert witness emerged in the context of nineteenth-century urban poison and insanity trials, when a strong link between expert status and professional status was established.[127] But who deemed an individual to be competent to take on the role of expert, and how was that role acknowledged? Following a study of the on-the-ground work done by doctors at crime scenes and their use of scientific aids to investigation, the chapter will use financial data not previously reflected in the historiography to show that the attribution of expert status was locally determined. The notion of who was an expert was relative to who was not: trust and credibility were vested in medical professionals by officers of the law, and since most homicide cases were not mysterious but required only good attention to detail, local practitioners could act as experts. This chapter contributes to the historical interest in forensic science and scientific policing,[128] but adopts a more practice-led than epistemological focus for the period before the First World War.

While new in itself, the analysis presented here dovetails with a broader re-evaluation of eighteenth- and nineteenth-century crime, policing and criminal justice practice that has been under way for two decades. However, its innovative examination of the contribution made by medical practitioners to the investigation and prosecution of violent crime goes further than the existing historiography, both in scope and detail: it demonstrates the longstanding and influential impact doctors in England and Wales had on the procedures of criminal justice, prosecution strategies, and jury expectations. This yields remarkable new findings about aspects of medical practice hitherto overlooked by historians of medicine, and offers criminal justice historians a fresh way to contemplate the professional links on which the criminal justice system depends. In bringing the various strands of the book together, the concluding chapter will review the main arguments and conclusions on the role of medico-legal practice in developing policing and courtroom processes, indicate their wider significance and ramifications and discuss the several directions in which future research might usefully go.

Notes

1 Samuel Farr, *Elements of Medical Jurisprudence* (London: T. Becket, 1788), 68. Dease was even more explicit than Farr: "the surgeon, when called on, has no alternative; he must either avow his ignorance, or deliver his opinion." See William Dease, *Remarks on Medical Jurisprudence: Intended for the General Information of Juries and Young Surgeons* (Dublin: James Reilly, 1793), p. 3.

2 Bruce P. Smith, "English Criminal Justice Administration, 1650–1850: A Historiographic Essay," *Law and History Review* 25 (2007), pp. 593–634; Greg T. Smith, "Recent Themes in English Criminal Justice History," *Manitoba Law Journal* 35 (2011–12), pp. 285–292.

3 A. H. Manchester, *A Modern Legal History of England and Wales* (London: Butterworths, 1980); J. H. Baker, *An Introduction to English Legal History*, fourth edition (London: Butterworths, 2002).

4 Clive Emsley, *Crime and Society in England 1750–1900*, fourth edition (Harlow: Pearson, 2010).

5 David Taylor, *The New Police in Nineteenth-Century England: Crime, Conflict and Control* (Manchester: Manchester University Press, 1997); David J. A. Cairns, *Advocacy and the Making of the Adversarial Criminal Trial 1800–1865* (Oxford: Clarendon Press, 1998); John H. Langbein, *The Origins of Adversary Criminal Trial* (Oxford: Oxford University Press, 2003).

6 Shani D'Cruze and Louise A. Jackson, *Women, Crime and Justice in England since 1600* (Basingstoke: Palgrave, 2009).

7 Pioneering studies include: Keith Wrightson, "Infanticide in Earlier Seventeenth-Century England," *Local Population Studies* 15 (1975), pp. 10–22; J. A. Sharpe, "Domestic Homicide in Early Modern England," *The Historical Journal* 24 (1981), pp. 29–48; J. M. Beattie, *Crime and the Courts in England 1660–1800* (Princeton: Princeton University Press, 1986); and J. S. Cockburn, "Patterns of Violence in English Society: Homicide in Kent 1560–1985," *Past & Present* 130 (1991), pp. 70–106.

8 Anna Clark, *Women's Silence, Men's Violence: Sexual Assault in England 1770–1845* (London: Pandora, 1987); Kim Stevenson, "'Most Intimate Violations': Contextualising the Crime of Rape," in *Histories of Crime: Britain 1600–2000*, ed. Anne-Marie Kilday and David Nash (Basingstoke: Palgrave, 2010), pp. 80–99; Garthine Walker, "Rape, Acquittal and Culpability in Popular Crime Reports in England, *c.*1670–*c.*1750," *Past & Present* 220 (2013), pp. 115–142.

9 The *Oxford Dictionary of National Biography* does not mention Dease's *Remarks on Medical Jurisprudence*, neatly highlighting the neglect of medical contributions to legal processes that existed until quite recently. See C. Creighton, "Dease, William (c. 1752–1798), Surgeon," *Oxford Dictionary of National Biography*, 23 Sep 2004, www.oxforddnb.com/view/10.1093/ref:odnb/9780198614128.001.0001/odnb-9780198614128-e-7398 (accessed 6 Dec 2017).

10 This comment was made by Walker in relation to rape, "Rape, Acquittal and Culpability," p. 115, but it holds just as well for all forms of interpersonal violence, which has clearly become less acceptable since the early modern period. See, for example, J. Carter Wood, "A Useful Savagery: The Invention of Violence in Nineteenth-Century England," *Journal of Victorian Culture* 9 (2004), pp. 22–42.

11 Douglas Hay and Francis Snyder, "Using the Criminal Law, 1750–1850: Policing, Private Prosecution, and the State," in *Policing and Prosecution in Britain 1750–1850*, ed. Douglas Hay and Francis Snyder (Oxford: Clarendon Press, 1989), pp. 3–52; David Philips and Robert D. Storch, *Policing Provincial England 1829–1856: The Politics of Reform* (London and New York: Leicester University Press, 1999); Andrew T. Harris, *Policing the City: Crime and Legal Authority in London, 1780–1840* (Columbus: Ohio State University Press, 2004); Ruth Paley, "Dragging the Law into Disrepute," in *Law in the City: Proceedings of the Seventeenth British Legal History Conference 2005*, ed. Andrew Lewis, Paul Brand and Paul Mitchell (Dublin: Four Courts Press, 2007), pp. 283–304.

12 John H. Langbein, "The Criminal Trial before the Lawyers," *University of Chicago Law Review* 45 (1978), pp. 263–316; Stephan Landsman, "The Rise of the Contentious Spirit: Adversary Procedure in Eighteenth Century England," *Cornell Law Review* 75 (1990), pp. 497–609; David Bentley, *English Criminal Justice in the Nineteenth Century* (London: Hambledon Press, 1998).

13 Lindsay Farmer, "Criminal Responsibility and the Proof of Guilt," in *Modern Histories of Crime and Punishment*, ed. Markus D. Dubber and Lindsay Farmer (Stanford: Stanford University Press, 2007), p. 52. See also Lindsay Farmer, "'With All the Impressiveness and Substantial Value of Truth': Notable Trials and Criminal Justice, 1750–1930," *Law and Humanities* 1 (2007), pp. 57–78. The increase in the length of trials, due to the inclusion of more witnesses and more extensive examination and cross-examination of both lay and expert witnesses, was evident to the jurist James Fitzjames Stephen in 1860: "On Trial by Jury, and the Evidence of Experts," in *Papers Read before the Juridical Society, Vol. 2, 1858–1863* (London: William Maxwell, 1863), pp. 236–249.

14 The study of the office of coroner was initiated by R. F. Hunnisett in a series of articles published in the late 1950s but especially in his *The Medieval Coroner* (Cambridge: Cambridge University Press, 1961), but over 50 years later had attracted little attention according to Pamela J. Fisher, "The Politics of Sudden Death: The Office and Role of the Coroner in England and Wales, 1726–1888," PhD thesis, University of Leicester, 2007, 7. The work of barrister and criminologist J. D. J. Havard focused closely on inquest procedure in the nineteenth and twentieth centuries: *The Detection of Secret Homicide: A Study of the Medico-Legal System of Investigation of Sudden and Unexplained Deaths* (London: Macmillan, 1960).

15 Indeed, Matthew Lockwood has recently argued that during the early modern period medical evidence was not particularly necessary for effective homicide investigation: *The Conquest of Death: Violence and the Birth of the Modern English State* (New Haven: Yale University Press, 2017), pp. 105–145.

16 Early research was carried out mainly by T. R. Forbes, a doctor who looked for evidence of medico-legal practice in coroner's inquisitions and selected trial transcripts. See, for example, Thomas Rogers Forbes, *Surgeons at the Bailey: English Forensic Medicine to 1878* (New Haven: Yale University Press, 1985); "Inquests into London and Middlesex Homicides, 1673–1782," *Yale Journal of Biology and Medicine* 50 (1977), pp. 207–220; "Crowner's Quest," *Transactions of the American Philosophical Society* 68 (1978), pp. 5–52; "Early Forensic Medicine in England: The Angus Murder Trial," *Journal of the History of Medicine and Allied Sciences* 36 (1981), pp. 296–309; "Coroners' Inquisitions from London Parishes of the Duchy of Lancaster: The Strand, Clapham, Enfield, and Edmonton, 1831–1883," *Journal of the History of Medicine and Allied Sciences* 43 (1988), pp. 191–203. See also Gary I. Greenwald and Maria White Greenwald, "Medicolegal Progress in Inquests of Felonious Deaths: Westminster, 1761–1866," *Journal of Legal Medicine* 2 (1981), pp. 193–264. The Greenwalds were also medical doctors.

17 Carol A. G. Jones, *Expert Witnesses: Science, Medicine, and the Practice of Law* (Oxford: Clarendon Press, 1994); Ian A. Burney, *Bodies of Evidence: Medicine and the Politics of the English Inquest, 1830–1926* (Baltimore: The Johns Hopkins University Press, 2000); Tal Golan, *Laws of Men and Laws of Nature: The History of Scientific Expert Testimony in England and America* (Cambridge, MA: Harvard University Press, 2004).

18 Catherine Crawford, "The Emergence of English Forensic Medicine: Medical Evidence in Common-law Courts, 1730–1830," DPhil thesis, University of Oxford, 1987; Jennifer Ward, "Origins and Development of Forensic Medicine and Forensic Science in England 1823–1946," PhD thesis, Open University, 1993.

19 Most studies focused on London, for example: Forbes, *Surgeons at the Bailey* and Stephan Landsman, "One Hundred Years of Rectitude: Medical Witnesses at the Old Bailey, 1717–1817," *Law and History Review* 16 (1998), pp. 445–494. Fisher's thesis offers a welcome national perspective: "Politics of Sudden Death," pp. 184–211.

20 Michael Clark and Catherine Crawford, eds., *Legal Medicine in History* (Cambridge: Cambridge University Press, 1994). Seven of the 13 chapters focus on England, covering the seventeenth century through to the twentieth.

21 Catherine Crawford, "Legalizing Medicine: Early Modern Legal Systems and the Growth of Medico-Legal Knowledge," in *Legal Medicine in History*, ed. Michael Clark and Catherine Crawford (Cambridge: Cambridge University Press, 1994), p. 108.

22 Julia Rudolph, "Gender and the Development of Forensic Science: A Case Study," *English Historical Review* 123 (2008), pp. 924–946; Carol Loar, "Medical Knowledge and the Early Modern English Coroner's Inquest," *Social History of Medicine* 23 (2010), pp. 475–491. This is because they examined sources other than inquisitions, which typically do not include evidence about post-mortems or the questioning of medical witnesses. Rather, as Krista Kesselring has pointed out (personal communication, 28 Dec 2017), information of this nature tends to appear in the records generated by "contested cases or other ancillary documents."

23 Keir Waddington, *An Introduction to the Social History of Medicine: Europe since 1500* (Basingstoke: Palgrave, 2011), pp. 3–15.

24 Mark S. R. Jenner and Patrick Wallis, "The Medical Marketplace," in *Medicine and the Market in England and Its Colonies, c. 1450–1850*, ed. Mark S. R. Jenner and Patrick Wallis (Basingstoke: Palgrave, 2007), p. 16.

25 Catherine Crawford, "A Scientific Profession: Medical Reform and Forensic Medicine in British Periodicals of the Early Nineteenth Century," in *British Medicine in an Age of Reform*, ed. Roger French and Andrew Wear (London and New York: Routledge, 1991), pp. 203–230.

26 Sara M. Butler, *Forensic Medicine and Death Investigation in Medieval England* (New York: Routledge, 2015).

27 Malcolm Gaskill, "The Displacement of Providence: Policing and Prosecution in Seventeenth- and Eighteenth-Century England," *Continuity and Change* 11 (1996), pp. 341–374; Vanessa McMahon, "Reading the Body: Dissection and the 'Murder' of Sarah Stout, Hertfordshire, 1699," *Social History of Medicine* 19 (2006), pp. 19–35. McMahon's pessimistic argument is undermined by Loar, "Medical Knowledge and the Early Modern English Coroner's Inquest." See also Lockwood, *The Conquest of Death*, pp. 111–123 and James Oldham, "The Jury of Matrons," *Georgetown Law* (Fall/Winter 2006), pp. 50–55.

28 Orna Alyagon Darr, *Marks of an Absolute Witch: Evidentiary Dilemmas in Early Modern England* (Farnham: Ashgate, 2011), pp. 209–225, 259.

29 David Harley, "Political Post-Mortems and Morbid Anatomy in Seventeenth-Century England," *Social History of Medicine* 7 (1994), pp. 1–28; David Harley, "The Scope of Legal Medicine in Lancashire and Cheshire, 1660–1760," in *Legal Medicine in History*, ed. Clark and Crawford, pp. 45–63.

30 W. B. Ober, "Infanticide in Eighteenth-Century England: William Hunter's Contribution to the Forensic Problem," *Pathology Annual* 21 (1986), pp. 311–319; Mark Jackson, "Suspicious Infant Deaths: The Statute of 1624 and Medical Evidence at Coroners' Inquests," in *Legal Medicine in History*, ed. Clark and Crawford, 64–86; Mark Jackson, *New-Born Child Murder: Women, Illegitimacy and the Courts in Eighteenth-Century England* (Manchester: Manchester University Press, 1996), pp. 84–109; Mary Clayton, "Changes in Old Bailey Trials for the Murder of Newborn Babies, 1674–1803," *Continuity and Change* 24 (2009), pp. 347–351. In their work on infanticide in early modern Cheshire, Dickinson and Sharpe focus little on medical evidence but do note that it became more important during the course of the eighteenth century: J. R. Dickinson and J. A. Sharpe, "Infanticide in Early Modern England: The Court of Great Sessions at Chester, 1650–1800," in *Infanticide: Historical Perspectives on Child Murder and Concealment, 1550–2000*, ed. Mark Jackson (Aldershot: Ashgate, 2002), p. 46.

31 Joel Peter Eigen, *Witnessing Insanity: Madness and Mad-Doctors in the English Court* (New Haven: Yale University Press, 1995); Dana Rabin, *Identity, Crime and Legal Responsibility in Eighteenth-Century England* (Basingstoke: Palgrave Macmillan, 2004).

32 Crawford, "The Emergence of English Forensic Medicine" and "A Scientific Profession"; Ward, "Origins and Development." Taylor began teaching in January 1831 when the spring lecture series commenced at Guy's: *Public Ledger and Daily Advertiser*, 10 Jan 1831, p. 1.

33 Olive Anderson, *Suicide in Victorian and Edwardian England* (Oxford: Clarendon Press, 1987), pp. 225–230 on the links between insanity and suicide; Katherine D. Watson, "Medical and Chemical Expertise in English Trials for Criminal Poisoning, 1750–1914," *Medical History* 50 (2006), pp. 373–390; Karen Jane Merry, "Murder by Poison in Scotland during the Nineteenth and Early Twentieth Centuries," PhD thesis, University of Glasgow, 2010.

34 The historiography suggests that apparently objective medical evidence of child rape was interpreted by doctors and jurors through a cultural framework of negative assumptions about working-class pubescent girls, allowing rape myths to influence legal decision-making. See J. B. Lyons, "Sir William Wilde's Medico-Legal Observations," *Medical History* 42 (1997), pp. 437–454; Louise A. Jackson, *Child Sexual Abuse in Victorian England* (London and New York: Routledge, 2000), pp. 71–89; Ivan Crozier and Gethin

Rees, "Making a Space for Medical Expertise: Medical Knowledge of Sexual Assault and the Construction of Boundaries between Forensic Medicine and the Law in Late Nineteenth-Century England," *Law, Culture and the Humanities* 8 (2012), pp. 285–304; Victoria Bates, *Sexual Forensics in Victorian and Edwardian England: Age, Crime and Consent in the Courts* (Basingstoke: Palgrave Macmillan, 2016).

35 G. K. Behlmer, "Deadly Motherhood: Infanticide and Medical Opinion in Mid-Victorian England," *Journal of the History of Medicine and Allied Sciences* 34 (1979), pp. 403–427; Tony Ward, "The Sad Subject of Infanticide: Law, Medicine and Child Murder, 1860–1938," *Social and Legal Studies* 8 (1999), pp. 163–180; Mary Beth Emmerichs, "Getting Away with Murder? Homicide and the Coroners in Nineteenth-Century London," *Social Science History* 25 (2001), pp. 93–100; Hilary Marland, *Dangerous Motherhood: Insanity and Childbirth in Victorian Britain* (Basingstoke: Palgrave Macmillan, 2004); Daniel J. R. Grey, "Discourses of Infanticide in England, 1880–1922," PhD thesis, Roehampton University, 2008, chapters 3 and 4.

36 Ian A. Burney, "A Poisoning of No Substance: The Trials of Medico-Legal Proof in Mid-Victorian England," *Journal of British Studies* 38 (1999), pp. 59–92; "Testing Testimony: Toxicology and the Law of Evidence in Early Nineteenth-Century England," *Studies in History and Philosophy of Science* 33 (2002), pp. 289–314; Tony Ward, "A Mania for Suspicion: Poisoning, Science, and the Law," in *Criminal Conversations: Victorian Crimes, Social Panic, and Moral Outrage*, ed. Judith Rowbotham and Kim Stevenson (Columbus: Ohio State University Press, 2005), pp. 40–56; Roger Smith, *Trial by Medicine: Insanity and Responsibility in Victorian Trials* (Edinburgh: Edinburgh University Press, 1981); Joel Peter Eigen, *Unconscious Crime: Mental Absence and Criminal Responsibility in Victorian London* (Baltimore: Johns Hopkins University Press, 2003).

37 Stephan Landsman, "Of Witches, Madmen, and Products Liability: An Historical Survey of the Use of Expert Testimony," *Behavioral Sciences and the Law* 13 (1995), pp. 131–157.

38 Katherine D. Watson, *Forensic Medicine in Western Society: A History* (Abingdon: Routledge, 2011), 46–50.

39 M. A. Crowther and Brenda M. White, "Medicine, Property and the Law in Britain 1800–1914," *The Historical Journal* 31 (1988), p. 856.

40 The turn to specialist experts was most visible in the fields of toxicology and psychiatry during the Victorian period and pathology in the early twentieth century. See Watson, "Medical and Chemical Expertise"; Ian A. Burney, *Poison, Detection, and the Victorian Imagination* (Manchester: Manchester University Press, 2006); Anne Crowther, "The Toxicology of Robert Christison: European Influences and British Practice in the Early Nineteenth Century," in *Chemistry, Medicine and Crime: Mateu J.B. Orfila (1787–1853) and His Times*, ed. José Ramón Bertomeu-Sánchez and Agustí Nieto-Galan (Sagamore Beach, MA: Watson Publishing International, 2006), pp. 125–152; Katherine D. Watson, "Criminal Poisoning in England and the Origins of the Marsh Test for Arsenic," in *Chemistry, Medicine and Crime*, ed. Bertomeu-Sánchez and Nieto-Galan, pp. 183–206; Ian A. Burney, "Bones of Contention: Mateu Orfila, Normal Arsenic and British Toxicology," in *Chemistry, Medicine and Crime*, ed. Bertomeu-Sánchez and Nieto-Galan, pp. 243–259; Joel Peter Eigen, *Mad-Doctors in the Dock: Defending the Diagnosis, 1760–1913* (Baltimore: Johns Hopkins University Press, 2016); Ian Burney and Neil Pemberton, "Bruised Witness: Bernard Spilsbury and the Performance of Early Twentieth-Century English Forensic Pathology," *Medical History* 55 (2011), pp. 41–60.

41 Norman V. Ambage, "The Origins and Development of the Home Office Forensic Science Service, 1931–1967," PhD thesis, University of Lancaster, 1987; Norman Ambage and Michael Clark, "Unbuilt Bloomsbury: Medico-Legal Institutes and Forensic Science Laboratories in England between the Wars," in *Legal Medicine in History*, ed. Clark and Crawford, pp. 293–313.

42 Keith Laybourn and David Taylor, *Policing in England and Wales, 1918–39: The Fed, Flying Squads and Forensics* (Basingstoke: Palgrave Macmillan, 2011); Amy Helen Bell, *Murder Capital: Suspicious Deaths in London, 1933–53* (Manchester: Manchester University Press,

2015); Alison Adam, *A History of Forensic Science: British Beginnings in the Twentieth Century* (Abingdon: Routledge, 2016); Ian Burney and Neil Pemberton, *Murder and the Making of English CSI* (Baltimore: Johns Hopkins University Press, 2016).

43 Cockburn, "Patterns of Violence," pp. 79–87 found that the greatest proportion of homicides were committed with either sharp or blunt instruments, or by beating/kicking, a finding echoed in my study.

44 The few works devoted to forensic issues are not concerned with the criminal courts: R. W. Ireland, "Eugene Buckley and the Diagnosis of Insanity in the Early Victorian Prison," *Llafur* 6 (1993), pp. 5–17; T. G. Davies, "Judging the Sanity of an Individual: Some South Wales Civil Legal Actions of Psychiatric Interest," *The National Library of Wales Journal* 29 (1996), pp. 455–467. An extremely brief consideration of 'forensic techniques' is included in Rachael Jones, *Crime, Courts and Community in Mid-Victorian Wales: Montgomeryshire, People and Places* (Cardiff: University of Wales Press, 2018), pp. 72–74. For a recent study of Welsh criminal justice history, see Richard W. Ireland, *Land of White Gloves? A History of Crime and Punishment in Wales* (Abingdon: Routledge, 2015).

45 Alun Withey, "Unhealthy Neglect? The Medicine and Medical Historiography of Early Modern Wales," *Social History of Medicine* 21 (2008), pp. 163–174; Alun Withey, *Physick and the Family: Health, Medicine and Care in Wales, 1600–1750* (Manchester: Manchester University Press, 2011); Stephen Roberts, "'Necessary Precautions': Public Health in Wrexham 1830–1848," *Transactions of the Denbighshire Historical Society* 45 (1996), pp. 59–88; Anne Borsay, ed., *Medicine in Wales c. 1800–2000: Public Service or Private Commodity* (Cardiff: University of Wales Press, 2003); Pamela Michael, *Care and Treatment of the Mentally Ill in North Wales, 1800–2000* (Cardiff: University of Wales Press, 2003); Pamela Michael and Charles Webster, eds., *Health and Society in Twentieth-Century Wales* (Cardiff: University of Wales Press, 2006).

46 Thomas Glyn Watkin, *The Legal History of Wales* (Cardiff: University of Wales Press, 2007).

47 Peter King, *Crime and Law in England, 1750–1840: Remaking Justice from the Margins* (Cambridge: Cambridge University Press, 2006), pp. 60–61. For a further example of this thesis see Peter King and Richard Ward, "Rethinking the Bloody Code in Eighteenth-Century Britain: Capital Punishment at the Centre and on the Periphery," *Past & Present* 228 (2015), pp. 159–205.

48 Fisher, "Politics of Sudden Death."

49 Grey, "Discourses of Infanticide"; Victoria L. Bates, "'Not an Exact Science': Medical Approaches to Age and Sexual Offences in England, 1850–1914," PhD thesis, University of Exeter, 2012.

50 Her thesis, completed at Queen's University Belfast in 2010, has since been published: Elaine Farrell, *'A Most Diabolical Deed': Infanticide and Irish Society, 1850–1900* (Manchester: Manchester University Press, 2013), pp. 48–71.

51 Nicholas Duvall, "Forensic Medicine in Scotland, 1914–39," PhD thesis, University of Manchester, 2013; Tim Siddons, "Suspected New-Born Child Murder and Concealment of Pregnancy in Scotland, c.1812–c.1930," PhD thesis, University of Edinburgh, 2013.

52 I am here drawing on the work of Mike Redmayne, *Expert Evidence and Criminal Justice* (Oxford: Oxford University Press, 2001), which notes that the goal of scientific evidence in the criminal process is to improve verdict accuracy.

53 Excellent examples include Beattie, *Crime and the Courts in England 1660–1800*, pp. 267–399; Emsley, *Crime and Society in England*, pp. 192–260; and John Minkes, "Wales and the 'Bloody Code': The Brecon Circuit of the Court of Great Sessions in the 1750s," *Welsh History Review* 22 (2005), pp. 679–685. For property crime, see Peter King, *Crime, Justice and Discretion in England 1740–1820* (Oxford: Oxford University Press, 2000), pp. 47–125 and pp. 221–258.

54 For a recent example see Patrick Polden, "Coroners and Their Courts," in *The Oxford History of the Laws of England, Vol. 11, The Legal System 1820–1914* (Oxford: Oxford University Press, 2010), p. 951. The chapter is at pp. 934–955.

55 Neither Burney, *Bodies of Evidence*, nor Fisher, "Politics of Sudden Death," have much to say about lawyers or the police.

56 This term refers to the uniformed, organised, paid police introduced in the late 1820s and 1830s. They were accountable to central or local government rather than parishes, they had a wider responsibility for law and order and contemporaries perceived them as new: David Taylor, *Crime, Policing and Punishment in England, 1750–1914* (Basingstoke: Macmillan, 1998), pp. 71–87; Emsley, *Crime and Society in England*, pp. 227–260.

57 Emsley, *Crime and Society in England*, p. 250.

58 Edward Umfreville, *Lex Coronatoria: Or, the Office and Duty of Coroners*, Vol. 2 (London: R. Griffiths; T. Becket, 1761), pp. 295–296, 510. The surgeon's contract with the parish covered his payment but, if not, any financial wrangling would be between him and the vestry.

59 Richard Burn, *The Justice of the Peace and Parish Officer*, third edition (London: Henry Lintot, 1756), p. 200.

60 Umfreville did not mention this, but 60 years later the practice was considered established: Charles Cottu, *On the Administration of Criminal Justice in England; and the Spirit of the English Government* (London: Richard Stevens and Charles Reader, 1822), p. 38.

61 Edward Umfreville, *Lex Coronatoria: Or, the Office and Duty of Coroners*, Vol. 1 (London: R. Griffiths and T. Becket, 1761), p. 206.

62 Umfreville, *Lex Coronatoria*, Vol. 2, pp. 314–316, 322–330 explains the wording necessary to ensure that an indictment or inquisition charged a particular offence.

63 Cottu, *On the Administration of Criminal Justice in England*, pp. 87–88.

64 Langbein, "The Criminal Trial Before the Lawyers"; John H. Langbein, "The Historical Origins of the Privilege against Self-Incrimination at Common Law," *Michigan Law Review* 92 (1994), pp. 1047–1085; David Lemmings, "Criminal Trial Procedure in Eighteenth-Century England: The Impact of Lawyers," *The Journal of Legal History* 26 (2005), pp. 73–82.

65 Langbein, *Origins of Adversary Criminal Trial*, pp. 167–170.

66 Ibid., p. 170.

67 T. P. Gallanis, "The Mystery of Old Bailey Counsel," *Cambridge Law Journal* 65 (2006), p. 173.

68 David Lemmings, *Professors of the Law: Barristers and English Legal Culture in the Eighteenth Century* (Oxford: Oxford University Press, 2000), p. 208.

69 Ibid., pp. 219–222; Langbein, *Origins of Adversary Criminal Trial*, pp. 258–284.

70 William Blackstone, *Commentaries on the Laws of England*, Vol. 4 (Oxford: Clarendon Press, 1769), p. 21.

71 Brian P. Levack, "Review of *Marks of an Absolute Witch: Evidentiary Dilemmas in Early Modern England*, by Orna Alyagon Darr," *Law and History Review* 30 (2012), p. 938.

72 John H. Langbein, "Historical Foundations of the Law of Evidence: A View from the Ryder Sources," *Columbia Law Review* 96 (1996), p. 1172.

73 Geoffrey Gilbert, *The Law of Evidence* (Dublin: S. Cotter, 1754); Thomas Starkie, *A Practical Treatise of the Law of Evidence, and Digest of Proofs in Civil and Criminal Proceedings* (London: J. & W.T. Clarke, 1824).

74 T. P. Gallanis, "The Rise of Modern Evidence Law," *Iowa Law Review* 84 (1999), p. 508.

75 Ibid., pp. 518–523.

76 Capel Lofft, ed., *The Law of Evidence by Lord Chief Baron Gilbert*, Vol. 1 (London: J. F. & C. Rivington, T. Longman, C. Dilly, W. Clarke & Son, and W. Otridge, 1791), p. 301.

77 Ibid., p. 302.

78 John Frederick Archbold, *A Summary of the Law Relative to Pleading and Evidence in Criminal Cases* (London: R. Pheney, 1822), p. 93.

79 Ibid., p. 110.

80 Henry Delacombe Roome and Robert Ernest Ross, eds., *Archbold's Pleading, Evidence and Practice in Criminal Cases, by Sir John Jervis*, twenty-sixth edition (London: Sweet and Maxwell, 1922), p. 451.

81 Assault was a misdemeanour and thus falls outside the purview of this project, although it could certainly involve medical witnesses.

82 The study of crime and criminals necessitates an investigation of the institutions that created and defined them. Thus, because criminals are identified, labelled and processed by the criminal justice system, its records provide a foundation for any historical investigation of criminality: R. S. Sindall, "The Criminal Statistics of Nineteenth-Century Cities: A New Approach," *Urban History* 13 (1986), pp. 28–36.

83 Daniel Duman, *The Judicial Bench in England 1727–1875: The Reshaping of a Professional Elite* (London: Royal Historical Society, 1982), 7; Susan C. Lawrence, "Entrepreneurs and Private Enterprise: The Development of Medical Lecturing in London, 1775–1820," *Bulletin of the History of Medicine* 62 (1988), pp. 171–192.

84 I am grateful to Anne-Marie Kilday for this insight.

85 Michael Steed, "The Core-Periphery Dimension of British Politics," *Political Geography Quarterly* 5 (1986), pp. s91–s103.

86 Richard Suggett, "The Welsh Language and the Court of Great Sessions," in *The Welsh Language before the Industrial Revolution*, ed. Geraint H. Jenkins (Cardiff: University of Wales Press, 1997), p. 153.

87 Silent corrections of factual or transcription errors in the Great Sessions and Old Bailey online databases were made.

88 Déirdre M. Dwyer, "Expert Evidence in the English Civil Courts, 1550–1880," *The Journal of Legal History* 28 (2007), p. 101; John H. Langbein, "The Prosecutorial Origins of Defence Counsel in the Eighteenth Century: The Appearance of Solicitors," *The Cambridge Law Journal* 58 (1999), pp. 314–365.

89 The selected years include the following: 1780–1789, 1805–1809, 1830–1839, 1840–1846, 1861, 1864, 1870–1875, 1881, 1884, 1891, 1894, 1900, 1904, 1911 and 1913. A small number of eighteenth-century murders classed as petty treason, and post-1834 cases that occurred in Essex, Kent or Surrey were also included. Manslaughter cases were excluded after the 1805–1809 set for reasons of scale: they outnumbered murder trials but were often shorter in length.

90 Clark, *Women's Silence, Men's Violence*, pp. 17–18 on the restricted coverage of the sexual details of rape in the *Proceedings* and in newspapers.

91 Andrew Hobbs, "When the Provincial Press was the National Press (c.1836–c.1900)," *International Journal of Regional and Local History* 5 (2009), pp. 16–43; on the increasing role played by lawyers as court reporters in the nineteenth century see Judith Rowbotham, Kim Stevenson and Samantha Pegg, *Crime News in Modern Britain: Press Reporting and Responsibility, 1820–2010* (Basingstoke: Palgrave, 2013), pp. 25–28, 32–33.

92 As James Mussell observes, "the digitization of large tracts of the nineteenth-century press has transformed the terms upon which we discover material and attempt to recover its meanings." See *The Nineteenth-Century Press in the Digital Age* (Basingstoke: Palgrave Macmillan, 2012), p. 28.

93 Judith Rowbotham and Kim Stevenson, "'For Today in this Arena . . .': Legal Performativity and Dramatic Convention in the Victorian Criminal Justice System," *Journal of Criminal Justice and Popular Culture* 14 (2007), p. 121.

94 Tim Hitchcock, "Confronting the Digital: Or How Academic History Writing Lost the Plot," *Social and Cultural History* 10 (2013), pp. 9–23.

95 Even allegedly full trial reports do not record all the evidence given in court. See for example two accounts of the same trial in 1740: the second contains more or different details including three additional defence witnesses; but the surgeon's evidence is the same in both pamphlets. *The Suffolk Parricide; being the Trial, Life, Transactions, and Last Dying Words, of Charles Drew, of Long-Melford, in the County of Suffolk* (London: J. Standen, 1740) and *The Genuine Trial of Charles Drew, for the Murder of His Own Father, at the Assizes held at Bury St Edmund's*, second edition (London: C. Corbett, 1740).

96 *Carmarthen Journal and South Wales Weekly Advertiser*, 20 Apr 1811, p. 4. The 'satisfactory proof' occupied 2 of 17 pages in the trial judge's notes: National Library of Wales (hereafter NLW), MSS 202D, Notebooks of Samuel Heywood, Vol. 10 (1811), pp. 26–42.

97 Emsley, *Crime and Society in England*, pp. 57–95.
98 Ibid., pp. 21–56 (p. 24).
99 In a widely influential article, Howard Taylor suggested that the police and government rationed murder prosecutions to save costs: "Rationing Crime: The Political Economy of Criminal Statistics since the 1850s," *Economic History Review* 51 (1998), pp. 584–588. See also Peter King, "The Impact of Urbanization on Murder Rates and on the Geography of England and Wales, 1780–1850," *Historical Journal* 53 (2010), pp. 675–678. Historians of infanticide stress the importance of the dark figure: see for example Anne-Marie Kilday, *A History of Infanticide in Britain c. 1600 to the Present* (Basingstoke: Palgrave Macmillan, 2013).
100 The last execution for rape occurred in 1836; between 1837 and 1867 there were on average about ten executions for murder each year, rising to nearer 17 per year in the period 1868–1899: see *Public Executions 1837–1868*, www.capitalpunishmentuk. org/1837.html (accessed 17 Dec 2017) and Steve Fielding, *The Hangman's Record, Volume One 1868–1899* (Beckenham: Chancery House Press, 1994).
101 Victor Bailey, *'This Rash Act': Suicide across the Life Cycle in the Victorian City* (Stanford: Stanford University Press, 1998), pp. 50–52, 66. In Kingston-Upon-Hull in the period 1837–1899, 13.1% of all suicide inquests included a post-mortem but half that number were conducted in the 1890s alone; and a higher proportion were carried out on those who died by poison or gunshot than by hanging or drowning. By contrast, Greenwald and Greenwald found that in the City of Westminster in the mid-1860s a minimum of 40% of inquests (on accident casualties) involved a post-mortem, but in cases of suicide the figure was only 11%. Their figure for homicide, 17%, is strangely low, probably because of the way they classified six cases in which the final verdict was not actually one of homicide: "Medicolegal Progress in Inquests of Felonious Deaths," pp. 208, 214–215.
102 John Tidd Pratt, *A Collection of the Late Statutes, Passed for the Administration of Criminal Justice in England* (London: W. Benning, 1827), pp. 4–5.
103 Fisher, "The Politics of Sudden Death," p. 19.
104 During the nineteenth century there were rarely more than 400 murders reported annually: Emsley, *Crime and Society in England*, p. 42.
105 Havard, *Detection of Secret Homicide*, pp. 77–96.
106 For an example of extensive cross-examination of all witnesses, including three doctors, at an inquest, see the case of William Price, who was accused of murdering a soldier: NLW GS 4/398/2/3–5, pp. 9–18, Breconshire, 1827. The attorney, Mr Middleton Powell, was probably acting on behalf of the army, not the accused.
107 Geraint H. Jenkins, Richard Suggett and Eryn M. White, "The Welsh Language in Early Modern Wales," in *The Welsh Language before the Industrial Revolution*, ed. Geraint H. Jenkins (Cardiff: University of Wales Press, 1997), p. 48.
108 In 1891 54.4% of the population could speak Welsh, but in 1901 only 15% were monolingual: G. E. Jones, *Modern Wales: A Concise History*, second edition (Cambridge: Cambridge University Press, 1994), pp. 211–212.
109 John Minkes has pointed out that from the inception of the Welsh law courts in 1543 as part of the process of unification between England and Wales, it was assumed that interpreters would be employed: "Wales and the 'Bloody Code'," pp. 673–674. Bills compiled by the clerks of assize of the North Wales Circuit in the first two decades of the nineteenth century show that the standard fee paid to court translators was 10s. 6d. per trial. Later in the century pre-trial translation was done by police officers, legal officials or civilians.
110 See for example the trial of John Roberts, reported in *The North Wales Chronicle*, 29 July 1853, p. 3: "As the prisoner spoke in Welsh, he [the coroner] translated it into English, and it was then taken down. He is positive that he gave a correct translation. After it was taken down, it was again translated into Welsh, and read over to the prisoner. It was translated as nearly as possible in the same words as the prisoner had used himself. After it had been read over to the prisoner, he put his name to it."

111 William Russell Oldnall, *The Practice of the Court of Great Sessions on the Carmarthen Circuit* (London: J. Butterworth, 1814), "The Practice of the Carmarthen Circuit," p. 24.

112 I am grateful to Sara Butler for this insight.

113 Drawing on recent historiography, Lynsey Cullen explains the distinction between anatomisation and post-mortem as lying in the explicit focus of the latter on establishing cause of death: "Post-Mortem in the Victorian Asylum: Practice, Purpose and Findings at the Littlemore County Lunatic Asylum, 1886–7," *History of Psychiatry* 28 (2017), pp. 283–284.

114 Jackson, *New-born Child Murder*, pp. 84–109; Siddons, "Suspected New-Born Child Murder," pp. 254–262.

115 William Wills, *An Essay on the Rationale of Circumstantial Evidence* (London: Longman, Orme, Brown, Green, and Longmans, 1838); Claire Valier, "True Crime Stories: Scientific Methods of Criminal Investigation, Criminology and Historiography," *British Journal of Criminology* 38 (1998), pp. 88–105; Barbara J. Shapiro, "Oaths, Credibility and the Legal Process in Early Modern England: Part Two," *Law and Humanities* 7 (2013), pp. 19–54.

116 The National Archives (hereafter TNA), ASSI 72/4, Regina v. Thomas Nash, Glamorgan, 1885. The surgeon, David Howell Thomas of Swansea, had been the main medical witness in six previous murder trials since 1865.

117 Jackson, *New-Born Child Murder*, pp. 70–72; Harley, "The Scope of Legal Medicine in Lancashire and Cheshire," pp. 53–55; Dickinson and Sharpe, "Infanticide in Early Modern England," pp. 45–47; Clayton, "Changes in Old Bailey Trials," pp. 347–351.

118 Shani D'Cruze, *Crimes of Outrage: Sex, Violence and Victorian Working Women* (London: UCL Press, 1998); Martin J. Wiener, *Men of Blood: Violence, Manliness and Criminal Justice in Victorian England* (Cambridge: Cambridge University Press, 2004); J. Carter Wood, *Violence and Crime in Nineteenth-Century England: The Shadow of Our Refinement* (London: Routledge, 2004); Desmond J. Newell, "Masculinity and the Plebeian Honour Fight: Dispute Resolution in Georgian England," PhD thesis, Oxford Brookes University, 2016, pp. 172–195.

119 TNA ASSI 65/10, Regina v. Robert Jones, Flintshire, 1876.

120 For example, a Staffordshire coroner sent a suspected murderer's clothes to Dr Francis Wrightson, an independent analytical chemist in Birmingham, to determine whether they were stained with blood. See TNA ASSI 6/10, Regina v. Richard Hale, Staffordshire, 1864.

121 Jackson, *New-Born Child Murder*, p. 86.

122 Ibid., p. 88.

123 R. J. Kellett, "Infanticide and Child Destruction: The Historical, Legal and Pathological Aspects," *Forensic Science International* 53 (1992), p. 9; Grey, "Discourses of Infanticide," pp. 151–175.

124 See for example Jackson, *New-Born Child Murder*, pp. 60–83 and Kilday, *A History of Infanticide in Britain*, pp. 52–58.

125 Farrell, *Infanticide and Irish Society*, pp. 120–177; Siddons, "Suspected New-Born Child Murder," pp. 185–203.

126 Daniel J. R. Grey has examined this issue from a feminist perspective in a narrow time period: "'What Woman Is Safe . . .?': Coerced Medical Examinations, Suspected Infanticide, and the Response of the Women's Movement in Britain, 1871–1881," *Women's History Review* 22 (2013), pp. 403–421.

127 Relevant secondary sources have been cited in notes 36 and 40. One might add: Tony Ward, "Law, Common Sense and the Authority of Science: Expert Witnesses and Criminal Insanity in England, ca. 1840–1940," *Social & Legal Studies* 6 (1997), pp. 343–362; Tony Ward, "Observers, Advisers, or Authorities? Experts, Juries and Criminal Responsibility in Historical Perspective," *The Journal of Forensic Psychiatry* 12 (2001), pp. 105–122; Arlie Loughnan and Tony Ward, "Emergent Authority and Expert Knowledge: Psychiatry and Criminal Responsibility in the UK," *International Journal of Law and Psychiatry* 37 (2014), pp. 25–36; Holly Easton, "Communities and Interactions in Nineteenth-Century Scottish and English Toxicology," MA thesis, University of Canterbury, 2017.

128 Adam, *A History of Forensic Science*, chapters 1 and 2; Burney and Pemberton, *Murder and the Making of English CSI*, chapters 1 and 2.

2 Medical education and forensic medicine

> It has been erroneously stated by some writers, that the science of medical jurisprudence, is nothing more than the application of the elementary branches of medicine to the elucidation of judicial investigations; and consequently that a scientific medical man must necessarily be a good jurist. This is not correct, inasmuch as the most scientific physicians and surgeons have proved to be the worst jurists, because they could not derive the requisite information on medico-legal science from the common systems of medicine or surgery, as it is only to be derived from works exclusively devoted to the subject.
>
> Michael Ryan, *A Manual of Medical Jurisprudence*
> (London: Renshaw and Rush, 1831), p. ix

When Dr Michael Ryan (1800–1840), lecturer on medical jurisprudence in one of the numerous private medical schools in London,[1] warned readers of his new textbook that the subject required specialist teaching, he was merely stating the obvious. Medical practitioners, particularly surgeons, were well aware that medico-legal practice was a unique undertaking that presented numerous pitfalls for the unwary but might be professionally rewarding for the proficient. As Catherine Crawford has shown, medical reformers of the early nineteenth century seized upon forensic medicine as the hallmark of a reformed and improved medical curriculum: it was thought to foster a critical attitude to evidence, was concerned to identify causation and helped doctors to establish their civic authority and social importance. It was one of few areas of public life "in which the medical sciences could be seen really to matter."[2] Reality often fell short of the ideal, however, because medical evidence was ignored, practitioners were reluctant to get involved or they experienced problems under cross-examination in court, contradicted each other or were simply ignorant.[3] And yet there was a growing expectation in the legal profession that, where relevant to a case, medical opinion was desirable.[4] Thus, as Ryan had suggested, doctors who got involved in medico-legal work needed to understand the requirements of the law, not just medical theory and practice. How then did they learn what those requirements were?

This chapter sets out to examine the place of forensic medicine in English medical education, and to uncover precisely what the average English practitioner was taught. From this, it concludes that the knowledge doctors had was sufficient to enable them to tackle a typical medico-legal case if called upon to do so. This approach circumvents the usual historiographical focus on 'expertise',[5] and, in so doing, repositions the argument away from negative comparisons with neighbouring countries considered more advanced such as Scotland, France and Germany in order to concentrate on what was typical in England and how that changed over the period under study. Thus, the chapter asks this: what did students know and how useful was it to them? The accent is not on professional expertise in and of itself, but on how those who possessed specialist knowledge imparted it to students destined to become general practitioners. An important finding derived from the teaching content delivered at four different points between the late eighteenth century and 1900 is that there was a consistent stress on infanticide, suggesting that the effort to control this offence, discussed in more detail in Chapter 4, was a particular spur for the development of forensic medicine and for the refinement of medico-legal practice.[6]

Teaching and learning forensic medicine: an overview

While a free market economy cannot produce the form of a medical innovation or specialisation,[7] in the analysis presented here, the notion of supply and demand clearly helps to explain a growing attention to training, procedures and courtroom presentation best exemplified by the burgeoning literature on forensic medicine. The first modern textbook in England – indeed, in the English language – appeared in 1788, an abridged version of a German work whose translator, the Somerset physician Samuel Farr, was well aware that he was breaking important new ground:

> As nothing of the kind hath ever been published in this country, I was willing to take the assistance of a learned foreigner, rather than travel a tract unbeaten by myself. I need say nothing about the utility of such a Work; it will readily be pointed out to every serious mind. Life and death are objects too important to be sported with in the manner they are sometimes: nor should the valuable connections of our fellow-citizens be ever sacrificed to the ignorance of the faculty, the caprice of a court, or the artifices of revenge and disappointment.[8]

Just over four decades later, forensic medicine had become a compulsory subject for students who intended to become general practitioners, many of whom – particularly in London – were taught by the growing number of teachers who had published their lectures as textbooks. Despite the fact that before 1815 medical students in England did not have "the benefit of any prescribed curriculum of study,"[9] those who were educated in Edinburgh, then the foremost British medical school,[10] could attend the weekly lectures delivered by Andrew Duncan (1744–1828), the first British lecturer on the subject and the first to publish a course synopsis.[11] One of his students, the Birmingham physician George Edward Male (1779–1845), later acknowledged the advantage gained from those lectures when he wrote his own textbook in 1816, a book B. T. Davis deemed "the first original and satisfactory work on the subject by an English author."[12] Male's book was shortly followed by those of Dr John Gordon Smith (1821), a three-volume work by Dr John Ayrton Paris and barrister John Fonblanque (1823), and the first British edition of a book by an American, T. R. Beck.[13] Although Smith's book was criticised for its lack of references,[14] that did not prevent him from publishing two subsequent editions within the decade – inspired perhaps by his status as England's first lecturer on forensic medicine, which he began to teach at the Webb Street medical school (St Thomas's Hospital) in 1823, or simply because the book proved popular.[15]

The year 1815 marked a turning point in English medical education: the Apothecaries Act introduced qualifying examinations for aspiring general practitioners. From 1 August, medical study required an apprenticeship of five years, attendance at lectures on anatomy, botany, chemistry, materia medica and physic, and six months' practical hospital experience over the course of up to seven years, after which men aged 21 or older were examined at Apothecaries' Hall in London; successful completion conferred a recognised medical qualification, the Licentiate of the Society of Apothecaries (LSA). To meet the demand caused by this new requirement, medical teaching in England expanded rapidly in London and large provincial cities,[16] with forensic medicine included on an ad hoc basis until January 1831, when a three-month second year course of lectures became compulsory for the LSA. Why did the Society introduce this obligation, and why at this time?

Jennifer Ward has explained that the late 1820s were a period of sustained agitation and lobbying by a small group that included the self-interested but increasingly isolated J. G. Smith; the equally self-interested and ultimately more successful first professor of materia medica in the new University of London (1828), Dr Anthony Todd Thomson (1778–1849), and the campaigning editor of *The Lancet*, future MP and would-be coroner Thomas Wakley (1795–1862). Their various calls for the addition of forensic medicine to the medical curriculum in London fell on deaf ears, however, until the summer of 1830, when two incidents coincided: Wakley's failed first attempt to be elected coroner for West Middlesex, and the inquest on a young woman, Catherine Cashin, who had died under the care of a quack doctor. The publicity from the inquest, at which Wakley represented Cashin's family, and the coronial campaign, when he used the case to highlight the importance of forensic knowledge, served to stimulate public opinion in favour of forensic medicine and its importance to medical education. Media attention reached a height in the last week of August, coinciding with the annual report of the committee appointed to consider the rules and regulations of the Society of Apothecaries. Although the report has not survived and there is no record of the discussion it prompted, on 9 September 1830 the Society announced that forensic medicine would become compulsory. Ward is surely correct in supposing that the "sequence of events is suggestive of some direct influence."[17]

This view is supported by a report in *The Morning Post*, which also indicates that comparisons were being made to another nation, probably Ireland or Scotland:

> Fully impressed with the many difficulties that obstructed their course, the Court of Examiners [were] . . . urging on slowly and deliberately such improvements in medical education as time or circumstances appeared to warrant . . . until they find themselves at length enabled to reach a standard of education, which, though far from perfect, presents such a system of study as may not, for some years at least, require any essential change; a system nearly approaching to that which has long been demanded from the parallel grade of practitioners in a neighbouring country. The Court of Examiners, in instituting the following regulations, do not by any means conceive that they are requiring the maximum of knowledge that might be expected from the apothecary, but merely that quantity of information which the general advancement of science demands, and certainly not more than is requisite to afford a just degree of security to those whose lives are entrusted to his care, including the majority of the inhabitants of every large city in the kingdom, and the bulk of the population throughout the country.[18]

Students in Ireland and Scotland were already required to study forensic medicine: in autumn 1829 it became an examined subject for those seeking qualification in surgery from the Royal College of Surgeons of Dublin, and on 1 August 1831 for those studying for the equivalent degree from the Royal College of Surgeons of Edinburgh; and, in 1833, the University of Edinburgh followed suit. The Royal College of Physicians did not include it in their diploma until 1836, however.[19] Most of those who qualified from these institutions were destined for careers as general practitioners, not as specialist surgeons or physicians, and became precisely the group most likely to be drawn into local medico-legal cases. In 1836 the Medical Witnesses Act authorised fees for medical testimony at coroners' inquests and the Births and Deaths Registration Act required causes of death to be registered, so that it began to look as though post–mortem examinations would become a routine feature of local inquests.[20] In delivering the theory, but with limited practical instruction in forensic practice, British medical education was preparing but not yet prepared to meet this challenge.

Anne Digby reminds us that despite the fact that professional development between 1815 and 1884 ensured that medical students had to be trained in both medicine and surgery in order to qualify as general practitioners, via the LSA or MRCS (Member of the Royal College of Surgeons), the Medical Act of 1858 required registered practitioners to be qualified in only one; dual qualification did not become a legal obligation until 1885, under the terms of the Amended Medical Act.[21] On 7 August 1859 the new Medical Council sanctioned a double qualification, which was jointly conferred by the Royal Colleges of Physicians and Surgeons; candidates were examined in anatomy, physiology, chemistry, materia medica, midwifery and medical jurisprudence.[22] The curriculum incorporated new subjects over the second half of the nineteenth century, reflecting intellectual developments in medicine and science, but forensic medicine remained an examined subject.[23] Although a single course could not guarantee competence in medico-legal matters, it is likely that late Victorian medical practitioners had some practical experience of chemical analysis and microscopic examination, but may not have been particularly proficient or have had access to the necessary apparatus once established in private practice. The public analysts, a role established on a national basis in 1872, possessed the necessary analytical skills but were employed principally in identifying adulteration, not murder.[24] Chapter 5 will examine the role played by chemical analysis and the public analysts, who were usually called upon in poisoning cases or to examine bloodstains. More typically, the police or other authorities sought out a doctor when a body was discovered and, unless an expert medico-legal practitioner was both necessary and available, that doctor became the main forensic witness in the case.

This raises an important question: just what were medical students taught about forensic medicine? In answering it, two points should be borne in mind. Firstly, doctors were expected to continue learning after completing their formal education, a task that medical publications facilitated;[25] and, secondly, the proliferation of textbooks of forensic medicine suggests a market for the practical knowledge they imparted. The most widely read and influential texts were undoubtedly those by Alfred Swaine Taylor, the lecturer, toxicologist and expert witness who did more than any of his mid-Victorian counterparts to advance the principles and practice of forensic medicine through his books and the example he set for others. It was his name that was most frequently mentioned by lawyers in cross-examination, probably because many had attended his lectures at Guy's Hospital,[26] and by other lecturers in their teaching; his books were widely published in numerous editions from 1836 until long after his death in 1880. Part of what made Taylor's textbooks so helpful was his explicit attention to the needs of the criminal justice system and its expectations of the medical witness, a demand that set forensic medicine apart from typical medical teaching and practice. But his works were eventually superseded: according to William Brend (1873–1944), who published *A Handbook of Medical Jurisprudence and Toxicology* for the use of students and practitioners in 1906 (the eighth edition appeared in 1941), those who required detailed information about illustrative cases or trial reports were recommended to the works of John Dixon Mann (1840–1912) and John Glaister (1856–1932),[27] the standard texts of the Edwardian era. What Brend offered was the information needed to pass the exam in forensic medicine and toxicology at the London University – and there was a great deal of information to learn: the book ran to nearly 300 pages.[28] In 1928 Brend was still stressing the importance to the general practitioner of "the various matters calling for the exercise of medico-legal knowledge which are most likely to be met with in everyday clinical experience,"[29] in essence merely updating Ryan's "requisite information."

This chapter uses textbooks and lecture notes to provide a detailed overview of what late Georgian and Victorian medical students were taught, and thus could reasonably be expected to understand, about matters that called for the exercise of medico-legal skill and knowledge, and the procedures to follow if they were called to attend a homicide. For the late eighteenth century the analysis relies upon the best-known of the few works available, texts by Farr, Duncan and William Dease; for the nineteenth century, printed and manuscript lecture notes have been consulted. While such sources do not prove that any given practitioner remembered what he had learned or was able to apply it effectively in conducting a forensic examination, it does afford a standard by which to assess the key ways in which medico-legal practice changed over the period between 1788, when Farr's book was published, and 1914. During the eighteenth century, the intellectual separation between surgery and medicine began to break down, so that those who gained a university medical degree had some training in anatomy and probably midwifery too. About 90 per cent of those who did not go abroad to study went to Edinburgh or Glasgow, which provided a fuller range of medical courses than the ancient universities did, but by the second half of the century, the teaching at Oxford and Cambridge was by no means lacking a clinical element. In contrast to the physicians, surgeons and surgeon–apothecaries were trained by apprenticeship: they paid a fee to a master to teach them for five or seven years, after which the more ambitious spent several months in London walking the wards of a hospital and attending lectures. They did not write a dissertation or take any examinations, but what it lacked in uniformity, apprenticeship made up for in practicality and hands-on experience.[30]

As the Victorian population grew, so too did the number of doctors and the institutions that trained them. By the end of the nineteenth century students in the United Kingdom could study at 1 of 35 medical schools of all kinds: approximately 7,000 students were for the most part spread between 23 hospital schools in London; the extramural medical schools of the universities of Glasgow and Edinburgh;[31] the English universities of London, Oxford and Cambridge and the medical schools in large northern cities including Leeds, Manchester, Liverpool and Birmingham.[32] The first medical school in Wales opened at Cardiff in 1894 and by the start of its first full year of operation had attracted 20 students.[33] Throughout most of the period covered by this book, therefore, doctors who practiced in Wales had probably studied elsewhere, while "many Scottish and some Irish trained doctors came to practise in England."[34] The medical press published details of the curriculum taught at some of these schools, particularly in London, and even printed entire lecture courses verbatim. The lectures delivered by Dr William Cummin (1800–1837) at the Aldersgate Street School are a case in point and will be used to examine the teaching of forensic medicine in the mid-1830s, just after the statutes of 1836 came into effect.

A fragment of a larger notebook compiled by Thomas Scattergood (1826–1900) between the late 1860s and the early 1890s provides detailed information about what he taught his students at the Leeds School of Medicine where, from 1869 to June 1888, he lectured on forensic medicine and toxicology. It was in these subjects that "he attained such eminence that as an expert his advice was constantly sought in medico-legal cases not only in Leeds, but in Yorkshire and in the North of England generally."[35] This document has no table of contents, formal introduction, conclusion or index: it is therefore impossible to determine how many lectures there were or how the contents changed over the years; but the occasional dates, insertions and marginalia suggest that Scattergood amended but did not significantly change the material, which seems to have been compiled between 1869 and the mid-1880s and includes some references to the medical literature he was reading. The notes offer a partial picture of what Scattergood believed students needed to know about forensic medicine, but give no real sense of how his lectures were delivered. Student notes compiled in Edinburgh around 1900 provide an important comparison: not only do they record a complete course of lectures, with the exam questions set by the lecturer, Professor Sir Henry Littlejohn (1826–1914), but they afford insight into the student's perspective on what he was learning: the author decided what to write in relation to what he heard Littlejohn – who lectured without notes – say.[36] He also noted class visits to the city mortuary, a valuable learning opportunity linked to Littlejohn's longstanding position as the city's police surgeon.[37] Given the large proportion of Edinburgh-trained doctors who worked in England and Littlejohn's influence on the teaching and application of forensic medicine,[38] the standards typical of Scottish medico-legal practice were essentially transferred south of the border to become part of the typical English experience.

The late eighteenth century

The works of Farr, Dease and Duncan serve as indicators of what medical prac-titioners, particularly surgeons, may have known about medico-legal matters in the period between 1788 and 1816, when Male's book appeared. Although we cannot presume that British doctors did not read some or all of the most highly regarded continental treatises, of which there were a not insignificant number,[39] it is more likely that publication and teaching in English stimulated the spread of knowledge about what was then known as medical jurisprudence. This was broader in scope than the parameters of forensic medicine established by the nineteenth century, as it included public health along with more obviously medico-legal issues of both a criminal and civil nature. However, by the 1780s British doctors were beginning to focus more on the needs of the courts, as Farr did in abridging the posthumous work of the German physician Johann Fried-rich Faselius (1721–1767), *Elementa Medicinae Forensis*.[40] Whether Farr consulted the Latin edition of 1767 or the German translation published the following year, he decided what to retain and how to organise the material. This resulted in a text that leaned towards criminal contexts and cut nearly all of the material on public health to produce a succinct description "of such tokens in the human body as are requisite to determine the judgment of a coroner, and of courts of law, in cases of divorce, rape, murder, etc."[41] The chapters on rape, infanticide and homicide comprise over half the book's length; about a third of the text is devoted to matters addressed from a largely civil perspective such as pregnancy, childbirth, malingering ("imposters") and insanity; and there is one good-sized chapter on public health.

Most of the chapter on rape was devoted to bodily signs, either of destroyed virginity in young girls (six signs) or that a woman was sexually experienced and thus "less to be believed upon a deposition for rape" (nine signs).[42] The chapter on infanticide focused first on the signs of recent delivery in the reputed mother, including genital swelling, vaginal distension, a flow of the lochia (vaginal bleeding which looked and smelled different from menstrual blood), the presence of breast milk and changes in the nipples. To determine whether the child was born alive or not, Farr listed 23 signs of stillbirth, ten of blood circulation and three of breathing. He acknowledged that the presence of air in the lungs was not conclusive evidence that the child had been born alive, and provided general instructions as to how a test was to be carried out by throwing the heart and lungs into moderately warm water to observe "how far they sink or swim."[43] Then he detailed the signs of a violent death, providing basic descriptions of the expected post-mortem indicators in cases of suffocation, wounds, skull injuries and blood loss when the navel cord was left untied. Most interestingly, he advocated a full post-mortem examination of the body in which the three principal cavities, the head, chest and abdomen, were opened and examined; the presence of blood in the heart, meconium and urine were all important signs of live birth.

Farr recommended that examinations in cases of suspected homicide be carried out in daylight, not necessarily where the body was found but in a "proper" place utilising proper surgical instruments;[44] and that a thorough external survey be carried out before the body was opened: the three main cavities, all wounds, nerves, blood vessels, and the brain were to be dissected, comprising of 16 individual steps. He adopted a narrow view of the possible methods of homicide, which "may be reduced to poisons, wounds, bruises, drowning, and strangulation," asserting that the first two were most common before giving a lengthy account of how to detect poisons and distinguish the lethality of wounds, including head injuries.[45] The types of weapons that could inflict various wounds were not considered; rather, Farr focused on whether wounds were always mortal or only in certain, possibly accidental, circumstances, which may have been especially helpful to surgeons called to testify at inquests. However, while the focus on wounds was not misplaced, that on poisoning was out of proportion to its frequency: as we will see in Chapter 3, poison was a rare method of murder in the eighteenth century and remained relatively exceptional in the nineteenth century, but fear of this secret and hard-to-discern crime led to a strong emphasis on toxicology in textbooks of forensic medicine.

William Dease also adopted a strong focus on wounds, poisoning and infanticide, for all of which a practical knowledge of anatomy was needed to ascertain cause of death. He was less systematic in presenting this information than Farr was, making his book harder to use as a practical guide, but he clearly advocated a stepped process of post-mortem examination, working in good light from a careful external inspection to dissection of the three main body cavities, beginning with the one in which the cause of death appeared to be situated. The head was to be shaved before scrutiny, and evidence of injury sought in the cranial bones, the brain and its membranes. This section of the book is shorter but a little more useful than Farr's advice, given the frequency with which head injuries led to criminal charges: based on 25 years' experience in which, Dease claimed, he had opened more heads than most practitioners,[46] the book linked cause of death to post-mortem appearances, enabling practitioners to distinguish the natural from the unnatural. However, like Farr he offered no advice about the questions that lawyers might ask. The next steps of the examination were to open the thorax and then the abdomen; a great deal of attention was devoted to the alimentary canal and symptoms of poisoning.[47] Then the text moved to a discussion of infanticide that merely summarised the well-known posthumous article by William Hunter (1718–1783), 'On the Uncertainty of the Signs of Murder, in the Case of Bastard Children', giving little concrete information about how to conduct a post-mortem or examine the lungs – as indeed Hunter had not, stating only that to make a firm judgment a doctor must have seen and dissected a number of deceased newborn infants.[48] The rest of Dease's short book adopted a rather vague and unduly informal tone in reviewing surgeons' duties in making reports and attending inquests. It is not hard to imagine that a doctor who found himself involved in a trial for infanticide during the 1790s would have turned either to Hunter or Farr, a continental textbook, or simply taken a chance on what he recalled from his student days.

We do not know what precisely British medical students learned about medico-legal questions prior to the publication in 1792 of a synopsis of the lectures given in Edinburgh by Andrew Duncan; he had then been teaching the subject for about two years, influenced by the continental practice of uniting medical jurisprudence with 'medical police', loosely defined as public health.[49] Three quarters of the course focused on forensic questions, with sections devoted to the criminal, civil and church courts (where the focus was on sex in relation to marriage); insanity was included under the civil heading, together with pregnancy, childbirth and feigned illness, thus mirroring Farr's content fairly closely. The questions that concerned the criminal courts related to homicide, infanticide, abortion and rape, for which internal and external examinations were required. Organised by topic, the lectures began with homicide by wounds, hanging, drowning, suffocation and poisoning. On infanticide, Duncan warned that it was difficult to prove; he noted but did not list the circumstances that proved stillbirth, and noted seven ways in which infants might be killed – by wounds, contusions, suffocation, drowning, an untied umbilical cord, cold or starvation.[50] The section on rape was adapted from European texts ("writers on the *medicina forensis*") and showed that lectures would address completed, attempted and pretended rape before switching to Latin to add the signs of virginity and defloration.

Duncan's synopsis does not, unfortunately, provide details of the characteristic anatomical signs that doctors were to look for in medico-legal investigations or how to go about this, only the general themes of his lectures, which were drawn from European textbooks. There is therefore no way to gauge their reception by students or whether the subject appeared overly theoretical or more (or less) complicated than it actually was. As an early champion of the unity of medicine and surgery,[51] however, Duncan might well have encouraged students to explore some of these issues in the Edinburgh hospitals or to visit the criminal courts when they were in session. His campaign for a chair in medical jurisprudence ended when his eldest son was appointed to the new post in 1807 as the most qualified individual at the time. Andrew Duncan junior (1773–1832), who had training in both medicine and surgery, made a success of his lectures, which were well received by students and medical practitioners alike and "greatly stimulated interest in this discipline in Britain."[52] At his death the national impact of his lectures on medical jurisprudence and medical police was acknowledged:

> He began to lecture in 1809, and by his lectures, and numerous papers in his journal, he gradually impressed on the public mind the importance of these subjects, and essentially contributed to the general estimation which they have since acquired, especially since they have been taught . . . by his favourite pupil and successor, Dr Christison.[53]

Robert Christison (1797–1882), an internationally renowned forensic toxicologist, further extended the authority of Scottish teaching and medico-legal practice through his *Treatise on Poisons* (1829), which became a standard work in English.[54] The influence of these innovative Scottish forensic educators reached deeply into England.

London 1836–1837

Despite the interest in forensic medicine fostered by the Duncans in Edinburgh, it was years before a course of lectures was introduced in London, the first being those of Dr J. G. Smith (1792–1833), who had graduated with honours from Edinburgh in 1810, served at Waterloo and then retired to London on half pay. There he was unable to practice medicine because he lacked English qualifications, but by 1823 he had begun to teach forensic medicine at the Webb Street medical school, possibly as a result of the publication of his *Principles of Medical Jurisprudence*.[55] Demand for lectures remained low until the Society of Apothecaries made them compulsory in a resolution that changed the nature of medical education in England. In London, new lecturers were appointed, and by the mid-1830s all 11 of the existing medical schools were offering lecture courses.

William Cummin, who received his medical degree in Dublin but had been lecturing at the Aldersgate school for several years,[56] gave a series 24 lectures on forensic medicine which were published in full in *The London Medical Gazette* between 1 October 1836 and 18 March 1837, just weeks before his death on 10 April from what appears to have been complications arising from an inflammatory disease. The course cost three guineas, somewhat less than the 4-guinea fee for the forensic medicine courses in most of the metropolitan schools,[57] but extended over a much longer period than the three months required by the LSA.

The course was cut short by his sudden death: there is no indication of how many lectures were planned, but the twenty-fourth was clearly not the last. The extant content is thus incomplete yet intriguing in its substantial focus on civil, sexual and obstetric problems, arranged in what Cummin termed a "simple and natural order."[58] There is no consideration of cause and manner of death except in relation to infanticide, on which Cummin had recently published a short monograph and reprinted William Hunter's article.[59] This suggests that the content focused on Cummin's particular area(s) of interest as well as those he expected would be most typically encountered in medical practice. Furthermore, he did not serve as a medico-legal witness, which probably explains the more civil emphasis in comparison to the courses offered by Scattergood and Little-john later in the century, both of whom drew extensively on their experience of death investigation in criminal cases. The lectures were reproduced verbatim, doubtless based on his own notes given Cummin's close association with the *Medical Gazette*, and they are liberally strewn with references to a wide variety of British and continental authors and cases.[60]

The lectures addressed the following topics and were numbered as follows: 1) Introduction: historical overview; nature, scope and importance of the subject. 2) Medical Evidence: an introduction to the legal system and courts, the rights and duties of medical men giving evidence, the importance of notes made during medico-legal examinations, and a concluding piece of sage advice: ultimately, one must be calm and prepared.[61] 3) and 4) Age: how to estimate it in a foetus; the stages of life. 5) Sex: its determination in the living and the dead. 6) Form and Identity: racial characteristics; identity of the living. 7) Identity: of the living and the dead, contested or uncertain. 8) and 9) Impotence: in males and females. 10–12) Rape and Unnatural Offences: physical proofs including microscopic observation of semen; evidence in virgins; similar signs in married women and prostitutes; detailed procedure for the examination of alleged victims and perpetrators; examples of trials for rape; sodomy (written in Latin to discourage prurient curiosity). 13) and 14) Pregnancy: physical signs on the female body; determining that the foetus is alive; complications; the stages of gestation; conditions under which women might be ignorant of their own pregnancy; criminal responsibility of pregnant women, where medical evidence was relevant only to states of mind, e.g. irritable temperament, melancholy, hypochondria. 15–19) Birth: recent delivery; concealment of birth – the law did not require proof of whether death occurred before, at, or after the birth;[62] what to look for in examining the reputed mother – only the discovery of a placenta in the uterus or vagina might be an acceptable sole proof that a woman had recently given birth, but usually a series of related proofs were required, including the presence of colostrum or breast milk, a lochial discharge, abdominal (stretch) marks, or changes in the size and shape of the uterus; labour in unconscious women; premature birth and the ability of babies to survive outside the womb (viability); "monstrous" births; multiple births; the laws of legitimacy; the length of gestation; stillbirth, abortion and miscarriage.

Lectures 20–22 were dedicated to infanticide, beginning with its history and status in law. There were two main medico-legal questions: whether or not the infant was born alive, and whether death was due to natural causes or the infliction of violence. To provide answers, doctors were first to seek proof that an infant had survived birth: indications included the state of the umbilical cord, food in the stomach, and the absence of meconium in the bowels. Evidence of stillbirth was provided by putrefaction or by negative tests for live birth. Then Cummin turned to the five ways to determine live birth through evidence of respiration, based on the fact that the lungs, heart and liver displayed tell-tale signs. These included the following: a) lung colour; b) lung volume, illustrated by two diagrams showing the visible change in their size and situation in the chest cavity consequent upon respiration (Figures 2.1 and 2.2);[63] c) a spongy feel and the presence of crepitation or discharge of air bubbles from the lungs by pressure under water; d) blood in the lungs and the ratio of their weight to the infant's total weight (Ploucquet's static lung test)[64] and e) the hydrostatic lung test. Cummin stressed the errors present in Hunter's classic paper,[65] the correct manner of conducting the test by floating the lungs and heart together, separately, whole and in pieces (if they float, the infant had breathed), the test's weaknesses (false positive results due to putrefaction, artificial respiration or breathing while in the birth canal) and how to counter them, particularly in the light of a recent discovery by A. S. Taylor.[66] Ultimately, students were told, "the hydrostatic test, in shewing that the child did breathe, has performed its office; *when* it breathed, and *where*, must be made out by other evidence."[67] If the lungs sank, wholly and in every part, the infant had never respired, but objections might be raised on the grounds of disease or the failure of the test despite the fact that the child was seen

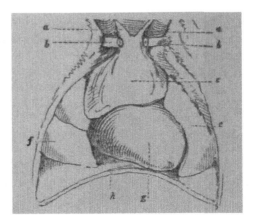

Figure 2.1 The chest cavity of a stillborn child

Source: William Cummin, *The Proofs of Infanticide Considered* (London: Longman, Rees, Orme, Brown, Green and Longman, 1836), p. 56. In this figure, *a* and *a* represent the horns of the thymus; *b* and *b*, the clavicles, with their anterior portions removed; *c*, the body of the thymus; *e* and *f*, the lungs; *h*, the diaphragm; and *g*, the pericardium. Openlibrary_edition OL24239708M.

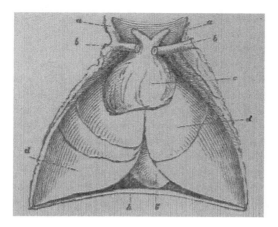

Figure 2.2 Changes in the volume and situation of infant lungs caused by the admission
    of air

Source: William Cummin, *The Proofs of Infanticide Considered* (London: Longman, Rees, Orme, Brown,
Green and Longman, 1836), p. 56. Openlibrary_edition OL24239708M.

to have been fully born and to breathe; in such cases only further experimental
or eyewitness evidence could remove the doubt.

Proof of respiration could be further established by examining the circulatory
system: characteristic changes took place in the arterial duct, the foetal blood
vessel that connected the two main arteries of the heart, the aorta and the pulmonary artery, and normally closed at birth. While this test could not state the
length of time that an infant had breathed (i.e. lived), in conjunction with other
tests it could determine whether the infant had *ever* respired. Diagrams were
provided to show the nature of the change that doctors were to look for in the
heart, indicating that anatomical knowledge based on dissection was essential.
Related changes were dismissed as being too slow to have any medico-legal
value at all, while those associated with the liver were far too unreliable. The
safety of medical evidence in cases of infanticide was guaranteed only by the
relationship between multiple proofs; as we will see in Chapter 4, a single test
was never sufficient.[68]

The following lecture reviewed and summarised the tests before turning to
the question of the cause and manner of death. Absence of obvious marks of
violence might suggest a natural death but a conclusive determination could
be made only on the basis of a full post-mortem inspection in which the head,
thorax and abdomen were opened and all the organs examined. The most
common method of murder was strangulation: the lungs and right side of the
heart would "almost always" be filled with dark blood, and bruises on the neck
would correspond to subcutaneous effusion (bleeding). The medico-legal signs
of suffocation were less clear-cut unless an object had been pushed down the

throat, but drowning presented signs that were easily recognised and usually but not always present: the lungs and right side of the heart were filled with blood, the brain was congested and the air passages full of froth; firm proof that an infant was alive when put into liquid was provided when the liquid was found in the stomach. In the case of death from blows, wounds and fractures, recent French research proved that a fall on to a paved floor from a height of eighteen inches caused parietal skull fractures in 80 per cent of stillborn test subjects,[69] an important finding in relation to a trial defence strategy which claimed that an infant had dropped on to its head when the mother gave birth suddenly while standing up. But these experiments did not match the clinical evidence: confirmed German case histories showed that babies born from a standing position did not hit the ground at a right angle, as in the French tests, but obliquely, so that none suffered skull fractures, let alone death. It was therefore difficult to distinguish accident from murder, and Cummin's suggestion as to how to do so was highly subjective: in cases of wilful murder, he claimed, fractures would be "much more numerous and extensive" and would be found on parts of the head where accident could not possibly produce them: the face, frontal or occipital bones, or the base of the skull itself. Crucially, from a medico-legal perspective, it was possible for skull fractures to occur naturally before or during labour, while deliberate violent twisting of the head left no external sign and could be identified only by post-mortem dissection of the neck.[70]

In what seems another rather hasty assumption, Cummin claimed that wounds inflicted on infants for murderous purposes were "generally confined to the head and neck," although puncture wounds to the heart were not unknown. All wounds were to be carefully inspected and measured, with a view to identifying the weapon that caused them, but an important problem arose in trying to ascertain when injuries had been inflicted, since those done soon after death often showed little or no appreciable difference from those done shortly before death.[71] Signs of burning before and after death were easily noticed and chemical analysis could afford proof of poisoning, but neglect was not recognised as a crime, although deliberate exposure or failure to tie the umbilical cord aggravated a charge of concealment of birth. Signs of violent death were generally indicated by wounds on parts of the body unlikely to sustain an accidental injury; and when such wounds, blows or burns indicated, by evidence of vital reaction (the physiological response of a living organism to a trauma), that the infant was not yet dead when they were inflicted.[72]

In his final two lectures Cummin introduced medico-legal problems of the mind, "opening a new and very important division of the course" centred on unsoundness of mind in civil and criminal cases. A centuries-old legal designation, *non compos mentis* (of unsound mind), embraced both derangement and intellectual disability but was so loosely defined that lawyers used it as a convenient opportunity to attack medical witnesses who could not state what precisely was to be understood by words like *unsoundness* or *insanity*. In Cummin's view it was incumbent upon the legal profession to specify the ideas comprehended under the term along lines established by medical knowledge,[73] but until that happened, he recommended that students should acquaint themselves with the key characteristics of the various types of mental unsoundness, summarised in a handy table. Those most relevant to criminal cases included dementia, mania and monomania, a form of partial insanity characterised by a delusion related to a particular idea whilst judgment on other subjects remained perfectly sound.[74] Three degrees of mania ranged from "reasoning madness" to complete intellectual confusion, but were distinguishable from monomania by their less fixed attention on a single wrong idea. All of his case studies were drawn from civil practice.

The course ended suddenly at this point, but an idea of what Cummin might have planned to cover in later lectures is suggested by synopses of courses delivered in the early 1830s by Robert Christison in Edinburgh and by Anthony Todd Thomson and barrister Andrew Amos (1791–1860) at the University of London. Cummin had dedicated his book on infanticide to Amos, whose lectures inspired him to study forensic medicine. Both courses included significant sections on poisons and the signs and causes of death but were otherwise quite similar to Cummin's in content, albeit structured differently.[75] Given the growing prevalence of poisoning in the 1830s and the importance of cause and manner of death in medico-legal investigations it would be surprising if Cummin did not lecture specifically on these topics, as students clearly needed the information. However, he died just at the point when forensic education reached a turning point, signalled in 1836 by the first of Alfred Swaine Taylor's publications. This book focused on wounds and cause of death, supported by evidence from homicide trials; a companion volume, which never appeared, was to cover toxicology, infanticide, abortion and insanity.[76] Then in 1844 Taylor published the first edition of a text hailed as the best and most complete treatise on medical jurisprudence in any language.[77] This dense tome, reasonably priced at 12s. but printed in type so small that it was difficult to read, covered poisoning, wounds and infanticide in 50 chapters, since they constituted more than three quarters of all medico-legal cases, while the remaining 16 chapters considered a miscellany of further topics including suffocation, rape, legitimacy and insanity; medical evidence in civil cases was omitted because it was comparatively rare.[78] Within four years the book had sold 4,000 copies.[79] Led by Taylor's example in instituting the subject as a "coherent whole,"[80] by the 1840s the academic study of forensic medicine had developed a decided focus on the criminal courts – an emphasis reflected in the course delivered by Thomas Scattergood 25 years later when he began teaching forensic medicine to students in Leeds.

Leeds c.1869–1888

Thomas Scattergood, the son of a Methodist clergyman, was born in Huddersfield, West Yorkshire, in 1826. In 1846 he was appointed to the post of assistant apothecary at the General Infirmary in Leeds, subsequently qualifying as MRCS and LSA, and then going into general practice in Leeds early in 1851, the same year he became a lecturer in chemistry at the Leeds School of Medicine, founded in 1831. By the late 1850s he was beginning to develop a reputation as a forensic expert, particularly with regard to poisoning, and he recorded his medico-legal work in three notebooks over a period of 40 years. He lectured on forensic medicine and toxicology from 1869 to 1888, but did not write a textbook or, indeed, publish much at all. But he devoted considerable energy to the development of the medical school: he was instrumental in its amalgamation with the Yorkshire College (established in 1874) and became the first Dean of the new Faculty of Medicine in 1884, a post he held until his death in February 1900.[81] However, his extant lecture notes indicate that his teaching was informed both by his own experience and up-to-date international literature: there are numerous references to Alfred Swaine Taylor, still England's most eminent medico-legal expert; but also to Johann Ludwig Casper (1796–1864), professor of forensic medicine at the University of Berlin and author of a four-volume handbook translated into English just before his death; Jean-Pierre Barruel (1780–1838), former head of the Paris medical faculty's chemical laboratory, on blood analysis; Theodor Billroth (1829–1894), a pioneering surgeon at the University of Vienna, on gunshot wounds; and H. Aubrey Husband's (1844–1933) student handbook of forensic medicine, published in 1874. Scattergood's own work on the Mary Ann Cotton serial poisoning case of 1872, in which four victims were exhumed, was cited in a lecture on adipocere, the waxy substance formed by the decomposing soft tissues in bodies subjected to moisture;[82] and it seems likely that other cases also found their way into his lectures.

The notebook's pagination runs consecutively from 1 to 24 (verso pages are not numbered), but the content appears to begin in the middle of a lecture, or series of lectures, on decomposition; the first distinct heading appears halfway down the first page. The contents are presented in detail below, to demonstrate what Scattergood intended to teach his students about the core aspects of medico-legal practice. There is no section on poisons, which he probably placed either before or after these lectures; nor are infanticide, sexual offences or insanity mentioned, although by this time all textbooks of forensic medicine included these discrete topics. It is possible that, like his contemporary at the University of Glasgow, Pierce Adolphus Simpson (1837–1900), Scattergood based his lectures on Taylor's *Principles and Practice of Medical Jurisprudence* (1865),[83] but his extant notes do not simply reproduce that text. Scattergood focused mainly on the determination of cause and manner of death, ordered the content to follow a logical route into and through the dead body and provided words of caution where necessary. His notes serve as a good introduction to the types of injuries found in the majority of murder cases encountered by medical practitioners, with a clear indication of the tasks they would be expected to undertake.

The first six pages cover decomposition, saponification, mummification and survivorship (which of two or more dead persons died first), none of which were likely to be problems that arose in typical inquest or criminal cases involving just one recently deceased individual. The next heading was the point at which Scattergood probably urged his students to pay close attention: "The question most important of all arises: what was the cause of death?" The section begins with a warning: "Sudden or violent deaths, and deaths attended by suspicion of foul play, neglect and malpraxis, constitute the greatest number of those on which the practitioner is called to give an opinion," leading to at least 25,000 inquests annually in England and Wales.[84] The lecture explained cause of death first in terms suggested by the French anatomist and pathologist Marie François Xavier Bichat (1771–1802), as typically arising from cessation of the function of the brain, heart or lungs, singly or in combination; proceeded to describe post-mortem appearances; and listed six ways in which death from violence could occur. These included the following: mechanical (crushing, gunshot wounds, "knocking down by trains"), neuroparalytic (shock), inflammatory (exhaustion caused by infected tissue), hyperaemic (excessive congestion of the brain or lungs caused by asphyxia or injury), anaemic (bodily weakness due to blood loss or starvation) and pyaemic (blood poisoning). Of course, more than one form might be present in any given case of sudden death.[85]

Students were then introduced to their central task as a medical witness, the examination of a body both externally and internally, and told to take note of all circumstances, not just the medical ones: "A medical witness may have not only to formally dissect a body by legal order, but, by having been called in on first alarm may be compelled to act as a witness to other and extrinsic circumstances," as for example the precise position of a weapon or of the body in relation to other objects, blood or other stains, odours and clothing. Then he turned to a detailed discussion of how to identify blood using chemical tests and a microscope,[86] suggesting five important medico-legal questions that the prac-titioner would have to answer. Firstly, was it human? "By the microscope [we] may say whether it is mammalian . . . but it would be unwise to assert . . . that any particular specimen was [animal or human] because [there is] no proportion between size of animal and its corpuscles." As to Barruel's claim that fresh blood mixed with acid emitted a distinctive scent unique to each species,[87] Scattergood was sceptical: "the sense of smell is the least reliable of all. . . . Moreover, we want an opinion not from *fresh* blood in *bulk* – but from *old* blood in *minute* portions." Next, was it menstrual or ordinary blood? Third, was it venous or arterial? The fourth question was moot: was it of male, female or child? "No difference exists." Finally, was the stain derived from a living or a dead body? "If coagulated fibrin is formed in the blood there is a strong presumption that it was derived rather from a living or a recently dead body."[88]

Scattergood then focused attention more closely on examining the body itself, starting with the external appearances. While official instructions for how to go about this existed in some European countries and in Scotland, where they were to be found "in Husband's manual,"[89] English doctors were given no such essential guide to follow.[90] Rather, medical practitioners relied on their student training and on Taylor's textbooks, to which Scattergood referred frequently. But this is not to say that he taught a derivative curriculum; rather, the lecture notes suggest a synthesis of contemporary knowledge structured according to his personal experience and preferred procedure. He began with identification: "If the body is that of an unknown person first note all marks which may be of use

in determining identity; this is of utmost importance before body is mutilated."
Students were next instructed to consider indicators denoting time of death,
including "warmth or warm places, pliancy or rigidity of several parts, flaccidity
of iris, softness of eye, smell, cadaveric lividity or staining, putrefaction," before
working their way into the body by examining the condition of its natural openings. The ears, nose, mouth, fauces, anus and genitals had to be checked in case
they held material such as faeces, semen or some object; "Cases are certainly
rare in which foreign bodies are found in these openings, but they do occur."
Contusions were to be distinguished from post-mortem lividity by making an
incision into them, the exact position and direction of wounds and marks of
vital reaction around them recorded, and then a systematic search conducted
from head to toe for bone fractures.[91] Only then was the body to be opened.

The method for examining a body internally was so well known as to require
"certain general rules only," one of which was that a post-mortem examination
should be made by at least two medical practitioners, another that the entire
body was to be examined thoroughly regardless of how obvious the cause of
death might be:[92]

1 The head is always to be opened, as well as chest and abdomen.
2 If examination does not reveal clearly cause of death, the spinal marrow
   must also be examined. When there is reason to expect cause of death
   in any particular cavity, open that first; otherwise begin with the head,
   then chest.
3 The condition of *every organ* must be noticed, whatever conclusion the
   appearances lead you to form.
4 The first thing to note on opening each cavity is the position of organs,
   the appearance and quantity of fluid effusion . . .
5 Don't fail to examine fauces larynx trachea oesophagus for foreign substances, marks of corrosion and
6 If suspicion of poisoning, tie double ligatures round the lower part of the
   oesophagus and round pyloric end of stomach, and remove it in a separate
   vessel . . .
7 Examine rectum for hardened faeces, sometimes important in reference
   to existence of recent purging.
8 Examine uterus and ovaries.
9 With regard to abdominal viscera, if stomach and intestines are inflamed
   note the extent and position of the [inflammation] and all marks of effusion of blood softening erosion perforation. NB: precision in all this as
   to observing and recording.
10 The greatest care must be used that organs preserved for further [exami-
   nation] must be put in perfectly clean vessels of glass or earthenware . . .
11 The utmost care must be taken to preserve the identity of objects, by not
   giving them into the keeping of others, but preserving under lock and
   seal up to and during time of analysis or delivery to someone authorized
   to take them.

12 Careful notes should be made of all appearances. These are generally with conscience dictated by the inspector of the body: if so they must be read over before the two parties separate, and signed.

The remaining lecture notes address specific causes of death, moving from the wounds commonly found in cases of violence, to the more typically accidental or downright unusual: fire, spontaneous combustion, lightning, cold and starvation. In keeping with his medico-legal focus, Scattergood was careful to highlight the difficulties that doctors might encounter in interpreting post-mortem results.

> When a person dies directly from a wound it is generally from bleeding and therefore the amount of blood lost will enable us to speak positively and is in this case a better guide than the mere appearance of the wound. . . . On the other hand if incised wounds are made a few minutes after death they will present much [the] same appearance as during life. Taylor found that 10 minutes after a limb had been amputated an incision made had but little of these appearances. . . . And in drowned bodies Casper avers that the most experienced may often hesitate to decide whether a wound was inflicted during life.[93]

Gunshot wounds were the most complicated,

> and as a rule cause the most dangerous of all wounds: they are both contused and lacerated & penetrating, with the additional evil that their course is often circuitous and often unknown or difficult to determine, and they are made by projectiles which may strike with the highest degree of force. . . . Besides this they often have an aperture of exit, as well as an entrance, and the projectile may remain in the body taking with it portions of clothing etc.[94]

The immediate causes of death from wounds were haemorrhage, shock or the destruction of a vital organ. Students were reminded that their legal duty was to provide a medical link between an injury and death:

> shock is sometimes the cause of death, when many injuries, any one of which is slight and unimportant have been inflicted. Thus death sometimes takes place after prize fighting, or after whipping or beating. This is most important to remember, that under such circumstances we are not bound to find severe or serious injuries in order to enable us to say that death was the result of the injury.[95]

This medico-legal convention explains why many cases of death arising from sudden fights were tried as murders but resulted in acquittal or a manslaughter verdict. Doctors were expected to state whether or not an injury inflicted by an assailant had caused death and, if it had, a murder trial was likely to follow.

Then, under the common law tradition, a grand jury might reduce the charge to manslaughter, but the ultimate responsibility for determining whether a fatal blow was struck with the premeditation required to support a murder conviction rested on the trial jury. Doctors had no formal role to play in determining the *motive* with which a fatal blow was delivered; that was for a jury to decide. But, as later chapters will show, medical practitioners frequently used the nature of wounds to draw conclusions about the possibility they had been caused intentionally, most often in cases of infanticide.

It was thus with good reason that Scattergood cautioned his students against imprecision:[96]

> [W]e should be prepared to give a distinct opinion as to whether death was or was not the result of injury: the law will admit one cause of death only; and to this if it be possible we should make up our minds. Other predisposing circumstances may be stated, and proper weight given to them as reasons why such and such injuries were more likely to be fatal, or more quickly fatal than under other circumstances they would have been; but we should be distinct in our opinion as to the actual cause the question being in our own minds would the deceased have been likely to die at the same time had he not received the wound. But at the same time if we cannot make up our minds as to the cause it is much better to say so distinctly and at first.

The difficulty of determining whether an injury or some other cause led to death was much greater if the wound was not immediately fatal but set up secondary effects such as haemorrhage, tetanus, blood poisoning or erysipelas: "When these are distinctly the consequence of the wound, the English law considers that the crime is still homicide."[97] Where the question was which of two wounds given by different persons or at different times had caused death, the answer was to rest upon "ordinary surgical principles"; if the second wound was in itself fatal, "but little difficulty can arise." In the case of "the question often put, which of two wounds was first inflicted," the answer had to be based on the particular circumstances surrounding the death. Students were again reminded of crucial legal points:

> Let it be distinctly understood then that within the limits of time just stated,[98] an aggressor is just as responsible for the effects of injury inflicted by him, as if death had taken place upon the spot; but if there be any doubt that the death is strictly & clearly traceable to the injury an acquittal may be looked for.[99]

Scattergood's next topic was how to determine when an injury had been inflicted: "It may in some cases be possible to say that death must have been immediate but with regard to many so called mortal injuries care must be taken not to pronounce too positively on this point."[100] The medical practitioner then had to identify the weapon with which an injury was caused; where no weapon was found, the form and character of the wound could be used to form a hypothesis.[101] Perhaps the most critical question in forensic practice was whether a fatal injury was accidental, suicidal or homicidal; Scattergood estimated a ratio of three or four suicides and 40 accidental deaths for every homicide in England and Wales.[102] Several indicators, mainly concerning the nature, direction and situation of the wound, permitted confident determination of the manner of death, but wounds of the throat might be particularly complicated because they were so often suicidal but easily inflicted by a killer to give the appearance of suicide. There was plainly no dependable rule: "A homicidal cut given in front will if given with right hand mostly be from right to left, but may be the other way."[103] But there were two reliable methods for estimating whether an injury had been inflicted before or after death: the colour gradations in bruises (ecchymosis), which might appear hours *after* death; and the location of any fractures, those of the skull or larynx being probably produced before death whereas ribs might easily be broken after death.[104]

This led to a lengthy consideration of death caused by wounds and mechanical injuries, a topic that included both fractures and ruptures or lacerations of the internal organs, but excluded burning and all forms of suffocation. This selection was based on Taylor's definition of a wound as a "solution of continuity" of any part of the body by external means, but also on recent legal decisions related to the 1861 Offences Against the Person Act, which obviously encompassed these types of injuries.[105] As has been shown elsewhere, the medical interpretation of the types of injuries embraced by the word 'wound' changed in relation to the Act, expanding from a purely surgical understanding as breaking of the skin by some instrument, to include most forms of bodily harm, although burns were always omitted.[106] As Scattergood explained to his students, the medical understanding of a wound did not necessarily match the legal understanding: "Lawyers may quibble about what a wound is in law, but a medical witness need never be at fault if he is able to define what he means by the word." He then examined the range of injuries that might be met with in medico-legal practice: bruises, contusions and ecchymosis; incised, punctured and lacerated wounds and, most complicated of all, gunshot wounds. It was important to preserve any foreign bodies removed from such wounds, and to determine whether a shot was due to suicide, accident or homicide: tell-tale signs included chemical residues left on the weapon, the shape of the bullet, and blackening of the skin around the entrance wound.[107]

The last ten pages of the lecture notes cover topics seldom met with in cases of homicide: burns and scalds, due primarily to accidents and for which medical evidence was rarely called at inquests;[108] fire, which caused mainly accidental deaths but was sometimes used by killers to hide their crime;[109] a few "marvellous instances" of spontaneous combustion, which Scattergood thought were probably due to drunken accidents;[110] death from lightning strikes (about 20 people per year in England and Wales) and death from cold, an infrequent medico-legal concern except when compounded by starvation, the final topic in the document. These were both uncommon methods but they could be used with criminal intent against children or the infirm.[111] The cases on which the rest of this book is based corroborate the rarity of these types of homicide throughout the period of study: a handful of deaths from fire resulted when a lighted lamp was thrown in anger at an adult, and a small number of children were allegedly starved to death. Typical murder cases involved wounds and injuries of some kind, just as Scattergood was teaching his students to understand, but one important category of wound was missing: head injuries were not singled out for discussion, at least not in the surviving notes.

Edinburgh 1900

While Scattergood's notebook has provided a partial but very detailed indication of the content of his lectures on forensic medicine, including illustrative case studies, national statistics, and frequent references to the works of a wide range of reputable medico-legal experts, especially A. S. Taylor, the student notebook on which this section concentrates offers a very different yet directly comparable perspective. It summarises Henry Littlejohn's lectures on forensic medicine, delivered daily Tuesday to Friday in the summer session, 1 May to 6 July 1900, at the University of Edinburgh. The author is unknown: it is supposed that the lawyer whose family donated it to the Signet Library received it from a previous student, as it was common for student notes to be passed on from one year to the next.[112] But since forensic medicine was then a required subject for both medical and law students it is difficult to identify whether the notes were taken by a medical student.[113] On balance, however, it is likely they were: careful recording of numerous medical details, such as the location of the liver and the definition of 'congested',[114] reference to the formal opinion as "the most important part and the part to which the lawyer looks" in a medico-legal report,[115] together with relatively light attention to legal precedent but frequent illustrative medical sketches seem to signpost the interests of a student who planned to become a doctor.

Although less detailed than Scattergood's lecture notes, the Edinburgh student notes present a complete summary of the course content at the Scottish university where the teaching of forensic medicine had been inaugurated in the late eighteenth century. By 1900, the widely experienced Henry Littlejohn had occupied the Regius Chair of Forensic Medicine at the University of Edinburgh since 1897, having previously taught the subject for 42 years in the Edinburgh extramural medical school. There, his popular lectures had been "frequently complemented with 'field demonstrations' to relevant locations,"[116] a tradition he continued at the university: the notebook records several excursions to the mortuary, the first occurring on the opening day of classes, and refers to recent deaths used as teaching material. Littlejohn took full advantage of the educational opportunities presented by fresh bodies, interrupting planned lectures when necessary; mentioned historic cases, both Scottish and English; cited the works of international medico-legal experts such as Taylor; pointed out differences in Scottish and English procedures and distributed printed copies of his own forensic reports as models of good practice.[117] The first mortuary visit, to see the body of a man who had cut his own throat, gives an indication of Littlejohn's teaching style: the student recorded many different points about the body and their medico-legal significance, but noted that the swollen stomach was not explained: "The fact was merely mentioned to us."[118] Oddly, there is no reference whatever to the ideal manner in which a post-mortem examination should be performed, even though Littlejohn held strong views about this,[119] suggesting that he communicated such information during mortuary visits, rather than in a specific lecture as Scattergood had. The student may not have taken good notes about autopsy protocols, but he did observe that Scottish criminal procedure required all post-mortems to be conducted by two doctors.[120]

The course was divided into 11 sections: wounds, burns, poisons, asphyxiating cases, asphyxia, rape, conception, pregnancy, delivery, infanticide and insanity.[121] Throughout, the emphasis lay on fatal cases. Thus, on the first day of teaching the section on wounds mentioned assault briefly before listing a series of general queries related mostly to the dead: is the case one of accident, suicide or murder?, was there power of locomotion and volition after severe injuries?, what was cause of death?, what was the fatality of wounds of various parts of the body?, what are the signs of death? and questions of identification. Manner of death was determined by position of the body, nature of its injuries, direction of the wound, position of any instrument, marks of blood, and evidence of a struggle.[122] These details were covered in a series of case studies on 2 May, along with brief indicators of the damage that various organs might sustain;[123] the next day focused on bruises and how to gauge their age and difference from post-mortem lividity.[124] Then the students were taken to the city mortuary to see the body of a 45-year-old woman who had drowned herself the day before. They examined her externally, finding rigidity, incipient putrefaction, silvery abdominal marks indicative of child-bearing and foam in the mouth resulting from water forcing its way down the windpipe; "If the body had been dissected we would have found water in considerable quantities in the stomach."[125] The meandering approach to wounds continued, taking in a wide variety of important signs and indicators of contusions, sprains, dislocations, fractures and incisions, punctured, lacerated and contused wounds, peppered with asides about the Burke and Hare murders, the Anatomy Act of 1832, the medical men of genius whom Littlejohn had met and numerous case studies.[126] Then they went back to the mortuary to examine a man who had thrown himself from a bridge: "The skull had been fractured, as could be felt by anyone who cared to feel his head above the left ear."[127] And this was still only the second week of the course!

Following some discussion of gunshot wounds, for which the student made a series of sketches to show how bullets passed through or ricocheted inside the head, and burns, ("wounds in the eye of the law") illustrated by a human leg exhibiting burns inflicted after death,[128] Littlejohn listed the causes of death arising from wounding. His list mirrored the one created by Scattergood decades earlier, with a couple of additions:

1. Primary: a) haemorrhage; b) shock, including death from a multiplicity of injuries without any mortal wound; c) mechanical injury. 2. Secondary:

erysipelas, tetanus, pyaemia; delirium tremens; operations; malum regimen [of the patient or practitioner].[129]

The last category was a defence specific to Scots law: a defendant in a homicide case could assert that bad medical treatment, not their actions, had caused the victim's death.[130]

The signs of death, due to cessation of the action of the heart, lungs or brain (for which Littlejohn provided 13 indicators) were less important than the time at which death had occurred, which could be determined by the body's temperature (cooling occurred at a rate of 1°F per hour), rigidity (rigor mortis began in the head and moved down the body) and state of putrefaction, for which rates were provided. Adipocere did not form before six weeks.[131] The teaching turned to identification of the living and the dead, including the use of footprints and the anthropometric methods of the Parisian criminologist Alphonse Bertillon (1853–1914), before another mortuary visit to examine an elderly man found in an advanced state of decomposition. Had the weather been hotter, the student noted excitedly, the smell would have prevented them from approaching the body.[132]

From this point onward, the notebook reflects what appears to have been either the considerable amount of attention devoted to infanticide during the rest of the course, or the student's particular interest in it. His notes on infanticide are interspersed with others on toxicology, asphyxiation, rape and insanity and give the impression that, together with poisoning, newborn child murder was a potentially problematic aspect of medico-legal practice – but more likely to be encountered by the average medical practitioner than other forms of lethal violence. Given that 27 per cent of the homicides that form the research basis for this book were cases of infanticide, the notes present us with a suitable means of examining the medico-legal standards associated with the investigation of the offence circa 1900. They show that Littlejohn's students were taught to assess the prospect that a dead infant had not been the victim of deliberate killing, how to ascertain whether a woman had given birth recently, and that there were two aims of a post-mortem examination: determination of live birth, in which the hydrostatic lung test played a key but not conclusive role; and proof that the child had been fully separated from the mother's body before death. This differed from the second of William Cummin's two main points, which was merely to ascertain whether death resulted from violence. As Daniel Grey's detailed study has shown, the issue of separate existence became a key battleground between doctors and lawyers from the 1830s, as a result of a series of legal decisions. Furthermore, inconclusive medical evidence in trials where separate existence had been claimed remained a problem acknowledged by medico-legal writers in both England and Scotland well into the twentieth century.[133] This point will be picked up again in Chapter 4.

The student's introduction to infanticide began on 25 May when

> We were shown the dead body of a newly-born female child which was found in a coloured linen sack early this morning in Queen Street Gardens.

There were no injuries on it and the naval (sic) string had been cut high up i.e. near to the mother. The mother must [therefore] have been conscious enough to cut the string for it is cut and not torn. It will be dissected to see whether or not it has breathed. If it has there is always the chance that it died of suffocation due to the mother's fainting shortly after delivery. But it being a female child, there is less chance of this for the labour which accompanies the birth is much easier in the case of females.[134]

This last statement, perhaps surprising to the modern reader, reflects a long-standing medical belief that "the birth of male children is attended with much greater danger than the birth of females," as a result mainly of their larger head size.[135] This raises the intriguing possibility that in some cases of newborns found dead, the victim's size or sex may have influenced the doctor's initial sense of whether or not a deliberate murder had been committed, and thus served inadvertently to shape or restrict the subsequent medico-legal investigation. Evidence of potential bias is obscured by the tendency for reports to refer to infants as 'it', not 'he' or 'she', but this is not a question that can be pursued using records generated by prosecutions.

On 30 May, following a lecture on poisons and the symptoms of poisoning, the students were again shown the body of the infant found in Queen Street Gardens. Even if stored at low temperature one would assume it was displaying some sign of decomposition, but, according to Taylor, "the distension of the lungs with gas from putrefaction cannot be easily overlooked or mistaken for the air of respiration."[136] Moreover, Littlejohn told them, it was impossible to get the air out of lung tissues once they had been filled by the normal process of human respiration.[137] Thus,

> The lungs were taken out and put to the test to see if they had breathed or not. The test is by floating: if they float the child has breathed. Both lungs were taken with the heart and placed in a large tank of water. They at once rose to the surface: one (the right) lung was cut off and the left lung and heart remained afloat. The heart is of course a heavy organ so this shews the buoyancy of the lungs. Then cut off the heart: it sinks at once and the lungs remain afloat. It is thus conclusively proved that the child has breathed, but a more careful examination will have to be made tomorrow to see if the breathing has only taken place in the maternal passages or if it was after complete separation. The result of this second [examination] was not such as to admit of any decided judgment as to whether or not the child did or did not breathe after complete delivery.[138]

On the following day

> We were shewn (sic) the lungs of a still-born child put to the lung test. They at once sank to the bottom. Were also shewn the body of a still-born child; it was a child of only 5 months 'making' and was not nearly mature.

The body had a very red unskinned 'rabbity' look, for the white skin does not form till the sixth month.[139]

But in an example of how Littlejohn made the most of the teaching opportunities afforded by the bodies brought into the city mortuary, once they had learned what they could from these infants the class did not discuss infanticide again for several weeks. The subject was then approached more systematically, beginning with the legal parameters of the crime: "Then we have concealment of pregnancy. The child must be born & dead before we can press this charge in Scotland. In England they are more logical and speak of concealment of birth."[140] There was an assumption that victims of infanticide were "always killed immediately on entrance into the world" because there was otherwise no point: "the neighbours hear the child cry, if she keeps it half an hour."[141] William Hunter's 'On the Uncertainty of the Signs of Murder, in the Case of Bastard Children' was held to be a turning point: "The government must prove that the child is born alive since 1783; before that the onus of proof fell on the woman."[142]

The signs of recent delivery were to be detected in two ways:

1) By the smell of the lochia in badly ventilated rooms. The lochia is a discharge of the newly delivered woman; 2) Then the breasts are large, full, and dark. The signs of recent delivery disappear in one week. Irritation of the womb may make the breasts full of milk: in fact the breasts of a woman who has borne a child are never quite empty of milk. But nothing but pregnancy will ever *fill* the breasts of a woman with milk. The appearances are almost unmistakeable.[143]

There was no suggestion that a doctor should presume to conduct an internal examination of a woman suspected of infanticide: by this time such an invasion of privacy was held to be illegal,[144] but as a later chapter will show, internal examinations – usually but not always carried out with the permission of the woman – were not uncommon in earlier decades. The easiest way to ascertain whether a recently delivered woman was the mother of a newborn was to match the child's umbilical cord "to see if it fits on to the end of the afterbirth discharge; if it does there is no doubt of the identity of the child as the newly born child of the mother who is in question."[145]

Then the student recorded interesting general observations about infanticide, indicating important legal distinctions between English and Scottish law. In England, it was irrelevant whether a premature child was viable, or had the capacity to live: if a child was "actually born and its body entirely in the world, it matters not whether it has been destroyed within a few minutes or not until several days after its birth"; English law required only proof that a child had lived, separated from its mother (the umbilical cord might still be attached), and then been killed.[146] But in Scotland, the statutory offence of concealment of pregnancy required proof of pregnancy up to a period when a child could be born alive,[147] and this meant that in Scottish medico-legal practice a child's viability became an additional point in law:

> To prove infanticide we must prove that the child is newly born. What guides us in this country? No settled period. For about a fortnight in this country the child is newly born. After this the charge is one of murder. The Crown has to prove live birth in all cases of infanticide. Secondly we must prove that the child was mature. What is a mature child? It should be 16 to 18 inches long, and of 6 to 8 lbs weight. The cord should be in the centre of the body. The testicles should be in the scrotum if a male. The hair and nails should be developed whether it is male or female. Thirdly the child must be healthy. Some infants are born dying from disease, e.g. their lungs are diseased. Unless there is absolute evidence that the child has lived there can be no charge. Respiration is the sign of live birth, both in civil and criminal law. The child is entered with a push into the world. It has to be pushed through the maternal passages: though a child is still connected with the mother it is murder by English law to kill it. This has never been brought up in our Courts. Whenever we have imperfect respiration the woman must be given the benefit of the doubt. We can't then state positively that the child has breathed.[148]

Surgeons in English cases, many of whom had trained in Scotland, also provided details of length, weight, hair and nails in support of the conclusion that an infant had not been born dead but had in fact been killed, as a prelude to their evidence about the cause and manner of death. This process will be explored at greater length in Chapter 4. While it is not possible to state with certainty that all the surgeons who provided these details had been trained in Scotland, it is safe to say that there was uniformity of practice across the two countries. The medico-legal problems associated with newborn child murder were essentially international; this is why textbooks published in England and Scotland made reference to European and even American research.[149]

Littlejohn also taught his students to be alert to signs that might exonerate an accused woman: if the umbilical cord was torn rather than cut it was probably a case of unassisted labour, so any violence may have been unintentional; infants were so easily suffocated that it was always necessary to check for any foreign body in the mouth, throat or air passages;[150] and the lung test itself might prove to be a mitigating factor:

> Notice that in trying the lung test we must divide the right lung into at least 16 and the left lung into 14 separate pieces. There are 3 lobes of the right lung and 2 in the left. Each piece must float and if every piece still floats after gentle and then severe pressure we can say positively that the child has had full and perfect respiration. If one piece does not float we must say that the respiration has been imperfect. The child enters the world with the mouth downwards: at the last struggle the mother may faint and the child may very

easily be drowned in the discharge which comes immediately after the birth and collects in the bed i.e. of course if she is unassisted. This is a perfectly sound plea in defence.[151]

This information was followed by a chillingly matter-of-fact comment: "The simplest way to kill a child is to put one hand over its mouth and to hold the nostrils tight with 2 fingers of the other hand";[152] but the student failed to record any suggested ways in which a doctor might identify this tactic.

While poisoning was not a common method of homicide,[153] death from asphyxiation features regularly among the cases collected for this study, so that the Edinburgh student's notes on this topic are as relevant as those on infanticide, although they are decidedly less detailed. Of the five forms of death by asphyxia – inhalation of carbon monoxide, hanging, strangulation (garrotting or throttling), suffocation (smothering or overlaying) and drowning – neither monoxide nor hanging feature in the homicides discussed in this book, being more typically associated with accidents or suicides. But the symptoms caused by these five different mechanisms were not very different:

> In all deaths by asphyxia the blood is very fluid and the post-mortem lividity is very well marked in consequence. The face is only a little congested. The teeth are usually close shut, and the tongue is often driven out against them so as to take an imprint of the insides of the teeth. Prof. Casper of Berlin first discovered this. The lungs are intensely congested in cases of death by asphyxia. The right side of the heart must be distended with dark blood and very fluid blood. Congestion refers to the tissues so we should say that the heart is distended. . . . The abdominal organs are more or less congested.[154]

Tardieu's spots (small spots of ecchymosis on the face, neck, chest and eyes) were external signs of death from overlaying, although in fact more commonly associated with strangulation,[155] while not every body taken out of water had died from drowning: without evidence of a struggle and signs of asphyxia it was impossible to reach a firm conclusion. Symptoms of drowning included water in the stomach and bronchi, froth in the windpipe, injuries on the fingers, sand under the fingernails and the speed at which post-mortem rigidity developed.[156]

Unlike Scattergood's lecture notes, the student notebook does not refer to the use of microscopy in the forensic examination of blood, which was not covered in Littlejohn's lectures; but it was cited as a key tool in the investigation of sexual offences. The topic of discussion on 16 June was rape, when the notes betray the stereotypical attitudes of the day: "After puberty, there must be a struggle. Any woman can resist the advances of a single male: she must resist to the utmost. . . . But whether or not she consents there are marks of violence on the private parts."[157] The belief that young girls suffered from a disease called leucorrhoea, indistinguishable from gonorrhoea, was recorded alongside the assumption that men infected with venereal disease had intercourse with children in a misguided attempt to cure themselves (Figure 2.3): "There is a false idea abroad that if a

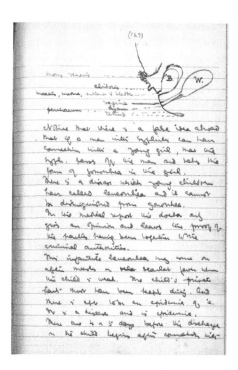

Figure 2.3 Extract from student notes on rape, University of Edinburgh, 16 June 1900

Source: The Signet Library, Edinburgh, L61: Notes on lectures on medical jurisprudence and forensic medicine, Sir Henry Littlejohn, 1900, p. 127. With permission from the WS Society.

man with syphilis can have connection with a young girl, that the syph[ilis] passes off the man and takes the form of gonorrhoea in the girl."[158] Medical students in Edinburgh were clearly absorbing the pervading theory of the early twentieth century to account for alarming numbers of children infected with gonorrhoea. As Roger Davidson and Lynn Sacco have demonstrated, by the 1890s sexual infections in young girls were easily diagnosed but difficult to explain away. By situating them as a product of uncleanliness or superstition (the 'virgin cure'), health-care professionals were able to disregard evidence of child sexual abuse within families.[159]

Despite this obvious reluctance to consider the reality of child rape, it seems that the medico-legal position was relatively straightforward, for the notes reflect a greater attention to the examination of adult (non-virgin) rape victims, including the use of the microscope:

> There is no injury here to the genital organs, for the male can very easily gain entrance without any pain to the woman. So we must look only for the evidence of a struggle and for seminal stains. In an examination of a

woman in the attempt to find evidence of rape we must examine the genital organs, then the body generally (particularly the thighs) and then the linen for blood or seminal stains. The body is examined to try to find evidence of a struggle. Semen is detected a) by characteristic odour when moistened, b) by being held up to light, c) by the microscopic exam[n] of the stain soaked in distilled water. The smallest scratches must be regarded in an exam[n] for rape [since] the nails of the man in endeavouring to separate the thighs will make small scratches.[160]

On the following day a proviso was added: "Notice that an ordinary physician is incapable as a rule to detect spermatozoa. His opinion should not be taken unless he is an expert microscopist."[161] It was for the courts to assess individual expertise, based on reputation, experience and credentials; but GPs at the time had been taught the use of the microscope and could consult books on medical microscopy. That by Dr Frank Wethered (1860–1928), for example, acknowledged the relevance of microscopy in medico-legal cases but referred readers to specialist treatises on medical jurisprudence.[162]

Much of the remaining lecture time was devoted to insanity. Following the classificatory system of the pioneering French psychiatrist Philippe Pinel (1745–1826), Littlejohn began with the type known as mania, which he associated more strongly with women than men and believed fellow doctors did not confront with sufficient vigour: "Where doctors fall short is that they neglect the premonitory symptoms,"[163] one of the most obvious of which was the existence of delusions.[164] Insanity could be distinguished from acute alcoholism by the presence of hallucinations – "delusions are when we act on the strength of a hallucination," but alcoholism might also be a form of insanity: "We have acute mania in cases of delirium tremens."[165] The second type of insanity was monomania, though "It used to be said that there was no such thing." Melancholia was defined as the monomania of depression, while homicidal monomania was "a very convenient plea but should not be accepted unless on very strong evidence of premonitory symptoms. It can't be taken in sudden fits or on account of some sudden impulse."[166] An even more detailed classification of the various forms of insanity followed, with some discussion of behaviours of interest to psychiatrists but not relevant to the investigation of murder, including kleptomania and pyromania. The last category was puerperal insanity, "a mania which comes in a month after delivery; it is accompanied by homicidal and suicidal tendencies." It is evident that Littlejohn expected his students to recognise the various degrees of mental incapacity, since in their private practice they might one day have to certify an individual as insane. This useful medico-legal information was laced with his personal, occasionally rather odd, opinion, such as the dangers connected with wet-nurses: Littlejohn seems to have believed, or at least led the student to believe, that insanity could be communicated through breast milk![167]

Littlejohn spent the last four days of the course discussing a range of diseases and their effects on various internal organs, with brief case studies. If the brevity of the student's notes is anything to judge by, he had begun to lose interest. This is unsurprising, given that the class exam had already been held. It comprised three questions, for which the student appears to have been well prepared:

1) Name the corrosive acids and state shortly their leading characteristics. 2) A person is found suspended from a rafter in the ceiling, and his feet are fully 12 inches from the floor, what are the appearances that would lead you to certify that there had been foul play? 3) What are the circumstances in which pregnancy comes up for discussion in civil and criminal courts? Mention any distinction that exists between English and Scottish procedure.[168]

Conclusion

Just as Michael Ryan had told his readers 30 years earlier, in 1865 Alfred Swaine Taylor prefaced his *Principles and Practice of Medical Jurisprudence* with a reminder that the law expected doctors to have "a fair average knowledge" not just of medicine "but of that which falls more peculiarly under the province of a medical witness"; it was a mistake to assume such principles were "spontaneously acquired, or . . . necessarily derived from the study of those isolated branches of medicine upon which medical jurisprudence is based."[169] While eighteenth-century medical students had little option but to absorb the principles in an ad hoc and essentially autodidactic fashion, their nineteenth-century successors had access to increasingly sophisticated textbooks, lecture courses, demonstrations, expert teaching and, finally, clinical experience. Admittedly, it was a slow start: in reminiscences published in 1874 J. F. Clarke, a student who studied under Ryan at the Gerrard Street school and later conducted his post-mortem, noted rather nonchalantly that he got involved in a murder trial because he was apprenticed to one of the first London police surgeons, and pointed out that the lectures on medical jurisprudence given by both Ryan and Thomson lacked originality.[170] Despite this, however, we can say with some confidence that, following the reforms of the early 1830s, the average British-trained general practitioner had access to a basic knowledge of forensic medicine and medico-legal practice, albeit shaped by idiosyncratic local teaching and an over-emphasis on written exams and book learning.

References to the publications of scholars in other countries, such as the well-known multi-volume work of the Berlin-based expert J. L. Casper, cited by Scattergood and Littlejohn in their lectures to students in Leeds and Edinburgh, demonstrate that teaching in forensic medicine was, like Western medical education in general,[171] international in its range and scope. The impact that this had on the English assimilation of medico-legal knowledge and the necessary elements of good practice should not be under-estimated. The English may have lagged behind the Scots and continental physicians in forensic matters in 1800, but by the 1830s they had begun to catch up, and by the mid-Victorian era there was little to distinguish the professionalism of English medico-legal experts such as A. S. Taylor from that of experts in other countries. The fact that so many textbooks were re-issued in revised editions, "in accordance with the results of recent scientific researches on subjects related to Forensic Medicine and Toxicology,"[172] shows that the discipline was evolving quickly and that English teaching kept abreast of the changes.

There has long been a tendency to dismiss English medico-legal knowledge and practice as inadequate,[173] but without careful scrutiny of what students were taught or how they applied that information in real cases such an evaluation is largely unhelpful: it provides few insights into how medico-legal practice was actually integrated into the legal system on an increasingly routine basis. This chapter has uncovered some of that missing information. The immediacy of the lecture notes on which it is based warrants the close attention to detail provided, for they give a clear sense of the developing content of medical education and the manner in which students were instructed about the key forensic aims, responsibilities, questions and problems that they might one day encounter as medical practitioners in England and Wales. As limited as their practical experience may have been, after the 1830s doctors did not approach forensic cases from a position of complete ignorance. They knew about infanticide and its key medico-legal pitfalls, building on the late eighteenth-century fascination with the hydrostatic lung test and the enduring impact of William Hunter's impassioned plea on behalf of accused women. They were taught that a post-mortem should always encompass the three main body cavities and told how to conduct such an examination systematically. Students were warned about the sorts of questions that lawyers might ask and on which legal and medical opinion might differ, and they were told to be prepared. What is therefore one of the most fascinating findings of this chapter is the consistent focus on poisoning, despite the fact that statistics of known cases show that it simply was not a common method of murder. While this suggests that historians of crime and forensic toxicology may not have been looking in all the right places, the lack of attention paid to head injuries is particularly interesting because they made up fully 21 per cent of the cases for which a cause of death was recorded, by contrast to poison's 3 per cent and the 15 per cent of stabbings. The following chapter considers the cases on which the rest of this book will focus.

Notes

1 Howard Brody, Zahra Meghani and Kimberley Greenwald, "Michael Ryan: A Biographical Summary," in *Michael Ryan's Writings on Medical Ethics*, ed. H. Brody, Z. Meghani and K. Greenwald (London and New York: Springer, 2009), p. 28. Ryan was associated with the school located in Gerrard Street, Soho.

2 Catherine Crawford, "A Scientific Profession: Medical Reform and Forensic Medicine in British Periodicals of the Early Nineteenth Century," in *British Medicine in an Age of Reform*, ed. Roger French and Andrew Wear (London and New York: Routledge, 1991), p. 210.

3 Ibid., pp. 213–218.

4 John Frederick Archbold, *A Summary of the Law Relative to Pleading and Evidence in Criminal Cases* (London: R. Pheney, 1822), p. 93: "in a matter of science, a person intimately acquainted with it, may be called upon to give his opinion as to the probable result or

consequence from certain facts already proved." The exemplar he gave was that of a surgeon called to confirm cause of death in a murder trial.

5 For example: Jennifer Ward, "Origins and Development of Forensic Medicine and Forensic Science in England 1823–1946," PhD thesis, Open University, 1993, pp. 84–92, 96–107; Stephan Landsman, "Of Witches, Madmen, and Products Liability: An Historical Survey of the Use of Expert Testimony," *Behavioral Sciences and the Law* 13 (1995), pp. 138–143; Daniel J. R. Grey, "Discourses of Infanticide in England, 1880–1922," PhD thesis, Roehampton University, 2008, pp. 159–161.

6 Mark Jackson found that the "need for medical evidence in cases of suspected new-born child murder contributed . . . to the emergence of legal medicine in England": *New-born Child Murder: Women, Illegitimacy and the Courts in Eighteenth-Century England* (Manchester: Manchester University Press, 1996), p. 85.

7 Mark S. R. Jenner and Patrick Wallis, "The Medical Marketplace," in *Medicine and the Market in England and Its Colonies, c. 1450–1850*, ed. Mark S. R. Jenner and Patrick Wallis (Basingstoke: Palgrave, 2007), pp. 12–16.

8 Samuel Farr, *Elements of Medical Jurisprudence* (London: T. Becket, 1788), vi.

9 *A Statement by the Society of Apothecaries, on the Subject of Their Administration of the Apothecaries' Act, with Reference to some Supposed Features of Sir James Graham's Promised Measure of Medical Reform* (London: Samuel Highley, 1844), p. 9.

10 Anne Digby, *Making a Medical Living: Doctors and Patients in the English Market for Medicine, 1720–1911* (Cambridge: Cambridge University Press, 1994), p. 54.

11 Matthew H. Kaufman, "Origin and History of the Regius Chair of Medical Jurisprudence and Medical Police Established in the University of Edinburgh in 1807," *Journal of Forensic and Legal Medicine* 14 (2007), p. 121; Andrew Duncan, *Heads of Lectures on Medical Jurisprudence* (Edinburgh: Neill & Co., 1792).

12 George Edward Male, *An Epitome of Juridical or Forensic Medicine: For the Use of Medical Men, Coroners and Barristers* (London: T. & G. Underwood, 1816), 3. The quotation is in B. T. Davis, "George Edward Male MD: The Father of English Medical Jurisprudence," *Proceedings of the Royal Society of Medicine* 67 (1974), p. 118. Davis dismissed William Dease's *Remarks on Medical Jurisprudence* (1793) as "inaccurate and unhelpful," pp. 117–118.

13 John Gordon Smith, *The Principles of Forensic Medicine, Systematically Arranged, and Applied to British Practice* (London: T. and G. Underwood, 1821); J. A. Paris and J. S. M. Fonblanque, *Medical Jurisprudence*, 3 vols (London: W. Phillips, 1823); Theodric Romeyn Beck, *Elements of Medical Jurisprudence*, second edition, ed. William Dunlop (London: John Anderson, 1825).

14 See Dunlop's preface in Beck, *Elements of Medical Jurisprudence*, p. xvi.

15 J. F. Clarke, *Autobiographical Recollections of the Medical Profession* (London: J. & A. Churchill, 1874), p. 413.

16 Thomas Neville Bonner, *Becoming a Physician: Medical Education in Britain, France, Germany, and the United States, 1750–1945* (Baltimore and London: Johns Hopkins University Press, 1995), pp. 166–173.

17 Ward, "Origins and Development," pp. 26–34, 46–49; quote on p. 34.

18 *The Morning Post*, 11 Oct 1830, p. 4.

19 Ward, "Origins and Development," pp. 34, 42; *The London Medical Gazette* 7 (1831), p. 539; Kaufman, "Origin and History," p. 123. See *Statement by the Society of Apothecaries*, p. 12 for details of the medical curriculum from 1 Oct 1835; forensic medicine was taught in the second summer session of the programme, 1 May to 31 July.

20 J. D. J. Havard, *The Detection of Secret Homicide: A Study of the Medico-Legal System of Investigation of Sudden and Unexplained Deaths* (London: Macmillan, 1960), pp. 47–51; Pamela J. Fisher, "The Politics of Sudden Death: The Office and Role of the Coroner in England and Wales, 1726–1888," PhD thesis, University of Leicester, 2007, pp. 192–203. Both point out that the promise of the Medical Witnesses Act was not realised for practical and financial reasons.

21 Digby, *Making a Medical Living*, p. 57.

22 John Struthers, *The Royal Colleges of Physicians and Surgeons under the Medical Act* (Edinburgh: Maclachlan and Stewart, 1861), p. 13.

23 Sir George Newman, *Some Notes on Medical Education in England* (London: HMSO, 1918), p. 24. In England medical education consisted of the following: Preliminary Scientific Studies (chemistry, biology, physics), Intermediate Medical Studies (anatomy, physiology, pharmacology) and Advanced Medical Studies (pathology, medicine or the practice of physic, surgery, obstetrics and gynaecology, preventive medicine, forensic medicine).

24 Sale of Food and Drugs Act (1875).

25 Digby, *Making a Medical Living*, p. 58. The fast pace of progress and the requirements of testimony at coroners' inquests prompted Dr R. G. Mayne's revised and expanded vocabulary: *An Expository Lexicon of the Terms, Ancient and Modern, in Medical and General Science: Including a Complete Medico-Legal Vocabulary* (London: John Churchill, 1860), preface. This book was advertised and endorsed in Alfred Swaine Taylor, *The Principles and Practice of Medical Jurisprudence* (London: John Churchill & Sons, 1865), p. 1187.

26 Lawyers and even judges attended his lectures: "Obituary: Alfred Swaine Taylor, MD, FRS," *BMJ*, 12 June 1880, p. 905.

27 John Dixon Mann, *Forensic Medicine and Toxicology* (London: Charles Griffin & Co., 1893), sixth edition revised by W. A. Brend 1922; John Glaister, *A Textbook of Medical Jurisprudence, Toxicology and Public Health* (Edinburgh: E. & S. Livingstone, 1902), fourth edition 1921; public health was dropped after the first edition. Dixon Mann was professor of forensic medicine at Owens College, Manchester; Glaister was professor of forensic medicine and public health at Glasgow University.

28 William A. Brend, *A Handbook of Medical Jurisprudence and Toxicology for the Use of Students and Practitioners* (London: Charles Griffin & Co., 1906).

29 William A. Brend, *A Handbook of Medical Jurisprudence and Toxicology for the Use of Students and Practitioners*, sixth edition (London: Charles Griffin & Co., 1928), preface.

30 Bonner, *Becoming a Physician*, pp. 39–42, 56–57; Digby, *Making a Medical Living*, pp. 52–53. Neither group was especially regulated: only those who set up practice in London were subject to scrutiny by the Company of Surgeons or the Royal College of Physicians.

31 M. Anne Crowther and Marguerite W. Dupree, *Medical Lives in the Age of Surgical Revolution* (Cambridge: Cambridge University Press, 2007), pp. 65–76. Students at the universities of Edinburgh and Glasgow had to attend courses of 50 lectures on medical jurisprudence; competition with the extramural classes meant that students could "shop around" for the best lectures (p. 66).

32 Bonner, *Becoming a Physician*, pp. 281, 295–296; *The Western Times*, 27 Dec 1894, p. 4; *BMJ*, 1 Sep 1894, pp. 497–498.

33 *South Wales Daily News*, 6 Dec 1894, p. 3.

34 Digby, *Making a Medical Living*, p. 13. See also Crowther and Dupree, *Medical Lives*, pp. 176–183: 60% of the students who matriculated at Glasgow and Edinburgh in the late 1860s and early 1870s, most of whom became GPs, were practising in England and Wales ten years after qualifying.

35 "Thomas Scattergood, M.R.C.S., L.S.A.," *BMJ*, 3 Mar 1900, p. 547; Brotherton Library, University of Leeds, Notes for Lectures on Forensic Medicine, MS 534/4.

36 The Signet Library, Edinburgh, L61: Notes on Lectures on Medical Jurisprudence and Forensic Medicine, Sir Henry Littlejohn, 1900.

37 Brenda M. White, "Littlejohn, Sir Henry Duncan (1826–1914), Medical Officer of Health and Expert in Forensic Medicine," *Oxford Dictionary of National Biography*, 23 Sep 2004, https://doi-org.oxfordbrookes.idm.oclc.org/10.1093/ref:odnb/40753 (accessed 23 Oct 2018). He was appointed police surgeon to the city of Edinburgh in 1854.

38 Ibid.; Anne Digby, *The Evolution of British General Practice 1850–1948* (Oxford: Oxford University Press, 1999), pp. 48–49.

39 Burkhard Madea, "History of Forensic Medicine: A Brief Introduction," in *History of Forensic Medicine*, ed. B. Madea (Berlin: Lehmanns Media, 2017), pp. 22–26. The author lists 22 "important books" in the history of forensic medicine of the seventeenth and

eighteenth centuries, almost all German. The list should be expanded to include French works, such as Jean Devaux, *L'art de faire les raports en chirurgie* (Paris: Laurent d'Houry, 1703). Joan Lane noted that the *Medical Register* of 1779 "listed sixty-five 'foreign books' as contemporary publications (thirty in Latin, twenty-four in French, seven in Italian, and two in German), presumably to draw practitioners' attention to these recent titles," from which we may conclude that at least some provincial doctors were reading these books: "A Provincial Surgeon and His Obstetric Practice: Thomas W. Jones of Henley-in-Arden, 1764–1846," *Medical History* 31 (1987), p. 338.

40 Johann Friedrich Faselius, *Elementa Medicinae Forensis*, ed. Christian Rickmann (Jena: Wilhelm Hartung, 1767). The translation by Christian Gottfried Langen was published at Leipzig in 1768.

41 Farr, *Elements of Medical Jurisprudence*, title page. I have not retained the extensive capitalisation.

42 Ibid., p. 45.

43 Ibid., p. 67.

44 Ibid., p. 74. "Proper" was not defined, but by the contrast made with where bodies were found (unstated, but often outdoors or at night), and in comparison to Dease's recommendation in *Remarks on Medical Jurisprudence*, p. 6, we may surmise that Farr meant on a table inside a building in natural daylight but not necessarily in a medical institution such as a hospital.

45 Ibid., pp. 82–114; quotation on p. 81.

46 Dease, *Remarks on Medical Jurisprudence*, p. 9.

47 Ibid., pp. 12–19.

48 Ibid., pp. 19–21; William Hunter, "On the Uncertainty of the Signs of Murder, in the Case of Bastard Children," *Medical Observations and Inquiries* 6 (1784), pp. 281–282.

49 Kaufman, "Origin and History," pp. 121–122; M. Anne Crowther and Brenda White, *On Soul and Conscience: The Medical Expert and Crime: 150 Years of Forensic Medicine in Glasgow* (Aberdeen: Aberdeen University Press, 1988), pp. 9–10.

50 Duncan, *Heads of Lectures*, pp. 5–6.

51 G. T. Bettany, "Duncan, Andrew, the Elder (1744–1828), Physician," *Oxford Dictionary of National Biography*, 23 Sep 2004, https://doi-org.oxfordbrookes.idm.oclc.org/10.1093/ref:odnb/8213 (accessed 21 Nov 2018).

52 Kaufman, "Origin and History," p. 123.

53 *The Edinburgh Evening Courant*, 24 May 1832, p. 2.

54 Brenda M. White, "Christison, Sir Robert, First Baronet (1797–1882)," *Oxford Dictionary of National Biography*, 23 Sep 2004, https://doi-org.oxfordbrookes.idm.oclc.org/10.1093/ref:odnb/5370 (accessed 21 Nov 2018).

55 Ward, "Origins and Development," p. 24.

56 *The London Medical Gazette* 20 (1837), pp. 86–87.

57 *The London Medical Gazette* 19 (1837), p. 26.

58 Ibid., p. 433.

59 William Cummin, *The Proofs of Infanticide Considered* (London: Longman, Rees, Orme, Brown, Green and Longman, 1836).

60 *The Morning Post*, 12 Apr 1837, p. 4. Cummin could read French and German: "William Cummin, MD," *The Gentleman's Magazine*, new series, 8 (1837), p. 95.

61 *The London Medical Gazette* 19 (1837), p. 41.

62 Ibid., pp. 514, 723. As Cummin noted in a later lecture, this feature of the charge of concealment of birth implied that in indictments for murder, i.e. infanticide, jurors would expect proof as to *when* the child died.

63 Ibid., p. 726. The images were originally published in and are here reproduced from Cummin, *The Proofs of Infanticide Considered*, p. 56. A similar pair of diagrams appeared in Taylor's *Principles and Practice of Medical Jurisprudence*, pp. 895, 914, 916.

64 In 1782 and in an expanded monograph, *Commentarius medicus in processus criminales super homicidio, infanticidio, et embryoctonia* (Strasbourg: A. Koenig, 1787), Wilhelm

Gottfried Ploucquet (1744–1814), professor of medicine at the University of Tübingen, proposed that respiration doubled the weight of the lungs in a newborn in relation to its total weight. The research of Alphonse Devergie (1798–1879), author of a two-volume work on forensic medicine published in 1836, proposed that in the stillborn the average weight of the lungs in proportion to the whole body would be 1/51, but 1/38 in the live born.

65 *The London Medical Gazette* 19 (1837), p. 755: "Dr Hunter was very imperfectly acquainted with the nature of the test which he attacked, and has fallen into several errors in the few pages which he devotes to a pretended examination of its merits; yet there was no one to answer him."

66 Ibid., p. 757: Taylor and a Mr Jennings of Leamington had independently and recently shown that "in the case of lungs that have naturally respired, even the smallest particles still remain buoyant – as long, in fact, as there is any portion of them not completely mashed."

67 Ibid., p. 758.

68 Ibid., pp. 759–762.

69 Ibid., p. 805.

70 Ibid., p. 806.

71 Ibid., pp. 806–807.

72 Ibid., pp. 807–808.

73 Ibid., p. 884. For an analysis of the evolving relationship between the legal and medical understanding of insanity see Joel Peter Eigen, *Witnessing Insanity: Madness and Mad-Doctors in the English Court* (New Haven: Yale University Press, 1995), chapters 2 and 3.

74 Monomania was identified by the French alienist Jean-Étienne Dominique Esquirol (1772–1840) in 1817: see Eigen, *Witnessing Insanity*, pp. 72–76. The table is in *The London Medical Gazette* 19 (1837), p. 885.

75 Robert Christison, *Syllabus of the Course of Lectures on Medical Jurisprudence Delivered in the University of Edinburgh* (Edinburgh: John Stark, 1831); Anthony Todd Thomson and Andrew Amos, *Syllabus of Lectures on Medical Jurisprudence in the University of London* (London: Joseph Mallett, 1830).

76 Alfred S. Taylor, *Elements of Medical Jurisprudence*, Vol. 1 (London: Deacon, 1836). This book was reissued in 1843 under the same title.

77 *British and Foreign Medical Review* 17 (1844), p. 228.

78 Alfred S. Taylor, *A Manual of Medical Jurisprudence* (London: John Churchill, 1844), pp. vi, ix.

79 Alfred S. Taylor, *Medical Jurisprudence*, second American edition (Philadelphia: Lea and Blanchard, 1850), p. iii (the preface to the third London edition, written in August 1848). I thank Chris Milroy for this reference.

80 "Obituary," p. 905.

81 "Thomas Scattergood, MRCS Eng., LSA," *The Lancet*, 10 Mar 1900, pp. 737–738; M. A. Green, "Dr Scattergood's Case Books: A 19th Century Medico-legal Record," *The Practitioner* 211 (1973), pp. 679–684. For a summary of some of Scattergood's forensic work, see Cassie Watson and Laura Sellers, "Thomas Scattergood: Forensic Toxicology in Victorian Yorkshire," *Legal History Miscellany*, 19 Dec 2017, https://legalhistorymiscellany.com/2017/12/19/thomas-scattergood-forensic-toxicology-in-victorian-yorkshire/ (accessed 21 Oct 2018).

82 The Cotton reference is made in Brotherton Library, MS 534/4, p. 2r.

83 Crowther and White, *On Soul and Conscience*, p. 24. The main headings in this text, spread over 87 chapters, were as follows: the dead body, poisoning, wounds and personal injuries, spontaneous combustion, asphyxia, pregnancy and delivery, legitimacy and paternity, infanticide, rape, insanity, and life insurance.

84 Brotherton Library, MS 534/4, p. 4r.

85 Ibid., pp. 4r–5v.

86 Ibid., pp. 6r–8v.

87 José Ramón Bertomeu-Sánchez, "Chemistry, Microscopy and Smell: Bloodstains and Nineteenth-Century Legal Medicine," *Annals of Science* 72 (2015), pp. 490–516.

88 Brotherton Library, MS 534/4, pp. 7r–9r.

89 H. Aubrey Husband, *The Student's Handbook of Forensic Medicine and Medical Police* (Edinburgh: E. & S. Livingstone, 1874). The sixth edition of this manual, in which medical police was replaced by public health, was published in 1895; a seventh appeared in 1904 as *Husband's Handbook of Forensic Medicine and Public Health* under new editors, much as A. S. Taylor's earlier textbooks were revised and reissued. Husband, who came from a long line of Jamaican coffee farmers, gained his medical degree from the University of Edinburgh in 1865 and emigrated to Canada in 1885 before returning to Jamaica in 1905 to run the family plantation: see Gordon Goldsborough, "Memorable Manitobans: Henry Aubrey Husband (1844–1933)," *Manitoba Historical Society*, 2014, www.mhs. mb.ca/docs/people/husband_ha.shtml (accessed 20 Oct 2018).

90 There is no evidence that Scattergood could read other languages, but he clearly read European publications in English translation. It is plausible to assume that he knew the key German manual, a copy of which is held by the University of Leeds: Rudolph Virchow, *A Description and Explanation of the Method of Performing Post-Mortem Examinations in the Dead-House of the Berlin Charité Hospital, with Especial Reference to Medico-Legal Practice*, trans. T. P. Smith (London: J. and A. Churchill, 1876).

91 Brotherton Library, MS 534/4, p. 9v (all quotations in this paragraph).

92 Ibid., pp. 10r–10v.

93 Ibid., p. 11r.

94 Ibid., p. 11v. The discussion of gunshot wounds continues for another page.

95 Ibid., p. 13r.

96 Ibid.

97 Ibid., pp. 12v–13r.

98 Ibid., p. 13v. He was referring to the legal rule which held that if an injured person survived their wound by a year and a day the accused could not be held guilty of murder: "The fixing of such a time is quite arbitrary, and medically speaking is absurd, as of course a man may die from wounds after a longer period than this (cases Taylor p. 570, Casper). In gunshot wounds especially this is not at all unusual."

99 Brotherton Library, MS 534/4, p. 13v (all quotations in this paragraph).

100 Ibid., p. 15v.

101 Ibid., p. 16r.

102 Ibid., p. 16v.

103 Ibid., p. 17r.

104 Ibid., p. 18r.

105 Ibid., p. 18v. "Late legal decisions seem to include fractures, dislocations and ruptures of internal organs as *wounds* within the meaning of the statute." Taylor is mentioned in marginalia but it is unclear which of his books Scattergood has cited.

106 Katherine D. Watson, "Is a Burn a Wound? Vitriol-Throwing in Medico-Legal Context, 1800–1900," in *Lawyers' Medicine: The Legislature, the Courts and Medical Practice, 1760–2000*, ed. Imogen Goold and Catherine Kelly (Oxford: Hart Publishing, 2009), pp. 65–68.

107 Brotherton Library, MS 534/4, pp. 18v–20r.

108 Ibid., p. 20v.

109 Ibid., pp. 20v–22v.

110 Ibid., p. 23r.

111 Ibid., pp. 23v–24r.

112 Signet Library, Notes on Lectures, letter from Alan Somerville to George Ballantyne, 8 Dec 1987.

113 In 1856 forensic medicine became a prerequisite for admission to the Faculty of Advocates, the professional association for Scottish lawyers: Katherine D. Watson, *Forensic Medicine in Western Society: A History* (Abingdon: Routledge, 2011), pp. 58, 61.

114 Signet Library, Notes on Lectures, pp. 5, 60v.
115 Ibid., p. 70.
116 Kaufman, "Origin and History," p. 127.
117 Six printed reports (1876–1899), five on rapes and one on infanticide, were pasted in at the back of the notebook.
118 Signet Library, Notes on Lectures, p. 4.
119 Henry D. Littlejohn, "How to Perform a Post-Mortem Examination: The Experience of a Lifetime, and Its Practical Teaching," *The Hospital* (5 Oct 1907), pp. 5–8, on p. 5 and *The Hospital* (12 Oct 1907), pp. 31–33.
120 Signet Library, Notes on Lectures, p. 45.
121 Ibid., p. 1.
122 Ibid., p. 3.
123 Ibid., pp. 5–9.
124 Ibid., pp. 10v–14.
125 Ibid., pp. 14v–16.
126 Ibid., pp. 17–40. Apparently Littlejohn had met only three geniuses, all Edinburgh professors: James Syme (1799–1870), Sir Robert Christison and Sir James Simpson (1811–1870).
127 Ibid., p. 42.
128 Ibid., pp. 46, 49v. In Scottish medico-legal practice, burns caused by fire or corrosives were considered wounds, the result of laws against acid throwing passed in 1825 and 1829 and adoption of the continental definition of a 'wound', which included every injury caused by some external action: Watson, "Is a Burn a Wound?"; Alexander Watson, *Medico-Legal Treatise on Homicide by External Violence*, second edition (Edinburgh: MacLachlan, Stewart & Co., 1842), pp. 18, 26.
129 Signet Library, Notes on Lectures, p. 51, with details provided on pp. 52–54.
130 *Black's Law Dictionary*, eighth edition, 2004, p. 3044; www.republicsg.info/Dictionaries/2004_Black%27s-Law-Dictionary-Edition-8.pdf (accessed 31 Oct 2018). The student noted drily that "if you knock a man down and injure him you must take your chance of the sort of medical skill available": Signet Library, Notes on Lectures, p. 54.
131 Signet Library, Notes on Lectures, pp. 58–62.
132 Ibid., p. 70.
133 Grey, "Discourses of Infanticide," pp. 156–159, 163–166, 168–175. See for example John Glaister, "The Law of Infanticide: A Plea for Its Revision," *Edinburgh Medical Journal* 41 (1895), pp. 1–18 and Harvey Littlejohn, "Respiration and the Proof of Live Birth," *Transactions of the Medico-Legal Society* 16 (1922), pp. 86–113.
134 Signet Library, Notes on Lectures, p. 70.
135 James Y. Simpson, "Memoir on the Sex of the Child as a Cause of Difficulty and Danger in Human Parturition," *Edinburgh Medical and Surgical Journal* 62 (1844), pp. 389, 407–416. See also William A. Guy and David Ferrier, *Principles of Forensic Medicine*, sixth edition (London: Henry Renshaw, 1888), p. 113.
136 Alfred Swaine Taylor, *The Principles and Practice of Medical Jurisprudence* (London: John Churchill & Sons, 1865), p. 911.
137 Signet Library, Notes on Lectures, p. 134. This point was made by Cummin in *The London Medical Gazette* 19 (1837), p. 726.
138 Signet Library, Notes on Lectures, pp. 80–81.
139 Ibid., p. 85.
140 Ibid., p. 131.
141 Ibid., p. 132. In 1837 William Cummin had reminded his students that Scottish law required "proof that the child has *cried*": *The London Medical Gazette* 19 (1837), p. 725.
142 Signet Library, Notes on Lectures, p. 132.
143 Ibid., pp. 131–132.
144 Daniel J. R. Grey, "'What Woman Is Safe . . .?': Coerced Medical Examinations, Suspected Infanticide, and the Response of the Women's Movement in Britain, 1871–1881," *Women's History Review* 22 (2013), pp. 403–421.

145 Signet Library, Notes on Lectures, p. 135.

146 Taylor, *Principles and Practice of Medical Jurisprudence*, pp. 885–887.

147 Husband, *Student's Handbook of Forensic Medicine*, p. 85.

148 Signet Library, Notes on Lectures, pp. 132–133.

149 As just two possible references, see, H. Aubrey Husband, *The Student's Handbook of Forensic Medicine and Public Health*, sixth edition (Edinburgh: E. & S. Livingstone, 1895), pp. 157–168; J. Dixon Mann, *Forensic Medicine and Toxicology*, third edition (London: Charles Griffin, 1902), pp. 144–152.

150 Signet Library, Notes on Lectures, p. 134.

151 Ibid., pp. 135–136.

152 Ibid., p. 137.

153 For an overview of the crime in England (540 cases, 1750–1914), see Katherine Watson, *Poisoned Lives: English Poisoners and Their Victims* (London: Hambledon, 2004); for Scotland (63 cases, 1800–1913), see Karen Jane Merry, "Murder by Poison in Scotland during the Nineteenth and Early Twentieth Centuries," PhD thesis, University of Glasgow, 2010.

154 Signet Library, Notes on Lectures, pp. 105–106.

155 Ibid., p. 108; Taylor, *Principles and Practice of Medical Jurisprudence*, p. 674.

156 Signet Library, Notes on Lectures, pp. 109–110.

157 Ibid., pp. 125–126.

158 Ibid., p. 127. According to the student, leucorrhoea "is a disease and is epidemic."

159 Roger Davidson, "'This Pernicious Delusion': Law, Medicine, and Child Sexual Abuse in Early-Twentieth-Century Scotland," *Journal of the History of Sexuality* 10 (2001), pp. 62–77; Lynn Sacco, "Sanitized for Your Protection: Medical Discourse and the Denial of Incest in the United States, 1890–1940," *Journal of Women's History* 14 (2002), pp. 80–104.

160 Signet Library, Notes on Lectures, p. 128.

161 Ibid., p. 129.

162 Frank J. Wethered, *Medical Microscopy: A Guide to the Use of the Microscope in Medical Practice* (London: H. K. Lewis, 1892), pp. 184, 313. Four years later Wethered became lecturer in medical jurisprudence at the Middlesex Hospital: *BMJ*, 10 Nov 1928, p. 875. In 1892 a copy of his book, later digitised, was purchased by George Harrison, a GP in Streatham Hill, London. *The Medical Register* (1891, p. 533; 1895, p. 603) reveals that Harrison qualified MRCS (1860) and LSA (1861). He is thus a perfect example of a GP who continued to educate himself long after going into private practice.

163 Signet Library, Notes on Lectures, p. 138.

164 For a detailed explanation of the importance of delusions in the history of the insanity defence, see Joel Peter Eigen, *Mad-Doctors in the Dock: Defending the Diagnosis, 1760–1913* (Baltimore: Johns Hopkins University Press, 2016), pp. 42–49.

165 Signet Library, Notes on Lectures, p. 139.

166 Ibid., pp. 139–140.

167 Ibid., p. 147.

168 Ibid. A handwritten table of poisons is on p. 162v.

169 Taylor, *Principles and Practice of Medical Jurisprudence*, p. xviii.

170 Clarke, *Autobiographical Recollections*, pp. 99–102, 136, 306.

171 Bonner, *Becoming a Physician*, pp. 346–348.

172 Dixon Mann, *Forensic Medicine and Toxicology*, third edition, Preface to the third edition (no page number).

173 A few examples should suffice: Christison, *Syllabus of the Course of Lectures*, p. 18; R. F. Hunnisett, "The Importance of Eighteenth-Century Coroners' Bills," in *Law, Litigants and the Legal Profession*, ed. E. W. Ives and A. H. Manchester (London: Royal Historical Society, 1983), p. 130; Thomas Rogers Forbes, *Surgeons at the Bailey: English Forensic Medicine to 1878* (New Haven: Yale University Press, 1985), p. 1; Catherine Crawford, "Legalizing Medicine: Early Modern Legal Systems and the Growth of Medico-Legal Knowledge," in *Legal Medicine in History*, ed. Michael Clark and Catherine Crawford (Cambridge: Cambridge University Press, 1994), pp. 89–90.

3 Locating patterns of medico-legal provision

We thus see how, both by the construction of our law and the practice of its functionaries, we are all involved largely in the duty of aiding the furtherance of justice. There can be no evasion. The law requires the aidance of medical skill, that it may be duly administered, and that skill it may require at the hands of any practitioner in the kingdom.

William Cummin, "Lectures on Forensic Medicine: Introductory lecture,"
London Medical Gazette, 19 (1836–37), p. 7

The knowledge that doctors contributed to criminal investigations, and that in turn they gained from working in the criminal justice system, stimulated the direction in which the medical profession itself developed. In Chapter 2 we examined this process through the medium of education, to explain how and why the academic teaching of forensic medicine emerged in response to the practicalities of medico-legal work. In this chapter we consider professional development from the perspective of the medical witnesses themselves, to identify the role played by specialist groups and the particular knowledge that they brought to bear on evolving forensic practices. To this end, the chapter sets out the range and character of the criminal cases on which the book is based. It uses a series of tables and graphs to summarise the collected data, identifies trends over time and highlights comparisons between regions, medico-legal practices and the medical practitioners involved in crime investigation. In so doing, it ascertains the different channels through which medico-legal testimony was obtained and provides short illustrative case studies of selected groups and individuals who contributed to the on-going process of establishing the meaning and value of forensic knowledge in the marketplace created by the criminal justice system.

As historians of medicine have pointed out, changes in professionalism can be explained by issues of supply and demand, and medicine is indeed a service amenable to market forces – but these need not be restricted to the internal content of medicine or the external economic needs of health care.[1] The legal system, as the organising structure, imposed expectations and responsibilities on the medical profession that the publication of dedicated texts and the introduction of specialist training were designed to meet, leading to the emergence in the nineteenth century of experts whose professional knowledge and experience exceeded that of the average doctor. Yet, as William Cummin informed his students in 1836, and the Manchester professor of forensic medicine John Dixon Mann confirmed in 1908, any medical practitioner could be called upon to use their professional skill in the service of the law, particularly in the coroner's court.[2] By the Edwardian period this expectation was viewed with disapproval by specialists like Dixon Mann, who advocated the appointment of regional forensic pathologists,[3] but that goal remained largely unachieved at a national level before the 1940s.[4] In the absence of a centralised provision, legal officials such as coroners, magistrates and the police turned to the medical professionals who were closest to hand, especially local surgeons and GPs; a much smaller group of medico-legal witnesses worked at institutions such as hospitals, workhouses and prisons, or held an official appointment as a police surgeon, which is thus far an under-studied area of medical practice. But most of the doctors involved in the forensic market came there by chance, and visited only once before disappearing back to regular practice, having participated in a knowledge exchange that had real impact and lasting effects on the lives of people in their local communities.

The criminal offences: number and location

A total of 2,615 criminal cases that occurred between July 1699 and December 1914 were collected using a systematic sampling system explained in the Introduction. This created a unique record set which, for the first time, brings together such a large number of violent crimes tried in three very distinct areas of the United Kingdom. Table 3.1 shows that the majority of these offences,

Table 3.1 Number of cases by Assize Circuit

Circuit	No. of Cases	Date of Offence
Old Bailey[1]	1368	Jul 1699–Feb 1913
Great Sessions[2]	308	Jan 1730–Oct 1830
North Wales[3]	186	Jan 1831–May 1914
South Wales	180	Jan 1837–Dec 1914
Oxford	544	Jan 1719–Jul 1914
Chester	26	Jan 1754–Mar 1824
Other	3	Jan 1740–May 1817
Total	2615	Jul 1699–Dec 1914

Source: Database of cases compiled from: The Proceedings of the Old Bailey, 1674–1913 (1700–1913); The National Archives, ASSI 6, ASSI 65, ASSI 72 (1719–1914); The National Library of Wales, Great Sessions gaol files (1730–1830).

1 Trials for crimes committed in: Middlesex; Essex; Kent; Surrey; on the high seas; other county; outside England.
2 Twelve Welsh counties (excludes Monmouthshire).
3 Includes Cheshire.

52.3 per cent, were tried at the Old Bailey in London; approximately 26 per cent of the cases occurred in Wales; 21 per cent in the counties of the Oxford Circuit, only 12 of which date from before 1806; and the remainder are in Cheshire. Three detailed trial reports from other parts of England complete the record set. Nearly half the cases in the database, 1,180 or 45.1 per cent, occurred in the period up to December 1799, and the rest after. The vast majority of the eighteenth-century data comes from London, 935 trials or 79.2 per cent. The geographical range of the data is presented in Table 3.2, showing the county in which each crime occurred and was subsequently tried. A small number of crimes committed elsewhere in England, or abroad, were tried at the Old Bailey: this was a result of Admiralty prosecutions in the eighteenth century, as when Richard Coyle was tried in 1737 for murder and piracy committed off the coast of Turkey;[5] but was mainly due to the effects of the Central Criminal Court Act of 1834, which transferred the power to try crimes committed within the jurisdiction of the Admiralty (i.e. at sea) to the Old Bailey, renamed the Central Criminal Court, and a statute of 1856 which allowed a crime committed outside London to be tried at the Central Criminal Court (see Appendix 1).

Of the numerous trials held at the Old Bailey, most were for offences committed in London.[6] This is unsurprising, given its sheer size and the innovations in policing and public justice instituted during the eighteenth century.[7] Elsewhere, certain counties accounted for a disproportionate amount of recorded crime, notably Cheshire, Glamorgan, Gloucestershire and Staffordshire. While their larger populations had some impact on crime rates, Peter King has shown that murder rates were highest in London and precisely these counties due to their rapidly developing industrial and urban centres, and lowest in rural areas such as those that characterised most of Wales and much of the Oxford Circuit.[8] The contrast between Glamorgan and the rest of Wales is stark: Table 3.3 shows that following the abolition of the Court of Great Sessions in 1830, the number of cases notified to the authorities in Glamorgan rose at a much faster rate than in the other Welsh counties. This may reflect reporting as much as reality, but it suggests there were likely to be more doctors and more medico-legal work to do in Glamorgan than anywhere else in Wales.[9] Compared to the figures for Monmouthshire, the next most populous county in Wales (albeit, by the 1880s, one of the smaller ones on the Oxford Circuit, see Table 3.25), the data reinforce the prominence of Glamorgan as a site of forensic practice in Wales.

In contrast to the clustering of more than half the cases under study in four counties and London, the geographical distribution *within* those areas was far more extensive. Table 3.4 lists the main towns in which the crimes occurred. In London, it was impossible to distinguish the precise location for well over half the cases, but where a name was provided many parishes and boroughs were represented; the table lists only those with a minimum of ten cases. In Wales and the Oxford Circuit, only seven towns met this minimum threshold, chief among which were Cardiff, Swansea and Wolverhampton. The towns and parishes named in this table account for approximately 42 per cent of the

Table 3.2 Location of offences, by county

Region or Circuit	County	No. of Cases
Old Bailey	Middlesex	1,239
	(of which, London	1,191)
	Essex	22
	Kent	25
	Surrey	62
	On the high seas	10
	Other English county	3
	Outside England	7
North Wales	Anglesey	29
	Caernarfonshire	39
	Denbighshire	38
	Flint	31
	Merionethshire	16
	Montgomeryshire	38
South Wales	Breconshire	45
	Cardiganshire	13
	Carmarthenshire	42
	Glamorgan	192
	Pembrokeshire	28
	Radnor	24
Oxford	Berkshire	45
	Gloucestershire	101
	Herefordshire	19
	Monmouthshire	46
	Oxfordshire	33
	Shropshire	59
	Staffordshire	173
	Worcestershire	68
Cheshire	Cheshire	165
Other	Hertfordshire	1
	Suffolk	1
	Warwickshire	1
Total		2,615

Source: As for Table 3.1.

Table 3.3 Wales – number of cases before and after the abolition of the Court of Great Sessions

County	1730–1830	1831–1914	No. of Cases
NORTH WALES			
Anglesey	20	9	29
Caernarfonshire	27	12	39
Denbighshire	30	8	38
Flintshire	26	5	31
Merionethshire	13	3	16
Montgomeryshire	28	10	38
SOUTH WALES			
Breconshire	30	15	45
Cardiganshire	10	3	13
Carmarthenshire	30	12	42
Glamorgan	54	138	192
Pembrokeshire	19	9	28
Radnorshire	21	3	24
Total	308	227	535

Source: As for Table 3.1.

Table 3.4 Principal location of offences, by town

Town	Borough/County	No. of Cases
London	London	672
	City of Westminster	94
	City of London	43
	Bethnell Green	19
	Clerkenwell	18
	Shoreditch	17
	Whitechapel	17
	Holborn	16
	Chelsea	15
	Stepney	14
	Spitalfields	13
	Hackney	10
	Wapping	10
Subtotal		958
Cardiff	Glamorgan	44
Swansea	Glamorgan	32
Wolverhampton	Staffordshire	21
Stockport	Cheshire	15
Merthyr Tydfil	Glamorgan	14
Birkenhead	Cheshire	13
Brecon	Breconshire	11
Subtotal		150
Total		1,108

Source: As for Table 3.1.

entire data set, but 291 towns not listed here appeared at least twice and only 63 towns were identified five or more times. This demonstrates, for the first time, just how widespread medico-legal work was and also how ad hoc it was likely to be: many surgeons were called upon but few had the opportunity to gain regular experience.

The offences for which medico-legal evidence was sought are set out in Table 3.5, which shows that murder and infant murder were the most numerous. The Introduction explained the selection focus on homicide and rape, as these crimes were the most likely to provide a systematic indication of local efforts to apply medico-legal principles at the pre-trial (inquest or committal hearing) and trial stages of the criminal justice process. It also described the difficulties created by the general nineteenth-century reluctance to report rape trials, which was compounded by issues of record survival. As a result, the medico-legal approach to rape in the Victorian era must be approached through cases that led to the victim's death. Also, although the online *Proceedings* of the Old Bailey include 537 cases classified as concealment of birth (1836–1913), these have been excluded from this project because only 12 specified the medical evidence yet did not add substantially to the information derived from trials reported more fully. The creators of the *Proceedings of the Old Bailey* resource believe that, in the nineteenth century, practice at the court "came to be marked by large numbers of very short trials, as a result of the rise of plea bargaining," even for serious crimes like killing.[10] This is very evident in cases of newborn child murder: women were committed for murder or manslaughter by a coroner or a magistrate; but if the grand jury had refused to indict for homicide, prosecutors (sometimes in consultation with the judge) agreed to accept a guilty plea for concealment of birth.

Table 3.6 sets out the context within which the criminal cases occurred; it is based on the underlying motive accepted by the court or indicated by the circumstances described in the depositions or press reports. The most common scenario that led to homicide was male fighting, mostly between men who had an established relationship; a smaller number of cases involved fights between strangers stoked by alcohol, local rivalries and extraordinarily short tempers. Many of these deaths were not intentional: one punch in a 'fair fight' could cause a fatal head injury. Parish constables and police officers became murder victims during affrays with groups of angry or drunken men; some of the angry drunks ended up dead as well. Certain murders occurred during the commission of another felony: a small number of rapes and approximately four times as many robberies led to murder, and gamekeepers or police officers were killed by gangs of poachers. Domestic violence frequently resulted in death, usually of wives, while petty treason mostly involved wives who had murdered their husbands. The attempt to discipline a subordinate, often a servant, child, or work colleague, created a small subset of victims, as did blatant child abuse. Money was a surprisingly infrequent motive for murder, while poverty led to some killings, particularly of children, that were simply sad: some parents seem to have felt that it was better for their child to die than live a life of destitution. Children featured frequently as victims of rape: they are slightly more prevalent than adult

Table 3.5 Type of offence, by circuit

Offence	Old Bailey	Great Sessions	North Wales	South Wales	Oxford	Chester	Other	Total
Murder	694	97	78	91	241	11	2	1,214
Manslaughter	20	26	15	23	79	5	–	168
Infant murder	283	120	55	21	132	5	–	616
Murder of a child	90	16	21	12	45	–	–	184
Manslaughter of a child	9	3	4	4	15	–	–	35
Rape	198	18	–	–	9	2	1	228
Attempted rape	1	12	–	–	1	2	–	16
Petty treason	16	1	–	–	–	–	–	17
Concealment of birth	–	1	4	6	10	–	–	21
Murder and manslaughter[1]	53	3	9	23	10	–	–	98
Rape and attempted rape	3	9	–	–	–	–	–	12
Assault	–	1	–	–	–	1	–	2
Other[2]	1	1	–	–	2	–	–	4
Total	1,368	308	186	180	544	26	3	2,615

Source: As for Table 3.1; excludes Old Bailey concealment of birth (1836–1913) cases.

1 Perpetrator(s) indicted for both offences separately. Often the second indictment was on the coroner's inquisition, indicating a difference of opinion between the committing magistrate and the inquest verdict.

2 Includes one charge of digging up a dead body (1809) and three of attempted murder (in 1805, 1829 and 1839).

Table 3.6 Context in which criminal offences occurred

Offence Context	Murder	Mansl.	Infant Murder & Conceal't	Murder & Mansl.	Murder or Mansl. of a Child	Petty Treason	Rape & Attempted Rape	Assault & Other	Total
VIOLENT ASSAULT									
Child abuse	2	1	1	2	16	–	–	–	22
Domestic violence	245	17	–	15	9	11	–	–	297
Discipline	54	4	–	6	19	1	–	–	84
Poaching	17	1	–	–	1	–	–	–	19
Robbery	100	1	–	–	4	2	6	–	113
FIGHTING									
Associates	200	79	–	44	3	–	–	–	326
Duel	19	1	–	1	–	–	–	–	21
Money	14	–	–	1	–	–	–	–	15
Police	44	3	–	2	1	–	–	–	50
Strangers	90	15	–	11	–	–	–	1	117
INFANT MURDER									
Newborn	–	–	509	1	4	–	–	–	514
Older infant	1	3	104	–	11	–	–	–	119
Older infant – poverty	–	–	16	–	3	–	–	–	19
SEX CRIME									
Rape	22	–	–	1	–	–	105	–	128
Rape – child victim	1	1	–	–	5	–	141	–	148
MISCELLANEOUS									
Accident	75	28	–	8	51	1	–	–	163
Money	65	2	4	2	14	1	2	1	91
Poverty	9	1	–	–	22	–	–	–	32
Other	176	8	1	4	51	1	1	4	246
Unknown	80	3	2	–	5	–	1	–	91
Total	1,214	168	637	98	219	17	256	6	2,615

Source: As for Table 3.1. 'Other' includes abortion, incest or mistaken identity murder, suicide, possible accident and random violence.

women in the sample because of the growing significance of childhood as a stage of life deserving special protection and the well-known barriers to prosecution that existed.[11] Until 1828, rape complainants had to prove both penetration and ejaculation; and until the late twentieth century the courts expected to hear that a victim had done everything physically possible to fight off the attacker.[12] These legal restrictions, combined with the cultural stereotypes associated with rape myths, made prosecution a difficult and demoralising endeavour for women, whose conduct was automatically subject to suspicion and scrutiny in ways that did not apply quite so readily to young children.[13] Of the other contexts in which crime occurred, a significant number of traffic accidents, especially in London, led to a trial for homicide; but medical evidence was unlikely to be needed because the cause of death was obvious and eyewitnesses could describe what had happened.[14] A small number of deaths resulted from accidents caused by the careless handling of weapons. Finally, the category 'Other' includes random acts of apparently motiveless violence, abortions that caused a woman's death, insane acts, murder-suicide pacts and a variety of unique circumstances that defy categorisation.

The precise relationship between victim and perpetrator, while interesting to historians of crime, is generally not relevant to medico-legal investigations, with the exception of infant murder, discussed in Chapter 4. However, the relationship between the prosecutor and the victim, shown in Table 3.7, gives a sense of who might have commissioned medical evidence. Coroners were responsible for securing medical evidence at their inquests; rape victims had to find their own medical witness but magistrates could instruct a doctor to provide a medical report; parish officials could ask the parish surgeon to conduct a forensic examination; and during the nineteenth century it was frequently the police who summoned a doctor when a medico-legal case arose. Curiously enough, Welsh coroners seem to have been particularly willing to prosecute homicide cases: 34 cases were prosecuted in the period 1754–1825, mostly in north Wales (Flintshire, Denbighshire and Merionethshire) after 1790; although only 14 of these cases could be included in the project database.[15] Robert Davies, surgeon and coroner in Flintshire, was particularly vigorous, acting as prosecutor in four cases of infanticide, three of manslaughter and one murder (1793–1807); but in 1806 he was fined for neglect of duty, having failed to hold an inquest on a miner killed by a falling stone in a coal-pit.[16] Table 3.7 should however be seen less as a core part of the evidence supporting the argument developed below and more as a pointer to the new research questions that can be asked of familiar records.

The coroner's officer

A word of caution should be sounded in relation to the procedure for convening inquests, given the advent in the Victorian period of the coroner's officer, who was a policeman tasked with determining whether a death warranted an inquest. When decided in the negative, the costs associated with inquests, payable by the borough or county (see Appendix 1), could be restricted. Since coroners

Table 3.7 Relationship of prosecutor to victim, by circuit

Circuit / Prosecutor	Old Bailey	Great Sessions	North Wales	South Wales	Oxford	Chester	Other	Total
Police – senior officer[1]	–	4	28	47	68	–	–	147
Police – junior officer[2]	–	7	12	16	42	8	–	85
Widow/widower	8	26	–	1	1	1	–	37
Parent	18	40	1	–	6	5	–	70
Employer	6	14	–	–	4	–	1	25
Coroner	–	14	–	–	–	2	–	16
Magistrate	–	2	–	–	–	–	–	2
Overseer of the poor	4	25	–	–	2	–	–	31
Churchwarden	4	12	–	–	1	–	–	17
Other official[3]	12	9	1	8	15	–	–	45
Other[4]	10	42	–	5	9	3	–	69
Victim	59	14	–	–	1	1	–	75
Sub-total	121	209	42	77	149	20	1	619
Unknown	1247	99	144	103	395	6	2	1,996
Total	1,368	308	186	180	544	26	3	2,615

Source: As for Table 3.1.

1 Includes parish head constable (Great Sessions); chief constable; police inspector or superintendent.
2 Includes parish constable (Great Sessions and Chester); police constable; police sergeant.
3 Generally lawyers e.g. Attorney General, Director of Public Prosecutions, Treasury Solicitor, magistrate's clerk, clergyman, inquest juryman, MO, unspecified parochial officer.
4 Includes accusers, first-finders, friends, pub landlords, relatives and spouses.

were unable to order a post-mortem examination without holding an inquest, a situation that did not change until 1926, coroners' officers acted essentially as gatekeepers, taking on a semi-forensic role in deciding that a case was not one for a full inquest.[17] In her study of suicide, Olive Anderson noted that post-mortems tended to be ordered more often by urban than rural coroners, probably because they "received a high proportion of their cases from public hospitals, and upon these they had the benefit of free medical evidence."[18] Under the terms of the Medical Witnesses Act 1836, if the deceased had died in any public medical institution such as a hospital or asylum, the institutional medical officer was expected to conduct the examination free of charge. Historians have long been aware of the nineteenth-century disputes between coroners and magistrates about the costs of the coroner system.[19] The battle was probably most intense during the 1840s and 1850s: the Inquest Expenses Act 1837 increased the fee payable to coroners and required counties to reimburse them for the full cost of inquests which, following the introduction of civil registration in the same year, led to increased numbers of inquests (since causes of death had to be certified) and thus to rising costs.[20] The introduction of the new police, most especially the County and Borough Police Act of 1856 which established county constabularies and swept away the old parish constables, offered magistrates a way to cut costs: they refused to pay for inquests that had not been sanctioned by the police.

Parish constables had been central figures in arranging inquests:[21] they informed the coroner of a death, summoned jurors and witnesses and rented premises in which to hold the inquest – tasks for which they were paid. The Act of 1856 changed this, as evidence from Berkshire and Oxfordshire demonstrates. In July 1856 the Chief Constable of the Berkshire constabulary, which had only been in existence since February, wrote to all county coroners to ask them not to pay police officers for organising inquests, but to send the bill to the county treasurer, to be credited to the police account. By employing only the police, rather than other individuals (i.e. parish constables), the sums paid would reduce the annual police rate. An Oxfordshire magistrate noted in a letter to the county clerk of the peace that the chief constable's missive had quickly had the desired effect: by intimating that all 'unnecessary' expenses would be disallowed, the coroners in Berkshire now always engaged the police.[22] Correspondence with officials in other counties shows that the question was one of national importance and that although some coroners were unhappy at having to work exclusively with the police, they were given little choice. The police thus gained an important role in inquest procedure: coroners' officers tended to be constables or sergeants who decided in practice whether an inquest should be held.

Coroners' officers are of interest to the history of medico-legal practice because they had the power to rule out the need for medical testimony in cases of accident and suicide, meaning that, to some extent at least, homicide investigations must have depended on their assessments at the scene of a sudden death. Surviving depositions indicate that the coroner for the city of Oxford at the turn of the twentieth century adopted a careful approach in his inquests, a large proportion of which were held in the Radcliffe Infirmary and thus included testimony from the house surgeon. Although the depositions are brief, it is clear that the coroner, Henry Frank Galpin (a solicitor), was concerned by the deaths of young children, and sought a medical opinion as to whether they were well cared for, particularly if they were insured. Where a family alleged poor medical care had contributed to death, Galpin was careful to explore the medical facets of the case thoroughly. But in some cases of suicide the coroner's officer, Sgt John Cross, provided the only semi-medical evidence on offer. When 57-year-old Joshua Fathers was found drowned in the Oxford Canal, the inquest heard testimony from his wife, a publican, the man who found his body and Cross, who testified that there was no suicide note and "no marks of violence."[23] Although coroners' officers could be highly experienced, and this sort of testimony was probably common, it does add a slightly different dimension to the history of medico-legal practice. Consider, for example, Sgt Cross's overtly medical testimony in the case of a child killed while playing on railway tracks. His evidence seemed very like that of a qualified medical practitioner, with two important exceptions: he neither stated the cause of death nor that it was his professional opinion that a specific disease or injury had led to death:

> I received the body of the deceased into my presence on Saturday the 16th. The skull of the body was smashed to pieces. There was a large hole in the left of the head. Most of the brains were missing. The left upper arm was broken. All the ribs below the 4th on the left were broken. The front part of the pelvis was smashed. The thigh was almost cut off at the groin. The left leg was smashed about 3 inches above the top of the boot. The right thigh was broken. Deceased was disembowelled.[24]

The main distinction between Cross's testimony and what one might expect from a doctor is that the stated cause of death, "died from being hit by a passing train of the GWR,"[25] is not a medical cause of death but a statement of the manner of death. Medicalised testimony by laymen was not unheard of in homicide cases, as we will see, and in some respects the coroner's officer had merely assumed a responsibility previously held by friends and neighbours of the deceased. However, in establishing the police as intermediates between the coroner and the public, coroners' officers changed the dynamics of the inquest system and thus the characteristics of homicide investigation. But their relative invisibility makes this difficult to study: they are only mentioned in 15 cases (1864–1911), mostly in Greater London; in one case in Berkshire (1884) and one in Swansea (1883), where the coroner's officer was a police inspector. In some of these cases it was the coroner's officer who sent for a medical practitioner, a choice that could have important consequences for an investigation reliant upon medical information about cause and manner of death. Anderson found that, in London, the emergence of coroners' officers as full-time investigators streamlined inquest proceedings and this, combined with greater use of post-mortems and expert witnesses, created a more professional, formal and expert investigation of suicide.[26] An experienced coroner's officer may also have been a valuable asset in homicide investigations, but in the absence of detailed information about their role in a national context, it is difficult to draw firm conclusions about their impact on the development of medico-legal practice.

Medical evidence in criminal trials: statistical overview

The lawyerisation of the criminal trial, a historiographical debate of keen interest to legal historians, clearly has a bearing on the history of medico-legal practice, but the exact mechanism of cause and effect remains uncertain. In a client-led analysis, John Langbein views it as a response to a failure to develop reliable and effective systems of pre-trial criminal investigation;[27] whereas Allyson May has considered it from the opposite perspective, as a development led by barristers who needed trial experience to advance their careers.[28] On the other hand, Barbara Shapiro stresses the central fact-finding role of the jury, who made decisions based on direct testimony and circumstantial evidence but, guided by judges in the eighteenth century, came increasingly to expect evidence sufficient to support their verdicts and overcome any reasonable doubt that attended the uncertainties of fact-finding.[29] These interpretations, based on published sources and London trials, do not consider the role played by surgeons, who pre-dated the lawyers as key personnel in criminal trials. The relevance of medical professionals to all three of the proposed explanations is evident in trials for felonious interpersonal violence: doctors contributed to pre-trial investigations, providing medical evidence to link a suspect to a crime; consequently, medical evidence was a significant part of the prosecution case presented to juries; and medical testimony was an important focus of examination and cross-examination by prosecution and defence counsel. Tables 3.8 and 3.9 show just how commonplace medical evidence in criminal trials was: the lawyerisation of the criminal trial was accompanied by an equally influential medicalisation.

The forensic evidence presented in court has been classified according to the type of examination conducted. A full post-mortem involved opening the three main cavities of the body: head, chest and abdomen, following a thorough external inspection, a procedure that was documented in all textbooks of forensic medicine from Samuel Farr's first English-language text of 1788 onwards.[30] But, as is clear from the tables and from Figures 3.1 and 3.2, not all medical practitioners did a full post-mortem, not even in the twentieth century. In many cases of homicide, the surgeon made an external examination only: this involved carefully looking at and perhaps probing a wound to trace its path, but no cutting. A larger number of cases involved opening part of the corpse, either the head or 'the body', meaning the chest or abdomen depending on where the injury was located. The depositions do not always specify precisely what was opened or that the surgeon did actually open the body, and so the tables include a separate count for cases where the balance of evidence leans toward the probability that the body was opened or a full post-mortem was carried out.

Table 3.8 The use of medical evidence, by type of offence

Offence / Evidence Type	Murder	Manslaughter	Infant Murder & Concealment	Murder & Manslaughter	Murder or Manslaughter of a Child	Petty Treason	Rape & Attempted Rape	Assault & Other	Total
External exam	208	12	88	16	44	5	3	3	379
Body opened	234	34	123	12	20	7	–	2	432
– Probable	2	–	3	1	–	–	–	–	6
Head opened	125	31	9	11	17	1	–	–	194
Full post-mortem	168	36	171	28	41	–	–	–	444
– Probable	102	15	35	14	21	–	–	–	187
None (surgeon)	104	26	23	9	28	3	4	–	197
No surgeon	104	9	138	1	12	–	101	1	366
Rape examination	–	–	–	–	1	–	128	–	129
Rape + external	3	–	–	1	–	–	2	–	6
Unknown	164	5	47	5	35	1	18	–	275
Total	1,214	168	637	98	219	17	256	6	2,615

Source: As for Table 3.1.

Table 3.9 Proportional use of medical evidence in homicide cases, by circuit

Circuit / Evidence Type	Old Bailey No.	%	Great Sessions No.	%	North Wales No.	%	South Wales No.	%	Oxford No.	%	Chester No.	%	Total No.	%
External exam	202	17.3	51	19.1	16	8.6	20	11.1	79	14.8	5	23.8	373	15.9
Body opened	185	15.9	31	11.6	52	28.0	23	12.8	134	25.2	4	19.0	429	18.2
– Probable	3	0.3	2	0.7	1	0.5	0	0	0	0	0	0	6	0.3
Head opened	75	6.4	8	3.0	18	9.7	16	8.9	75	14.1	2	9.5	194	8.3
Full post-mortem	129	11.1	8	3.0	68	36.6	58	32.2	180	33.8	1	4.8	444	18.9
– Probable	98	8.4	2	0.7	18	9.7	49	27.2	19	3.6	1	4.8	187	8.0
None (surgeon)	122	10.5	23	8.6	8	4.3	12	6.7	28	5.3	0	0	193	8.2
No surgeon	134	11.5	108	40.4	4	2.1	1	0.6	12	2.2	5	23.8	264	11.2
Rape examination	0	0	1	0.4	0	0	0	0	0	0	0	0	1	0
Rape + external exam	1	0.1	0	0	1	0.5	0	0	1	0.2	0	0	3	0.1
Unknown	216	18.5	33	12.4	0	0	1	0.6	4	0.8	3	14.3	257	10.9
Total	1,165	100	267	99.9	186	100	180	100.1	532	100	21	100	2,351	100

Source: As for Table 3.1; includes all categories of homicide; excludes circuit category 'Other'.

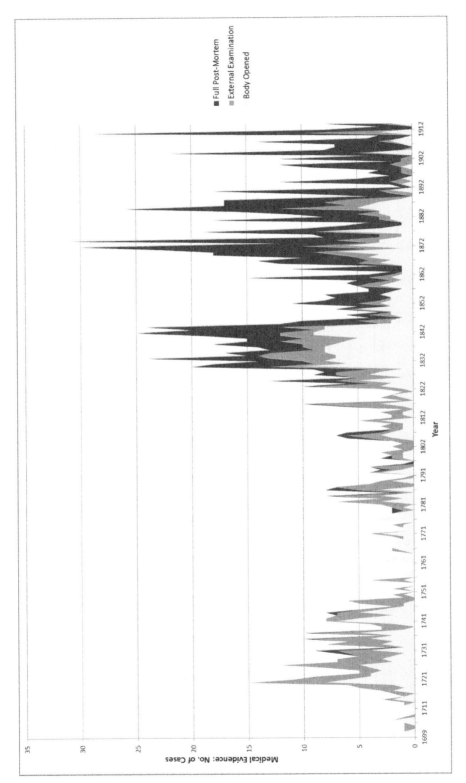

Figure 3.1 Use of medical evidence in homicide cases, 1699–1914

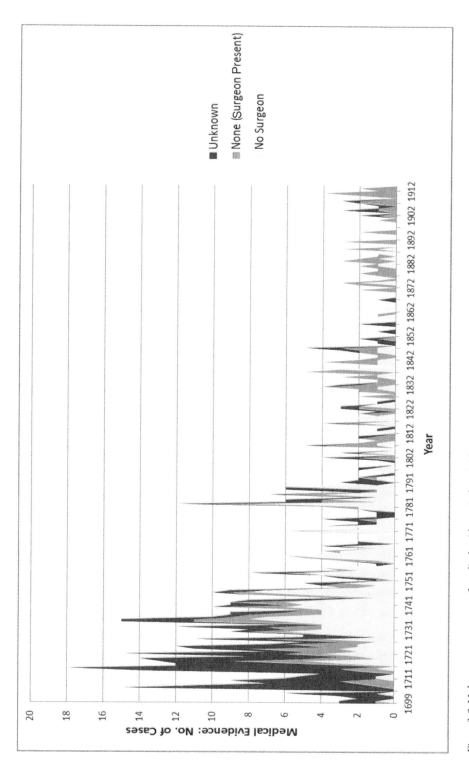

Figure 3.2 Unknown or non-use of medical evidence in homicide cases, 1699–1914

The regular use of the term 'post-mortem' by medico-legal witnesses dates from the early 1830s, excepting a single earlier example of 1827 when a surgeon in Hanley, Staffordshire, made a "post-mortem of the head,"[31] suggesting that his understanding of the term was still developing – it is not used to refer to a partial examination. The substitution of the old-fashioned and unspecific 'opening' by a modern scientific term can be linked to broader currents in medical history, especially the late-eighteenth-century rise of pathological anatomy,[32] but relates more specifically to the development of forensic medicine as a specialist discipline. As we saw in Chapter 2, systematic teaching in forensic medicine began in the early 1830s when new examination requirements were instituted for medical students in England, Scotland and Ireland, leading to the proliferation of textbooks on the subject. A comparison of three important books published before and after the watershed demonstrates the magnitude of the intellectual change that the term 'post-mortem' represents. The first truly original textbook in English, published by Dr G. E. Male in 1816, did not use the term 'post-mortem' at all; the third edition of J. G. Smith's text, published in 1827, used it only as an adverb (appearances post-mortem, examination post-mortem); but in 1836 the first book by the pioneering medico-legal writer Alfred Swaine Taylor referred to 'post-mortem examination' and 'post-mortem appearances' as though their significance was self-evident. It was: William Cummin's introductory lecture on forensic medicine at the Aldersgate School of Medicine, in October 1836, referred to a "post-mortem report," and the Medical Witnesses Act enabled coroners to "direct the performance of a post-mortem examination" of the deceased.[33] By 1836, many doctors could be expected to have a satisfactory understanding of the meaning and medico-legal importance of the post-mortem examination, and central government had made provision to pay for it. Figure 3.1 confirms the chronological association between the introduction of forensic medicine to English medical education in January 1831 and the use of post-mortem examination in homicide cases: the distinct spike around 1830 pre-dates the two statutory innovations of 1836, the Medical Witnesses and the Births and Deaths Registration Acts. The higher proportion of post-mortems after 1830 can be attributed to the effects of the statutes but also to increased professional interest and capability among doctors.

Yet this did not mean that every case thereafter involved a forensic examination. In a total of 197 cases, no medico-legal evidence was reported even though a medical professional was present. This tended to occur when death followed a period of 'languishing', often under medical care following a serious injury. For example, when Robert Leaver was shot by a highwayman in July 1699 a surgeon probed the wound "and found that the Bullet was lodged in his Guts, and that all such Wounds were always Mortal,"[34] but did not open Leaver after he died. Nearly 56 per cent of such cases occurred before 1800, but the remainder were evenly spread across the following century. This was because when a person who had been under medical care died, the coroner summoned that practitioner to give evidence but did not necessarily have to ask him to perform a post-mortem.[35] The last occasion on which this occurred was in January 1913, when two teenage victims of a fire caused by arson died from shock in the London Hospital; the house surgeon testified to their injuries but did not mention making a post-mortem examination, presumably because it was not necessary to conduct one – the cause and manner of death were painfully obvious.[36]

Table 3.8 shows that a total of 366 trials (320 of which took place before 1800) proceeded without a male surgeon to provide forensic testimony. A midwife testified as the sole medico-legal witness in 74 of these trials, one for rape and 73 for infant murder; only one of these trials occurred after 1800 (see Table 4.8 in Chapter 4). Thus, with the exception of eighteenth-century rape and newborn child murder cases, surgeons were regular and preferred participants in criminal trials throughout the period of study. Table 3.9 presents a regional comparison of the presence of surgeons in homicide trials, showing the use of medical evidence as a proportion of the cases in each assize circuit. This reveals that cases in which no surgeon testified were most prevalent in the Welsh Court of Great Sessions 1730–1830, where 40.4 per cent of homicide depositions did not record testimony from a surgeon. The region with the next highest proportion of cases without medical evidence was the palatinate of Chester, at 23.8 per cent, but the sample size of 21 cases is rather too small to enable firm conclusions to be drawn. Although there were a sizeable number of medical practitioners in late eighteenth-century Wales – Appendix 2 names the 113 medical men practising in Wales in 1783, based on the list compiled for the *Medical Register*,[37] this amounted to considerably fewer per head of population than in the neighbouring county of Cheshire, where 59 practitioners were identified.[38] By contrast, nearly a quarter of all medical practitioners in England and Wales in 1783 were located in London (968/4134, 23.4 per cent).[39] However, the *Medical Registers* of 1779–1783 did not include all active practitioners:[40] the depositions taken in criminal cases yield the names of nine additional medical men who were not included on the register published in 1783, rendering it an incomplete source for late eighteenth-century Welsh medical history. It would therefore be unwise to conclude that lack of access to medical practitioners in peripheral regions explains the differences revealed by Table 3.9.

For the Welsh Great Sessions in the period 1800–1830 the figures tell a more positive story: of 77 homicide cases, only eight did not record medical testimony (10.4 per cent), with six cases for which this information is unknown. After 1830 there was very little difference between the regions: the figures for the Old Bailey, where 365 of the homicide cases in the period 1831–1914 occurred, are 11 (no surgeon present, 3.0 per cent); 13 (information unknown, 3.6 per cent) and 26 (no post-mortem but a surgeon was present, 7.1 per cent). The last group resulted from the growing frequency with which victims were taken to the hospital, a service often performed by police constables using public conveyances such as carts, cabs or ambulances.[41] Cardiff was unique in having a hospital ship, the *Hamadryad*, founded in 1866 under the impetus of Dr Henry J. Paine, who served the city at various times as police surgeon, prison medical officer and magistrate.[42] The *Hamadryad*'s attending surgeon became a medico-legal witness in two cases when seamen were stabbed to death.[43] The docks were a constant hotspot for violence between sailors, contributing to Cardiff's prominence in Table 3.4. The three circuits – Oxford, North and South Wales – can only be compared directly for the period 1831–1914, as the Introduction explained. When 95 homicide cases that occurred on the Oxford Circuit before 1831 are extracted and the figures adjusted, they reveal that, jointly, the number of cases in which no medical evidence was sought was a mere 1.2 per cent, or ten cases out of the total 803. On the basis of these findings, we can confidently conclude that, after 1830, medico-legal practice was at least as common in the peripheral regions of England and Wales as it was in London.

Collectively, these figures suggest that the loss of the courts of Great Sessions in 1830, when Wales and Cheshire were absorbed into the English assize system, had an effect not just on legal practice and personnel but on medico-legal practice too. The late eighteenth and early nineteenth centuries were periods in which crime investigation was becoming more effective and systematic, represented by the increasingly regular use of medical evidence. Recent research on the courts of Great Sessions in Wales and Cheshire in precisely this period has identified some notable trends which, though not framed in relation to crime investigation per se, are certainly suggestive of on-going changes in such practices. James Sharpe and J. R. Dickinson found that, in Cheshire, the late eighteenth century was an important period of transition: fatal violence came increasingly to be seen as unacceptable behaviour associated mainly with the lower orders, leading to more individualised approaches to interpersonal violence at trial.[44] Furthermore, these scholars forged a more explicit link to medical evidence in homicide prosecutions: "a number of cases from the later eighteenth century do show the opinions of medical men being afforded greater respect."[45] Meanwhile, in his quantitative work on Great Sessions, John Walliss identified a distinct difference between Wales and Cheshire: in the Principality, "almost as many persons brought to court to be tried for murder were discharged on No True Bill as were found guilty";[46] but in Cheshire the equivalent proportion was just under 21 per cent and indictments for interpersonal violence rose noticeably between 1800 and 1830.[47] Although indictments cannot tell us precisely how crimes were investigated, Langbein's conclusion that "pre-trial examination helped dispose of weak cases without trial while reinforcing the evidence of cases that went to trial" would seem to suggest one of the core reasons for this difference.[48] One gains the impression that the criminal justice system was being used more systematically and more efficiently to prosecute homicide in Wales and Cheshire by the first decades of the nineteenth century.

Before 1830 both areas were peripheral to England and especially to London, but they were integrated within a regional legal structure: they had their own judges, procedures, court officers and training standards for attorneys. Few barristers practiced in Wales, but those who did also practiced on the Oxford or Northern Circuit in England; similarly, although there were few attorneys in Wales, there were many of them in border counties such as Cheshire and Gloucestershire, and their professional practice probably crossed borders.[49] But Great Sessions came under sustained attack in the late eighteenth century; the judges in particular were singled out for criticism on the grounds of political cronyism and intellectual inferiority, although with little justification for either accusation.[50] After 1830 however, differences in standards and customs were eliminated as the practice of the law underwent a slow process of professionalisation and the two new Welsh assize circuits adopted English ways: 15 judges travelled the circuits of England and Wales; barristers began to specialise and those intended for the criminal law joined a circuit upon being called to the bar; attorneys took charge of all the pre-trial details of a case and retained a barrister on behalf of their clients.[51] The standardisation of legal procedures and personnel coincided with national developments in medical education, the provision of funding for medical evidence at inquests, and the introduction of the new police (see Appendix 3), creating a greater consistency of medico-legal practice across England and Wales in the nineteenth century.

Figure 3.2 demonstrates the declining number of homicide cases where no medical evidence was presented or for which the information is lacking; a significant reduction in both these categories is discernible around 1750 and again in the 1790s. This is due to two related factors: most of the eighteenth-century homicide cases in the database, 733 out of the total 949 (77.2 per cent, 1699–1799) are Old Bailey trials, but neither the Old Bailey nor Great Sessions (Wales or Cheshire) records were surveyed thoroughly for the whole century; the sampling system used for London favoured the decades up to 1740 and the 1780s. So the falling number of cases in which no medical evidence was recorded may signify actual changes in investigative practice at mid-century, but it also reflects the increasingly detailed trial reporting introduced by the publisher of the *Proceedings* between the 1730s and 1780s.[52] For the period after 1800, however, the data is more geographically balanced as London comprises only 30.2 per cent (433 out of 1,435) of the cases. Figure 3.2 can therefore be considered a true reflection of nineteenth-century practice across *all* the regions in the study: medico-legal testimony was rarely omitted from Victorian and Edwardian homicide investigations. Only 46 cases (3.2 per cent, 1804–1888) included no surgeon at all, half before and half after 1830; and further research might be able to provide more information about the 29 cases for which this information is unknown. Finally, in 146 cases (1836–1914) a surgeon used the term 'post-mortem examination' but the information provided does not consciously specify that all three body cavities were dissected. This may be an issue related to reporting: it is more frequent in Old Bailey trial proceedings (81 cases), which are not necessarily full accounts of all that was said in court.[53] In other areas of the country, it seems to relate to cases where the cause of death appeared obvious to a casual observer, with drowning (11 cases) or stab wounds and head injuries (27 cases) being most common in this regard. This does not mean that the medico-legal examination in such cases was slipshod, however: surgeons focused their efforts on trying to determine what the manner of death was, so that opening all three body cavities was a lesser priority than careful study of other physical signs. For example, when Olive Beasley, 40, was found dead on the floor of her kitchen at Dudley, Worcestershire, in April 1872, the cuts in her throat left no doubt about the cause of death and suspicion fell immediately on her estranged husband. But recent events suggested that she might have committed suicide: she had been embroiled in an adulterous affair with a family friend and had previously attempted to cut her own throat. Two surgeons conducted the post-mortem and were concerned to establish whether she might have killed herself: the balance of evidence – bruises on her arms and cuts on her hands – indicated that she had not, but one surgeon "had seen such extraordinary things done by suicides that it was difficult to judge." Under cross-examination at the trial, he admitted that "A person committing suicide would cut the throat in the same direction as a person cutting from the back. He would not say that all the wounds might not have been caused by the deceased herself." The husband was acquitted to popular acclaim.[54]

Medical witnesses

The names of hundreds of doctors appear in the depositions collected and collated for this project, marking another innovative contribution to the history of medicine and criminal justice history. In 652 cases there was no name provided: these include all of the cases listed in Table 3.8 as unknown or in which no surgeon was present (641); the remaining 11 were cases where the circumstances suggested a surgeon had been present or a rape examination was made by a midwife or laywoman. In 84 cases, all but 11 of which were trials held at the Old Bailey before 1760, a medical witness was present but no name was given. At least 593 cases involved two or more medical practitioners (1714–1914); the larger proportion, 376 (63.4 per cent) occurred after 1830 but it is clear that many medical men called upon to conduct a forensic examination did so in the company of another doctor. Sometimes this occurred by chance because both had arrived independently at the scene of a crime and were then obliged to act in a medico-legal capacity; but at other times by design, when one doctor corroborated the findings of another. In Chapter 2 we saw that in the 1870s Thomas Scattergood was teaching his medical students that a post-mortem examination should be performed by two practitioners; although this advice did not appear in textbooks of forensic medicine before the 1880s,[55] the practice would seem to make good sense, albeit complicated by the issue of payment. As will be discussed briefly here and again in Chapter 5, the costs associated with medico-legal work were a concern to the authorities who had to pay for it, and the Medical Witnesses Act did not encourage coroners to appoint pairs of doctors to conduct post-mortems. Their right to do so was finally clarified by the Lord Chancellor in February 1894, when he noted that under the terms of the Coroners Act 1887, coroners had the right to summon as many medical witnesses as they deemed expedient.[56] For now, however, it is more important to consider who these practitioners were and where they actually came from. To that end, Table 3.10 lists the institutional affiliations or specialist status that could be identified for individuals who appeared as medico-legal witnesses. The numbers prove conclusively that medico-legal work was most often conducted

Table 3.10 Specialist practitioners, by circuit

Circuit Practitioner	Old Bailey	Great Sessions	North Wales	South Wales	Oxford	Chester	Total
Midwife	137	34	2	2	10	1	186
Expert[1]	98	–	43	24	54	–	219
Infirmary surgeon	26	–	11	12	19	–	68
Hospital surgeon	113	–	9	14	10	–	146
House surgeon[2]	–	–	–	–	10	–	10
Parish surgeon	28	–	–	–	8	–	36
Police surgeon	71	–	9	14	20	–	114
Workhouse MO	17	–	1	6	11	–	35
Total	490	34	75	72	142	1	814

Source: As for Table 3.1.

1 Includes mental health (PMO, asylum MO, psychiatrist), medicine (pathology, surgery) and science (chemistry, toxicology, ballistics).
2 Institution not specified.

by the men who are *not* included in the table, that is, GPs and their eighteenth-century equivalent, the 'surgeon' or 'surgeon-apothecary'. In other words, the local medical man was generally the first on the scene and became the de facto medical 'expert'.

At least 167 surgeons provided evidence in two or more cases, but for the majority this amounted at most to three court appearances. Table 3.11 lists the 15 practitioners who appeared in four or more cases. The fact that six of these surgeons were active in London before 1730 reflects the way in which the records were sampled but also the fact that fatal assaults were endemic in a densely populated city in which male violence was "part of an accepted code of masculine behaviour" and thus a means by which to affirm personal honour. Robert Shoemaker charted the decline in per capita homicide rates in London, which he believes may be ascribed in large part to a lessening tendency by men to resist law enforcement or to engage in fatal violence sparked by matters of honour. Furthermore, the habit among gentlemen of carrying swords began to decline in the 1720s and 1730s. His figures, adjusted for population growth, show the rate declining from the 1740s.[57] Secondly, London was well served by medical practitioners, but the fact that the *Proceedings* refer to certain medical men simply as 'Mr So-and-so the surgeon' suggests that these practitioners were

Table 3.11 Surgeons involved in four or more forensic cases

Name	Affiliation/Residence	Dates of Cases	No. of Cases
James Joseph Buist	Police surgeon, Cardiff	1901–1912	11
George Coldham	Covent Garden, London	1728–1736	5
William Cox[1]	London	1725–1731	5
William Henry Freer	Stourbridge, Worcestershire	1827–1837	4
Ludwig Freyberger	Pathologist, Great Northern Central Hospital, London	1904–1911	5
Richard Harding	Hanley, Staffordshire	1827–1841	5
Matthew Jennette	Police surgeon, Birkenhead	1851–1872	4
John Perkins	London	1720–1749	8
Matthew Pierpoint	Worcester Infirmary	1830–1844	6
John Rayner	Stockport Infirmary	1838–1853	4
Simon Snowd	London	1723–1741	5
David Howell Thomas	Workhouse and Prison MO, Swansea	1865–1895	7
Henry Vaughan	Saint Giles in the Fields, Middlesex	1721–1722	4
Thomas Wallace	Police surgeon, Cardiff	1891–1900	4
John Westbrook	Workhouse,[2] St Margaret's, Westminster, London	1719–1744	8

Source: As for Table 3.1.

1 Includes two appearances as a defence witness.
2 From its foundation in 1726.

well known in the city; case details indicate that their surgical skill was called upon to try to save victims who languished some hours or days before death. At that point, the patient's doctor became the state's medico-legal witness. This began to change in the nineteenth century, as a small group of specialists emerged. This is most evident in the careers of the pathologist Dr Ludwig Freyberger (1865–1934), of whom we will hear more in Chapter 5, and police surgeon Dr James Joseph Buist (1864–1943), who "acquired considerable experience in medico-legal matters during his association with the city police" in Cardiff, where he also served as a district medical officer.[58] Buist was the sole medical witness in 6 of the 11 cases he testified in, served alongside a hospital surgeon in four others and was brought in as an expert to observe the postmortem in a case of wife murder in 1904: the main medical witnesses deposed at the inquest were the local doctors whom the husband alerted to his wife's death.[59] Buist was the quintessential example of an urban medico-legal expert who became so on the basis of his practice as a police surgeon: all of his cases involved deaths that had occurred in Cardiff, and although he taught forensic medicine at the medical school founded in the city in 1893, his expertise was largely confined to the city itself; he did not publish a textbook or memoire, nor apparently any articles.

The numbers in Table 3.10 refer to individuals, not criminal cases, of which there are fewer due to overlap; where one specialist practitioner was involved, there was often another. 'Specialist' is used to denote expert witness status of the type discussed in Chapter 5 or an institutional affiliation, both of which were on the whole remarkably infrequent. In total, the records reveal that very few men self-identified as having any formal institutional appointment. When the figures are considered in relation to cases, the total number involving one or more doctors who held an official post is 410: these include those attached to a workhouse, the police, a hospital/infirmary or who served as a parish surgeon or invited expert witness. The low number of parish surgeons and the fact that only ten of them appeared before 1800 is both interesting and surprising, given Edward Umfreville's suggestion that they might refuse to attend an inquest without payment, but Joan Lane provides an alternate explanation. She found that, in late eighteenth-century Warwickshire, forensic duties were performed by a small group of practitioners who carried out post-mortem examinations and gave evidence at inquests; although in theory anyone could do so, in practice medico-legal work in the county was more selectively undertaken.[60] However, while it is clear that some individuals became involved in several cases over a period of years, the balance of the evidence collected here shows that GPs local to the vicinity of the crime did most of the work. This might entail a journey of up to five miles in more rural areas, though rarely further, or it might mean simply walking from a few streets away. Some medical practitioners literally happened upon the scene of a crime as they were going about their business: "I was passing through Palmer Street, I saw a crowd, and went into this house, and into the room on the ground floor – I there saw a female infant – I found it covered with the soil of the privy," Henry Taynton testified at the Old Bailey during a trial in 1844.[61] But he was not the only doctor on the scene: Daniel Ross "went with a policeman to No. 44, Palmer Street, and saw the prisoner there – she was in a very weak state – we did all we could for the child – I have heard Mr Taynton's evidence, and concur with him in the opinions he has expressed."[62] Daniel Ross (1812–1877), who had qualified LSA in 1839 and MRCS in 1843, was for 40 years one of the best-known medical practitioners in East London, where he built a successful practice: he became a police surgeon (almost immediately upon going in to practice, apparently), registrar of births and deaths for Shadwell and Wapping, Public Vaccinator and surgeon to five (burial) clubs.[63] His role as a police surgeon was just one of the local niches that he occupied, and probably the earliest, in a bid to establish a professionally profitable career.[64]

A mere 15.7 per cent of cases involved a specialist practitioner of the type noted in Table 3.10. The majority occurred after 1830 due to the introduction of police surgeons, who will be discussed in more detail in the next section of this chapter, and the growing number of hospital and workhouse infirmary posts.[65] There were more of these in London than anywhere else: in 1832 at least 54 London parishes had their own workhouse,[66] but in south Wales 20 per cent of Poor Law unions avoided building a workhouse for 30 years after the Poor Law Act of 1834 directed them to do so.[67] According to Megan Evans and Peter Jones, Welsh poor law unions were on the whole "far more likely to resist or delay building a workhouse than their English counterparts";[68] and in the absence of a workhouse, there was no workhouse medical officer to take on medico-legal work. By mid-century there were nine medical schools in London and 13 elsewhere in England.[69] Only one of these, at Bristol, was located within the Oxford Circuit region, but the medical school at Birmingham proved an occasional source of expertise for authorities in Staffordshire and the schools in Liverpool and Manchester were similar sources for legal officials in Cheshire and north Wales, as were other specialists based in these cities. However, cross-border consultations did not occur frequently and when they did, tended to involve a public analyst, since many of those in counties along the Welsh border held joint appointments in two or more districts. The advent of the railways made it easier to send organic samples from one town to another and this became typical practice in poisoning cases requiring toxicological expertise;[70] but unless poison was suspected there was rarely any reason to call in an expert.

Experts 'worked' homicide investigations mostly in addition to the local surgeon who had conducted the post-mortem, rather than in conjunction with another of the specialists counted in Table 3.10. In other words, the data display little evidence of the expert teamwork that came to exemplify forensic practice in the twentieth century.[71] Of the 214 cases in which an individual testified in an expert capacity, 100 testified about the sanity of the accused, 38 were toxicologists and the rest were experts in pathology or surgery, but the post-mortem examination had been conducted by a local doctor. There were 38 exceptions in which a hospital surgeon or police surgeon had done the post-mortem.

Although these data do not lend strong support to the conclusion that forensic autopsies were routinely conducted by a small group of individuals, nor even that "most courts preferred a specialist,"[72] Joan Lane's findings for Warwickshire remain intriguing. They suggest that, to resolve the issue, a wider range of cases should be studied in a more localised area such as a single county.

Finally, a word about the spaces and places in which post-mortem examinations were conducted is in order. The depositions rarely provide much information about this, but it is clear that during the eighteenth century and earlier decades of the nineteenth, bodies were examined where they were found, if that was at home, or where they were taken for the inquest, often the outbuilding of a public house. Exhumed bodies were examined in churches or churchyards. These locations, even private homes, were permeable to the public, who gathered to watch. In 1733 the proximity of the crowd to the surgeon examining a body in London was such that "In leaning over the Bed the Mob press'd so hard upon me, that I was in Danger of having my Legs broke, so that I could not be so particular in my Observation as I could have been."[73] Inquest jurors were required by law to view the body, but then withdrew to another part of the premises to hear evidence and await the surgeon's report. If a victim had died in a hospital or workhouse infirmary, the inquest was held in a suitable room in the building and the post-mortem was conducted in the institution's dead-house. Police stations began to serve as convenient places to take victims in the nineteenth century; the forensic examination probably took place in one of the cells, though by the early 1890s some police stations, such as those in Bute Street, Cardiff and at Dudley in Worcestershire, had a mortuary. The word itself was introduced in 1862, in a conscious effort to distinguish this modern type of building from the dead-houses associated with pauper burials, but purpose-built mortuaries were not common before the 1875 Public Health Act enabled local authorities to use public funds to construct them. Pam Fisher has charted the pattern of mortuary building in London, where the needs of the medico-legal examination proved influential:

> The first beneficiaries of these new buildings were coroners and local doctors, and their influence is clearly demonstrated by the development of the court, mortuary and post-mortem room complex, which became the preferred design from around 1875, wherever a site permitted.[74]

However, only 61 cases named a venue identified as a mortuary, the first in London in 1874. A total of 21 of these cases occurred in London, and a further 19 in Glamorgan; mortuaries outside London were cited in relation to crimes committed in boroughs, where hospitals and larger police stations were located. Access to a mortuary depended entirely on where a victim had died, however: until 1926, bodies could not be transported across sub-districts within a coroner's jurisdiction.[75] Although the era of the kitchen-table post-mortem had vanished, it seems likely that key distinctions between the conditions in rural and urban locations remained by the end of the period under study.

Police surgeons

The small number of doctors who worked as police surgeons in England and Wales form one of the most interesting yet hitherto under-studied groups of medical practitioners of the Victorian and Edwardian periods. The role originated in London as a means of providing medical care to serving and retired police officers, but it soon gained a forensic aspect when constables on the beat or, in more serious cases, their superior officers called upon the local police surgeon when a medico-legal examination appeared necessary. Uniquely positioned, police surgeons occupied "a potentially influential role in the criminal justice system, falling between medical and legal functions";[76] yet, with the exception of practitioner studies that focus largely on their twentieth-century heyday or recent travails,[77] there were until now no academic studies of the role or the individuals who held it. To some extent this results from the fact that their experience, and thus expertise, varied from person to person: it was never a full-time job, but rather one seen as an adjunct to general practice. An appointment as a police surgeon exploited one of Anne Digby's "local niches," useful to doctors seeking to supplement their income from fee-paying patients, but the service provided has always been grounded in "informality in administration and arbitrariness in selection, training and quality control."[78] There were no set criteria for becoming a police surgeon, positions were not necessarily filled via open competition, and there were no centrally held national lists of those occupying the posts. According to Jennifer Ward, an "organised system of police surgeons was slow to develop in the provinces,"[79] but no one has really studied those based outside London, perhaps because only the London police surgeons created records that are still extant.[80] But the role of police surgeon was introduced into other parts of England and Wales in the 1830s and 1840s, as references to them and advertisements for posts demonstrate.[81] The work was potentially fascinating for those interested in forensic matters: police surgeons assessed living victims of violence (e.g. rape or physical assault), attended sudden deaths and examined the body, collected forensic evidence and testified in court.

The earliest known example of the employment of a police surgeon dates from 1805, when "a medical officer was paid £100 per annum to examine recruits and give medical attention to the Mounted Bow Street Patrol."[82] Neither John Beattie nor David Cox discuss this appointment in their detailed histories of the Bow Street Runners, from whom the mounted patrol, founded in 1805 by Sir Richard Ford, the chief magistrate at Bow Street, soon became entirely separate when the Home Office took over their management.[83] The name of the first appointee is unknown, although it was probably John Andrews, a surgeon in Greek Street, Soho. He was succeeded in 1821 by (Sir) John Fisher (1788–1876), his former apprentice, with whom he had been in practice and who had served as his deputy for 15 years.[84] On the formation of the Metropolitan Police in 1829, into which a large portion of the Bow Street patrol was incorporated, Fisher was appointed chief surgeon to the new force. He took up the post on 19 April 1830 at a salary of £350, and retired in 1865 on £800, having negotiated several pay rises over the years. The salary was initially based on that of an army surgeon,[85] as doubtless the job title was too: the doctors appointed to look after the men in the 17 (increased to 20 in 1865) police divisions were called divisional surgeons. Until 1914, appointments to these posts were made by the Home Secretary on the recommendation of the Commissioner, who followed the advice of the Chief Surgeon.[86] The number of divisional surgeons increased steadily as the strength of the force rose: in April 1847 there were 62 divisional surgeons, rising to 100 by 1872; in February 1888 there were 133; and in December 1893 there were 140.[87] They were appointed to a particular police station and paid an annual rate per policeman assigned to it, based on each man's rank. By the 1890s the surgeons were paid extra fees if required to attend an officer injured on duty at night, when called in by police to attend casualties in the streets, for attending court and in "difficult cases"[88] – about which we will learn more in Chapter 5. In the view of the then Commissioner, Sir Edward Bradford, "it may be said that the appointment is much sought after and it would appear therefore that even if its direct emoluments are not satisfactory its indirect advantages are considerable."[89]

One of those advantages was access to fascinating clinical and forensic cases, but it was hard work that was, as noted for Daniel Ross earlier, often combined with other posts. Charles Graham Grant (1864–1935), a wiry and athletic Scot who could hold his own in a fight, was a successor to Ross as police surgeon in Shadwell and Wapping. He applied for the job in September 1897 but was not told he had been appointed; a constable simply turned up on his doorstep in January 1898![90] Grant was also MO to the Post Office in his part of East London, and for a year he looked after the health of the 'Rats', the men who built the Rotherhithe Tunnel, completed in 1908. In 1910 he was called to the bar. But most of the tales included in his 1920 memoire, *The Diary of a Police Surgeon*, concerned the various interesting cases he was involved in, which included no fewer than five murders between July 1902 and October 1904. In the last of these, the murder of newsagent Emily Farmer, Grant testified at the Old Bailey to the fact that he had conducted the post-mortem with the assistance of a local GP but was not an expert like Professor Pepper of St Mary's Hospital, who had not seen the body but formed his opinion on the time of death from the written evidence alone.[91] The distinction between expert witnesses of Pepper's calibre and those who, like Grant, had a great deal of first-hand proficiency in investigating crime will be discussed in Chapter 5. Indeed, Grant's expertise was such that he published *Practical Forensic Medicine: A Police-Surgeon's Emergency Guide*, in 1911.

There is next to no information about the role of the police surgeon elsewhere in Victorian England and Wales, but police forces certainly implemented some means of assessing the health of recruits and looking after the men. Under the terms of the Municipal Corporations Act 1835 and the County Police Act 1839, town councils and county magistrates were empowered to set up and fund police forces, and were responsible for paying medical practitioners when such assistance was required. According to Ralph Summers, a twentieth-century police surgeon, a chief surgeon who reported to the local Watch Committee or Police Committee headed up a team of 'divisional surgeons', the number of which depended on the area covered and the volume of work this entailed.[92] In a small borough like Hastings, only one surgeon was needed, and he was not paid very well: in 1861 John Underwood sought a salary of £8 per year as a police surgeon.[93] But larger police forces did employ divisional surgeons, and Liverpool and Manchester advertised the positions in local newspapers. In 1863 a surgeon was to be appointed to the North Division of the Liverpool City Police at a salary of £105 including "medicine, leeches, and all remedial appliances";[94] while in Sheffield a post with the borough police was advertised at £40 in the same year.[95] The position of surgeon to the C and D Divisions of the Manchester City Police was advertised at £60 per annum in 1872,[96] but a similar advertisement for the Wigan police force did not state the salary.[97] By the late 1880s the position of surgeon to the A and B Divisions of the Manchester police was worth £100, "to include all cost of dispensing and drugs."[98] Other industrial cities in the Midlands and North also had police surgeons, some of them controversial figures. In Birmingham, James Vose Solomon became embroiled in a disagreement with the city's Watch Committee over his rejection of a highly experienced police officer whom he deemed "too slightly built" to take on the "rough fellows about the town."[99] In Hull, Joseph Brownridge was attacked in an anonymous letter to the press that accused him of being under-qualified for his role as police surgeon because he was not a Licentiate of the Society of Apothecaries.[100] He was in fact duly qualified under the terms of the Medical Act 1858, as he gained the MRCS that very year; but he had not necessarily completed a course of lectures on forensic medicine as those who qualified LSA had. This was potentially detrimental to his ability to carry out the medico-legal duties of a police surgeon. There were police surgeons in Wales, too, though none as experienced as J. J. Buist, and most not directly referred to as police surgeons in the depositions. During the investigation into the murder and dismemberment of Sarah Hughes by Cadwalader Jones in Merionethshire in 1877, two surgeons performed the post-mortem and gave evidence, but at no point was their status as police surgeons mentioned.[101] However, Edward Jones and Humphrey Lloyd Williams later sought "more adequate remuneration" of the expenses they incurred during Jones's trial at Chester Winter Assizes.[102]

It is clear that forensic duties were, from an early date, considered part of the job of a police surgeon. In London, John Leeson (b. 1801; surgeon to G Division) was testifying in trials at the Old Bailey in the 1830s, and in 1831 J. F. Clarke, then apprenticed to the surgeon to F Division, Charles James Snitch, represented him at the post-mortem on Carlo Ferrari, the 'Italian Boy' victim of the London Burkers, John Bishop and Thomas Williams.[103] Snitch himself testified at inquests and trials in the early 1830s.[104] In Birkenhead, Matthew Jennette (1802–1885), an honorary surgeon at the local infirmary, was appointed surgeon to the city police in February 1844 and held the post for about 30 years.[105] He testified in at least four murder trials between 1851 and 1872, in the last of which the defendant was a police constable charged with the manslaughter of a man whose daughter he had raped while on duty.[106] Jennette seems to have been a confident forensic witness, but as neither of his qualifications required formal training in forensic medicine, he may well have had to learn on the job.[107] In total, 80 different police surgeons testified in 114 cases in the period 1839–1914, mostly in London (Table 3.10). It would seem sensible for a police constable faced with a dead body to summon either his local police surgeon or the nearest practitioner, and there was every chance that constables knew the doctors who practiced in their patrol area. In the early 1890s coroners in London invariably asked the first doctor on the scene of a homicide to conduct the post-mortem,[108] so it was important that a competent choice was made; but evidence from both London and the provinces suggests that when a senior officer arrived at the scene he sent for the police surgeon, presumably having made a considered judgement about the likely complexity of the case. This is what happened when Olive Beasley was found dead in 1872, as discussed previously. Her sister found the body, noting "we must have a policeman and a doctor;" a neighbour fetched PC Hughes, who in turn went for local GP James Fisher and then for the Chief Superintendent who, when he arrived, immediately sent for the police surgeon, Thomas Frederic Higgs. Both doctors testified at the inquest, committal hearing and trial.[109] The police directed this investigation much as they would today, and both medical men were called as witnesses. But this bore a cost that coroners were not necessarily willing to pay. In a London double homicide in 1896 both a local GP and the divisional surgeon attended the scene, the latter at the request of the police inspector; but the coroner only paid the fee for the doctor who had arrived first, the GP, and did not take evidence from the other. The divisional surgeon had to seek reimbursement from the Metropolitan Police, to cover examining the bodies, assisting at the post-mortem and attending the inquest.[110]

Historians of Victorian and Edwardian crime and policing have overlooked police surgeons far too readily. For some, the role was doubtless a stepping-stone to a more lucrative or socially ambitious appointment, but for others, it was an area of professional practice carried out diligently over many years. On the evidence given, it is possible that police surgeons participated in the early stages of some crime investigations in which they did not appear as formal witnesses, because coroners did not need to pay them in order to bring the case to a satisfactory conclusion. If they did not appear at an inquest, they might have given evidence at a subsequent committal hearing;[111] but they might not. It is also probable that some medical witnesses were police surgeons who simply did not mention the fact or, if they did, it was not recorded.[112] Until this group of forensic practitioners can be studied in more detail it will not be possible to fully assess their contribution to the history and development of medico-legal practice.

Medical coroners

The Introduction noted the resurgence of academic interest in the office of coroner as, over the past 20 years, historians have used the records generated by inquests, and public debates about the office itself, as a means to examine death investigation and wider aspects of socio-political history.[113] Work on the nineteenth-century inquest has not failed to note its growing medicalisation: larger numbers of doctors put themselves forward for election to coronerships, albeit often unsuccessfully, and medical evidence became more prevalent.[114] Yet, with the exception of the celebrated Thomas Wakley, who in 1839 became the first medically trained coroner in London, we know relatively little about those who preceded him in the role of medical coroner. Roy Hunnisett observed that in the second half of the eighteenth century, all seven of the Wiltshire county coroners were medical men; but their bills merely served to convince him of "the backwardness of forensic medicine in England," because post-mortems were performed in only 8 of their 2,779 inquests – probably the cases in which homicide was suspected at the outset.[115] More recently, Pam Fisher noted that around one quarter of county coroners in the late eighteenth and early nineteenth centuries were members of the medical profession,[116] and her subsequent research on a Shropshire coroner suggested that the reason for this might lie in a civic determination to secure reliable medical evidence at inquests: "As there was no legal requirement to summon a medical witness, some boroughs and counties seem to have found an alternative solution: to appoint a medical man as coroner."[117] This persuasive theory casts Hunnisett's findings in a new light: the Wiltshire bills may reflect the coroners' resolve to carry out their own medico-legal examinations *except* when there was a pre-existing suspicion of murder, as prosecutions required medical evidence obtained under oath, not simply informal, if professional, opinions.[118]

Systematic analysis of the extensive archival data compiled for this book identified 38 medical coroners. They are listed in Appendix 4, and their election dates confirm Fisher's findings about the late eighteenth-century origins of the medical coroner. Her earliest example is Dr Stephen Hemsted, who served as a county coroner in Berkshire from 1773 to 1810,[119] whereas the earliest appointments in the appendix, three in Wales and one in Herefordshire, date to the 1790s. Five more medical coroners were elected in Wales during the first two decades of the nineteenth century, and another in Gloucestershire where, later in the century, a member of the Grace dynasty of medical cricketers held the office. The fact that Welsh doctors seem to have seen the role as desirable is a novel and interesting finding, but for the purposes of this book the main question concerns what effect, if any, medical training had on their inquests. Is there evidence that, despite the fact that Umfreville's handbook did not countenance the practice, these doctor-coroners provided medical evidence to the inquests over which they presided?

The coroner in the well-known case of Mary Morgan, who was executed for newborn child murder in Radnorshire in 1805, was a surgeon. The endorsed list on the back of the indictment against her reveals that Hector Applebury Cooksey, who was also surgeon to the gaol, was the only man among the four prosecution witnesses; the other three were Morgan's fellow servants.[120] Their depositions are extant but there is none from Cooksey, which explains why Anne-Marie Kilday noted only three witnesses in her study of this case.[121] The medical evidence that exists in writing is minimal, merely the dimensions of the wound that Morgan inflicted on the throat of her infant; yet this was clearly a murder and a medical witness would have been sought. As there was no other male witness, none of the female witnesses was a midwife but Cooksey was a surgeon, we can conclude – in the absence of evidence to the contrary – that Cooksey acted as both coroner and medical witness in this case. A similar situation seems to have occurred in the case of Mary Williams, who was tried for newborn child murder in Carnarvonshire at the summer Great Sessions of 1817. Edward Carreg, a surgeon who had been elected coroner in October 1816, presided over the inquest in April 1817, when the jury found that Williams had concealed the birth but that there was insufficient evidence to determine how the child died. If any medical evidence was provided, it must have come from Carreg and was evidently inadequate: a magistrate opened his own inquiry and called in another surgeon, who concluded that the child was born alive and then suffocated. Williams was convicted of concealing the birth and sentenced to two years in prison.[122] Carreg was no stranger to the coroner's court: he had appeared as the medical witness in a murder case in September 1816 and testified at the trial in April 1817.[123] Six years later, however, he had ceased to practice medicine and when called to the scene of a murder he "did not examine the wounds, but desired the surgeons to do it."[124]

Other medical coroners in Wales could be more overt about combining the roles, but it was never common practice in homicide investigations. In Flintshire, Peter Parry, then just embarking on a long period of service that culminated in 1874 when he died as Britain's oldest coroner, presided over an inquest at which he served as the medical witness; he then prosecuted the defendants.[125] In 1814 in Gloucestershire, William Trigg also served as the medical witness at an inquest he conducted,[126] as did Benjamin Williams in Breconshire in 1825,[127] having given up private practice two years earlier when he was elected. Benjamin Meredith Bradford appears to have been a recently elected coroner when he gave evidence at a murder trial in Monmouthshire in 1835,[128] but as a franchise coroner he dealt with far fewer cases than the county coroners did. In 1861 the salaries of the three coroners in the county were set under the County Coroners Act of 1860: Bradford's was £7, but William Brewer (who was also a surgeon) was to earn £317 14s. 3d. and Thomas Hughes's salary was to be £164 15s. 8d.[129] In May 1867 Dr James Teague assisted at the post-mortem in a case of newborn child murder in Gloucestershire, having examined the suspected mother and been present at the crime scene as the police searched it – information revealed in the inquest depositions but not mentioned at the committal hearing. In fact, he had been the first legal authority at the scene because of geography: he lived in Blakeney, just over a mile from the hamlet of Etloe where the death occurred.[130]

In 1877 the newly elected coroner for the city of Oxford, Edward Law Hussey, was criticised by a judge for returning an inquest verdict of murder on a man he had attended as a doctor,[131] but the risk of conflating patients, victims and perpetrators must have been a constant if remote possibility for medical coroners.

In 1878 it was clear that Edward Mills Grace knew the suspect when he held an inquest on a victim of newborn child murder: "He himself could say that the young woman had, on a previous occasion, been confined very quickly." The evidence against the accused mother could go either way: the jury had to decide whether the head injuries were inflicted deliberately, bearing in mind "it was also possible that the woman was taken so suddenly that she was unprepared."[132] Dr Grace provided relevant information, given the infant had died from head injuries which might have occurred during birth; however, it should have been given by someone who had been formally called as a witness, because any statement not made on oath was not evidence.[133] This was the last occasion in the project database on which a medical coroner gave evidence to an inquest.

Fisher pointed out that the proportion of medical coroners declined steadily during the nineteenth century to about 20 per cent by 1851.[134] The timing dovetails with a trend highlighted by Gordon Glasgow: the office now carried considerable status and had become profitable, so that there were many more contested elections for county coronerships, particularly in large jurisdictions.[135] But the cost of such elections was usually too high for doctors to compete with solicitors, and ultimately the medicalisation of the inquest developed away from medical coroners, towards the use of specialist facilities (mortuaries) and pathologists.[136] In any event, medical coroners did not play an important medico-legal role in homicide cases, quite properly restricting their involvement to administrative aspects of the inquest. On the very few occasions when this did not happen, it was usually because the coroner was so newly elected that the boundary between his two roles – coroner and doctor – had not yet settled. Although Drs Cooksey and Teague might have behaved differently, given their years of experience, Teague simply happened to be first at the scene of the crime and lost no time in calling in the police and another surgeon. Cooksey, by contrast, may have had little alternative but to bring his own medical knowledge to bear on the case before him, as there appear to have been few medical practitioners in Radnorshire at that time. Criminal depositions of 1810 reveal the presence of a physician in Presteigne and a surgeon in Rhayader (probably the same man listed as the town's sole practitioner in the *Universal British Directory* in 1798),[137] but both towns were over 20 miles from Glasbury where the crime occurred and there is (as yet) no evidence that the physician was in practice in 1804. However, Cooksey was then practising as a surgeon in Presteigne and was possibly both the nearest medical man and the coroner, deciding therefore to combine the tasks at hand. At any rate, no law prevented a coroner from supplying medical evidence to his own inquest, although it was undoubtedly bad practice.

Female medical witnesses

Midwives served as medico-legal witnesses in a total of 186 cases: 161 in the period 1701–1799 and 25 in the period 1805–1910. Most of their testimony was given in cases of infanticide or rape and most appeared at the Old Bailey. Table 3.12 identifies their regional prevalence in the criminal cases included in

Table 3.12 Midwives as medico-legal witnesses

Offence / Circuit	Old Bailey	Great Sessions	North Wales	South Wales	Oxford	Chester	Total
Murder	4	1	–	1	–	–	6
Infant murder	92	30	2	1	10	1	136
Rape	38	1	–	–	–	–	39
Attempted Rape	1	1	–	–	–	–	2
Murder & Manslaughter	1	–	–	–	–	–	1
Rape & Attempted rape	1	–	–	–	–	–	1
Manslaughter of a child	–	1	–	–	–	–	1
Total	137	34	2	2	10	1	186

Source: As for Table 3.1.

the study and shows just how complete their exclusion from the courtroom was after 1830, judging by the figures for the Welsh and Oxford circuits, a phenomenon that will be examined in more detail in Chapter 4. Adrian Wilson has argued that the growth in man-midwifery during the eighteenth century was driven by patients, not medical practitioners,[138] but that was not the process that informs these findings – only 29 of the witnesses identified himself as a man-midwife. Rather, it seems that female midwives were not asked to provide medico-legal testimony with any regularity after the middle of the eighteenth century, and this must be related to two factors. Firstly, in rape cases the victim or her parents chose to consult a surgeon and, even if she had also seen a midwife, it was the surgeon who was bound over to appear in court. Secondly, only surgeons could conduct post-mortem examinations, an increasing necessity in cases of infant murder when the question of live birth could mean the difference between life and death for an accused mother. Midwives were not replaced by man-midwives in forensic practice; they were replaced by general surgeons and GPs.

The earliest occasion on which the body of a newborn infant was opened by a surgeon was in 1717, when Ann Hasle was tried at the Old Bailey, accused of drowning her child. The court heard evidence from a midwife, who stated that the appearance of the body was largely natural, and then from an unnamed surgeon who had opened the body and found there was no water in it. Unusually for the time, Hasle mounted a vigorous defence: she was married and thus outside the scope of the statute of 1624 that rendered unmarried women who gave birth in secret liable to be convicted of murder; and she called another midwife to testify to her intention of having the child. This changed the focus of the prosecution, as the deliberate murder of a live-born infant now had to be proved:

> And the chief Stress of the Matter then being whether the Child was murthered by her before putting into the Copper, or alive when she put

it in: As to the first, the Evidences generally agreed there were no visible Tokens of any Violence offered to the Infant; and as to the latter, the Judge being of Opinion it was not alive when it was put in, because of what had been before testified, that at its being opened there was no Water found in the Body of it. A Surgeon being call'd to give his Opinion on the Matter, confirm'd his Lordship's Opinion, deposing upon Oath he was of Opinion that no human Body could be drowned without receiving some Quantity of Water into the Body, and consequently the Child could not be alive when put into the Copper. The Matter being thus, that there was no sufficient Proof that she had either murthered the Infant, or that it was born alive, tho' the Action was so unaccountably inhuman, for which she gave but little Satisfaction, the Jury acquitted her of the Indictment.[139]

Julia Rudolph considers this case an example of "the erosion of female knowledge and authority with the rise of male medical expertise and a 'culture of dissection'"; but her more important point, taken in a broader sense, is that anatomical knowledge could serve as a form of protection for defendants in court.[140]

The marketplace created by the criminal justice system favoured male practitioners; or, put another way, those who used the criminal justice system seem to have preferred male surgeons in cases of crimes against the person. Even some midwives gave this advice, presumably knowing that a court appearance might ensue. In 1781 for example, when 11-year-old Hannah Serjeant was raped in Denbighshire her mother sent for the local midwife, who advised her to get a surgeon. As a result, a rape examination was conducted by Thomas Griffiths, a surgeon-apothecary in Wrexham, who concluded that Hannah had certainly been a victim of "violence from some man."[141] Some mothers went straight to a surgeon, as Margaret William did when her daughter Mary was raped in Dolgellau, Merionethshire, in 1773:

> that upon her return home from begging about one of the clock on Tuesday the second day of March instant, she found her daughter Mary Richard had been crying, she immediately asked her what was the matter with her. She answered, Robert Bach did something very bad with me, he took up my clothes over my head and hurt me with something behind; then this examinant took the said Mary Richard to a surgeon.[142]

The surgeon in this case was not named, but it is extremely significant that rape victims in Welsh towns had what appears to have been ready access to surgeons. Thomas Griffiths was one of those not included in the *Medical Register* of 1783, even though he was practising at Wrexham just two years earlier: either he had died, moved to England (there is no one of that name on the Welsh list), or he was simply overlooked when the register was compiled.

Some midwives possessed anatomical knowledge and surgical skills, Sarah Stone (c.1680–after 1737) of Somerset and London being a well-known example;[143] but Chapter 4 will show that when midwives appeared as medico-legal witnesses it was in addition to, not in the place of or as an equal to, a male practitioner. However, the pattern of their disappearance from the records, reflecting their exclusion from formal processes of body examination, is more puzzling. Midwives appeared sporadically in nineteenth-century trials for infant murder in Wales and the Oxford Circuit, but not in Cheshire or other parts of northern England.[144] They were consulted more regularly in London until the 1830s when they all but disappeared from trial records. This was evidently a product of conscious choices made by regional law officers: in most parts of the country the investigating authorities did not choose to ask a midwife to provide medico-legal evidence; or, after about 1770, did not ask the attending midwife questions of a medico-legal nature. In London, the last verified occasion on which a midwife answered questions of a forensic nature occurred in 1833 and involved a living body, not a dead one: Marian Allan, a widow and midwife, confirmed that she was present when the parish surgeon examined a mother suspected of newborn child murder, and that this woman had the appearance of one who had given birth eight or nine days earlier. Only the surgeon testified about the dead infant.[145] Why exactly London practice changed so abruptly is uncertain, but the timing is suggestive: the Metropolitan Police force was founded in 1829 and with it the role of the police surgeon; medical education, including obstetrics, expanded greatly in London during the first few decades of the nineteenth century; and so did the number of doctors practising in or near the capital, more of whom had studied forensic medicine.[146] These broader currents led to changes in the way in which crime was investigated, and in the expectations placed on medical professionals by the courts.

Apart from midwives, only two women appeared as medico-legal witnesses, both in murder cases. In 1751 a surgeon's widow, Elizabeth Vaughan of Machynlleth in Montgomeryshire, appeared as the sole medical witness following the death of a man stabbed several times in a dispute over cattle. He lived at Pennal in Merionethshire, about four miles away, and asked her to attend him as a medical practitioner; given his surname was also Vaughan it is remotely possible they were related. But there was nothing she could do to save his life and the justice of the peace who took the depositions in the case was clearly intrigued by this woman's presence. Her answer indicates the question he put to her: "That the reason of this examinant's having attended the said Mr Vaughan is because she has some knowledge in surgery, which she acquired in the lifetime of her late husband, who was a surgeon and apothecary."[147] The fact that she signed her deposition attests to Elizabeth Vaughan's status as an educated woman. Her husband William had appeared as a medico-legal witness in 1737, after a man was stabbed in the street following a quarrel at an inn. William Vaughan told the coroner that he had been two miles from home attending a patient when a special messenger was sent to fetch him; despite the best of his skill, the victim died three days later.[148] Both cases were typical of eighteenth-century practice – local practitioners attended local victims and then became forensic witnesses; but the presence of a female surgeon was exceptional.

The other case involving a female doctor occurred in 1907 when Dr Margaret Douglas French, the resident medical officer of the Haywood Hospital in Burslem, Staffordshire,[149] treated a woman who had allegedly drowned her five-year-old daughter in a canal and attempted to drown herself: Emma Lucas, 37, was rescued and resuscitated by a passing coal miner but her child died at the scene. Dr French presented her post-mortem findings at the inquest on 17 December and again six days later at the committal hearing when, cross-examined by Lucas's solicitor, she stated that in her opinion the prisoner was not in a fit state to give evidence. Margaret French had qualified at the University of Durham just three years earlier and had not held her post in Burslem for long: in April 1906 she was employed by the Hull City Asylum when she applied for a position at the Kingseat Asylum, which had opened near Newmachar in Aberdeenshire in 1904.[150] She plainly had experience of psychiatric conditions, but it was not her specialist knowledge that was called for in the Lucas case. The responsibility for conducting the forensic examination of a dead child and certifying that a suspect was unable to give evidence on her own behalf was entrusted to Dr French because of her position as the MO at the hospital nearest to the scene of the crime. But it may well have been her asylum experience that prompted her to question Emma Lucas about what had happened, although the answers she got were of doubtful validity given the mental and physical state the woman was in at the time.[151]

Dr French did not provide the only medical opinion in this case. While Emma Lucas was on remand at HMP Stafford, a period of just over two months, the prison medical officer, Dr Percy R. Mander, kept her under careful observation and on 29 February 1908 he submitted his report to the Director of Public Prosecutions, as required under the terms of Prison Standing Orders issued in 1900 and 1902: Mrs Lucas was fit to plead, as she understood the charges (of murder and attempted suicide) against her and was capable of instructing counsel; but she was of unsound mind at the time the offences were committed, notwithstanding the fact she had since improved both mentally and physically.[152] At her trial in March the grand jury rejected the bills, but the judge ordered her trial for murder to proceed on the inquisition, since two "tribunals" had found there was a case to answer. The "lady resident medical officer" gave her testimony as to both the victim's cause of death and the statements made by the accused, but it appeared from other evidence that the allegation of murder could not be sustained: no one had seen Emma Lucas push the child into the water and it might have been an accident.[153] Dr Mander was not mentioned but, consequent upon the standing orders must have been in court. Emma Lucas was acquitted and Dr French disappeared from the assize courts, although she returned twice to the coroner's court in 1912 to testify about the accidental deaths of two children.[154] She immigrated to Saskatoon, Canada, sometime between 1935 and 1939 and died there in 1950.

Homicide in medico-legal practice: statistical overview

The vast majority – 90 per cent – of this book's 2,615 cases involved the murder or manslaughter of an infant, child or adult (Table 3.5). As the Introduction explained, homicide offers a clear means of identifying and querying patterns in medico-legal practice and provision in the investigations for which it was most likely to be used. In these last sections, therefore, a collective overview of the cases is presented to provide insights into the forensic evidence produced for the courts, the developing use of specialist witnesses and scientific tests and the ways in which medical knowledge could work for, not just against, defendants. Some of these strands will be examined in greater depth in the following two chapters, which will demonstrate the growing sophistication of forensic investigations in cases of infant murder (Chapter 4), the key crime around which forensic practice developed and matured in the eighteenth and nineteenth centuries; and the emerging role of the 'expert witness' (Chapter 5), which helped to solidify the relationship between the police and forensic practitioners in criminal investigations. As an example of the ways in which location – both spatial and historical – could influence forensic practice, the chapter concludes with a short study of the links between medicine and crime at one point in time, 1881, a year selected to represent the regional variations in policing and medical provision that underpinned the foundations of medico-legal practice and helped to shape its professional development.

Cause of death

In any case of homicide, one of the most important medico-legal facts that the courts required was a clear cause of death, which is why the post-mortem examination was so important: doctors needed to prove the nature and consequence of the injuries sustained by the victim, to help establish the act alleged against a defendant. Earlier in this chapter we considered the extent to which post-mortems were carried out; here, we explore the information they revealed. Tables 3.13 and 3.14 list the main causes of death identified in homicides: head injuries and stabbing were most common, accounting for nearly 37 per cent of all victims; but stabbing was more clearly associated with adults. Infants, on the other hand, were killed by strangulation or suffocation. These differences are presented in Table 3.15: babies and children were more likely than adults to be killed by forms of asphyxia, including drowning. This could sometimes lead to assumptions both favourable and unfavourable to a defendant, for example that a child found in water had drowned (possibly accidentally), or that a newborn infant who bore no marks of violence had been strangled or smothered (a typical cause of death in eighteenth-century indictments, sometimes on flimsy evidence).[155] Children were victims of forms of homicide less easily inflicted on adults, such as starvation; conversely, because they were rarely killed in spontaneous fights, they did not often get stabbed. Adults were regularly beaten to death in instances of spousal violence and male fighting. Adults and children, but not babies, died more frequently from head injuries caused by deliberate violence than any other method of killing, indicating that perpetrators tended to lash out more with blunt weapons than with blows and kicks.

The places in which dead infants tended to be found – privies, roads, bodies of water or open ground – the resultant decomposition and the well-known

Table 3.13 Main cause of death in cases of homicide

Offence / CoD	Murder	Manslaughter	Infant Murder & Concealment	Murder & Manslaughter	Murder or Manslaughter of a Child	Petty Treason	Rape & Attempted Rape	Total
Beat/kick	149	40	3	20	10	1	–	223
Broken neck	8	4	–	–	1	–	–	13
Cut throat	75	1	36	–	22	1	–	135
Drowned	23	1	60	2	41	–	–	127
Head injury	283	71	52	32	58	2	–	498
Multiple injuries	58	4	24	2	7	1	–	96
Poison	53	–	14	1	11	1	–	80
Shot	133	4	–	3	11	–	–	151
Stabbed	305	12	7	26	5	11	–	366
Starved	5	2	3	1	6	–	–	17
Strangled	31	1	144	–	12	–	–	188
Suffocated	10	2	117	–	8	–	–	137
Other	58	19	74	11	20	–	1	183
Unspecified	23	7	103	–	7	–	–	140
Total	1,214	168	637	98	219	17	1	2,354

Source: As for Table 3.1. Excludes all 261 cases in which the victim did not die; includes 1 rape case where the child victim died before the trial.

Table 3.14 Main cause of death in cases of homicide, by circuit

CoD \ Circuit	Old Bailey	Great Sessions	North Wales	South Wales	Oxford	Chester	Other	Total
Beat/kick	122	39	7	15	36	4	–	223
Broken neck	2	2	1	2	5	1	–	13
Cut throat	67	6	11	12	37	2	–	135
Drowned	39	14	21	12	40	–	1	127
Head injury	206	40	41	43	163	5	–	498
Multiple injuries	47	8	9	8	24	–	–	96
Poison	22	11	21	3	23	–	–	80
Shot	74	12	15	15	33	1	1	151
Stabbed	256	11	13	34	52	–	–	366
Starved	9	–	2	–	6	–	–	17
Strangled	65	79	14	4	24	2	–	188
Suffocated	72	12	13	7	30	3	–	137
Other	96	19	11	22	33	2	–	183
Unspecified	89	14	7	3	26	1	–	140
Total	1,166	267	186	180	532	21	2	2,354

Source: As for Table 3.13.

Table 3.15 Cause of death – percentage by age of homicide victim

Cause of Death	Adult (%)	Infant (%)	Child (%)
Beat/kick	14.0	0.5	4.6
Broken neck	0.8	0	0.4
Cut throat	5.1	5.6	10.0
Drowned	1.7	9.4	18.6
Head injury	26.0	8.2	26.4
Multiple injuries	4.3	3.8	3.2
Poison	3.7	2.2	5.0
Shot	9.4	0	5.0
Stabbed	23.7	1.1	2.3
Starved	0.5	0.5	2.7
Strangled	2.1	22.6	5.4
Suffocated	0.8	18.4	3.6
Other	5.9	11.6	9.6
Unspecified	2.0	16.1	3.2
Total	100	100	100

Source: As for Table 3.1. Infant denotes up to 1 year in age; child denotes age of 1 year or more.

difficulties of establishing a specific cause of death in newborns[156] meant that surgeons sometimes could not specify a precise cause of death. This occurred in 103 cases, 73 of them (70.9 per cent) before 1831. The fact that it continued to happen after medical students began to receive training in forensic medicine is related to the fact that infant murder involved other, more important forensic issues to do with whether the infant had been born alive, rendering cause of death sometimes of lesser importance than it was in respect to older victims. Thorough forensic examinations were performed, as we will see in Chapter 4, but their main aim was to establish live birth, not an exact cause of death. It was otherwise unusual for a trial to proceed without reference to a well-defined medical cause of death: this happened only six times after 1830, when the body was too burned or decomposed to permit an accurate determination.

This is not to say that surgeons might not have done more; but they sought to provide the forensic evidence required by the court, not *all* the possible evidence. When Samuel Middleton was tried in June 1902 for the murder of his wife at Webheath (a village outside Redditch) in Worcestershire, the main confirmation of how she actually died came from admissions made by Middleton himself: he had beaten her about the head with a poker (or a hatchet, it was uncertain which) in a drunken rage and then set the house on fire, later telling a police officer "I have done my doom." The Redditch doctor "instructed" by a police inspector to examine the body, described it fully but did not state a cause of death or, apparently, try to determine whether she was alive when the fire began, as the press suggested she was.[157] While good practice might have demanded such detail,[158] it was not actually necessary: the victim could be identified by her size and clothing and had clearly not died a natural death. Moreover, Middleton had condemned himself in several inadvisable remarks to witnesses, and circumstantial evidence connected him to the arson; he met his doom on the scaffold at Worcester on 15 July 1902.

Uniquely among victims, infants sometimes died from neglect rather than a wilful act, summed up by the coroner's verdict of 'lack of attention at birth'. Such cases, along with blood loss caused by failure to tie the umbilical cord, and stillbirth, are included in the category 'Other'. This group also includes crush injuries sustained in traffic accidents, disease (usually an infection) consequent upon prior injury and references to wounds that do not cite a particular cause of death. One child rape victim died from a fever in 1741, three weeks after being discharged from a workhouse infirmary in London. She had been treated for venereal disease with mercury compounds and the surgeon "opened" her, possibly fearing his drugs had killed her, but more likely as a means of establishing whether the rapist should instead face a murder charge.[159]

In cases involving obvious causes of death such as stabbing, throat cutting or shooting, there was generally little forensic mystery; the key issue was the legal question of whether the accused had committed the act intentionally. Medicine could sometimes shed light on this, as for example by providing an estimate of the amount of force required to inflict fatal injuries, noting an unusually weak constitution in the victim, counting the number of separate wounds to prove they were made in a sustained attack or by confirming that injuries were not survivable. Head injuries were common, although their effect was not always as dramatic as those inflicted on his family by an insane father in 1878: the surgeon told magistrates that

> The wounds I have described would be quite sufficient to cause instant death and would be likely to be caused by an instrument similar to the axe produced. The other organs were perfectly healthy. I could have formed an opinion as to the cause of death without making a post-mortem examination.[160]

In other words, when brain matter oozed from the skull, there could be little doubt about the cause of death. This is why the proportion of homicides in which only the head was opened remained quite high throughout the nineteenth century, as Figure 3.3 shows.

This chart should serve as a reminder of just how prominent head injuries were in medico-legal practice – and yet, they did not attract controversy. This is because medical practitioners had long been aware that complete failure of one of the three essential organs, the brain, lungs and heart, fairly speedily interfered with the function of the other two, leading inevitably to death.[161] This medical understanding was also reflected in the use of selective forensic examination relative to other modes of death. Figure 3.3 depicts a total of 806 cases in which a body was opened or an external examination was made in place of a full post-mortem (excluding opening of the head only). Over the whole period 1699–1914, 180 of these cases involved stabbing as the cause of death; the next most common form of killing was beating and kicking (102 cases). But when these statistics are considered for the period 1831–1914, the numbers tell a more specific story. Table 3.16 shows that selective body examination was used most frequently in cases of shooting, stabbing and throat

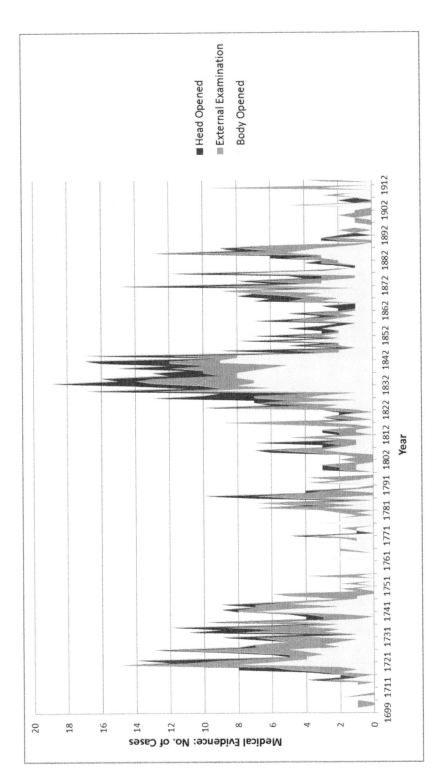

Figure 3.3 Use of selective medical evidence in homicide cases, 1699–1914

Table 3.16 Use of selective medical evidence in homicide cases, 1831–1914

Offence CoD	Murder	Manslaughter	Infant Murder & Concealment	Murder & Manslaughter	Murder or Manslaughter of a Child	Total	%
Beat/kick	13	11	–	3	1	28	7.6
Broken neck	2	–	–	–	–	2	0.5
Cut throat	32	1	9	–	13	55	14.9
Drowned	5	–	11	–	11	27	7.3
Head injury	17	1	3	1	3	25	6.8
Multiple injuries	5	1	2	–	2	10	2.7
Poison	21	–	4	–	4	29	7.8
Shot	41	1	–	1	3	46	12.4
Stabbed	58	6	1	7	1	73	19.7
Starved	–	2	2	–	1	5	1.4
Strangled	3	–	8	–	2	13	3.5
Suffocated	–	–	16	–	1	17	4.6
Other	4	6	15	–	3	28	7.6
Unspecified	–	–	11	–	1	12	3.2
Total	201	29	82	12	46	370	100
Absolute Total	557	103	310	61	137	1,168	–
Proportion (%)	36.1	28.2	26.4	19.7	33.6	31.7	–

Source: As for Table 3.13. Selective medical evidence includes external examination and opening the body; excludes head opening.

cutting, which were modes of killing that (with the exception of throat cutting) affected adults disproportionately to infants and children. It is not too surprising that some doctors felt a full post-mortem was unnecessary in such cases: many wounds were very obvious and their fatal nature evident from their extent and position; if death had not been immediate, it soon followed from heart failure caused by blood loss. Similarly, a surgeon might push the intestines back in and sew up a stab wound to the belly, but it was still a justifiable assumption that when the victim died, it was because they had been stabbed in the belly. On the other hand, a more thorough post-mortem was needed if the victim had languished for some days or even weeks, as that cast doubt on the cause of death: pre-existing disease or secondary infections gave jurors pause for thought. And the cause of death was much less obvious in the rarer methods of murder, such as poisoning and starvation, compelling a full post-mortem. Table 3.16 suggests that although partial post-mortem examinations might have been due to professional ineptitude or financial parsimony, they were equally likely to be grounded in a robust medical understanding of the deadly effects of certain types of wounds.

Medicalised testimony by lay witnesses

Laymen understood some of this, which explains the findings presented in Tables 3.17 and 3.18, showing the use of medicalised testimony by lay witnesses as an absolute number of cases in which it occurred and as a proportion of all cases over the course of the period under study. This was not a usual phenomenon by any means, but although it became less common in the nineteenth century – as one would expect, due to the rising importance of formal forensic evidence presented by doctors – it was never entirely eliminated. As an example, consider this testimony from the Old Bailey in 1737: "Counsel: What sort of a noise was it? Walker: Like the groans of a dying man." And another witness heard the victim's blood spurting: "I heard the gushes of blood run from the orifices, as if a bung-hole had been made in his body."[162] These witnesses, one of whom put his hand into the stab wound the victim suffered, knew that a sword thrust straight through the breast near the heart must prove fatal. In some cases the medicalised nature of a layman's testimony was more overt than this, as for example in a trial for infant murder in 1754:[163]

> I thought I had seen children newly born more perfect, there being very little hair on its head, and the nails on its fingers not so big as on newborn children I have seen; it was a small child. By the position the child lay in it might have come from her as she sat on the vault, for the head was downwards, and seemed to be a good deal buried in the soil. I also observed what follows the child [i.e. the placenta] lying near its feet, or betwixt the legs, and the navel-string was found to be broke, not cut, about five or six inches from the child's body; a good deal of blood had gone down the vault, more than I perceived anywhere else.

Table 3.17 Medicalised testimony by lay witnesses per circuit, 1699–1914

Period	Old Bailey	Great Sessions	North Wales	South Wales	Oxford	Chester	Total
1699–1729	74	–	–	–	–	–	74
1730–1759	74	39	–	–	–	1	114
1760–1789	33	12	–	–	1	2	48
1790–1809	8	4	–	–	–	–	12
1810–1829	–	14	–	–	7	1	22
1830–1839	7	–	1	–	8	–	16
1840–1849	9	–	1	1	3	–	14
1850–1859	–	–	1	1	1	–	3
1860–1869	–	–	1	–	7	–	8
1870–1879	5	–	4	2	13	–	24
1880–1889	1	–	3	2	6	–	12
1890–1899	1	–	–	1	–	–	2
1900–1914	8	–	–	1	3	–	12
Total	220	69	11	8	49	4	361
Proportion 1831–1914 (%)[1]	8.5	–	5.9	4.4	9.2	–	–

Source: As for Table 3.1. Total includes 48 cases of rape/attempted rape (1707–1786, one GS and the rest *OBP*).

1 Total (1831–1914) as a proportion of all cases for the period 1831–1914: Old Bailey, 31/365; North Wales, 11/186; South Wales, 8/180; Oxford Circuit, 41/447.

Table 3.18 Proportion of medicalised testimony by lay witnesses, 1699–1914

Period	No. of Cases involving lay medical opinion	Total No. of Cases	Proportion (%)
1699–1729	74	434	17.0
1730–1759	114	427	26.7
1760–1789	48	272	17.6
1790–1809	12	109	11.0
1810–1829	22	167	13.2
1830–1839	16	225	7.1
1840–1849	14	184	7.6
1850–1859	3	87	3.4
1860–1869	8	111	7.2
1870–1879	24	195	12.3
1880–1889	12	162	7.4
1890–1899	2	74	2.7
1900–1914	12	168	7.1
Total	361	2,615	13.8

Source: As for Table 3.1.

This male witness was particularly observant, providing a mixture of fact and opinion that differed very little from the evidence given by a midwife in the same trial; and we will see in the next chapter just how closely these details matched those emphasised by surgeons. However, the majority of the cases enumerated in Table 3.18, 74.9 per cent, occurred before the 1830s, the decade that heralded significant changes in forensic procedure due to the new emphasis on medical evidence at inquests and on training doctors to provide it, discussed earlier in this chapter and in Chapter 2. When laymen gave evidence of a medical nature later in the nineteenth century, it was generally a spontaneous means of expressing what they had seen and the importance they attached to it. This was more likely to occur when the sanity of a defendant seemed doubtful (54 out of 91 cases, 59.3 per cent): neighbours and relatives tended to comment about the individual's demeanour, behaviour and family history. But even when a perpetrator was seen to behave very strangely or to appear "like a madman," that did not mean they were actually insane or even that all the lay witnesses had reached the same conclusion. Judges and jurors did, however, take account of these impressions: perpetrators who appeared to be depressed, maniacal or suffering from delusions were likely to be confirmed as insane at trial, regardless of any contrary medical opinion. Joel Eigen has convincingly demonstrated that common-sense understanding of insanity and criminal responsibility still solidly reinforced jury decision-making in the nineteenth century,[164] while Tony Ward noted the importance of common sense to the knowledge that fact finders, i.e. jurors, applied when deciding whether a (courtroom) narrative was plausible. The observations made by doctors had to compete with legal and lay interpretations of the events in question: professional authority might persuade a judge and jury to set aside their common-sense construal,[165] but Eigen and Ward agree that experts on mental illness tended to look for and accept the same signs of insanity that the general public did, albeit with a veneer of class bias. Defendants of higher social status were more likely to be deemed insane, but people of any class who were members of a group believed to be prone to insanity, such as epileptics, new mothers and those with a family history of lunacy, most easily met the accepted criteria. Perhaps uniquely in forensic practice, verdicts in 'insanity trials' were shaped by shared lay and medical beliefs about what a prisoner knew they were doing and what they believed about the outcome of the act.

Specialist evidence and expert witnesses

Nineteenth-century prisoners considered insane by their friends could not confidently expect to make a successful defence on the grounds of insanity if they did not display one of the principal accepted signs of lunacy: mania, melancholia and, especially, delusions.[166] Of the total of 271 cases in which insanity was alleged, 76 trials, 65 of which occurred after 1830, ended in a guilty verdict. Fourteen defendants were convicted of a lesser offence, all after 1830. Only 17 perpetrators were acquitted. But the insanity plea was clearly becoming more frequent and successful: 118 defendants were found not guilty on the grounds of insanity, the majority (96) after 1830; and of the 37 who were too mentally ill to plead to their indictment, all but two were after 1830. Four cases were abandoned, one perpetrator was found to have no case to answer, and the outcome in four others is unknown, possibly because the perpetrators were removed from the criminal justice process because they were insane. Changes in prosecutorial procedure towards the end of the century played a key role. In 1885, the office of the Director of Public Prosecutions was made responsible for the conduct of all capital prosecutions. Under pressure from the Home Office, which had had to issue far too many reprieves from execution for insane convicts, the public prosecutor began to seek medical advice about prisoners' sanity *before* trial.[167] The usual practice was to obtain a written report from the MO of the asylum nearest the town where the trial was held; however, prison medical officers are generally more visible in the records because of their role in observing prisoners held on remand. By the First World War, according to Tony Ward, the PMO had become the principal courtroom adviser on insanity, displacing asylum MOs,[168] but this shift occurred earlier in London, where the redoubtable MO of Newgate Gaol, Gilbert McMurdo (1799–1869), was a regular, often unsympathetic expert witness at the Old Bailey from 1830 to 1855.[169] He was followed into the courtroom by the MOs of Brixton, Clerkenwell and Holloway prisons, while his successor at Newgate, John Rowland Gibson (1814–1892), testified in over 80 trials at the Old Bailey between 1856 and 1882. Prison medical officers were also important experts on mental health in the courts of the Oxford Circuit and South Wales from the middle of the nineteenth century, whereas in Cheshire and North Wales the asylums at Chester (1829) and Denbigh (1848) supplied staff with the necessary expertise.

Table 3.19 Use of a formal medical defence of insanity in homicide trials, by circuit

Crime \ Circuit	Old Bailey	Great Sessions & Chester	North Wales	South Wales	Oxford	Total
Murder	33	–	10	6	20	69
Infant murder	15	–	5	2	8	30
Manslaughter	–	–	–	–	1	1
Murder of a child	18	–	7	5	12	42
Manslaughter of a child	–	–	–	1	–	1
Murder + manslaughter	1	–	–	–	–	1
Total	67	–	22	14	41	144
Proportion (%)[1]	5.7	0	11.8	7.8	7.7	–

Source: As for Table 3.1.

1 Total as a proportion of all homicide cases on these circuits: Old Bailey, 67/1166; North Wales, 22/186; South Wales, 14/180; Oxford Circuit, 41/532. For the period 1831 onward, the figures for London are 53/365 (14.5%), and for the Oxford Circuit, 41/447 (9.2%). Calculating an average proportion inclusive of Great Sessions and Chester would produce a meaningless figure, given the absence of formal insanity defences on these circuits.

Table 3.19 provides a count of cases in which a medical professional, but not necessarily an expert on mental illness, gave evidence about the sanity of a defendant. However, few defendants called doctors to speak on their behalf, relying instead on relatives and neighbours. The table shows that this must be what occurred in Wales prior to the abolition of Great Sessions: there were 11 homicide cases in which the perpetrator was believed to be insane, but no medical witness testified to this at any of the trials. However, this did not mean that allegations of insanity were not explored: in 1816 Griffith Roberts was indicted at Carnarvon for the murder of his young son, but neither the coroner nor magistrates had bound the witnesses to appear at his trial. However, one of the magistrates, David Ellis Nanney, was also Attorney General of the North Wales circuit, and it seems likely to have been at his urging that, "being also deemed proper to have witnesses to prove the sanity of the prisoner and other facts," subpoenas were issued for four more witnesses, all of whom were farmers. It is possible that the surgeon-coroner, Edward Carreg, also testified to Roberts' insanity, but clearly the witnesses expected to do so were laymen.[170] There is too little data for the Chester Great Sessions to determine whether this was a regional or a particularly Welsh way of assessing sanity at this time, but the fact that the nineteenth-century Welsh circuits sought medical opinions on sanity at approximately the same rate as in London and the Oxford Circuit is certainly telling. As we discovered in relation to the use of the post-mortem examination, after the abolition of Great Sessions the Welsh counties adopted English procedures. A similar effect seems to have been felt in relation to the insanity defence, but the Welsh could not rely on the staff of asylums until much later in the century. In Wales, institutional provision for the mentally ill did not become the norm until the early twentieth century, and the number of asylums remained limited even after national legislation of 1845 required all counties to provide for the insane. Not only was the rate of building slow, with only eight asylums constructed before the First World War, but the typical Welsh response to the County Asylums Act was to enter into agreement with a neighbouring county in Wales or in England; sometimes with more than one county. This meant that the nearest asylum medical officer might be much further away than the nearest prison medical officer, but GPs were always closest to hand. For example, the North Wales Lunatic Asylum at Denbigh, opened in 1848, served the insane poor of five counties,[171] but in the early 1860s its resident MO appeared in only one of the three trials in the region that involved an insanity plea.[172] In South Wales, where the first county asylums were not constructed until the mid-1860s (for Glamorgan, and an asylum at Carmarthen that served three counties), GPs remained the de facto 'experts' on mental illness until the 1880s, when both asylum and prison MOs began to appear at trials with noticeable regularity following the changes instituted by the Director of Public Prosecutions. Their increased presence in court is reflected in Table 3.21: the number of cases in which a defendant's insanity was suggested by lay witnesses is compared to the number of formal medical opinions offered, suggesting that laymen could recognise insanity and articulate it in relation to the accepted medico-legal elements of criminal irresponsibility.

With its far greater number of practitioners, London led the way in the use of medical evidence of insanity in murder trials, and especially that provided by experts who developed their proficiency in prisons. When the figures in Table 3.19 are adjusted to enable a direct comparison between all four regions in the period 1831 to 1914, the greater proportion of insanity trials in London (14.5 per cent) is evident; and a prison medical officer was one of the expert witnesses, or the sole expert, in 41 of these 53 trials. On the Oxford Circuit, 21 of the 41 insanity pleas were supported by the testimony of a prison medical officer; the earliest example, in 1832,[173] originated in Stafford where a new prison opened in 1794. Asylum medical officers were less prominent in the assize courts: six trials involved the testimony of both an asylum MO and a PMO, but only three trials heard testimony from an asylum MO alone.

Tables 3.20 and 3.21 show the frequency with which medical witnesses gave testimony that helped to create a defence to the charge alleged. The figures relate to an active contribution to a trial, not simply failure to conduct a forensic investigation. Examples include a specific finding that helped to exonerate a defendant, or an acknowledgment that the medical witness had been unable to confirm a relevant fact, such as live birth in cases of newborn child murder, or a cause of death linked to the defendant's act(s). This did not require a distinct defence witness, though some defendants were able to call surgeons to testify on their behalf. Rather, medical testimony favourable to the defence was often elicited during the course of evidence given for the prosecution, especially in trials for infant murder; Table 3.20 shows that this was the most typical type of offence in which a medical defence occurred. If, in his examination-in-chief or under

Table 3.20 Use of a medical defence, by circuit and offence

Offence	Old Bailey	Great Sessions	North Wales	South Wales	Oxford	Chester	Total	%	% of Offence Type
Murder	136	1	13	10	32	–	192	39.3	15.8
Manslaughter	6	1	4	1	8	–	20	4.1	11.9
Infant murder	99	4	16	9	30	1	159	32.6	25.8
Murder of a child	24	2	7	6	12	–	51	10.4	27.7
Manslaughter of a child	–	1	–	1	3	–	5	1.0	14.3
Rape	42	–	–	–	–	–	42	8.6	18.4
Attempted rape	1	–	–	–	–	–	1	0.2	6.25
Petty treason	1	–	–	–	–	–	1	0.2	5.9
Concealment of birth	–	–	2	2	3	–	7	1.4	33.3
Murder + manslaughter	7	–	1	3	–	–	11	2.2	11.2
Total	316	9	43	32	88	1	489	100	

Source: As for Table 3.1. Percentage of offence type calculated in relation to Table 3.5, 'Total' column.

Table 3.21 Proportion of medical defences, 1699–1914

Period	Total No. of Cases	Cases citing a Medical Point in Defence	Proportion (%)	Defendant Insanity	
				Suggested	Defence
1699–1709	65	7	10.8	4	0
1710–1719	155	34	21.9	5	1
1720–1729	214	61	28.5	7	5
1730–1739	206	28	13.6	7	3
1740–1749	151	22	14.6	6	0
1750–1759	70	11	15.7	0	0
1760–1769	64	11	17.2	1	0
1770–1779	82	12	14.6	0	0
1780–1789	126	23	18.2	8	3
1790–1799	47	6	12.8	1	0
1800–1809	62	11	17.7	4	2
1810–1819	54	5	9.2	3	1
1820–1829	113	10	8.8	3	0
1830–1839	225	35	15.6	23	12
1840–1849	184	25	13.6	21	8
1850–1859	87	12	13.8	7	4
1860–1869	111	19	17.1	18	10
1870–1879	195	49	25.1	39	25
1880–1889	162	47	29.0	41	27
1890–1899	74	15	20.3	15	10
1900–1914	168	46	27.4	58	34
Total	2,615	489	18.7	271	145

Source: As for Table 3.1. Suggested insanity as layman's view; defence of insanity on medical evidence.

cross-examination, a surgeon admitted that an infant might have died for want of medical assistance at birth, this amounted to a defence on medical grounds. It weakened the prosecution claim that the defendant had deliberately committed murder by providing a persuasive alternative narrative to explain how death had occurred. When a post-mortem had been made and two practitioners concurred, such testimony was unassailable. Or defence-oriented evidence could focus on the accused by providing evidence of temporary insanity. Essentially, a prosecution was destined to fail if it could not establish that an illegal act had been committed and that the act had been committed purposefully. Consider, for example, this testimony from a murder trial at the Old Bailey in 1787:

> Mr Gillis and Mr Rider, surgeons, who were called in after to inspect the body of the deceased, deposed, that the marks on the body were a rasure

[scrape] of the skin on the right foot, a bruise on the same knee, and a contusion over the left eye; these marks, they said, did not appear the result of
violence, they were rather to be accounted for by a fall; for if the contusion
in the forehead had been occasioned by a blow, she could not have fallen
forward so as to hurt her knee at the same time.[174]

Murder trials accounted for the largest proportion of medical defences, closely
followed by infant murder; the phenomenon was otherwise relatively infrequent
except in eighteenth-century rape trials. If a child victim did not show evidence
of penetration, this amounted to a medical defence: a jury could, with some
justification, conclude that the act of rape had not been completed. Defence
counsel knew exactly how to elicit the answers they needed, as this trial from
1768 demonstrates:

> Q. Do you think it possible for a man to lie with a child of eight years old,
> without an extension or laceration of the part? Barrel [a surgeon]. No, it
> is not possible. Q. Do you think a man's applying his prepuce to a girl of
> that age, might give her the foul disease without penetration? Barrel. Yes,
> the disorder is communicable, if the two parts touch one another, the dis-
> order may be emitted by that means. Q. If the child had been penetrated
> two months ago, must not her parts have been so uneasy, it must have been
> discovered by the weakness of the parts? Barrel. Yes, it would. Q. If a child
> had been forced by a man, must it not be immediately found out? Barrel.
> Yes, it must. Acquitted.[175]

Medical defences were more usually made on physical than mental grounds
until the late nineteenth century. Table 3.21 demonstrates that the proportion of
cases which included a medical defence was fairly consistent, with the exception
of the 1720s when a large number of trials at the Old Bailey heard testimony
from midwives and surgeons who were unwilling to commit themselves to a
firm opinion, or from lay witnesses who confirmed a pre-existing disorder. This
phenomenon arose as a result of insufficient pre-trial preparation, and it is not
surprising that it diminished after 1730, when lawyers began to appear more
regularly in court. The growing sophistication of late Victorian police investigations helps to explain the rising proportion of insanity defences in relation to
all medical defences. Defendants who could afford to hire partisan expert witnesses were not numerous, and weaker cases had been removed by magistrates'
committal hearings designed to determine whether the evidence was sufficiently
strong to justify a trial.

Table 3.22 provides a count of instances in which an expert witness was
employed. These cases were identified in accordance with the definition established in the Introduction: expert witnesses were a unique class of witness whose
professional experience permitted them to testify to both fact and opinion.
Prison and asylum medical officers fulfilled this role in insanity trials, and their
increasing presence – largely in response to statutory initiatives such as the

Table 3.22 The presence of expert witnesses in criminal cases over time

Period	No. of Cases employing an Expert	Total No. of Cases	Proportion (%)
1699–1829	11	1,409	0.78
1830–1839	13	225	5.8
1830–1836	10	162	6.2
1837–1839	3	63	4.8
1840–1849	25	184	13.6
1850–1859	7	87	8.0
1860–1869	9	111	8.1
1870–1879	30	195	15.4
1880–1889	38	162	23.5
1890–1899	28	74	37.8
1900–1914	58	168	34.5
Total	219	2,615	8.4

Source: As for Table 3.1.

Prison Acts of 1865 and 1877, and the role adopted by the Director of Public Prosecutions – accounts for about half of all cases from the 1870s onward. Analytical chemists and toxicologists served as expert witnesses in trials for criminal poisoning, the 1840s being a notoriously poison-ridden decade:[176] 24, or 30 per cent, of the 80 poisoning homicides in the database occurred in the 1840s. This crime in particular stimulated a recognisable pattern in the development of the expertise needed to detect it: as new chemical tests were introduced and perfected, the number of men who had the skill to use them most effectively contracted, making forensic toxicology a much more restricted area of medico-legal practice than was required in other forms of homicide.[177] Other expert witnesses were drawn from the ranks of hospital consultants in pathology, surgery or obstetrics; professors of forensic medicine; the tiny group of Home Office Analysts, a role created in 1872, and the Home Office Pathologist, an appointment that originated when Professor Augustus J. Pepper (1849–1935) of St Mary's Hospital in London became consulting surgeon to the Treasury in the mid-1890s.[178] Access to men who had the requisite expertise was facilitated by the growing number of hospitals and medical schools in England, the location of which sometimes required magistrates to call upon experts from outside the county.[179] Birmingham, Liverpool and Manchester were particularly well situated for Cheshire and counties in the Oxford Circuit, but such consultations were on the whole quite rare. In fact, at just 219, the overall number of cases in which a recognised expert gave evidence is small enough to allow us to conclude that the majority of homicide cases were resolved without recourse to expert witnesses.

It is perhaps more instructive to consider the use of specialist tests, identified in Tables 3.23 and 3.24. Again, the absolute numbers are low, with the exception

Table 3.23 Specialist tests, by circuit

Circuit Test	Old Bailey	Great Sessions	North Wales	South Wales	Oxford	Chester	Total
Blood	11	1	8	11	17	–	48
Gun	3	–	–	1	–	–	4
Lung	54	13	35	19	66	4	191
Microscope	7	–	4	6	9	–	26
Poison	15	4	19	4	21	–	63
Other[1]	8	–	1	1	5	–	15
Total	98	18	67	42	118	4	347
Proportion (%)[2]	7.2	5.8	36.0	23.3	21.7	15.4	

Source: As for Table 3.1. Includes 305 cases in which a single test was used and 20 cases where two or more tests were used (see Table 3.24).

1 Includes soil analysis, experiments on animals and bones, weapons matched to wounds, fingerprint analysis (one case, 1908) and blood spatter analysis.
2 Total as a proportion of *all* cases. If the Old Bailey cases are considered only for the period after 1830, the proportion becomes 65/365 = 17.8%; for the Oxford Circuit, 109/447 = 24.4%.

Table 3.24 Use of multiple specialist tests, by circuit

Test \ Circuit	Old Bailey	North Wales	South Wales	Oxford	Total
Microscope & Blood	4	2	4	3	13
Microscope & Poison	–	1	1	–	2
Microscope, Poison & Lung[1]	–	–	1	–	1
Microscope, Blood & Other[2]	–	–	–	1	1
Microscope & Gun	1	–	–	–	1
Blood and Poison	1	–	–	–	1
Blood and Other	–	–	–	1	1
Total	6	3	6	5	20

Source: As for Table 3.1.

1 A case of infant murder in Pembrokeshire, 1895; the tests were carried out by a public analyst from Swansea.
2 A case of murder in Herefordshire, 1885; for more details, see Chapter 5.

of the hydrostatic lung test: this was used in 30 per cent of all cases of infant murder and concealment of birth between 1729 and 1914, its purpose being to help establish whether an infant had been born alive and then murdered. This test will be discussed at length in the next chapter, to reveal its central role in the development of medico-legal practice across England and Wales. Other tests, for blood and biological stains such as semen, ballistics and trace evidence identified under a microscope, will be discussed in Chapter 5, in relation to the emergence of forensic science. In this chapter, we are principally interested in what the statistics can tell us. As a proportion of all cases, the use of specialist tests was higher in Wales than elsewhere; but these tests were, in all regions, carried out mainly by local practitioners, not experts. Furthermore, when the lung test is isolated, the numbers suggest that with the exception of poisoning, few tests were used. When poisoning is in turn subtracted, differences between North and South Wales emerge, the former showing no evidence of the use of a microscope or test for blood before 1873 – a Cheshire case in which two Lancashire-based experts conducted tests for blood and trace evidence in the case of a murdered police officer.[180] In fact, 51 of the North Wales circuit cases (76 per cent) in which a forensic test was used occurred in Cheshire, the largest and most criminal county in the circuit; the six Welsh counties between them accounted for only 16 tests in total. In South Wales, Glamorgan dominated the figures, accounting for 22 of 42 instances, or 52.4 per cent; the occasional use of tests other than for poison and live birth began in the 1870s. On the Oxford Circuit, such testing occurred sporadically in the 1830s and 1840s, but more consistently from the 1870s onward. Remarkably, London does not appear predominant in the use of specialist tests, but rather the opposite. This is probably related to the fact that, as Table 3.14 shows, a large proportion of London cases involved the most uncomplicated modes of death, inflicted on victims in circumstances that were anything but mysterious.

Explaining patterns: crime, medicine and policing in 1881

As a means of concluding this chapter, Tables 3.25 and 3.26 present a snapshot of crime statistics and medical and police provision in 1881, providing an illustrative overview of the regions under study at the end of the nineteenth century. The year is representative of the demographic context within which medico-legal practice developed during the Victorian era, as the national population expanded and migration to towns swelled the number of city dwellers. By 1881, two thirds of the population of England and Wales was classified as urban, living in towns with populations of at least 3,000, and one third as rural. The English population was concentrated around London and the great towns of the Midlands and north, while the Victorian Welsh population lived mainly in the north-east and the valleys of the south; the rural mid and west areas were sparsely populated. These demographic changes necessitated what David Taylor identified as a "significant extension of police powers" in the second half of the century, accompanied by an increase in the number of policemen that outpaced the rate of growth in the overall population.[181]

The number of doctors also increased rapidly at this time: Anne Digby tabulated a steady upward trend amounting to a rise of 34 per cent. However, although their absolute numbers did not keep pace with the overall population, which soared per doctor from 1,028 to 1,539 over the period between 1851 and 1911,[182] there was an over-supply of trained doctors "in relation to effective demand for their services."[183] In order to make a living in the crowded medical marketplace, doctors tended to set up practice in towns, where they could attract the most patients; rural areas were comparatively poorly served.[184] Table 3.25 shows the differences in population, and numbers of police and doctors, in relation to the reported number of homicides in 1881. This suggests that the need for medico-legal testimony, and consequent development of medico-legal expertise, was regionally contingent: the largest number of detected homicides occurred in the counties where the most doctors and police officers were based: London, Cheshire, Glamorgan and Staffordshire. This outcome in turn explains the range of towns in which medico-legal cases were found to be most prominent (Table 3.4). Medico-legal practice was intimately bound up with the development of the medical and police professions.

National crime statistics for 1881 also help to demonstrate why medico-legal practice in England and Wales developed certain patterns of provision, including a general reliance on local GPs rather than specialists or experts, and a consistent focus on the crime of infant murder. Table 3.26 summarises the national homicide statistics derived from notifications to the police. Bearing in mind the usual provisos about unreported or unrecorded crime, the table shows three important points. Homicide was relatively uncommon, comprising 18.2 per cent of the total 2,879 offences against the person; the majority of cases were instances of

Table 3.25 Number of police, medical practitioners, and homicide indictments in 1881, in order of decreasing population

County	Population	Police	Medical Practitioners	Murder	Manslaughter	Concealment of Birth
Inner London & City	3,816,483	9,354	6,146	–	–	–
Middlesex	380,814	1,026	457	5	30	3
Staffordshire	1,006,758	755	476	3	11	2
Cheshire	622,365	594	407	4	8	1
Gloucestershire	525,167	594	438	0	4	2
Worcestershire	383,011	292	298	0	5	0
Shropshire	265,890	190	197	1	0	2
Berkshire	247,892	262	179	0	0	2
Oxfordshire	181,570	146	119	0	0	0
Herefordshire	118,147	106	94	0	0	0
WALES						
Glamorgan	518,383	444	276	3	10	2
Monmouthshire	234,332	196	121	0	3	0
Caernarfonshire	123,781	75	111	0	1	0
Denbighshire	112,940	84	84	0	0	0
Carmarthenshire	111,255	67	68	3	0	0
Cardiganshire	95,137	46	53	0	0	0
Pembrokeshire	83,679	85	47	0	1	2
Montgomeryshire	76,196	42	61	0	0	0
Merionethshire	68,278	39	62	0	0	1
Breconshire	54,140	41	36	0	2	0
Flintshire	45,774	27	23	0	0	0
Anglesey	35,141	19	26	0	0	0
Radnorshire	18,523	13	15	0	0	1
Total	9,125,656	14,497	9,794	19	75	18
National Total	25,974,439	32,508	21,172	61	224	67

Source: 1881 Census of England and Wales, Table 4: Area, Houses, and Population of Civil Parishes in the several Registration Sub-Districts in 1871 and 1881; and Table 10: Occupations of Males and Females in the Division and its Registration Counties;[185] *Judicial Statistics 1881, England and Wales* (London: HMSO, 1882), pp. 45–50.

Notes: Medical practitioners include physicians, surgeons, GPs, assistants and students. [186] Homicide figures are for the calendar year 1881 and so do not match those in Table 3.26 precisely. Figures for Middlesex include London: the Metropolitan Police District incorporated the entire county in 1840. On 1 January 1881 the total strength of the Metropolitan Police force was 10,893.[187]

Table 3.26 Murders reported by the police in England and Wales, 1880–1881

Offence	Counties	Boroughs	London	Total	Coroners' Returns
Murder: over 1 year	41	26	11	78	193
Murder: under 1 year	16	24	49	89	92, of which 43 in Middlesex
Manslaughter	77	80	94	251	168
Concealment of birth	67	14	25	106	N/A
Justifiable homicide					5
Total	201	144	179	524	458

Source: *Judicial Statistics 1881, England and Wales* (London: HMSO, 1882), pp. xiv, xxiii, 42.

infant murder and manslaughter arising from male-on-male fights or reck-less behaviour; and the largest proportion (34.2 per cent) of these homicides occurred in London. Police reports classified cases according to trial verdicts, and this explains the difference from inquest statistics: crimes indicted as murder resulted in conviction for concealment of birth or manslaughter,[188] whereas the concealment finding was not among those returned by coroners to the Home Office. The inquest statistics nonetheless identify the same national pattern: a significant proportion of all homicide victims, 11.9 per cent, were infants killed in Middlesex, which until 1889 included all of London for administrative purposes. The importance of London/Middlesex, Cheshire, Glamorgan and Staffordshire as dense areas of population, police, doctors and crime is evident.

Conclusion

This chapter has demonstrated the integral role played by medical practitioners in the investigation of homicide since the early eighteenth century, and identi-fied the various institutions that employed them. It has explained the nature of the forensic examinations they conducted, provided a numerical assessment of the frequency with which they did so, and shown how this increased over the course of the eighteenth century and, especially, following crucial changes in criminal procedure instituted in the 1830s and 1870s. Doctors were routinely called upon by the coroners, magistrates and police officers who investigated homicide, becoming part of a functional relationship clearly established as an essential, effective instrument of the criminal justice system. Local surgeons were the pivot on which this process balanced; but in larger cities or specialised cases involving allegations of insanity or poisoning, a group of experienced experts developed. As forensic practice and the sites associated with it became more institutionalised and formalised, away from public houses and back bedrooms to a closer association with hospitals, mortuaries and laboratories, the chang-ing perception of what appropriate forensic practices were contributed to the development of the modern adversarial trial. Medical witnesses were subjected to more penetrating questioning by prosecution and defence counsel, and judges worked harder to explain to jurors the importance of the medical testimony they heard. The value of forensic evidence cannot be underestimated: it could seal a defendant's fate or enable them to walk free.

The new findings presented here point to a pattern of professionalisation that developed over the course of two centuries. Stimulated by the practical requirements of forensic work and fostered by the knowledge exchanges that occurred during homicide investigations and criminal trials, medico-legal expertise operated within a network of increasingly specialised and sophisticated techniques and roles. Local GPs formed the largest group in this network, acting as de facto experts on the basis mainly of their qualifications and professional identity. A much smaller number of doctors took up multiple, specialist responsibilities: medical coroner; prison medical officer and expert on insanity; hospital consultant and toxicologist; police surgeon. As more searching questions were asked about crime and culpability, and more conclusive evidence was demanded in murder trials, the criminal justice system relied progressively more intently on the expertise provided by forensic practitioners who, in turn, honed their knowledge and skill through practical application. Women were excluded from this network during the eighteenth century, as male surgeons took over the role that midwives had held, and they were not readmitted until the twentieth century.[189] Those outside the medical profession were eased out of medico-legal decision-making, with one exception: the Victorian coroner's officer was usually a member of the other key group entrusted with the investigation of crime – the police.

During the course of the nineteenth century, the selection of the doctors who performed medico-legal examinations fell increasingly to the police: after 1856, when every county had a force, it was usually the first police officer at a scene who summoned a surgeon. Given financial considerations, it was logical to call upon surgeons who already had some public role, such as police surgeon, or who worked in a public institution, or who was personally known to the individual officer(s). Thus, while coroners and magistrates were successively displaced by the police as homicide investigators, the role played by surgeons increased in tandem with the growing authority of the police. There were regional differences, to be sure. Rural counties such as Oxfordshire and Herefordshire did not have much violent crime but supported large numbers of medical doctors, in contrast to even more rural Radnorshire, where very few doctors or policemen lived. By comparison, the small area bounded by the towns of Wolverhampton, Dudley, West Bromwich and Walsall in the Midlands was subject both to high levels of fatal violence (36 cases in these four towns alone) and intensive policing. Dudley, Walsall and Wolverhampton had police surgeons from the late 1860s if not earlier; in 1881 a police force of 135 men served Wolverhampton's population of just under 76,000 souls, in a more heavily policed society than existed in most counties (see Table 3.25 and Appendix 3). From the late 1820s to the early 1840s one of Wolverhampton's constables, Richard Diggory, investigated at least nine homicides and prosecuted six of the defendants. The town offers a particularly good example of the relevance of the history of policing to local medico-legal practice: following the creation of its town police force in 1837 (reformed in 1842), policing in Wolverhampton became so effective that more crime was brought to light.[190] In the case of violent crime, their role was linked to that of the medical profession: across England and Wales, people who came across the aftermath of a homicide wasted little time in fetching a policeman *and* a doctor.

The opportunity for doctors to develop medico-legal expertise existed to a greater extent in larger towns, particularly London, and within particular types of institutions, especially asylums, hospitals and prisons. After the 1830s, however, a uniformity of practice developed as Wales was integrated into the English assize system, medical practitioners were paid for their examinations and students were increasingly better trained in a process examined in Chapter 2. Cross-border consultations were surprisingly infrequent: permeability existed between England and Wales, and between the counties in both countries, but legal authorities tended to rely on local practitioners and experts located nearest the assize town where the trial was to be held. The exception to this occurred in the relatively rare instances of criminal poisoning, when a small number of experts were consulted on a national level.[191] Most homicide victims, however, were killed in far from inexplicable circumstances, and deaths from head injuries, stabbing and beating posed few forensic difficulties. What both chapters have pointed to, however, is the importance of infant murder and the hydrostatic lung test in forensic medicine and medico-legal practice. The former was both very frequent and subject to specific legal questions that posed particular forensic problems which the lung test was designed to address. These problems, and the forensic techniques adopted to solve them, will be examined in the following chapter.

Notes

1 Mark S. R. Jenner and Patrick Wallis, "The Medical Marketplace," in *Medicine and the Market in England and Its Colonies, c. 1450–1850*, ed. Mark S. R. Jenner and Patrick Wallis (Basingstoke: Palgrave, 2007), pp. 5–6.

2 J. Dixon Mann, *Forensic Medicine and Toxicology*, fourth edition (London: Charles Griffin, 1908), pp. 4–5.

3 Ibid., p. 4; Alfred S. Taylor also suggested this: *The Principles and Practice of Medical Jurisprudence* (London: John Churchill & Sons, 1865), p. xxxiii.

4 The term 'Home Office List' (of approved forensic pathologists) was introduced in 1944: Peter Hutton, "A Review of Forensic Pathology in England and Wales: Submitted to the Minister of State for Crime Prevention, March 2015," p. 18.

5 *OBP*, trial of Richard Coyle, ref. t17370224-1.

6 Table 3.2: 87.1% (1,191 of 1,368 trials).

7 Lance Bertelsen, "Committed by Justice Fielding: Judicial and Journalistic Representation in the Bow Street Magistrate's Office January 3–November 24, 1752," *Eighteenth-Century Studies* 30 (1997), pp. 337–363; Andrew T. Harris, *Policing the City: Crime and Legal Authority in London, 1780–1840* (Columbus: Ohio State University Press, 2004); J. M. Beattie, "Sir John Fielding and Public Justice: The Bow Street Magistrates' Court, 1754–1780," *Law and History Review* 25 (2007), pp. 61–100.

8 Peter King, "The Impact of Urbanization on Murder Rates and on the Geography of England and Wales, 1780–1850," *Historical Journal* 53 (2010), pp. 685–686.

9 David J. V. Jones, *Crime in Nineteenth-Century Wales* (Cardiff: University of Wales Press, 1992), pp. 69–73 notes that, not only was violent crime statistically most prevalent in Glamorgan and Monmouthshire, but it was strongly associated with urban areas.

10 Tim Hitchcock and Robert Shoemaker, "Making History Online: The Colin Matthews Lecture for the Public Understanding of History," *Transactions of the Royal Historical Society*, 6th series 25 (2015), p. 85.

11 Garthine Walker, "Rape, Acquittal and Culpability in Popular Crime Reports in England, c.1670–c.1750," *Past & Present* 220 (2013), pp. 115–142; Louise Jackson, *Child Sexual Abuse in Victorian England* (London and New York: Routledge, 2000), pp. 18–22.

12 Kim Stevenson, "'Most Intimate Violations': Contextualising the Crime of Rape," in *Histories of Crime: Britain 1600–2000*, ed. Anne-Marie Kilday and David Nash (Basingstoke: Palgrave, 2010), pp. 83–84.

13 On rape myths and their continuing significance, see Joanna Bourke, *Rape: A History from 1860 to the Present* (London: Virago Press, 2007), pp. 21–85.

14 Craig Spence, *Accidents and Violent Death in Early Modern London 1650–1750* (Woodbridge: The Boydell Press, 2016), pp. 42–62 discusses the urban response to sudden violent death. Vehicles were the sixth most common cause of accidental death in Spence's sample, but form the majority of the accident cases in my database.

15 The 34 cases were retrieved from National Library of Wales, Crime and Punishment, https://crimeandpunishment.library.wales/ (accessed 8 Jun 2019).

16 NLW GS 4/1015/8/2, Rex v. Robert Davies, Flintshire, 1806.

17 Cassie Watson, "Death's Gatekeepers: The Victorian Coroner's Officer," *Legal History Miscellany*, 30 July 2016, https://legalhistorymiscellany.com/2016/07/30/deaths-gatekeepers-the-victorian-coroners-officer/.

18 Olive Anderson, *Suicide in Victorian and Edwardian England* (Oxford: Clarendon Press, 1987), p. 27.

19 J. D. J. Havard, *The Detection of Secret Homicide: A Study of the Medico-Legal System of Investigation of Sudden and Unexplained Deaths* (London: Macmillan, 1960), pp. 38–65.

20 Pam Fisher, *An Object of Ambition? The Office and Role of the Coroner in Two Midland Counties, 1751–1888* (Leicester: Friends of the Centre for English Local History, 2003), p. 29.

21 Havard, *Detection of Secret Homicide*, pp. 141–143.

22 Oxfordshire History Centre [OHC], COR VIII/3: As to coroners summoning juries and witnesses etc. through medium of county police, 1857.

23 OHC, Coroner/City/1901 (Accl 1344), inquest on Joshua Fathers, 21 Jan 1901.

24 OHC, Coroner/City/1901 (Accl 1344), inquest on Frederick Henry Mobey, 18 Feb 1901.

25 The GWR was the Great Western Railway (company, 1833–1948). There was also a sketch of the scene and testimony from the train driver and various eyewitnesses. The cause of death, in modern terms, was 'multiple injuries', based upon the multiplicity of the injuries described. I thank Chris Milroy for this information.

26 Anderson, *Suicide*, pp. 257–259.

27 John H. Langbein, *The Origins of Adversary Criminal Trial* (Oxford: Oxford University Press, 2003), p. 333.

28 Allyson May, "Advocates and Truth-Seeking in the Old Bailey Courtroom," *Journal of Legal History* 26 (2005), p. 85.

29 Barbara Shapiro, "The Beyond Reasonable Doubt Doctrine: 'Moral Comfort' or Standard of Proof?" *Law and Humanities* 2 (2008), pp. 149–173.

30 Samuel Farr, *Elements of Medical Jurisprudence* (London: T. Becket, 1788), p. 77.

31 TNA ASSI 6/1/1, Rex v. John Hill, Staffordshire, 1827, testimony of Thomas Alban Maguire.

32 Keir Waddington, *An Introduction to the Social History of Medicine: Europe since 1500* (Basingstoke: Palgrave, 2011), pp. 110–115.

33 The textbooks by Male, Smith and Taylor are cited in the Bibliography; electronic copies were searched for the term 'post-mortem'. For Cummin, see *London Medical Gazette*, 19 (1836–37), p. 4; in the Act, see section 1.

34 *OBP*, trial of Edmond Tooll and Brian Sullivan, ref. t17000115-19.
35 Medical Witnesses Act 1836; Coroners Act 1887; Dixon Mann, *Forensic Medicine and Toxicology*, fourth edition, pp. 3–4.
36 *OBP*, trial of Morris Loufer and Samuel Loufer, ref. t19130304-48.
37 Compiled from *The Medical Register for the Year 1783* (London: Joseph Johnson, 1783), pp. 124–126. The names of practitioners identified during the course of this project have been added.
38 *The Medical Register for the Year 1783*, pp. 55–56. In 1780 the population of Wales was approximately 530,000 including Monmouthshire (where there were an additional 23 medical practitioners); in Cheshire it was about 170,000.
39 Anne Digby, *Making a Medical Living: Doctors and Patients in the English Market for Medicine, 1720–1911* (Cambridge: Cambridge University Press, 1994), pp. 13–14. The population in 1760 was about 750,000; when the first modern census was taken in 1801, it was 1,096,784 in greater London.
40 Joan Lane, "The Medical Practitioners of Provincial England in 1783," *Medical History* 28 (1984), pp. 354, 370; Joan Lane, "A Provincial Surgeon and His Obstetric Practice: Thomas W. Jones of Henley-in-Arden, 1764–1846," *Medical History* 31 (1987), p. 335; Digby, *Making a Medical Living*, p. 21.
41 The New Poor Law allowed for the treatment and care of emergency cases, and casualty wards were established in public hospitals and workhouse infirmaries. On ambulances in Victorian London, see Matthew L. Newsom Kerr, "'Perambulating Fever Nests of Our London Streets': Cabs, Omnibuses, Ambulances, and Other 'Pest-Vehicles' in the Victorian Metropolis," *Journal of British Studies* 49 (2010), pp. 283–310.
42 "Death of Dr Paine," *Western Mail*, 16 Jan 1894, p. 6.
43 TNA ASSI 72/9, Regina v. Gaetano Cuirollo and Petro Gustra, 1869 and ASSI 72/39/2, Rex v. Hugh MacLaren, 1913 (both Glamorgan).
44 James Sharpe and J. R. Dickinson, "Homicide in Eighteenth-Century Cheshire," *Social History* 41 (2016), pp. 192–209.
45 James Sharpe and J. R. Dickinson, "Coroners' Inquests in an English county, 1600–1800: A Preliminary Survey," *Northern History* 48 (2011), p. 267.
46 John Walliss, "Wales and the 'Bloody Code': The Courts of Great Sessions, 1805–30," *Welsh History Review* 27 (2014), p. 40.
47 John Walliss, "Crime and Justice in Georgian Cheshire: The Chester Court of Great Sessions, 1760–1830," *Journal on European History of Law* 6 (2015), pp. 45, 48–49. The figures provided are as follows: concealment of birth (4 guilty, 2 no bill), manslaughter (75 guilty, 14 no bill), murder (18 guilty, 4 no bill); out of 200 indictments, there were 68 acquittals and one case was not prosecuted. Seven cases each of murder and manslaughter were discharged in other ways, e.g. by proclamation (released without trial or verdict).
48 John H. Langbein, "Shaping the Eighteenth-Century Criminal Trial: A View from the Ryder Sources," *University of Chicago Law Review* 50 (1983), p. 81.
49 Philip Aylett, "A Profession in the Marketplace: The Distribution of Attorneys in England and Wales 1730–1800," *Law and History Review* 5 (1987), pp. 1–30.
50 W. Llewelyn Williams, "The King's Court of Great Sessions in Wales," *Y Cymmrodor* 26 (1916), pp. 38–47.
51 Daniel Duman, *The Judicial Bench in England 1727–1875: The Reshaping of a Professional Elite* (London: Royal Historical Society, 1982), pp. 8–13, 22–25; W. Cornish et al., *The Oxford History of the Laws of England, Vol. 11, The Legal System 1820–1914* (Oxford: Oxford University Press, 2010), pp. 1030–1031, 1041–1043, 1047–1050.
52 Publishing History of the Proceedings, www.oldbaileyonline.org/static/Publishinghistory.jsp (accessed 8 Jun 2019).
53 "The Value of the Proceedings as a Historical Source," www.oldbaileyonline.org/static/Value.jsp (accessed 13 Jun 2019).
54 *Berrow's Worcester Journal*, 27 Jul 1872, p. 7, testimony of James Fisher. See also ASSI 6/13, Regina v. Felix Beasley, Worcestershire, 1872, testimony of James Fisher and Thomas Frederic Higgs (police surgeon).

55 I can find no reference to this advice in Taylor's textbooks, but it is explicit in the works of C. M. Tidy (1882, Vol. 1, p. 4) and Dixon Mann (1893, p. 20).

56 R. Henslowe Wellington, *The King's Coroner Being the Practice and Procedure in His Judicial and Ministerial Capacities*, Vol. 2 (London: Baillière, Tindall and Cox, 1906), p. 25.

57 Robert B. Shoemaker, *The London Mob:Violence and Disorder in Eighteenth-Century England* (London: Hambledon and London, 2004), pp. 168–176; quotation on p. 168.

58 *Western Mail*, 29 Dec 1943, p. 3.

59 TNA ASSI 72/30, Rex v. David Edwards, Glamorgan, 1904.

60 Joan Lane, "A Provincial Surgeon," pp. 337–338.

61 *OBP*, trial of Julia Eliza Scales, ref. t18440506-1386.

62 Ibid.

63 Royal College of Surgeons, *Plarr's Lives of the Fellows*: Ross, Daniel (1812–1877), ref. RCS: E003151.

64 Anne Digby, *The Evolution of British General Practice 1850–1948* (Oxford: Oxford University Press, 1999), pp. 259–275 on the diversification of appointments to supplement fee income in a competitive medical market.

65 Eighteenth-century workhouse MOs took on forensic cases: Archdall Harris, surgeon to St Margaret's workhouse, testified in 13 inquests; in 1790 he was paid 1 guinea to attend and open a body. See Kevin Siena, "Contagion, Exclusion, and the Unique Medical World of the Eighteenth-Century Workhouse: London Infirmaries in Their Widest Relief," in *Medicine and the Workhouse*, ed. Jonathan Reinarz and Leonard Schwarz (Rochester and Woodbridge: University of Rochester Press, 2013), pp. 31–33.

66 David R. Green, *Pauper Capital: London and the Poor Law, 1790–1870* (Farnham: Ashgate, 2010), p. 63.

67 Megan Evans and Peter Jones, "'A Stubborn, Intractable Body': Resistance to the Workhouse in Wales, 1834–1877," *Family & Community History* 17 (2014), p. 109.

68 Ibid., p. 103.

69 Digby, *Making a Medical Living*, pp. 12–13; this figure includes Oxford and Cambridge.

70 Katherine D. Watson, "Medical and Chemical Expertise in English Trials for Criminal Poisoning, 1750–1914," *Medical History* 50 (2006), p. 386.

71 Ian Burney and Neil Pemberton, *Murder and the Making of English CSI* (Baltimore: Johns Hopkins University Press, 2016), pp. 136–139.

72 M. A. Crowther and Brenda M. White, "Medicine, Property and the Law in Britain 1800–1914," *The Historical Journal* 31 (1988), p. 856.

73 *OBP*, trial of Sarah Malcolm, ref. t17330221-52, testimony of Thomas Bigg.

74 Pam Fisher, "Houses for the Dead: The Provision of Mortuaries in London, 1843–1889," *The London Journal* 34 (2009), p. 11.

75 Ian A. Burney, *Bodies of Evidence: Medicine and the Politics of the English Inquest, 1830–1926* (Baltimore: The Johns Hopkins University Press, 2000), p. 176 n.19.

76 Yvonne Bradshaw, Stephen P. Savage, Graham Moon and Kathleen Kelly, "A Different Sort of Doctor: The Police Surgeon in England and Wales," *Social Policy & Administration* 29 (1995), p. 122.

77 R. D. Summers, "History of the Police Surgeon," *The Practitioner* 221 (1978), p. 387 claimed they were a "fundamental and indispensable part of any police team in cases where forensic medicine is involved." But just three decades later they seemed to be largely a thing of the past as 31 out of 39 police forces no longer had police surgeons: Martin Ernest Barrett, "Historical Development and Contemporary Dilemmas of a Police Surgeon," LL.M. thesis, University of Central Lancashire, 2012, p. 104. The position is still important in London, but changes imposed by the Police and Criminal Evidence Act 1984 caused costs to spiral; the part-time nature of the work, lack of training and poor facilities were notable problems: Michael Knight, "Changes to the Police Surgeon Service in Recent Years," *Medico-Legal Journal* 70 (2002), pp. 95–107.

78 Bradshaw et al., "A Different Sort of Doctor," pp. 132–133.

79 Jennifer Ward, "Origins and Development of Forensic Medicine and Forensic Science in England 1823–1946," PhD thesis, Open University, 1993, p. 70; her focus is mostly on the largest group, based in London.

80 Ralph D. Summers, *History of the Police Surgeon* (London: Association of Police Surgeons of Great Britain, 1988), pp. 8–9. I would like to thank Fraser Joyce for sharing a copy of this hard-to-find publication with me.

81 The following are some early references to police surgeons or the decision to appoint one: *The Norfolk Chronicle and Norwich Gazette*, 22 Sep 1838, p. 2 (Norwich); *The Warwick and Warwickshire Advertiser*, 4 Apr 1840, p. 1 (Birmingham); *The Bolton Chronicle*, 29 Aug 1840, p. 4 (Manchester); *The Bolton Chronicle*, 18 Dec 1841, p. 3 (Bolton); *The Liverpool Mail*, 6 Jan 1844, p. 5 (Birkenhead).

82 Summers, *History of the Police Surgeon*, p. 1.

83 David J. Cox, *A Certain Share of Low Cunning: A History of the Bow Street Runners, 1792–1839* (Abingdon: Routledge, 2010), pp. 36–38; J. M. Beattie, *The First English Detectives: The Bow Street Runners and the Policing of London, 1750–1840* (Oxford: Oxford University Press, 2012), pp. 176–177.

84 "Sir John W. Fisher, FRCSE," *BMJ*, 1 Apr 1876, p. 429; TNA HO 45/1896: Police: Chief surgeon, increase of salary, 1847–1848, petition from J. W. Fisher to Sir George Grey, 25 Jan 1847; G. C. Boase, "Fisher, Sir John William (1788–1876), Surgeon," *Oxford Dictionary of National Biography*, 23 Sep 2004, https://doi-org.oxfordbrookes.idm.oclc.org/10.1093/ref:odnb/9502 (accessed 31 Dec 2017).

85 HO 45/1896, petition from Fisher to Grey, 1847. Summers, *History of the Police Surgeon*, p. 3 queried the terms chief surgeon and divisional surgeon: "one would have thought Physicians would have been more appropriate"; see p. 2 for the date of appointment.

86 R. D. Summers, "History of the Police Surgeon," *The Practitioner* 221 (1978), p. 384.

87 TNA MEPO 2/321: Medical: Divisional Surgeons Salaries, 1893–1895, Memo on divisional surgeons' salaries, n.d. but probably April 1894. There were 64 divisional surgeons in 1851, see TNA HO 45/4320: Police: Salary of surgeon in chief raised from £600 to £800, letter from J. W. Fisher to Sir George Grey, 22 Dec 1851. The cost in 1892–1893 amounted to £4521 12s.

88 MEPO 2/321, Letter from Sir Edward Bradford to the Home Secretary, 10 Aug 1893.

89 Ibid.

90 Graham Grant, *The Diary of a Police Surgeon* (London: C. Arthur Pearson Ltd., 1920), pp. 13–14.

91 *OBP*, trial of Conrad Donovan and Charles Wade, ref. t19041114-47.

92 Summers, *History of the Police Surgeon*, p. 3.

93 East Sussex Record Office, dhbe/DH/B/136/966: letter from John Underwood to Robert Growse, town clerk, 8 Apr 1861, https://discovery.nationalarchives.gov.uk/browse/r/h/A13532331.

94 *Liverpool Daily Post*, 14 Oct 1863, p. 7.

95 *Sheffield Daily Telegraph*, 7 Nov 1863, p. 4.

96 *Manchester Evening News*, 27 Feb 1872, p. 1.

97 *Wigan Observer and District Advertiser*, 9 Sep 1870, p. 4.

98 *Manchester Courier and Lancashire General Advertiser*, 22 Jan 1887, p. 2.

99 *The Birmingham Daily Post*, 18 Jun 1862, p. 3.

100 *The Hull Packet*, 23 Nov 1860, p. 6; *The Medical Register for 1859* (London: General Medical Council, 1859), p. 40.

101 TNA ASSI 65/10, Regina v. Cadwalader Jones, Merionethshire, 1877.

102 Gwynedd Archives, Meirionnydd Record Office, ZQS/H1878/86: letter signed by Edward Jones MD and A. (sic) Lloyd Williams, 29 Dec 1877, https://discovery.nationalarchives.gov.uk/details/r/a4bf796a-db12-45a1-82be-d47c92c4ccd8.

103 J. F. Clarke, *Autobiographical Recollections of the Medical Profession* (London: J. & A. Churchill, 1874), pp. 101–102.

104 For example: an inquest reported in the *Berkshire Chronicle*, 25 May 1833, p. 4; and the trial of Sarah Drew for attempted newborn child murder, *Public Ledger and Daily Advertiser*, 9 Jul 1832, p. 3. She was acquitted, but the details of this case were not reported in the *Proceedings of the Old Bailey*, see ref. t18320705-107.

105 *Liverpool Mercury*, 23 Dec 1885, p. 6; *The Liverpool Mail*, 10 Feb 1844, p. 3; TNA MH 13/267/182, folios, pp. 370–372, letter from Matthew Jennette to The General Board of Health, 22 Jun 1849.

106 TNA ASSI 65/8, Regina v. Robert Moore, Cheshire, 1872. This disgrace to the uniform was convicted and sentenced to 20 years.

107 He was a Licentiate of Apothecaries' Hall in Dublin 1828 and MRCS 1829.

108 TNA MEPO 2/229: Metropolitan Police: Divisional Surgeons: Post-mortem examinations fees 1889–1900, executive branch memo 8 Feb 1890. Exceptionally, in V Division the divisional surgeon generally attended in addition to any other surgeon. This might explain why Dr James Adams was so frustrated with the police, as described in Chapter 5.

109 TNA ASSI 6/13, Regina v. Felix Beasley, testimony of Sarah Jones at the committal hearing, Dudley, 10 Apr 1872.

110 MEPO 2/229, post-mortem on bodies of James and Emma Riley and attending inquest by Dr Miller, King's Cross, July 1896. Miller was paid 3 guineas; examining the bodies in situ took 45 minutes each.

111 TNA ASSI 6/49/4, Rex v. William Buckler, Staffordshire, 1914: Dr Harry Shore, MOH and police surgeon for the borough of Walsall, was present at the post-mortem, was not called as a witness at the inquest, but did testify at the committal hearing.

112 See, for example, TNA ASSI 6/13, Regina v. Ellen Gardner, Staffordshire, 1871. The depositions do not mention that John Henry Love was surgeon to the county police at Tettenhall, but a newspaper report did: *Nottingham Journal*, 3 Jan 1872, p. 8.

113 To the works of Burney, Butler, Fisher and Lockwood cited in the Introduction, and Spence cited in n.14 earlier, I would add the series of articles and pamphlets by the late Gordon Glasgow, e.g. G. H. H. Glasgow, "The Election of County Coroners in England and Wales circa 1800–1888," *Legal History* 20 (1999), pp. 75–108.

114 Gordon H. H. Glasgow, "The Campaign for Medical Coroners in Nineteenth-Century England and Its Aftermath: A Lancashire Focus on Failure (Part I) (published in two parts)," *Mortality* 9 (2004), pp. 150–167; Gordon H. H. Glasgow, "The Campaign for Medical Coroners in Nineteenth-Century England and Its Aftermath: A Lancashire Focus on Failure, Part II," *Mortality* 9 (2004), pp. 223–234; Pamela Jane Fisher, "The Politics of Sudden Death: The Office and Role of the Coroner in England and Wales, 1726–1888," PhD thesis, University of Leicester, 2007, chapters 4 and 7.

115 R. F. Hunnisett, ed., *Wiltshire Coroners' Bills 1752–1796* (Devizes: Wiltshire Record Society, 1981), pp. xlvii–li (quotation on p. li); R. F. Hunnisett, "The Importance of Eighteenth-Century Coroners' Bills," in *Law, Litigants and the Legal Profession*, ed. E. W. Ives and A. H. Manchester (London: Royal Historical Society, 1983), p. 131.

116 Fisher, "Politics of Sudden Death," pp. 100–107.

117 Pamela Fisher, "Edmund Whitcombe and the Detection of Homicide in Georgian Shropshire," *Family & Community History* 14 (2011), p. 15.

118 Ibid.; see also Edward Umfreville, *Lex Coronatoria: Or, the Office and Duty of Coroners*, Vol. 2 (London: R. Griffiths and T. Becket, 1761), p. 295: "If the Inquiry be of the Death of one Man by another, and it be doubtful, whether the Wound be mortal or not, you ought to have a Surgeon, to be present and attend with you, to examine and shew the Wound; and who should likewise attend the Coroner and give his Evidence upon Oath."

119 Fisher, "Politics of Sudden Death," pp. 101–102.

120 NLW GS 4/533/3, Rex v. Mary Morgan, Radnorshire, 1805; Patricia Parris, "Mary Morgan: Contemporary Sources," *The Radnorshire Society Transactions* 53 (1983), p. 58.

121 Anne-Marie Kilday, *A History of Infanticide in Britain c. 1600 to the Present* (Basingstoke: Palgrave Macmillan, 2013), p. 126.

122 NLW GS 4/280/2, Rex v. Mary Williams, Carnarvonshire, 1817.

123 NLW GS 4/280/2, Rex v. Griffith Roberts, Carnarvonshire, 1816.

124 *Bristol Mercury*, 25 Aug 1823, p. 2.

125 NLW GS 4/1019/1, Rex v. John Evison and Benjamin Hiles, Flintshire, 1816. Parry was elected in January 1816 and the murder took place in April.

126 TNA ASSI 6/1/3, Rex v. Esther Gardner, Gloucestershire, 1814.

127 NLW GS 4/397/4, Rex v. John Evans, Breconshire, 1825.

128 TNA ASSI 6/2, Rex v. Martha Llewellin, Monmouthshire, 1834.

129 *Hereford Journal*, 9 Jan 1861, p. 5.

130 TNA ASSI 6/11, Regina v. Rosanna Hammonds, Gloucestershire, 1867; *Gloucestershire Chronicle*, 25 May 1867, p. 5. He lived at Blakeney: *Gloucester Journal*, 21 Dec 1867, p. 8.

131 *Bradford Observer*, 5 Jul 1877, p. 8.

132 *Bristol Mercury*, 15 Oct 1878, p. 3.

133 Wellington, *The King's Coroner*, p. 67.

134 Fisher, "Politics of Sudden Death," p. 100.

135 Glasgow, "Election of County Coroners," p. 78.

136 Glasgow, "Campaign for Medical Coroners, Part II," p. 227.

137 *The Universal British Directory of Trade, Commerce and Manufacture*, Vol. 5 (London: The Patentees, 1793–1798), p. 163. This was William Rees, apothecary, probably the William Rice identified as a surgeon in 1810: NLW GS 4/534/1, Rex v. David Roberts, Radnorshire, 1810; the killing occurred at Llanddewi Ystradenni, about 11 miles from Rhayader (which is 28 miles from Glasbury, versus the 20–21 miles' distance between Presteigne and Glasbury). The county was just as poorly populated with doctors in 1881: see Table 3.25.

138 Adrian Wilson, "Midwifery in the 'Medical Marketplace'," in *Medicine and the Market in England and Its Colonies, c. 1450–1850*, ed. Mark S. R. Jenner and Patrick Wallis (Basingstoke: Palgrave, 2007), pp. 166–168.

139 *OBP*, trial of Ann Hasle, ref. t17170717-18.

140 Julia Rudolph, "Gender and the Development of Forensic Science: A Case Study," *English Historical Review* 123 (2008), pp. 945–946.

141 NLW GS 4/59/7, Rex v. Stephen Tailor, Denbighshire, 1781.

142 NLW GS 4/302/2, Rex v. Robert Roberts, Merionethshire, 1773.

143 Robert Woods and Chris Galley, *Mrs Stone & Dr Smellie: Eighteenth-Century Midwives and their Patients* (Liverpool: Liverpool University Press, 2014), pp. 93–98.

144 Mark Jackson, *New-Born Child Murder: Women, Illegitimacy and the Courts in Eighteenth-Century England* (Manchester: Manchester University Press, 1996), pp. 70–72; David Harley, "The Scope of Legal Medicine in Lancashire and Cheshire, 1660–1760," in *Legal Medicine in History*, ed. Michael Clark and Catherine Crawford (Cambridge: Cambridge University Press, 1994), pp. 53–55; J. R. Dickinson and J. A. Sharpe, "Infanticide in Early Modern England: The Court of Great Sessions at Chester, 1650–1800," in *Infanticide: Historical Perspectives on Child Murder and Concealment, 1550–2000*, ed. Mark Jackson (Aldershot: Ashgate, 2002), pp. 45–47.

145 *OBP*, trial of Catherine Weeks, ref. t18330704-33.

146 Digby, *Making a Medical Living*, pp. 12, 20.

147 NLW GS 4/299/4/46, Rex v. Lewis Bellis and William Bellis, Merionethshire, 1751.

148 NLW GS 4/179/4, Rex v. David Nicholas, Montgomeryshire, 1737.

149 This cottage hospital for the sick poor opened in June 1887, and included a mortuary: *The Birmingham Daily Post*, 21 Jun 1887, p. 4.

150 *The Aberdeen Daily Journal*, 25 Apr 1906, p. 7.

151 TNA ASSI 6/43/2, Rex v. Emma Lucas, Staffordshire, 1907; *The Medical Register for 1907* (London: General Medical Council, 1907), p. 632, lists her address as St Andrew's Rectory, Canterbury (probably her father's home).

152 TNA ASSI 6/43/2, Rex v. Lucas, report of Dr P. R. Mander.

153 *The Lakes Chronicle*, 11 Mar 1908, p. 7.

154 *The Staffordshire Sentinel*, 27 Feb 1912, p. 2 and 19 Apr 1912, p. 5.

155 Current medical opinion considers the five classic signs of asphyxial death too non-specific to be useful, but the term itself was generally used to denote interference with respiration: see Christopher M. Milroy, "A Brief History of 'Asphyxia'," *Academic Forensic Pathology International* 5 (2015), pp. 254–265.

156 R. J. Kellett, "Infanticide and Child Destruction: The Historical, Legal and Pathological Aspects," *Forensic Science International* 53 (1992), p. 16.

157 TNA ASSI 6/37/1, Rex v. Samuel Middleton, Worcestershire, 1902, testimony of Edward Mathews; *Manchester Courier and Lancashire General Advertiser*, 25 Jun 1902, p. 9.

158 J. Dixon Mann, *Forensic Medicine and Toxicology*, third edition (London: Charles Griffin, 1902), pp. 265–267.

159 *OBP*, trial of John Senor, ref. t17410828-63.

160 TNA ASSI 6/16, Regina v. Joseph Harris, Worcestershire, 1878, testimony of George Peat Dunn, 15 Feb 1878.

161 Farr, *Elements of Medical Jurisprudence*, pp. 98–99; Dixon Mann, *Forensic Medicine and Toxicology*, third edition, p. 32.

162 *OBP*, trial of Edward Johnson, Nicholas Williams, Lawrence Senett, Nicholas Wolf, Pierce Butler and John Bryan, ref. t17370224-2.

163 *OBP*, trial of G. H., ref. t17540227-51.

164 Joel Peter Eigen, *Mad-Doctors in the Dock: Defending the Diagnosis, 1760–1913* (Baltimore: Johns Hopkins University Press, 2016), pp. 174–178.

165 Tony Ward, "Law, Common Sense and the Authority of Science: Expert Witnesses and Criminal Insanity in England, ca. 1840–1940," *Social & Legal Studies* 6 (1997), pp. 344, 352–353.

166 Joel Peter Eigen, "Diagnosing Homicidal Mania: Forensic Psychiatry and the Purposeless Murder," *Medical History* 54 (2010), pp. 433–456.

167 Ward, "Law, Common Sense," p. 349; David Bentley, *English Criminal Justice in the Nineteenth Century* (London: Hambledon Press, 1998), pp. 86–87; House of Commons Debates, 17 Mar 1884, vol. 286 cols. 40–41, http://hansard.millbanksystems.com/commons/1884/mar/17/law-and-justice-the-director-of-public (accessed 17 Aug 2017).

168 Ward, "Law, Common Sense," p. 351.

169 Eigen, *Mad-Doctors in the Dock*, pp. 89–92; Eigen, "Diagnosing Homicidal Mania," pp. 449–451.

170 NLW GS 4/280/2, Rex v. Griffith Roberts, Carnarvonshire, 1816, bill of costs.

171 Pamela Michael, *Care and Treatment of the Mentally Ill in North Wales, 1800–2000* (Cardiff: University of Wales Press, 2003), pp. 2–5.

172 TNA ASSI 65/6: Regina v. Robert Jones, Carnarvonshire, 1861 (the Denbigh Asylum MO testified); Regina v. Grace Evans, Denbighshire, 1860 and Regina v. Sarah Edwards, Flintshire, 1861 (local doctors testified).

173 TNA ASSI 6/2, Rex v. Thomas Hart, Staffordshire, 1832.

174 *OBP*, trial of Sampson Thomas, ref. t17870912-91.

175 *OBP*, trial of William Allam, ref. t17680907-40.

176 Victoria M. Nagy, "Narratives in the Courtroom: Female Poisoners in Mid-Nineteenth Century England," *European Journal of Criminology* 11 (2014), pp. 214–215; Katherine D. Watson, "Criminal Poisoning in England and the Origins of the Marsh Test for Arsenic," in *Chemistry, Medicine and Crime: Mateu J.B. Orfila (1787–1853) and His Times*, ed. José Ramón Bertomeu-Sánchez and Agustí Nieto-Galan (Sagamore Beach, MA: Science History Publications, 2006), pp. 186–188.

177 Watson, "Medical and Chemical Expertise."

178 Pepper first undertook forensic autopsies at the request of the coroner Dr G. Danford Thomas: Royal College of Surgeons, *Plarr's Lives of the Fellows*: Pepper, Augustus Joseph (1849–1935), ref. RCS: E004458. I can find no formal record of his appointment as consultant to the Treasury, but in February 1895 he was sent by the Treasury to examine a defendant (*The Huddersfield Daily Chronicle*, 14 Feb 1895, p. 4) and in December 1896

he was identified as a consulting surgeon to the Treasury (*The Dover Express*, 11 Dec 1896, p. 8).

179 For example, in 1876 surgeons in North Wales sent a liver to the resident surgeon of the Liverpool Royal Infirmary: TNA ASSI 65/10, Regina v. Robert Jones, Flintshire, 1876.

180 TNA ASSI 65/9, Regina v. James Buckley, Cheshire, 1873. The experts were William Crawford Williamson, Professor of Natural History at Owen's College, Manchester and Prof. James Campbell Brown of the Liverpool Medical School. The defendant was acquitted and no other suspect was ever identified.

181 David Taylor, *Crime, Policing and Punishment in England, 1750–1914* (Basingstoke: Macmillan, 1998), p. 88. For a good account of the development of professional policing in the second half of the nineteenth century, see pp. 88–105.

182 Digby, *Making a Medical Living*, p. 15.

183 Digby, *Evolution of British General Practice*, p. 23.

184 Ibid., p. 28.

185 Census data retrieved from www.visionofbritain.org.uk/census/table/EW1881AGE_M10 and www.visionofbritain.org.uk/census/table/EW1881POP2_M4?u_id=10061325&show=DB&min_c=1&max_c=13 (accessed 26 Aug 2018).

186 The national total when students and assistants are excluded is 15,116.

187 *Accounts of Receipt and Expenditure of Metropolitan Police, 1880–81*, p. 17. The discrepancy of some 500 officers is explained by the fact that some parts of the Metropolitan Police District were in other counties (Essex, Kent, Surrey and Hertfordshire).

188 *Judicial Statistics 1881, England and Wales* (London: HMSO, 1882), p. xxiii. The number of murders reported by the police was 167 for the year ending 29 Sep 1881. The coroners' returns were for the year ending 31 Dec 1881.

189 The first female police surgeon in Britain was appointed in 1927: K. D. Watson, "Wells [née Perry], Nesta Helen (1892–1986), Physician and Police Surgeon," *Oxford Dictionary of National Biography*, 23 Sep 2004, https://doi-org.oxfordbrookes.idm.oclc.org/10.1093/ref:odnb/58141 (accessed 12 Jul 2019).

190 Roger Swift, "The English Urban Magistracy and the Administration of Justice during the Early Nineteenth Century: Wolverhampton 1815–1860," *Midland History* 17 (1992), pp. 83, 86.

191 Watson, "Medical and Chemical Expertise."

4 Infant murder in medico-legal practice

When called upon in a case of this kind, [a medical man] should make the following inquiries: . . . Was the child abandoned to the cold, famished, or suffocated? Was linen prepared for its reception? Was the labour difficult? Did the foetus reach its full time? Is it perfect? Are there any bruises, punctures, or marks of violence visible on the body of the child? Was there any unusual flooding? In what state is the mother? Was the cord tied on the part of the child? Was the ligature made before or after its death? Does the blood discovered come from the mother, or the child? Are there any swellings or stoppages in the throat or trachea? Has the child died of convulsions, or any other disease? Was the child born alive? Did it ever breathe? Was it capable of living when born? How long did it live after birth? What were the causes of its death? Did they occur before or after birth, or during delivery? Was the placenta healthy?

George Edward Male, *An Epitome of Juridical or Forensic Medicine*
(London: T. and G. Underwood, 1816), pp. 93–94

There is a large and international historiography on the crime generally known as infanticide, the murder of an infant, but academic curiosity has tended to focus on the socio-legal and gendered facets of this distinctive crime and few historians have addressed its forensic aspects in much detail. Those who have done so have identified two principal areas of medico-legal interest: the mental health of the accused killer, who was usually the victim's mother,[1] and the medical difficulty of establishing the time and manner of death in newborns,[2] considered a key factor in the declining rates of conviction observed after the middle of the eighteenth century.[3] In fact, scholarship on this subject actually encompasses two separate groups of victims, based on age and the context in which the crime took place, and this distinction is crucial to understanding the forensic investigation of this type of murder. Although previous chapters employed the term 'infanticide', which historians tend to use in reference to the murder of an infant at birth, its legal meaning was established only in 1938 by the Infanticide Act, which defined a form of manslaughter committed by mothers who killed their own child aged up to one year. As Mark Jackson has pointed out, the more accurate contemporary phrase in the eighteenth century was 'newborn child murder', neonaticide in modern parlance; such cases were of particular forensic interest because they "raised a substantially different set of legal, medical and social issues from those raised by the suspicious death of older children."[4] This was due to the effects of an earlier statute: the Act to prevent the Destroying and Murthering of Bastard Children of 1624 created a new capital offence – what historians now call newborn child murder – aimed squarely at single women. Its draconian provisions reversed the normal evidential standards required in a criminal trial by introducing "a presumption of murder in cases in which an unmarried mother gave birth in secret and the baby was later found dead, even though the infant might have been stillborn or died of natural causes."[5] This established a need for medical testimony, as some judges and jurors sought proof that an infant had been born alive and then deliberately killed, and the inclusion of this kind of proof became conventional practice in English trials for newborn child murder by the 1760s.[6] Both the trials of married mothers and for the murder of older infants took place under the normal common law expectation that the prosecution must prove that the accused killed the victim purposefully, to which a defendant could plead in mitigation insanity or lack of intent, or simply deny any role in the death. For this second group of infant victims, the medical question of live birth was irrelevant and the cause of death was often obvious.

The legal position in England and Wales changed in 1803 with the repeal and replacement of the harsh Jacobean statute by Lord Ellenborough's Act. Although the new law still singled out unmarried women who gave birth in secret, it placed their trials for infant murder on the same legal footing as other murder trials: the prosecution had to prove the murder, not just the secret birth. Moreover, a defendant acquitted of murder could be convicted of concealing the birth of her child, even one that had been stillborn, finally giving jurors an acceptable alternative to the death penalty: the maximum sentence was two years' imprisonment. This provision was extended to married women by the Offences Against the Person Act of 1828, which rendered it unnecessary to prove whether the child died before, at, or after its birth and had the intended effect of encouraging more convictions. Nineteenth-century criminal statistics indicate that prosecutions and convictions for concealment of birth began to rise,[7] as juries reached this verdict even in the face of what appeared to be persuasive evidence of murder. In this new legal landscape the importance of medical evidence expanded: doctors were now required to confirm live birth and deliberate murder, both of which were issues that a woman's mental state might affect if the former led to a special kind of temporary insanity and so caused the latter. Significantly for medico-legal practice, these medical questions were complicated by a key legal condition: in order for a murder to occur, a newborn victim had to have a wholly separate existence from the mother. In other words, no murder could exist in law, unless the infant's body had been expelled fully from the birth canal and had independent circulation,[8] and unless the child had breathed on its own before being killed, although the placenta and umbilical cord might still be attached to the mother.[9] Daniel Grey has revealed what fertile ground this provided for defence barristers looking for a chink in the prosecution's armour, a challenge that doctors sought to meet by successive refinements of tests for live birth and independent respiration, principally the hydrostatic lung test.[10] But this was not the only manner in which doctors contributed to the investigation of newborn child murder, and textbooks of forensic medicine, such as that by Dr George Edward Male, suggested a range of questions about the mother, child and crime scene to which practitioners should seek answers.

The analysis below therefore considers two types of homicide, for which the collective term 'infant murder' is used. The larger group comprises victims of newborn child murder, the killing of an infant at or within one day of birth by the mother acting alone or, less commonly, with someone else. In the nineteenth century the term 'infanticide' was equivalent to newborn child murder,[11] but is here used to denote a second group, infants who were killed within one year of birth by a parent, relative or unrelated person. There was no typical age for these infants, who could be days, weeks or months old, but together they formed a forensically distinct victim category for which there was no need to prove live birth or separate existence, as lay witnesses could attest to that. Instead, their deaths often highlighted the perpetrator's mental health or sometimes raised questions about the cause of death, for example in the prosecution of baby farmers.[12] Most historical studies focus on one group or the other,[13] but this chapter will examine the medical contribution to the investigation of infant deaths in England and Wales from three related forensic perspectives: the crime scene, the mother and the infant. Age was a starting point, as there were specific stages of medically relevant types of evidence needed depending upon the physical state of the victim, when and where they were found, and their immediate cause of death. Newborns and older babies required different forensic approaches so medical practitioners directed their attention mainly to the victim's body; but doctors also helped to determine that a suspected woman had recently given birth, taking over a role previously performed by laywomen. A doctor's work could even extend to the examination of a crime scene, a duty increasingly associated with the nineteenth-century police. In order to demonstrate the evolution of these practices, the final section of this chapter considers the presentation and reception of medical evidence in court, using a series of case studies from across the eighteenth and nineteenth centuries.

Characteristics of infant murderers

Samuel Farr's first English-language textbook of forensic medicine devoted one chapter to infant murder, noting that it occurred at one of three distinct stages in the process of labour and birth: just before birth, as a form of abortion; at the time of delivery; or very soon after birth.[14] This reflected the common experience of the day, shaped by popular awareness of the 1624 statute that identified infant murder as the crime of unmarried mothers. This underlying assumption helps to explain the characteristics of the indicted perpetrators, who included a large number of widows and servants: these women and girls had the most to lose if they bore a bastard but were probably the easiest to identify, given their relatively tenuous status in the local community. This did not change after the law was relaxed in 1803, and a number of historical studies have explained why such mothers might choose to kill an illegitimate infant through shame or fear of losing their job and reputation.[15] Some women killed newborns to solve the problem of unwanted pregnancy, perhaps raging at a situation forced upon them by a man who seduced then abandoned them. Others destroyed their infant in a moment of unreasoning panic, even temporary insanity, brought on by the shock and pain of labour and consequent psychological distress. Still others may well have acted from a sense of altruism, believing death a better alternative to the stigma and poverty associated with bastardy.[16]

It is impossible to pinpoint why some mothers decided to commit newborn child murder while many others did not, but a single reason was rarely to blame.[17] Anne-Marie Kilday has identified four main motives for newborn murder: shame and isolation, economic factors, malicious intent and psychological factors. The social disgrace and loss of reputation associated with illicit pregnancy was compounded by the unwelcome financial burden that bastardy posed to communities; thus, if a mother feared the financial repercussions of losing her job, being unable to get work or to maintain the child, she might resort to infant murder. For some women, murder was simply a means to an end, committed with deliberation and intent as a solution to a problem. Others suffered from irrationality bordering on insanity as a result of their fear, shame and the process of giving birth. Medical practitioners, among them William Hunter,[18] believed that for some women this caused a peculiar mixture of emotional and psychological symptoms that could result in the child's death; in the nineteenth century a new mental illness associated with pregnancy, puerperal insanity, entered the medical lexicon and served as an explanation for a wide variety of child killings, as discussed later. However, regardless of the precise motive(s) for any individual crime, the combination of socio-legal factors that shaped infant murder created a predictable pattern of prosecutions: the vast majority of those charged were mothers, specifically the women who were unable to escape, hide the crime or convince suspicious neighbours to remain silent.

The extensive data collected here reflects this pattern. Tables 4.1 to 4.3 identify the perpetrators in 637 cases of infant murder and concealment of birth that occurred in the years 1701–1912: the mother was involved in almost every case, accused solely or with another person in 600 or 94.2 per cent of all cases. They were the sole defendant in nearly 87 per cent of the cases and about 80 per cent of all victims were newborns. Of older infants killed by their mothers, a small group (16 cases) were the victims of women who gave birth in a workhouse and left with a healthy child whom they immediately killed, usually because of poverty and despair. Only 12 fathers stood trial, most (75 per cent) for killing an older baby. Of 55 cases involving multiple perpetrators, the victim's mother was one of the accused in 46 cases. They tended to be indicted with their child's father (18 cases); one of their own parents, usually their mother (12 cases); or an employer, friend or other family member (15 cases). One father was indicted with his new wife. Tables 4.4 to 4.6 summarise trial verdicts and support the conclusions reached by previous studies in demonstrating that capital convictions were not common and partial verdicts, particularly for concealment of

Table 4.1 Perpetrators of infant murder

Offence \ Circuit	Old Bailey	Great Sessions	North Wales	South Wales	Oxford	Chester	Total	%
INFANT MURDER								
Mother	252	104	46	17	113	4	536	84.1
Father	5	2	2	–	3	–	12	1.9
Other family[1]	17	13	5	3	13	1	52	8.1
Unknown	2	1	2	–	2	–	7	1.1
Other[2]	6	–	–	1	–	–	7	1.1
Master/mistress[3]	–	–	–	–	1	–	1	0.2
Servant/apprentice[4]	1	–	–	–	–	–	1	0.2
CONCEALMENT								
Mother	–	1	3	4	10	–	18	2.8
Other family	–	–	1	2	–	–	3	0.5
Total	283	121	59	27	142	5	637	100

Source: As for Table 3.1. Cases involving co-accused have been classed as 'other family'.

1 Includes 46 mothers acting with another person.
2 Baby farmers or others who had no familial relationship with the victim; most had monetary motives, but one was insane.
3 Accused employed the victim's mother; probable malicious prosecution made 18 months after death.
4 Child abuse (victim aged 10 months).

Table 4.2 The context for cases of infant murder

Context \ Circuit	Old Bailey	Great Sessions	North Wales	South Wales	Oxford	Chester	Total	%
INFANT MURDER								
Newborn infant	233	112	34	13	91	5	488	76.6
Older infant	39	8	17	7	33	–	104	16.3
Older infant – poverty	6	–	3	–	7	–	16	2.5
Money	2	–	1	1	–	–	4	0.6
Unknown	1	–	–	–	1	–	2	0.3
Other[1]	1	–	–	–	–	–	1	0.2
Child abuse	1	–	–	–	–	–	1	0.2
CONCEALMENT								
Newborn infant	–	1	4	6	10	–	21	3.3
Total	283	121	59	27	142	5	637	100

Source: As for Table 3.1.

1 A child killed in the womb by an external blow in 1724.

Table 4.3 The context for cases of infant murder: perpetrator's sex and relationship to victim

Context Relationship and Sex	Newborn Infant	Older Infant	Older Infant – Poverty	Money	Unknown	Other	Child Abuse	Total
MOTHER ALONE	459	76	16	–	1	–	–	552
FATHER ALONE	3	9	–	–	–	–	–	12
OTHER FAMILY								
One woman	2	3	–	–	–	–	–	5
One man	–	3	–	–	–	–	–	3
Woman and man	16	5	–	–	1	–	–	22
Two women	17	2	–	1	–	–	–	20
More than 2 other people	6	1	–	–	–	–	–	7
UNKNOWN								
Man	–	–	–	–	–	1	–	1
Unknown	3	1	–	–	–	–	–	4
Woman	–	1	–	–	–	–	–	1
Two women	1	–	–	–	–	–	–	1
OTHER								
Woman	–	2	–	1	–	–	–	3
Woman and man	1	–	–	1	–	–	–	2
Two women	–	1	–	1	–	–	–	2
Master	1	–	–	–	–	–	–	1
Female servant	–	–	–	–	–	–	1	1
Total	509	104	16	4	2	1	1	637

Source: As for Table 3.1. 'Other family' includes the mother acting with someone else in the 49 cases with multiple perpetrators.

Table 4.4 Trial verdicts in cases of infant murder

Circuit Verdict	Old Bailey	Great Sessions	North Wales	South Wales	Oxford	Chester	Total	%
INFANT MURDER								
Guilty	41	6	7	3	12	1	70	11.0
Not guilty	157	54	13	4	34	1	263	41.3
Not guilty – insane	14	1	3	1	11	–	30	4.7
No bill	–	38	6	3	16	1	64	10.0
No prosecution	2	5	2	–	4	–	13	2.0
Guilty – concealment	44	9	13	8	32	–	106	16.6
Guilty – manslaughter	14	–	3	1	5	–	23	3.6
Guilty of attempt	1	–	1	–	–	–	2	0.3
Unknown	1	3	3	–	10	1	18	2.8
Unfit to plead	1	–	2	1	1	–	5	0.8
Prosecution abandoned	2	–	1	–	4	–	7	1.1
Multiple verdicts[1]	6	4	1	–	3	1	15	2.4
CONCEALMENT								
Guilty	–	1	2	2	6	–	11	1.7
Not guilty	–	–	1	2	4	–	7	1.1
No bill	–	–	–	1	–	–	1	0.2
Unknown	–	–	–	1	–	–	1	0.2
Multiple verdicts	–	–	1	–	–	–	1	0.2
Total	283	121	59	27	142	5	637	100

Source: As for Table 3.5.

1 Different verdicts for multiple defendants in 15 trials.

Table 4.5 Trial verdicts according to the defendant's relationship to the victim

Verdict	Relationship Mother	Father	Other Family	Unknown	Other	Master/Servant	Total	%
Infant Murder								
Guilty	63	1	4	–	2	–	70	11.0
Not guilty	235	4	21	2	1	–	263	41.3
Not guilty – insane	22	4	3	–	1	–	30	4.7
No bill	57	1	4	1	–	1	64	10.0
No prosecution	8	–	1	4	–	–	13	2.0
Guilty – concealment	102	–	4	–	–	–	106	16.6
Guilty – manslaughter	20	1	–	–	1	1[1]	23	3.6
Guilty of attempt	1	–	1	–	–	–	2	0.3
Unknown	17	1	–	–	–	–	18	2.8
Unfit to plead	4	–	1	–	–	–	5	0.8
Prosecution abandoned	6	–	1	–	–	–	7	1.1
Multiple verdicts	1[2]	–	12	–	2	–	15	2.4
Concealment								
Guilty	9	–	2	–	–	–	11	1.7
Not guilty	7	–	–	–	–	–	7	1.1
No bill	1	–	–	–	–	–	1	0.2
Unknown	1	–	–	–	–	–	1	0.2
Multiple verdicts	–	–	1	–	–	–	1	0.2
Total	554	12	55	7	7	2	637	100

Source: As for Table 3.5.

1 Child abuse by a teenage female servant (victim aged 10 months).
2 Effectively a verdict of not guilty in a Carnarvonshire case, 1873: Grace Davies was committed for murder by the coroner but for concealment by a magistrate; at the assizes the grand jury threw out the bill for concealment and the prosecution offered no evidence on the inquisition.

birth, were preferred; but outright acquittal was the most likely outcome for all perpetrators, especially parents. A significant number of cases never reached a courtroom at all,[19] dismissed by a grand jury for lack of evidence, sometimes under clear direction from the judge.

There was an important distinction in trial verdicts according to the victim's age: the murder of a newborn was far less likely to lead to conviction than the murder of an older baby; but individuals who killed older babies were more likely to be found insane or guilty of manslaughter (Table 4.6). Two related factors explain this. Firstly, during the nineteenth century puerperal insanity came to be accepted as a complication of pregnancy and childbirth. This medical condition, characterised by severe depression and violent outbursts, could strike women of any age, class or marital status and lead to potentially fatal outcomes for themselves, their child or other family members.[20] Although men could not benefit from this gendered disease, cases of paternal infanticide were often mitigated by insanity and drunkenness, especially if the man had previously been a good father.[21] Secondly, if mental illness was not a cause, infanticide defendants had to explain apparently deliberate murder but received little or none of the inherent sympathy that prevailed in cases of newborn child murder. Moreover, there could be no question of the victim's legal status as fully born: 65 per cent of indictments (78 infants in 120 cases) specified the victim's name and 82.5 per cent their age, the youngest being four days old. This blocked a defence commonly used in cases of newborn child murder.

If convictions for murder were rare, executions were even rarer: 74 defendants in 71 cases received a death sentence, half before 1800 and half after. This group comprised 65 mothers, of whom 25 were executed, 34 reprieved, two died in gaol and the fate of four others is uncertain; two fathers (one executed in 1879, the other reprieved in 1904); two grandmothers (one transported in 1835, the other executed in 1874); an uncle (reprieved) and four baby farmers, all of whom were hanged. Of the executed mothers, four suffered in the nineteenth century: a Welsh teenager whom the judge made an example of in Radnorshire immediately after Lord Ellenborough's Act came into effect;[22] two Londoners, one of whom had murdered her child of six weeks,[23] and a woman executed in 1834 for killing her child aged 12 days.[24] The last woman executed anywhere in Britain for the murder of her own infant was Rebecca Smith, a poisoner, in 1849.[25] As a consequence of the 1624 statute, a higher proportion of those sentenced in the eighteenth century were executed: two in Cheshire, one in Gloucestershire, one in Carmarthenshire and the rest in London, between 1702 and 1778; only two of these women had not killed a newborn.

This overview reinforces important conclusions reached by Randolph Roth in relation to New England: parent-child relationships became violent at different times for different reasons. A child's risk of being murdered was highest on the first day of life, after which the risk declined dramatically as parents and carers bonded with the child. Most cases were domestic and most perpetrators were related to the victim; non-relatives rarely killed children unless from mental illness or some financial or sexual motive. In the nineteenth century, children became an economic liability for many families and were therefore at risk if their parents viewed them as a burden or, conversely, were forced by poverty to consider

Table 4.6 Trial verdicts according to the victim's age

Verdict \ Age	Newborn Infant	%	Older Infant	%	Older Infant – Poverty	%	Money	Unknown	Other	Child Abuse	Total
ALL OFFENCES											
Guilty	49	9.6	24	23.0	6	37.5	2	–	–	–	81
Not guilty	231	45.4	31	29.8	6	37.5	–	1	1	–	270
Not guilty – insane	5	1.0	23	22.1	2	12.5	–	–	–	–	30
No bill	58	11.4	6	5.8	–	–	–	1	–	–	65
No prosecution	10	2.0	3	2.9	–	–	–	–	–	–	13
Guilty – concealment	105	20.6	1	1.0	–	–	–	–	–	–	106
Guilty – manslaughter	12	2.3	8	7.7	1	6.25	1	–	–	1	23
Guilty of attempt	–	–	2	1.9	–	–	–	–	–	–	2
Unknown	18	3.5	1	1.0	–	–	–	–	–	–	19
Unfit to plead	1	0.2	3	2.9	1	6.25	–	–	–	–	5
Prosecution abandoned	7	1.4	–	–	–	–	1	–	–	–	7
Multiple verdicts	13	2.6	2	1.9	–	–	1	–	–	–	16
Total	509	100	104	100	16	100	4	2	1	1	637

Source: As for Table 3.5.

altruistic killing. Geographical mobility increased the risk: pregnant women could arrive in a strange town by rail, give birth, kill the child and leave.[26] A version of this phenomenon is observable here: four bodies wrapped in parcels were left on trains or railway platforms and another was thrown from a moving train; five women travelled by train to dispose of a body in another town; and four bodies were dumped on railway waste ground. Mobility gave perpetrators additional options and could pose problems for investigators. When a Lancashire police surgeon suggested that a dead infant found in a parcel on a platform at Manchester's Victoria Station was suffocated in Cheshire while the mother was travelling from Southport to Manchester, Lord Justice Baggallay stopped the trial because there was no evidence the child died in Cheshire. At the same time, he "severely condemned the manner in which the prosecution had been got up. It seemed to him that the whole prosecution had been conducted by the medical man."[27] Despite the judge's apparent doubt that any murder had been committed, the defendant was tried at Liverpool two weeks later, convicted and sentenced to death. The judge in that trial, Mr Justice Denman, was favourable to the medical evidence of suffocation, and the jury returned its verdict in a mere eight minutes.[28]

Jurisdictional issues of this kind did not occur often in cases of infant murder: it was more common for perpetrators to abandon bodies in nearby roads, fields or bodies of water, or to attempt burial at home. Those who were too exhausted or who were discovered before they could dispose of the body, simply left it where it lay in a privy, chamber pot, or bed, or in a box hidden somewhere in the home. In the absence of a body and a confession it was impossible to prove murder, though not concealment, so the pattern of cases tried at the assizes reflects the perpetrators' failure to hide both the victim and the relationship between them. The large proportion of London cases, 44.4 per cent (Table 4.1), is therefore most probably due to its immense population (Table 3.25), the anonymity that the city offered unmarried women seeking to hide a pregnancy,[29] and the greater resources available to investigate the crime. By contrast, the proportionally large number of cases prosecuted in mainly rural Georgian Wales suggests the role played by inquisitive neighbours in bringing the crime to light, an effort that the coroners, overseers and churchwardens who prosecuted the suspects supported. The records of the Court of Great Sessions show that public officials prosecuted 18.3 per cent of indictments for infant murder but only 9 per cent of other homicides.[30] Broken down further, of 121 cases of infant murder and concealment tried at Great Sessions (Table 4.4), the relationship between the prosecutor and the accused was identified in 76 cases: 48 of the prosecutors were local office holders, including constables.[31]

Given that the circumstances which led to infant murder reflect economic, demographic and cultural realities, Table 4.4 raises a surprising finding: relatively few cases of infant murder were prosecuted in South Wales, despite the fact that the region experienced significant in-migration, urbanisation and industrialisation, particularly in the most populous and criminal county, Glamorgan. Moreover, the large number of cases identified in North Wales is due mainly to the fact that the circuit included Cheshire, which accounted for 72.8 per cent (43) of the infant killings and an equivalent proportion of convictions (19 out of 26). It is possible that some of the deficit is due to undiscovered crime or missing records for cases indicted as concealment of birth. However, Richard Ireland has detected a tendency to keep certain types of sexual or family-based offences, including infant murder, out of the courts and within community control,[32] David Jones noted that assize juries rarely treated infant murder with the seriousness accorded to other murders,[33] and Russell Grigg identified late Victorian news reports of the discoveries of dead babies which show that infant murder seems to have been selectively notified to the authorities.[34] Collectively these historians' work suggests that it is likely that socio-cultural beliefs about the London-imposed criminal justice system, rather than about infant murder per se, changed in nineteenth-century Wales. The loss of Great Sessions, the Rebecca disturbances protesting high taxes and tolls in the early 1840s, the 'treachery of the Blue Books' when a scathing public report on Welsh education caused national outrage in 1847, religious divisions and, doubtless, other factors too all made the law of England seem a less appropriate venue for resolving issues of Welsh moral failing. It was therefore only the extreme – in the eyes of the community – cases that were handed over for formal justice.[35] The detailed reasons for this cannot be explored in this book, and they do not affect the findings apropos medico-legal practice, but the reduced number of formal cases indicates that doctors in Victorian Wales acquired fewer opportunities to investigate infant murder than their eighteenth-century or English counterparts did.

Forensic characteristics of infant murder

The investigation of infant murder engaged five broad areas of medical knowledge, corresponding to the evidence required to support a murder charge. Thus, medical witnesses had to prove that a) the infant was born alive; b) was fully developed, showing indicators of viability and maturity, c) and had had a fully separate existence from the mother at the time of death. Medical witnesses were then expected to d) identify and explain the nature and origin of any marks of violence on the infant's corpse, and e) determine the cause of death. Evidence of prematurity and stillbirth led to acquittals, as did inconclusive evidence of live birth and separation, and the suggestion that physical injuries might have been produced by or during labour or after death. In their work on eighteenth-century trials for newborn child murder, both Mark Jackson and Anne-Marie Kilday have concluded that judicial authorities considered medical evidence important but its inherent uncertainty undermined it; most verdicts ultimately hinged on circumstantial evidence and factors that lay outside the scope of medicine.[36] Daniel Grey and Tim Siddons have shown that many of the same questions and problems were associated with nineteenth-century trials; the latter also considers the medical evidence gained from examining suspected women.[37] However, the historiographical focus on weaknesses associated with the forensic investigation of newborn child murder over-simplifies and homogenises the complicated medical contribution to the identification of infant murder, which took place at three physical sites: the crime scene, and the bodies of the mother and the victim. Table 4.7 lists the main elements that comprised the investigation

Table 4.7 Questions and indicative signs in the medico-legal investigation of infant murder

A		The Scene
1	Noises	i. Of a woman in labour
		ii. Of a newborn child's cry
2	Where was the child born?	i. Evidence of delivery while mother was sitting on a privy?
		ii. Did the child drop from the mother at a height?
3	Presence of blood	Quantity of blood; clots; stains
4	Placenta	Evidence that a child was fully born; possible indication of a live full-term birth if there was no defect
5	Odour	The distinctive lochial discharge
6	Possible weapon	i. Is it blood-stained or not?
		ii. Can it be linked to the suspect?
7	The physical space	i. Indoors or outdoors; possibilities posed for accidental injury
		ii. May contain respirable matter (e.g. soil) which if found in the infant's mouth, nose or thorax supplied evidence of live birth
		iii. Evidence of preparation for the birth, e.g. baby clothes

B		The Mother
1	Did she exhibit signs of recent childbirth?	i. Layman's assessment of her size
		ii. Layman's assessment of her bloody clothes, legs, hands
		iii. Medical examination of her:
		a) Breasts (presence of milk, condition of nipples)
		b) Genitalia (open cervix, stretched vagina, tears, lochial discharge)
		c) Abdomen (flaccidity, stretch marks, swollen uterus, retained placenta)
		iv. Medical assessment of her degree of weakness
2	When did she give birth?	Circumstantial evidence provided by lay witnesses: noises heard, absences, bloodstains
3	What was her physical condition at the time she gave birth?	Was she weak, young, or mentally ill?
4	What was her mental condition at the time she gave birth?	i. Was this her first child?
		ii. Were there signs of derangement?

C		The Infant
1	Was the child newly born, or older?	i. Evidence provided by lay witnesses: older infant known to others/seen alive?
		ii. Newborn found alive?
		iii. External examination: presence of umbilical cord or placenta

(Continued)

Table 4.7 (Continued)

2	If the child was a newborn, was it born at full term and viable? [A 7-month child was viable.]	i. Physical development: a) Size: average length (18 inches) and weight (6 lbs) b) Hair and nails c) Anatomical development
		ii. Could the mother have supposed it to be a miscarriage?
3	Was the child born alive?	i. Post-mortem examination sought evidence to answer this question by considering: a) The condition of the internal organs b) The hydrostatic lung test c) The presence of meconium in the stomach d) The condition of the umbilical cord e) The three principal cavities of the body were to be opened: head, thorax, abdomen ii. External examination suggested live birth if the child had grasped anything in its hands; if bruises had formed or scratches healed; if meconium was found on or near the body
4	When was the child born?	i. Circumstantial evidence provided by lay witnesses ii. Medical evidence of age at death and/or time since death a) Healing of the umbilical cord b) Size and development
5	Did the child have a separate existence from the mother at the time of death?	The condition of the umbilical cord: torn, cut, or tied off; if body, cord and placenta still joined together, may indicate a rapid birth
6	What was the condition of the body?	i. Were there external marks of violence on it? a) If yes, what were the marks and where were they located on the body? b) Were the marks of violence inflicted before, at or after death? c) What instrument(s) might have inflicted the marks of violence? d) Could instrument(s) found at the scene have inflicted the documented injuries? ii. Were there internal marks of violence in the body? iii. If the body was found in water, was the victim alive or dead before entering the water? iv. If putrefaction had commenced, it was possible to prove respiration but potentially difficult to establish cause of death
7	What was the cause of death?	External and/or post-mortem examination by a surgeon
8	What was the anner of death?	i. Could death have occurred due to unintentional action(s)? ii. If yes, what were those actions?

of infant murder according to these three contexts. The scene could be an important means of linking suspect to victim even when the perpetrator was not the mother; an accused woman's physical and mental condition might ameliorate her ability to form a criminal intent; and the victim's cause and manner of death were essential details. Lay witnesses sometimes provided medical information and doctors occasionally offered factual non-medical evidence; but this was far more common in the eighteenth and early nineteenth century than in later decades, when judges and lawyers restricted questions of a medical nature to male medical professionals.

The (crime) scene

The scene of a suspected homicide is usually overlooked in the historiography of infant murder, but it was a site of medico-legal investigation populated by laymen, doctors, coroners and police officers – though not magistrates, who did not visit crime scenes during committal proceedings. In one of the few works that consider "doctors in the detection of infanticide cases," Clíona Rattigan included 1930s crime scene photographs and sketches in her study of Ireland in the first half of the twentieth century: these depict indoor and outdoor scenes where bodies were discovered, minus the bodies; they look very similar to the nineteenth-century English crime scene sketches discussed in Chapter 5. Although Rattigan's analysis of the doctor's role in detecting crime is brief, she makes several important points. Doctors could be the first to come into contact with unmarried mothers who had killed an infant when they treated these women in their bedrooms, entering "what had, in effect, become a crime scene." Similarly, doctors attempted to find the baby's body and reported cases to the police; sometimes they accompanied police officers to a suspect's home to establish whether she had recently given birth.[38] English and Welsh records confirm these actions and point out that doctors were rarely alone at a crime scene; rather, they were called in by a member of the public or the suspect's household, or by a police officer, any one of whom might already have noted some of the points listed in Table 4.7.

Most women, not just those who had had children, could recognise key indicators of childbirth. The quantity of blood found at the scene was one of the most tell-tale signs, as it pointed to the fact that "something more than ordinary" had happened: neither a miscarriage nor normal monthly bleeding but the birth of a child.[39] In Carmarthenshire in 1786 neighbours noticed blood running under the door of Jane Thomas's house; they refused to accept her explanation that she had had a miscarriage and pressed her until she told them where her child, still alive, was concealed.[40] The context within which such a bloody scene was evaluated was crucial: prior suspicion of unacknowledged pregnancy shaped the popular interpretation of bloodstains, mysterious noises and sudden absences. A lump of flesh could be correctly identified as a placenta, proof positive that a child had been born, and then laymen searched bedrooms, cellars, gardens and privies for hidden bodies, weapons and baby linen in an attempt to find further confirmation. Doctors entered these locations at the request of local people, a coroner or the police, to give their professional assessment of the conclusions to be drawn from the evidence discovered, none of which could independently prove deliberate murder. In the absence of an eyewitness, audible cries could not be taken as proof of live birth in the legal sense of complete separation from the mother, because a child could cry while still partially in the birth canal,[41] but bloody marks on a floor might indicate that a woman had given birth while standing up, lending support to an assertion that the child had been accidentally injured in the fall. If the position or severity of a head wound did not support this scenario, deliberate violence could be presumed.[42] Forensic practitioners had been aware of this possibility since at least the 1830s when, as we saw in Chapter 2, William Cummin had warned his students of it. Furthermore, in such cases the umbilical cord would be ruptured, not cut, as also when mothers claimed to have given birth while sitting on a privy. The unlucky infant might be suffocated in the mud, ordure or soil, but the position of the body and firmness of the soil could be used to evaluate the truth of this claim.[43]

The mother

In order to prove a charge of infant murder, the prosecution had first to establish that an accused woman was the mother of the child in question. The principal indicators did not change much over the course of two centuries: lactation and other physical signs in her abdominal and genital areas, blood stains on her clothes and body and a sudden reduction in size (see Table 4.7). The latter two signs were generally obvious to lay witnesses and remained a focus of popular attention, but during the eighteenth century, the woman's body gradually came more securely under formal male medical observation as witnesses called in man-midwives or surgeons (Table 4.8). In the nineteenth century, working with coroners or the police, doctors took on the role – once exercised by neighbours – of questioning the reputed mother and urging her to confess. This however was a practice fraught with danger: not only was it illegal to examine a woman without her consent, a fact widely acknowledged by the 1860s,[44] but statements made in the absence of a formal caution against self-incrimination were inadmissible in court. Most depositions are fairly silent on the means by which surgeons made a physical examination of a suspected woman, but occasionally they reveal a battle of wills. In 1832 two surgeons wanted to examine Ann Radley in her bed: they turned aside the bedclothes to reveal a bloody knee but she would not allow them to touch her. One threatened force whereas the other tried to persuade her, but still she refused, exclaiming "I will take care that no man concerns me"; then they gave up.[45] In 1844 a surgeon in Gloucestershire told Harriet Tarling that she must either be examined or he would search her boxes; she chose the latter option and the dead body of her infant was discovered.[46]

Some women submitted angrily to such importuning, some revealed their breasts readily enough but drew the line at an internal examination; still others were probably too traumatised to make much resistance. The lecture notes

Table 4.8 Midwives and surgeons in trials for infant murder, 1699–1914

Period	Total No. of Cases	Midwife	Surgeon	Midwife & Surgeon	No Medical Person[1]
1699–1709	7	2	0	0	5
1710–1719	19	12	0	2	5
1720–1729	27	18	0	5	4
1730–1739	41	18	3	4	16
1740–1749	26	12	2	3	9
1750–1759	24	6	4	5	9
1760–1769	28	6	7	4	11
1770–1779	20	3	8	4	5
1780–1789	20	2	8	5	5
1790–1799	24	0	16	2	6
1800–1809	24	0	19	1	4
1810–1819	28	1	19	4	4
1820–1829	34	0	30	2	2
1830–1839	54	0	48	5	1
1840–1849	44	0	40	0	4
1850–1859	36	0	33	1	2
1860–1869	41	0	38	3	0
1870–1879	50	0	48	2	0
1880–1889	38	0	34	3	1
1890–1899	13	0	13	0	0
1900–1914	39	0	37	1	1
Total	637	80	407	56	94

Source: As for Table 3.1. The first case occurred in Dec 1701, the last in Dec 1912.

1 Includes cases where a medical practitioner may have been present but was not mentioned in the trial account.

examined in Chapter 2 do not comment on the issue of consent, but Alfred Swaine Taylor's textbooks began to discuss it in the 1860s,[47] and by the 1870s surgeons were taking more care to seek permission before carrying out intrusive physical inspections for the distinctive and mostly unequivocal signs of recent childbirth. These were summarised in evidence presented at an inquest in 1844:

> The breasts were full, nipples turgid and the areolae around them wide and dark coloured, skin of the belly relaxed and thrown into folds and the skin interrupted by dark coloured brown streaks – the round form of the half contracted womb could be felt at the lower part of the belly – the external parts of generation swollen and torn, the outlet dilated, the mouth of the womb open and the margin relaxed, lochia present.[48]

Most doctors attempted to extract some breast milk, which was a sign of childbirth that a woman who already had children could explain away on the grounds that she was still breastfeeding.[49] There was a medical response to this, however: according to a surgeon speaking in 1841, the milk of a new mother would be greater in quantity and richer in quality than it would be after a few years.[50] But the question of whether or not a woman had previously had children was more important in relation to the possibilities it afforded defence counsel, for the underlying assumption was that the shock to the mother of an unfamiliar, painful ordeal might have contributed to the death of her illegitimate infant. A first child implied inexperience and ineffective management of the birth process, so that a defendant "might have committed the act imputed to her without being herself conscious of it, or of the consequences that would be likely to ensue."[51] Similarly, youth, infirmity or mental incapacity all provided possible explanations for a mother's failure to care properly for a newborn that subsequently died. Only medical evidence of extreme pre-mortem violence could counteract this suggestion, but the cases of decapitation described in the last section of this chapter demonstrate how easily judges and juries could be persuaded that such violence was neither wilfully inflicted nor the immediate cause of death.

Although the signs of recent childbirth were easily recognised, they were known to disappear within two weeks and often much faster.[52] This meant that a woman arrested after that period had elapsed had a good chance of escaping prosecution for murder, as it would be almost impossible to prove she was the mother of the infant in question. The same factor made the estimation of precisely *when* a woman had been delivered a matter of conjecture, but the potential remained to prosecute for concealment: a jury needed only to be convinced that she had been pregnant and given birth in secret.

Table 4.9 shows that a defendant's sanity was not much discussed before the 1870s, when expert testimony about mental illness became more frequent as a result of the Prison Acts of 1865 and 1877, which instituted routine medical examinations for prisoners.[53] Those who were found to be insane before trial or who became insane in prison could be transferred to a county asylum or to Broadmoor Criminal Lunatic Asylum, which opened in May 1863 with eight female patients, six of whom had killed or wounded their own child.[54] A defence on the grounds of insanity was more likely to be made, and more likely to be accepted by the courts when the victim was not newborn (Table 4.10).[55] In 1927 a junior medical superintendent at Broadmoor reported that 43 per cent of the female patients admitted during the period 1900–1925 had been charged with child murder; in the same period, nursing mothers accounted for over 25 per cent of the murders committed by individuals who were not considered responsible for their actions.[56] Most of these women suffered from puerperal or lactational insanity – they had not killed newborns but older infants or young children – and 77 per cent were married. He therefore disagreed with

> the statements that are to be found in most text-books to the effect that illegitimacy is a potent factor in the causation of the insanities of childbirth, but it is only fair to take into consideration that murders committed by unmarried mothers often take place at the time of the confinement, or very

Table 4.9 Insanity in trials for infant murder, 1699–1914

Period	Total No. of Cases	Insanity of Defendant Suggested	Proportion (%)	Expert Evidence of Insanity
1699–1709	7	–	0	–
1710–1719	19	1	5.3	–
1720–1729	27	–	0	–
1730–1739	41	1	2.4	–
1740–1749	26	3	11.5	–
1750–1759	24	–	0	–
1760–1769	28	–	0	–
1770–1779	20	–	0	–
1780–1789	20	–	0	–
1790–1799	24	–	0	–
1800–1809	24	–	0	–
1810–1819	28	1	3.6	–
1820–1829	34	1	2.9	–
1830–1839	54	7	13.0	–
1840–1849	44	2	4.5	1
1850–1859	36	1	2.8	–
1860–1869	41	3	7.3	1
1870–1879	50	8	16.0	1
1880–1889	38	11	28.9	7
1890–1899	13	4	30.8	3
1900–1914	39	12	30.8	8
Total	637	55	8.6	21

Source: As for Table 3.1. All defendants, of which 45 were mothers.

shortly after, and that at the trial the charge is frequently reduced to one of concealment of birth, and the question of the sanity or otherwise of the prisoner is not raised by the defence.[57]

Dana Rabin and Hilary Marland have shown that pleas of temporary insanity and puerperal insanity were met with increasing acceptance in eighteenth- and nineteenth-century trials,[58] and Tony Ward has explained how the 1922 Infanticide Act adapted medical theories about mental illness and its association with childbirth to fit a long-standing social consensus about the criminal responsibility of women who killed their infants.[59] This amounted to an admixture of lay and medical opinion about temporary insanity which posited a direct link between gender and crime. In so doing, it provided a neat explanation for the two main types of infant murder committed by mothers. More recently, legal scholar Arlie Loughnan has demonstrated how "acts of infanticide have come to be read as an instantiation of abnormality for criminal law purposes." This is because the mental incapacity associated with child bearing could affect both the 'sad' young woman who killed her illegitimate infant at birth and the 'mad' married woman who killed a child while suffering from depression or mania following childbirth. By ascribing both acts to insanity, society as a whole was reassured that otherwise incomprehensible deeds had a logical explanation.[60] Table 4.10 shows that insanity was invoked more frequently and successfully by women who had killed an older infant, but was adaptable to the accepted narrative of newborn child murder. Eighteenth-century popular understandings of frenzy or being out of one's mind were augmented in the nineteenth century by a new disease entity, puerperal insanity, supported by the opinion of medical professionals and, increasingly, expert evidence given by prison medical officers and psychiatrists. But the small number of cases in the sample, amounting to just 8 per cent of the total, suggests that insane offenders were either diverted from the criminal justice system before trial or indicted solely for concealment; they are therefore not amenable to systematic study using the records generated by murder trials.

There were only five cases before 1830, two of which occurred in Wales. One woman was married and suffering from what London obstetrician Robert Gooch (1784–1830) was soon to define as puerperal insanity:[61] in 1818 Ann Jones was not prosecuted for scalding her baby in a pot of boiling water.[62] In 1747 Elizabeth Price was tried for the murder of her illegitimate child and found to be "not of sane mind and understanding." The coroner's inquisition deemed her a "reputed ideot," and the indictment named only one female witness.[63] Three cases tried in England resulted in two acquittals and a commuted death sentence. Prosecutions between 1830 and 1914 resulted in a conviction rate of 32.5 per cent, mostly for the lesser offences of concealment or manslaughter. Of the four women convicted of murder after 1830, one became insane following the trial and probably was so at the time of the crime;[64] two alleged to

Table 4.10 Verdicts in trials of insane mothers for infant murder

Verdict	Newborn Infant	Older Infant	Older Infant – Poverty Motive
Guilty	2	1	2
Not guilty	1	4	–
Not guilty – insane	5	15	2
No prosecution	–	1	–
Guilty – concealment	6	–	–
Guilty – manslaughter	1	1	–
Unfit to plead	1	2	1
Total	16	24	5

Source: As for Table 3.1.

be suffering from puerperal mania that the prison medical officer could not confirm, were reprieved;[65] another was considered by the jury to be guilty but "in a frenzied state of mind at the time the act was committed" and was also reprieved.[66] Visible signs of derangement almost certainly enabled the family and friends of women who killed infants to identify a mental illness that doctors also recognised as a legitimate medical condition, so that some cases were not heard at the assizes. By 1885, as a local GP informed the judge at a trial in Carnarvon, "it was a well-known thing that pregnant women were often temporarily affected with madness, leading them to all kinds of violent deeds" for which they were not accountable, an opinion with which the local prison medical officer agreed.[67]

Ultimately, cases that called for medical evidence concerning mental illness were far less common than those which required evidence concerning the bodies of the woman and, especially, the child.

The infant

The first fact to be established was whether the child was newly born, as that determined the subsequent course of the investigation. Older infants presented far fewer evidentiary problems, for the obvious reason that there was no need to prove live birth. Most newborns were found with the umbilical cord and sometimes the placenta still attached, providing clear evidence of separation from the mother but not necessarily of live birth. Some newborns were found alive, however, and cared for until death, when the medico-legal examination could begin. In both circumstances it was important to establish that the child had been viable in order to lend support to the conclusion that it was living and entirely born when murdered.[68] English law made no distinction on the basis of the period of gestation, but received knowledge held a seven-month child to be viable: the chance of natural death was assumed to be lower than it would be in a child born at under seven months. In assessing maturity, eighteenth-century midwives and surgeons cited four factors: the length and weight of the body, and the presence of hair and nails. The stages of foetal development were known and could in theory have been used to determine foetal age, but there is no evidence that surgeons did so.[69] In the nineteenth century external features such as hair and nails occupied less prominence in medico-legal reports, but anatomical development was rarely noted; the focus lay on measured size and the results of a thorough post-mortem examination dedicated to establishing live birth and cause of death.

The question of the child's size could be extremely important. If it was particularly small there was a possibility that a first-time mother had genuinely mistaken childbirth for a miscarriage, but if it was abnormally large that was a reason to presume accidental death due to the ensuing difficult labour, especially for a woman trying to deliver herself. In 1793 a parish man-midwife in London told the court that a large child might get stuck, "and when the child sticks so it stops the circulation between the mother and the child, and destroys the child ninety-nine out of an hundred."[70] And a large child would necessarily fall with more force if the mother was delivered in a standing position or in a privy.[71] To counter defences made on the basis of size surgeons could refer to the maturity of the placenta or note that head injuries were not due to a fall but a blow from an object of some sort. But once the presumption of deliberate murder was undermined, it was very difficult for surgeons to provide incontrovertible evidence of intentional harm and the usual outcome was an acquittal or conviction for concealing the birth. Defence counsel were skilled at identifying the areas of weakness in trials for newborn child murder and at asking questions that bypassed the particular to focus on the universal; even some of the questions posed by prosecuting counsel elicited responses that provided a persuasive defence on medical grounds. These instances were quantified in Table 3.20, which showed that a medical defence was presented in 26 per cent of infant murder trials and 33 per cent of trials for concealment.

The weakest part of the prosecution case was the question of live birth and separate existence, for which surgeons regularly utilised the hydrostatic lung test as a source of evidence. This surgical test excluded midwives, who could not open bodies, from a key part of the trial and it is no coincidence that their withdrawal from the courtroom coincided with the ascendancy of lawyers and surgeons (Table 4.8). The first explicit reference to the use of the lung test in England was at the Old Bailey in 1729 when "John Hanby, a Surgeon, depos'd, That he view'd the Child, and it did appear to be at its full Time, and to be Born alive; and that upon making Trial of a Piece of the Lungs put into Water, it was buoyant, and did not sink; and that he did not observe any visible Marks of Violence on the Child."[72] The first reference to the lung test in Wales was made in 1755: an apothecary in Brecon "having opened the cavity of the thorax, taken out the lungs, put them in a pail of water, and they floated upon the surface of the water," leading him to conclude that the baby had been born alive.[73] The test was used in 191 trials, five of which did not involve newborn victims – lung tissue in an unopened body was not affected by decomposition. Figure 4.1 charts the geographical distribution over time and seems to show London moving away from its use, but this is probably an artefact of the reporting practices of the court reporters at the Old Bailey: the medical details were simply not included. Figure 4.2 indicates that the test was used regularly right up until the First World War and that, although it was not cited in a majority of cases, if anything it came to be relied upon more during the nineteenth century. At the turn of the twentieth century the test was so well entrenched in medico-legal practice that a pathologist, Dr Ludwig Freyberger, used it on an infant that had been dead three days in order to conclude that

> the child had a separate existence, my reasons for so saying, being that the birth of the child appeared to have been rapid, and that the lungs were perfectly inflated, which could not have taken place if the child had not had a separate existence: it must have breathed deeply and fully.

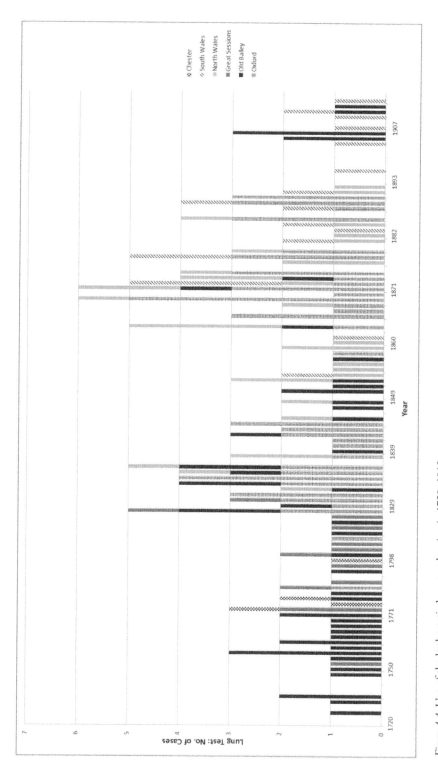

Figure 4.1 Use of the hydrostatic lung test by circuit, 1720–1912

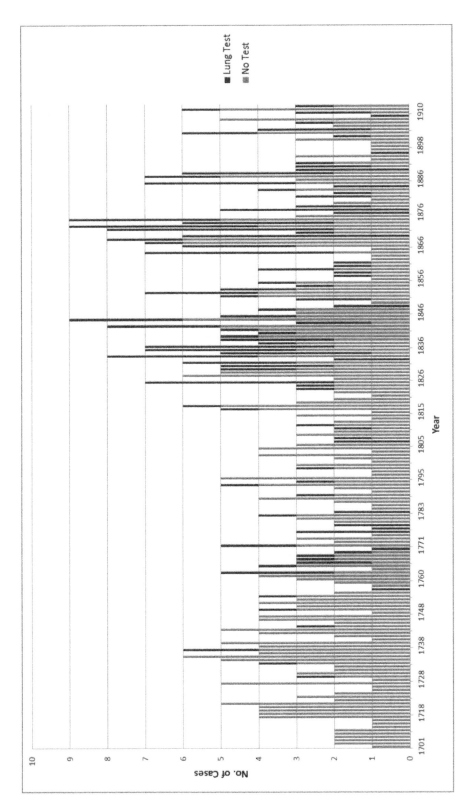

Figure 4.2 Use of the hydrostatic lung test as a proportion of all infant murder cases, 1701–1912

The general practitioner who had first seen the body told the court that he had no way of knowing whether the child had a separate existence,[74] suggesting that the lung test had become an accepted part of *expert* forensic practice.

Yet, its use was always controversial due to the essential tension between the evidence it could deliver and what the law required from it. Some surgeons dismissed the test altogether, as in 1771 when London surgeon Jonathan Wathen told the court that he "did make an experiment on the lungs, which was formerly thought decisive; but now that opinion is exploded, that a child that had been still born had not the lungs inflated with air."[75] Others were willing to admit that the experiment could not necessarily be relied upon but still had a good opinion of it, though they might not "like to stake the life of a fellow-creature on it."[76] How then could another surgeon, again testifying at the Old Bailey, tell the court in 1871 that as the lungs had never been inflated, "therefore the child had never breathed; that is an infallible test"?[77] The difference lies in what it was that the test was being used to prove. During the eighteenth century it was taken as evidence of live birth and therefore by extension separate existence, but by the middle of the nineteenth century it was recommended for use solely to establish that respiration had occurred, as support for the claim that a child had been born alive. But additional evidence of live birth was necessary because the law demanded proof that the child had been fully expelled from its mother's body. Over the course of a century the state of the lungs changed from a proof of live birth to presumptive evidence only, because a child could in theory remain partly in the mother whilst the head was outside and breathing. This was medically unlikely, but in a court of law a barrister could make much of the distinction. Table 4.11 summarises the medical evidence derived from the examination of infant lungs that was formally recognised in 1788 and 1884, showing the detail that was added by intervening developments in microscopy and pathology. If a child had died immediately after birth, however, John Dixon Mann warned readers of his textbook in 1902, it was "out of the power of medical evidence to *prove* that it was born alive, whatever reasons there may be for inclining to that opinion."[78]

But this irresolvable problem did not stop doctors from trying to provide evidence of live birth and deliberate murder. Despite the lack of medical consensus as to its inherent effectiveness, the Figures show how widely the lung test was used. Local surgeons introduced refinements garnered from their student training or from textbooks. By the early 1870s floating pieces of the lungs was common, as was floating the lungs and heart together, to demonstrate a degree of buoyancy that could only be caused by sustained breathing. In 1874 a surgeon in Berkshire went to heroic lengths to conduct this test: finding that the lungs and attached heart floated in water, he placed a piece of lung between two boards and pressed it with a 56lb weight, aided by the weight of a policeman. This piece likewise floated in water, leading to the conclusion that "the child had a separate independent existence from its mother."[79] A police officer provided similar assistance in a Gloucestershire case four months later: the lungs were divided into small pieces and placed in a towel, then the surgeon "with help

Table 4.11 Medical evidence derived from the examination of infant lungs

General Appearance of Lungs that have breathed, 1788	*General Appearance of Lungs that have breathed, 1884*	*General Appearance of Lungs that have not breathed, 1884*
1 Colour approaching to white (as opposed to red)	Light colour (rose-pink, pale pink, light red, or crimson)	Dark colour (black-blue, maroon, or purple) resembling liver
2	Pulmonary alveoli distinctly visible to the naked eye, or with a magnifying lens of low power	Pulmonary alveoli not visible to the naked eye
3	Crepitate, or crackle freely	Do not crepitate or crackle when squeezed or cut
4	Contain a good deal of blood, which escapes freely when cut into	Contain little blood, therefore little escapes when cut into
5	The blood present is freely mixed with air, and therefore appears frothy	The blood present is not frothy, unless there is putrefaction
6 Lower density; will tend to float in water; are so expanded that they fill up the cavity of the thorax	Float in water (the parts which have been expanded, or have breathed, float); if fully expanded they will even keep the heart afloat	Sink in water, unless putrid, and often even then
7	The air cannot be squeezed out	Bubbles of gas caused by putrefaction can be squeezed out, and as they escape are usually noted to be of large size

Source: Adapted from S. Farr, *Elements of Medical Jurisprudence* (London: T. Becket, 1788), pp. 55, 58; C. M. Tidy, *Legal Medicine*, Vol. 3 (New York: William Wood, 1884), p. 170.

from Supt Phillpotts (sic) made a very firm compression of the pieces, removed them from the cloth, put them in water and found them buoyant," indicating full respiration and independent circulation.[80] The point of these exertions was to prove that the lungs contained so much air that the child must have respired for a period of time long enough to confirm separate existence, a quarter of an hour at least, but in both cases the defendants were convicted of concealing the birth, not murder. A clue to this outcome is provided by a marginal note made by the prosecuting barrister in the second case: "no sure test."[81]

Further evidence that the lungs contained air due to the effect of sustained breathing rather than attempted resuscitation or putrefaction was obtained by squeezing them to produce crepitation, a crackling sound. This indicator was introduced to medico-legal practice in the 1830s: it was used for the first time in a Monmouthshire case of December 1834, having been noted almost in passing in Michael Ryan's textbook of 1831, but cited several times in Taylor's textbook of 1844.[82] Although the lungs remained the central focus of medico-legal attention, evidence from the post-mortem examination of other internal organs began to be cited as confirmation of live birth. The presence of milk or meconium (the distinctive faeces of a newborn infant) in the stomach, the absence of meconium from the intestines or finding it on or about the child were all strongly suggestive of survival after birth as swallowing and defecation were physiological actions unlikely to occur after death.[83] By the early twentieth century some surgeons floated the stomach as well as the lungs and heart, but this was uncommon despite promising results from German research and some important English support.[84] The condition of the umbilical cord was more useful: if it had been properly cut and tied, the child must have been fully born; if it was untied the volume of blood lost pointed to independent circulation, since the dead do not bleed. Healing of the cord could be used to gauge an approximate age, information that was useful in cases of infanticide when the victim's identity was unknown. Age could be estimated from the child's size if the cord had healed.

Bruises and healed scratches or fractures were also indicators of live birth, but while it was easy to prove that they had not been caused by the medico-legal examination, it was very difficult to prove that they were not of perimortem origin, caused by a fall during the birth or the mother's attempt to deliver herself.[85] The colour of the lungs offered more positive yet still not definitive evidence: those of the foetal state were a uniform brownish colour, while a mottled appearance of various reddish hues was peculiar to lungs that had breathed. Victorian textbooks provided a clear overview of the expected colour differences and the information provided was extremely consistent, suggesting that after the 1860s there was little or no research done on this topic.[86] The size and position of the lungs within the chest cavity, discussed in Chapter 2, was a more reliable and easily perceptible sign that doctors were trained to recognise, but depositions do not provide much detail about colour changes or lung size. This is possibly because the courts discouraged 'terms of art' and unnecessary detail, or because they were so fixated on the hydrostatic lung test, or simply because doctors included this type of information tacitly within their general conclusions about respiration. Finally, clenched hands were considered proof of life: as Samuel Farr noted in 1788, a child could only grasp something if it was live-born.[87] This sign was mentioned in 19 cases. In the earliest of these, a trial at the Old Bailey in 1717, a midwife took the opposing view, that it was a sign of stillbirth; but surgeons held it to be a sign of a convulsive movement made during life, generally in reaction to asphyxiation. Unless the child was actually clutching something, however, such as fabric or vegetation, the information was largely immaterial.

The remainder of the medical evidence concerning the body of a dead infant focused on whether there were any wounds, how and when they were made, and the cause of death, from which the manner of death, from accident, natural causes or homicide, was determined. Essentially, medical witnesses were expected to provide both a medical opinion and an explanatory narrative to support the conclusion that death resulted from intentional violence, a necessary prerequisite for a charge of murder. But throughout the entire period, judges, jurors and defence counsel sought confirmation that the prosecution narrative was the only plausible account; the conviction statistics presented in Table 4.4 show that often it was not. In cases that hinged on whether the umbilical cord was cut or torn, juries were willing to believe that, notwithstanding the most appalling injuries, an infant had suffered unintended violence during the birth process, and a torn cord suggested lack of planning. It was difficult to provide a precise estimate of when violence had been inflicted, so evidence of fatal wounding did not necessarily prove murder as it might have occurred after death or while the child was still partially in the vagina. If a doctor was certain only that injury was incurred around the time of birth, jurors took this to mean that the child was in all probability not fully separated from the mother. Accidental strangulation by the umbilical cord was often used as a defence, although it was possible to provide medical evidence to disprove this: indentations from a ligature would be discernible, the skin would not be abraded, and if the child died from constriction of the cord during delivery, then the lungs retained their foetal appearance.[88] When Mira Cresswell, 24, was tried in 1878, her defence counsel argued for accidental strangulation, probably more in hope than expectation: the baby girl was found with a petticoat string tied tightly round her neck, and although the surgeon admitted that if the string had been tied there immediately after death it might have caused the same marks, the jury was not convinced. Cresswell was convicted of manslaughter and sentenced to ten years.[89]

Marks around the throat could, alternatively, be construed as unintended, caused during self-delivery. It was also possible for a newborn to be suffocated in the mother's birthing discharges if left face down, another unintentional and thus non-criminal occurrence that might befall a woman who gave birth alone. When a victim was found in water, the presence of foreign substances in the throat, windpipe or stomach indicated death by drowning, but medical witnesses had to be alert to the fact that the body might have been thrown into the water after death from some other cause. It was usually more straightforward to identify the cause of death in an older infant than a newborn, since the question was not complicated by the issue of live birth; the post-mortem indications were largely the same as in adults. When a body was found days or weeks after death, decomposition made the medical examination more difficult but by no means impossible: the hydrostatic lung test could still be used and there were only five reported cases of failure to conduct a complete post-mortem because the body was too putrefied. When the cause of death was asphyxia (by suffocation, drowning or strangling), as it was in approximately 50 per cent of all cases of infant murder (see Table 4.12), interest turned once again to the lungs, as their condition was an important diagnostic in all forms of asphyxial death.[90]

Finally, we should note an important point: jurors were reluctant to convict where no specific cause of death was stated or when it was related to the

Table 4.12 Cause of death in cases of infant murder

Cause of Death	Newborn	%	Infant	%	Infant (Poverty)	%
Beat/kick	3	0.6	–	–	–	–
Cut throat	29	5.7	6	5.5	1	6.25
Drowned	24	4.7	30	27.3	6	37.5
Head injury	42	8.2	10	9.1	–	–
Multiple injuries	21	4.1	3	2.7	–	–
Poison	1	0.2	11	10.0	2	12.5
Stabbed	5	1.0	2	1.8	–	–
Starved	–	–	2	1.8	1	6.25
Strangled	132	25.8	10	9.1	2	12.5
Suffocated	92	18.0	24	21.8	1	6.25
Other	61	11.9	11	10.0	2	12.5
Unspecified	101	19.8	1	0.9	1	6.25
Total	511	100	110	100	16	100

Source: As for Table 3.1. Infant denotes up to 1 year in age.

circumstances in which the birth had taken place, or when the condition of the lungs was involved. Table 4.13 shows the high proportion of acquittals associated with asphyxial deaths and with cases where the cause of death was stated to be the very generic 'lack of assistance at birth' or the descriptive but medically meaningless 'by throwing into a privy', albeit that implied death from asphyxiation. How can we explain this medical imprecision? To a small extent it was related to lack of medical training: there was no male medical witness in 12 of the 63 cases that lacked a precise medical cause of death, although a midwife was present in seven of these. A similar number of eighteenth- and early nineteenth-century cases were stated by a medical witness to have been stillbirths and might not have been prosecuted at all, one supposes, were it not for some local feeling against the accused women. An unknown number of cases may simply reflect lack of detailed reporting. But a significant proportion of the imprecision was due to the narrow boundary between life and death in a newborn infant, who might die easily for reasons that were either too obvious to investigate or too difficult to pin down. "It is possible that a child may die in 2 or 3 minutes without any visible cause," surgeon John Evans told an inquest at Cardiff in 1883; use of the hydrostatic lung test had provided no information about the cause of death, which was either lack of care during the birth or suffocation in the privy.[91] It seems reasonable to conclude, therefore, that the circumstances in which cases of newborn child murder occurred fixed the path of the subsequent medical examination, at the same time creating the conditions under which a jury would find it easiest to reach a verdict of 'not guilty' despite the best efforts of medical practitioners to prove live birth, separate existence and deliberate

Table 4.13 Trial verdicts according to the main causes of death in cases of newborn child murder

Cause of Death / Verdict	Head Injury	%	Drown	%	Strangle	%	Suffocate	%	Unspecified	%	Other	%
Guilty	7	16.7	3	12.5	10	7.6	11	11.9	6	6.0	4	6.6
Not guilty	9	21.4	11	45.8	58	44.0	45	48.9	64	64.0	25	41.0
Not guilty – insane	1	2.4	1	4.2	–	–	–	–	1	1.0	2	3.3
No bill	2	4.8	4	16.7	27	20.4	8	8.7	6	6.0	7	11.4
No prosecution	–	–	1	4.2	3	2.3	1	1.1	2	2.0	2	3.3
Guilty – concealment	17	40.4	2	8.3	18	13.6	16	17.4	17	17.0	13	21.3
Guilty – manslaughter	3	7.1	–	–	4	3.0	2	2.2	–	–	2	3.3
Unknown	2	4.8	1	4.2	6	4.5	5	5.4	2	2.0	2	3.3
Unfit to plead	–	–	–	–	–	–	–	–	–	–	1	1.6
Prosecution abandoned	–	–	–	–	1	0.8	1	1.1	1	1.0	2	3.3
Multiple verdicts	1	2.4	1	4.2	5	3.8	3	3.3	1	1.0	1	1.6
Total = 451	42	100	24	100.1	132	100	92	100	100	100	61	100

Source: As for Table 3.5. 'Other' includes mainly lack of assistance at birth, stillbirth, throwing into privy, or a mixture of possible causes.

murder. The forensic investigation of newborn child murder was shaped by the acute entwining of its socio–legal and medical characteristics,[92] in essence, and the rest of this chapter examines that relationship through a series of individual and collective case studies.

The case against Jane Williams, Montgomeryshire, 1734

In February 1734 several women in the borough of Llanfyllin confronted Jane Williams, a widow who had become noticeably smaller in size following an alleged sickness, with their suspicion that she had recently given birth. If true, she had borne a bastard and it seemed all too likely she had "made away with the child." They demanded that she allow them to "search" her; in particular, they wished to examine her breasts. Williams obliged by baring one, but refused to allow anyone to "draw or suck it." What they saw was enough to convince the women that the allegation was true: there was milk in her breasts but no sign of a child. When Williams was placed under arrest on suspicion of murder, three women went by order of a justice of the peace into her house to examine her linen, shift and petticoats, all of which showed "marks or sign of the birth of a child."[93]

While Jane Williams was in custody her female neighbours again challenged her to provide an explanation, and finally she confessed to burying a stillborn girl in her house. The women unearthed the body, but were terrified and did not actually touch it. That task fell to two local medical men: Richard Griffiths, whom the depositions and recognisances state to be a "gentleman" of Llanfyllin but who was actually an apothecary, as noted by the clerk of assize on the back of the indictment against Williams, and surgeon Edward Neale. Griffiths confirmed that the body bore signs of wilful murder: the neck was dislocated and there were several marks of violence on the throat and under the left ear. Neale provided more detail of the injuries and a cause of death:

> he observed marks of violence on the throat & neck of the said female child the skin being chafed off as it had been with a hand in two severall places. And believes that the said child was strangled or choaked. And further sayth that he believes the said child was come to his [sic] full time and that the hands of the [said] child were open and its fingers extended, which as this deponent says is a sure sign that the sayd child was born alive according to the best of this deponent's experience and knowledge.[94]

This together with her signed confession was enough to convict Williams under the statute of 1624, and she was sentenced to death. There is no record of her execution but it seems likely that it was carried out: just five years later Elinor Hadley was executed at Carmarthen for the same offence.[95] Of the three Welsh women hanged for murder during the period 1735–1799, two suffered in the 1730s, suggesting that the country's later notable lenience to women who killed was not yet established,[96] as well as the danger of admitting any wrongdoing.

More unusually for the time, however, Hadley's conviction rested on the testimony of a single female witness whose evidence enabled an inquest to determine that the male child had been born alive and assaulted around the head. An eyewitness to live birth rendered medical evidence technically superfluous, while the cause of death was evidently obvious. There were 53 cases of newborn child murder in which there is clear indication that neither a surgeon nor midwife was present, the last of which occurred in Gloucestershire in 1842; in another 40 cases it is unknown whether a surgeon was involved or not. Lack of professional medical evidence was a risk to successful prosecution but not a total bar: 6 of the 53 cases resulted in a guilty verdict of some kind, the last in 1804 when Ann Smith was convicted of concealment at the Old Bailey.[97]

Neither laymen nor midwives, no matter how skilled, could provide evidence derived from *inside* the victim's body; only a surgeon had the necessary skill to do that. Coroners and magistrates recognised this and obtained medical evidence in 71 per cent of all cases of infant murder, a lower but nonetheless comparable figure to the equivalent proportion in cases of murder and manslaughter, 80.5 per cent (Table 3.8). Although midwives often testified in eighteenth-century trials for infant murder, serving as medico-legal witnesses in 47.9 per cent of inquests or trials before 1800 (113 cases of 236), they acted as the *sole* medico-legal witness in only 78 of these trials, 50 of which occurred *before* 1740. By mid-century medical evidence was seen as necessary and best provided by surgeons, who quickly supplanted midwives in court: only 23 midwives appeared in nineteenth-century trials, all but one as a secondary witness to medical facts proved by a surgeon.[98]

Lay women and medical men

Women remained key investigators of other women's bodies throughout the eighteenth century and well into the next. In 1783 Ann Husband constantly denied being pregnant despite local suspicion, so was permitted to remain in her employer's household until finally she appeared so near delivery that a midwife, Margaret Sayer of Hungerford in Berkshire, was called. By evening, Ann appeared "greatly reduced in her waste and size" but the three female investigators found nothing in her box. So Sayer "had recourse" to her breasts, "from the nipples of which issued milk very freely which she declared herself a stranger to." Pressed to confess, Ann admitted that "some little matter" had come from her and was in the privy. A search of the excrement revealed a face; removed and cleaned, the body had a small bruise near the left eye, probably inflicted by the coal rake used to get it up. The women observed blood coming from the mouth, but the men who removed the body saw no marks on it. The child appeared to be full-term, but Ann claimed that her labour came on five weeks early, so suddenly that the child was born in just ten minutes while she was in the privy; she did not hear it cry. Another servant confirmed that Ann had returned from the privy within ten minutes "very much disordered," and baby clothes found in her box four days later suggested she intended to keep the child.[99]

All of this amounted to a solid defence to murder;[100] the medical evidence was at most peripheral. Margaret Sayer could not be certain that the child was born alive, but knew from her own midwifery practice that it was possible to give birth to a dead child suddenly in a privy. Surgeon Edward Duke viewed the body and

> tried the old experiment of putting the lungs in water before the [inquest] jurors . . . and by the swimming thereof he is confirmed from his private opinion on the different authors on surgery and particularly that of Dr Albert Haller a very celebrated writer that the said child was born alive. Altho' he admits he has heard that the experiment of the lungs is quite disused and exploded either as substantial or corroborative evidence one way or the other.[101]

Surgeons all over England and Wales admitted that the hydrostatic lung test was disused, distrusted, out-dated or "exploded" – yet continued to use it. One reason for this was the physiological change that occurred in infant lungs once breathing began. The recent translation of a well-known textbook by Swiss anatomist Albrecht von Haller (1708–1777) stated that the lungs of newborns, "being dilated from the air, change from a small dense body, sinking even in salt water, into a light spungy floating fabric, extended to a considerable bulk with air, and of a white colour."[102] These changes were distinctive and provided secure evidence of live birth in a medical sense; Samuel Farr noted them in his textbook of 1788. The problem was that in the legal sense live birth meant breathing occurred after the child was wholly separated from the mother's body, and the lung test could not prove this; nothing short of eyewitness testimony could. This dichotomy was one that lawyers readily exploited: the direct question of whether a child was alive after birth was one many surgeons either declined to answer or admitted could not be known absolutely. Those who ventured to respond in the affirmative could be undermined by the well-known, and still to this day, difficulty of ascertaining the cause of death in newborn children.[103]

The trial of Martha John, Pembrokeshire, 1808

On 16 January 1808 an inquest was held on the death of a newborn girl at Rudbaxton in Pembrokeshire. After hearing evidence from five witnesses, four women and surgeon William Harris, the jury concluded that the child was murdered by a stab wound to the neck inflicted by her unmarried mother, Martha John, who had given birth alone and in secret. John was tried at Haverfordwest three months later, when a second count alleging murder by strangulation was added to the indictment.[104] Her trial was held on 13 April before John Balguy (c.1746–1833), the junior of the two judges on the Carmarthen Circuit,[105] but his fellow judge, the chief justice Samuel Heywood, was in court and took verbatim notes in one of 33 notebooks in which he recorded details of the trials over which he presided in the years between 1807 and autumn 1820. These notebooks clearly indicate that Heywood and Balguy were often in court together: Heywood recorded some of the trials over which Balguy presided, as in Martha John's case, and noted Balguy's occasional interjections about points of law during his own trials. This provides a valuable window into the prosecution of and judicial perspective on a trial for newborn child murder and Heywood's transcript of the proceedings against John has therefore been transcribed in full.[106] Line breaks in the document indicate the questions posed to witnesses, but the questions themselves were not recorded. There is no sign of a translator, and given how anglicised Pembrokeshire was it is likely the proceedings took place entirely in English.[107] Quite how Heywood managed to record so much detail in longhand as the witnesses testified may seem astonishing to modern readers unaccustomed to such exertions, but it was typical of judicial practices of the day.[108] Through him, we can take a seat in the court's public gallery.[109]

Thursday 13 April
Tried by Balguy J. – Rex v. Martha John
Indictment 11 January last for murder of her female bastard child by inflicting a wound on the throat with a penknife. 2nd Count for strangling it with her hands
The Attorney General and Owen for prosecution
Taunton & Lord for prisoner
Attorney General stated case: Evidence of child born alive will depend on 1 Surgeon's Evidence – 2 the blood – & 3 the cutting of the throat – for you to say what weight to be given to that evidence – child at full age & size

JANE SMITH: Housekeeper to Mr Phelps – 10 January – prisoner a servant a housemaid – single woman. About month before 10 January I asked her whether she was with child – she said no. I had farther conversation but not in particular – never but that once on that subject.

Saturday 9 January she went from Mr Phelps to see her father – he lives near Johnston 6 or 7 miles off, she returned Sunday evening about 8 o'clock. I saw her come into the kitchen, no more conversation she was much fatigued wet & dirty – She said so and it was so, she went to bed about 9. Next morning she did not come down at usual time, her usual time 7 o'clock. As soon as I had dressed myself I went up to see her – she was in bed, I observed blood on the floor. I asked her how she was. She said she had been ill in the night but much better – *she said she was in a particular way.* I went down and sent Ann Davis to her.

I saw her on Monday – 12 or 1 – nothing particular. Saw her Tuesday about her work when I came down stairs. On Wednesday I was sent to examine her room, she followed me up. I had not desired her to follow. She asked me what I was looking for – I told her my master and mistress *suspected she had miscarried, she said no.* I went down and met my mistress on stairs, I had said nothing further to prisoner before I left room. I went up with my mistress, prisoner was there she said *she had miscarried*, in answer to a question from my mistress. I did not hear the question but she said she had miscarried to me. My mistress then asked her where she had put the miscarriage, she said in the scullery. Nothing more passed on this subject. Wednesday evening she complained of great pain in her breast but said nothing further. *I went into scullery Wednesday morning, found nothing there.*

On Thursday morning I was sent by master and mistress both to know where she had put the miscarriage. I asked her she said it was in scullery and if I would wait till she got better she would show it me. Nobody present. Mr Phelps my master a Magistrate.

When I returned from scullery on Thursday I did not go to her. On Thursday prisoner sent to me about 11 or 12, I asked if she wanted me, she said yes – she said *if you will go to that trunk you will find it* – a large trunk in the room. I asked her for key, *she said it was not locked* – it was a trunk belonging to the room, I opened it and *found a child arranged in a linen cloth, lying on its back, dead*. I took it out box and laid it in window, I went downstairs to inform master I had found it.

I went upstairs and fetched child down to the nursery. I turned the child uncovered it – a *scratch on the right side of the neck* – *the skin was close together* – it looked like a scratch I did not observe. I observed blood in mouth and upon nowhere else. Child was a very small child but had nails on its fingers and hair on its head. Went back into prisoner's room she asked where child was, I told her in nursery. *She said what of it?* I told her there was a mark on the child's neck, she said she knew nothing of it – *but when she was nigh at pains she put her hands on both sides of the child's neck to assist herself, she might have hurt it with her nails but not intentionally*. I asked her when child born and she said it might be about 4 on Monday morning.

On Tuesday she washed part of her blanket. In the trunk I *found a little shirt and 2 little caps, one not finished*. This was when constable searched box. Nothing found in room besides, *but a knife in the window* – found on Thursday or Friday a round pocket knife.

[Cross-examined] On Sunday she walked to her father both there and back, very much fatigued. I am mother of a family, I can't say that fatigue has tendency to produce premature labour.

Two other maids Ann Davis and Joyce Williams slept in same room; usual for a child to cry immediately on birth – present at a great many and never knew an instance to contrary. The trunk in her bedroom – pointed to it – not locked – *she told me she had never locked it*.

I observed no blood about the neck. I had heard the prisoner *had had a child before*. No [male] servant in the family – that child I have heard is now living. The knife had a round end which she said she used to trim the candles with, it was a rusty knife. Another knife was found in another trunk but it seemed not to have been opened for many months, I examined it very particularly.

The shirt and cap were baby's linen. Character of prisoner for humanity and tenderness remarkably good. Young children in the house of Mr Phelps, she was more tender and affectionate to them than any other servant, my own three children when they came to house would rather go to her than me.

JOYCE WILLIAMS: On Sunday when she went to bed if she was any better – she said she was very poorly. I awoke in night – *not awaked by noise.* I heard her very poorly – *she was sitting up in bed.* Said to me in night, moonlight – she groaned – oh dear, oh dear – only a little noise. I asked her what was matter, she only groaned. I said no more, *I did not hear any other noise – or faint one* – I don't know she was out of bed.

I was first in kitchen in morning, I saw some spots of blood. I saw child on Thursday – *like a scratch on its neck*; I did not observe it [narrowly?], some spots of blood on face.

ANN DAVIS: Went to bed at 10; in night I saw her go out between 5 and 6. In morning she desired me to do her work and clean the parlour for she was very poorly. Prisoner did not come down on Monday. On Tuesday she came down, on Thursday I saw prisoner's bed – I looked at it, I saw marks of blood upon it. I washed sheet, a good deal of blood upon it. I asked her how she could have it of herself – and she said the Lord assisted her.

WILLIAM HARRIS: Surgeon in Haverfordwest. Sent to Mr Phelps (Witness here) Friday 15th Feb [sic] to see a child – I opened it – I tried the usual experiment.

(Not permitted by Court to go on.)

I observed child – impossible to say it was born alive or dead – at full term – but that might be & yet born dead. A wound in neck – which to casual observer might appear only a scratch. Tried with blunt end of knife, & it gave way – very deep – put finger at wound didn't come out at the wound – laying the sides open I could see it go deep – must be by a sharp instrument a cut right through into aesophagus. Sufficient to occasion death – external jugular vein was cut through – could not be done with the nail of any person – it was so deep.

[Cross examined] Wound when first I saw it was closed & appeared scratch – I introduced handle of knife which showed it was deep & I introduced little finger into wound & it came out. A wound in aesophagus alone would not cause immediate death. The division of the jugular vein would have occasioned instant death. If child alive must have been considerable effusion of blood. I was told woman seemed [undecipherable]. I saw it 10 o'clock Friday. Great exertion would hasten delivery – as walking great way. Possible a child not full time is not so strong if birth premature but mother more likely to be injured than child by it. The child was a female.

[From the Bench] The child had hair & nails – children may have hair & nails at 7 months ½ here every appearance was of child at full time.

MARTHA LEWIS: A child shewn to Mr Harris it was Martha John's child – I was not present.

MRS JANE SMITH CALLED AGAIN: 1st I took the child into nursery – & then into servants hall – I had key of room till Friday morning – it was locked on Thursday I locked key & I unlocked it on Friday morning, don't recollect I locked it again. Mr Harris was in servants hall. The child was carried into servants hall – after longer 2 hours in nursery – it remained unlocked in servants hall till evening – I unlocked it at 8 or 9 o'clock in morning.

Both the murder & concealment were summed to the jury together – & the jury found not guilty as to murder but guilty of concealment – & imprisoned 12 calendar months.

The judge's perspective

For this period, Heywood's notebook affords the most detailed account available for a criminal trial held at Great Sessions. It provides insights into the reactions of eyewitnesses to the crime and to the reception of the medical evidence by the court; it also corrects the verdict reported in the press as a full acquittal.[110] It shows that Martha John was ably defended, possibly via a dock brief although her employer John Phelps clearly had the means to hire counsel for her, and that her barristers tried to undermine the prosecution's account on both moral and medical grounds. This Welsh defendant, at least, was no more disadvantaged than the average English defendant at the time. Most importantly of all, Heywood's notes demonstrate that prosecuting counsel intended to construct the case largely on medical evidence: that the child was born alive and viable and then her throat was cut. An equally fascinating corollary informs us that Balguy refused to hear testimony of live birth based on the lung test the surgeon carried out; but we are not told why. It is possible that Balguy placed no confidence in it: other judges, and indeed surgeons, had been dismissing it for years. Perhaps he recognised that the circumstances surrounding the death of Martha John's infant lent themselves to a conviction for concealment of birth whereas murder was impossible to prove; he had already read the depositions, which do not survive in the archives, and the prosecution's own witness William Harris undermined the case when he admitted it was impossible to say whether the child was born alive or dead. None of the medical evidence was underlined, suggesting that in Heywood's opinion it was less compelling than that concerning the defendant's reported actions. Again, this is not unexpected: eighteenth- and early nineteenth-century judges exercised wide discretion in conducting trials and sentencing prisoners; many were preoccupied by a practical need for speedy exemplary justice and wanted to avoid difficulties of legal interpretation that might puzzle juries.[111] Had it not been for the statutory revision just five years earlier, in fact, Martha John might well have been acquitted; for her, the law functioned as Lord Ellenborough had intended it should.

A final clue to the judges' thinking in this case is provided by Heywood's notes of a similar trial over which he presided in spring 1814 when Margaret Francis, a servant girl, was tried for newborn child murder at Carmarthen. The prosecuting counsel – the attorney general William Owen (1775–1851) and William Oldnall (c.1784–1833), do not seem to have had much faith in their own case, opening it by stating there was "not strong evidence of child being born alive – surgeon of opinion child was born alive, from what is not now relied," then going on to suggest that since the child was found at the back of a privy where it could not have fallen and the prisoner had denied being pregnant, there had been a concealment.[112] The surgeon, Willoughby Dixie of Kidwelly, seems to have made only the most cursory of external examinations, concluding from the state of the umbilical cord that it "might have broke by the gravity of the child falling at the birth,"[113] though he had never heard of a mother being delivered while sitting on a privy. There were no marks of violence on the body, which had the hair and nails indicative of a full-term birth. Since Dixie did not perform the hydrostatic lung test, what was it that was unreliable? This could only be the evidence of live birth and viability. And so, Heywood tells us, "I summed up for no concealm[en]t – no *act* done by the woman to conceal only denied before and after delivery – see *Act* but Oldnall says Lawrence ruled no provision for child bed linen it be proof of concealment no[te]d Qn if he is right."[114] The jury disregarded Heywood and convicted Margaret Francis (who had no defence counsel) of concealment and she was sentenced to three months in the house of correction. This seems a little harsh, given that Heywood expected the jury to acquit her, but demonstrates how the law at this time was in the process of being shaped by the rulings of judges like Balguy, Heywood and Sir Soulden Lawrence, a contemporary of Lord Ellen-borough on the court of King's Bench.

Evidence from later trials shows that where there was no obvious indication that fatal wounds had been deliberately inflicted with some weapon, judges were willing to believe that observable injuries might have happened accidentally during labour, precisely as Martha John had claimed. In 1839, for example, two surgeons stated it was "highly improbable" that injuries to the baby's neck had been caused by the mother's hands as she delivered herself; but they had admit-ted to the coroner that it was possible,[115] and the judge seized on this in his remarks to the grand jury. Judges' observations on the cases before them were made immediately after the grand jury was impanelled at the opening of each assize and were usually reported in the mid-nineteenth-century press. They are particularly useful to historians because they represent the earliest opportunity that a judge had to influence the direction that a criminal case might take, and so they provide clues both to the legal complexity of a case and to the judge's opinion. As John Walliss has pointed out in relation to the operation of the Bloody Code, prisoners were funnelled away from execution at any one of five separate stages in the criminal justice process: before indictment; by a grand jury; or at trial, sentencing or pardoning.[116] Judges had the authority to guide the outcome of all but the first of these stages, and, having read the depositions before the court opened, used their 'charge' to the grand jury to indicate their views on the most serious or complex cases.[117]

By the 1830s judges instructed grand jurors to focus on two questions: "whether the unfortunate infant was born alive, and whether you are satisfied that its death was caused by the wilful act of the party accused."[118] Thus, when Ann King was indicted for newborn child murder at the Worcestershire assizes in July 1839, Baron Alderson told the grand jury precisely what to do:

> I do not conceive you will find much difficulty here, as it appears the child was born alive. The question for your consideration will be whether the injuries which the child received, and of which it died, were wilfully and designedly inflicted by the mother. This fact must be arrived at with the greatest possible caution, – with much calmness, – and the most dispassionate inquiry. Your regard for humanity will lead you to consider the agony of the mother at the moment of delivery – accompanied as it must be with much fear, and unassisted in the birth by a medical gentleman, or any one of her own sex. You must also bear in mind that, in the agony of child-bearing, a very little violence might inflict sufficient injury to cause the death of the child. In recommending these particulars to your consideration, I feel confident that you will discharge your duty in the most dispassionate manner, and with the greatest compassion and regard to humanity of which the case will admit.[119]

"A very little violence" is, nonetheless, violence; but Alderson's point – which appears anything but dispassionate – was that although the surgeons attributed death to strangulation, no wilful intent could be proved. And so the grand jury took their cue, throwing out the bill of indictment. Seven of the 18 cases of concealment of birth included in Table 4.5 were originally indicted as murder but the charge was downgraded by a grand jury. Table 4.6 indicates that findings of 'no bill' were regular but not typical outcomes: about 14 per cent of cases of newborn child murder that passed the scrutiny of an inquest or committal hearing never made it to trial, halted mainly by the decision of a grand jury. The last occasion on which this occurred was during the proceedings against Emily Combes, charged with the murder of her newborn son at Iron Acton in Gloucestershire in 1889. The medical evidence confirmed this as a case of sudden delivery in a privy: "My opinion is that the child died from suffocation, I think the woman must have been confined on the closet and the child was suffocated in the soft soil beneath. I am quite sure the child was born alive."[120] Other evidence persuaded the inquest jury that this was a murder: Combes did not alert her family that something untoward had occurred and when the body was found next day she tried to bribe a witness not to report it to the police. At the assizes, Baron Pollock told the grand jury "he did not think the evidence sufficient to support a charge of murder,"[121] an observation that obviously planted a strong seed of doubt, for the jurymen then decided that the facts could not even sustain a bill for concealment of birth.[122] The medical evidence was unequivocal – the child was full-term and viable – but the circumstances in which the birth occurred were subject to interpretation modified by obvious sympathy for a young woman whose mother claimed she did not know and never looked at what had come from her as she sat on the privy.[123]

Anne-Marie Kilday has described the 'moral panic' of the 1850s and 1860s that arose in relation to the leniency shown in trials for newborn child murder,[124] a leniency which one local newspaper editor ascribed to two factors: "there is great difficulty in procuring legal proof of wilful infanticide, to which we must add that there is still greater difficulty in getting juries to convict."[125] Trial jurors were expected to reach a decision according to their interpretation of the facts, but the evidence was first summed up for them by the judge, who commented on the facts and the law applicable to them.[126] So even if a woman was indicted for murder by a grand jury, there was still a good chance that she would be acquitted. Judges consistently discouraged trial juries from supposing that "the act of the prisoner was the cause of the death of the child, when there was another alternative consistent with her innocence,"[127] and seem frequently to have been prepared to imagine that the medical evidence before them invited some less horrific explanation than deliberate murder. When Margaret Bracegirdle, the cook at a school in Knutsford, Cheshire, killed her newborn during the night in March 1876, it did not take long for others in the household to find the bloody body, decapitated and stuffed into a box; Bracegirdle quickly confessed to a police officer that the infant was born alive.[128] A surgeon confirmed this, stating that the child had lived "some minutes" before suffering a blow to the head from a flat instrument (causing a blood clot), and was then decapitated with an axe – the sequence of events deduced from the fact that blood would not flow over the membranes of the brain to form a clot *after* the child was dead.[129] At the assizes, however, the Lord Chief Baron, Sir Fitzroy Kelly, told the grand jury that although this extraordinary case was certainly one for a trial jury, "he earnestly hoped that sooner or later they would have reason to believe that what may have led to this decapitation, or been the means of bringing about the child's death, would turn out to be an accident."[130] Under what accidental circumstances an infant's head might be cut off with an axe, he did not say, and Victorian men perceived this as a crime that fell short of murder: Bracegirdle was convicted of concealing the birth and imprisoned for 15 months.[131] In a similar case tried at the Old Bailey in 1905, in which "somehow the head came away from the body," Mr Justice Jelf ruled that there was no evidence of murder, despite the fact that experienced police surgeon Charles Graham Grant was absolutely positive that the cause of death was skull fracture and that "it is not possible that the head could have been severed from the body in any way except by cutting." The case was perhaps weakened when Grant, who had earlier avowed that the amount of blood on the brain indicated a blow "given during legal life," admitted – in response to a question put by prosecuting counsel – that the injury might have been caused before the child had completely separated from the mother, resulting in death after complete separation.[132] The law of murder still applied,[133] but the case for concealment was instead put to the jury and the defendant was convicted.

Grand jurors had a fourth option: in cases where a mother showed such lack of care that her actions amounted to gross negligence they could find a bill for manslaughter. Alternatively, a trial jury could return a verdict of manslaughter against a defendant charged with murder. When this occurred the medical evidence of live birth, separate existence and some fatal act or omission was unambiguous; defence counsel or the judge himself suggested that the facts fell short of murder yet remained very serious. But only 11 cases of this type were discovered: the perpetrators were imprisoned for up to two years in all but three instances, in 1874, 1878 and 1903. The lengthy sentences meted out in the 1870s are explained by the heightened concern about infanticide,[134] "the prevailing sin of the day" according to the judge who sentenced Emma Handley to ten years,[135] while 30 years later Louisa Beaumont got five years for abandoning her screaming newborn, placenta and umbilical cord still attached, on a doorstep in December. The medical evidence proved she had recently given birth and that the child suffered head injuries which could not have been due to a fall (unless the mother had then trodden on it), but were probably caused by a blow with a blunt object.[136] But most mothers were given the benefit of the doubt in cases of newborn child murder (Tables 4.5 and 4.6), aided by judicial paternalism, the perennial problem of separate existence, and the option of pleading guilty to concealment. The tolerance this encouraged is summarised by a comment made by the Lord Chief Justice as he sentenced a woman to 12 months' hard labour in 1909: "they must be very careful that in their desire to protect infant life they did not do more than absolute justice in connection with any particular case."[137]

The importance of plain speaking: the trial of Hannah Mottram, Cheshire, 1833

There was nothing remarkable about the circumstances of Hannah Mottram's crime, but the report of her trial for newborn child murder at the Chester assizes highlights one of the most important aspects of medico-legal practice: plain speaking in court. The problem of contradictory and faulty medical evidence was clearly recognised in the early decades of the nineteenth century,[138] and as teaching expanded to accommodate the compulsory curriculum set by the Society of Apothecaries in 1831, textbooks and lectures on forensic medicine took up the issue of how a doctor should present evidence in court. Apart from accuracy and preparedness, there were two basic points to remember: simplicity and directness. Both were essential, because judges, lawyers and jurors were unfamiliar with (and likely to be confused or annoyed by) scientific and technical terms.[139] But this message had not reached the two surgeons who testified at Mottram's trial in August 1833.

Concealing a birth

Hannah Mottram, (21) a pale cadaverous looking woman was indicted for having secretly disposed of the body of her male illegitimate offspring, born alive, by throwing it into a pit; a second count alleged the child to have been born dead, and charged the prisoner with concealing the birth. The prisoner was indicted for the murder of the child, but the Grand Jury ignored the bill.

The facts of the case are extremely short. On Sunday morning, the 16th of June last, as Sarah Winstanley and another little girl were going to Great Budworth church, in passing a pit about a quarter of a mile from the residence of the prisoner, they saw something floating in the water just under the surface. They got a stick and pulled it out, and on examination it proved to be the body of a male infant wrapped up in two stockings and tied with a string. They left the body and went on to church. Joseph Burgess, a farmer residing at Pickmere, found the body as he was going to church. It was delivered to a constable, and an inquest held on the 18th of June, in consequence of which Thomas Perris, the special high constable of Budworth, apprehended the prisoner the following day at her father's house. On examination of her person by a surgeon, he found milk in the breasts, and the state of the vagina was such as is usual after a recent delivery. She admitted that she had had a child, but requested him to keep it secret. The surgeon who attended the coroner's inquest proved that the child had an extensive wound in the throat, sufficient to have caused death. There was no evidence that the child was born alive. [The pedantic style in which medical men give their evidence on these occasions is very amusing. The two last witnesses were admirable specimens of this variety of the genus 'Chirurgieun'; their technical phraseology called for the interposition of the Court to render their evidence intelligible to the 'Hoi Polloi'. Take for example: the brother of the worshipful fraternity of the probe and pestle, who examined the prisoner's person, could not state, in plain English, that he found milk in her breasts, but that *upon applying one extremity of a glass tube to the areola and his lips to the other, and exhausting the receiver, a whitish fluid exuded from the excretory duct of the lacteal gland*!!!]

The jury found the prisoner guilty. The learned Judge in passing sentence, said he feared that it was not only for the purpose of concealing her own shame that she disposed of the body of this infant, but of concealing an act of violence committed upon it. Under the circumstances, he felt it imperative upon him to inflict the full measure of punishment imposed by the statute, which was two years imprisonment with hard labour.[140]

Who were these "admirable specimens" of the medical profession? James Dean was a surgeon in Winnington, a village outside Northwich about six miles from Pickmere; and Joseph Hill was a surgeon and man-midwife in Lymm, about nine miles from Pickmere in the opposite direction. This in itself is interesting, as these distances were longer than most of those encountered in this part of the country. Normally a medical man was based in the same village or town, or had travelled three to five miles at most, but Hill came from further away, summoned by a magistrate to examine Mottram. Dean had testified at the inquest on 18 June when he made an external examination of the body, which had begun to putrefy; he did not conduct a post-mortem and so could not use the lung test, possibly because he did not know how or that it could be done on a decomposing corpse, or did not think it necessary given there was no suspect in custody. The inquest returned a verdict of murder against a person unknown, but the high constable's inquiries yielded Mottram's name and he got a warrant to search her bedroom, where the most suspicious thing he found was evidence that she had recently repaired her bed by sewing pieces of clean fabric around it. This was enough to justify a committal hearing, however, at which Hill testified on 22 June. He reported having "examined her breasts and applied a glass to the nipple, which glass he sucked and a small quantity of milk exuded from the nipple." He concluded she had had a child within the month and revealed that during the examination she had admitted this but asked him to say nothing; he asked her if she cut its throat and she answered, faintly, that she had.[141] This was an aspect of medico-legal practice seen in cases of newborn child murder when a surgeon asked a suspect to admit giving birth or to say where she had hidden the child. But voluntary admissions did not have strong evidentiary status when not signed or corroborated by other evidence in the case,[142] and Mottram was probably lucky that Dean could not testify that the child had most likely been born alive.

Dean was the senior of these two surgeons, having been in practice before August 1815.[143] Hill was 20 years younger: born around 1806, he qualified LSA and MRCS and set up practice in Lymm sometime after 1829; he had died by February 1859.[144] Neither one appeared in another medico-legal case. It is possible that one or both of them had taken a course of lectures in forensic medicine, depending on where they did their training; but if they did, the experience did them little good. Hill at least sought to impress the court with his medical acumen but succeeded only in making himself a figure of fun. This unfortunate consequence of inexperience was one that later medico-legal writers tried hard to eliminate: by the middle of the nineteenth century textbooks included long sections on medical evidence, setting out the responsibilities of doctors and the expectations placed on them at inquests, committal hearings and trials, in the knowledge that any general practitioner might have to give evidence one day, and should be properly prepared to do so.[145] Given the frequency with which cases of infant murder occurred,[146] the medical difficulties of proving the offence, and the fact that judges and lawyers were becoming increasingly knowledgeable about forensic matters, it is easy to see why such emphasis was placed on this crime in the lecture courses considered in Chapter 2.

The jury's perspective

Medical testimony had to be equally clear and unambiguous during the pre-trial investigation, so that coroners, inquest juries and magistrates had the most accurate information possible when deciding whether a suspect should be committed for trial. Jurors were active participants, as befit a public inquiry, but while this fact has been recognised in relation to early modern inquests,[147] we have less information about their interventions in nineteenth-century inquests. However, it is clear that, despite the growing presence of solicitors, inquest jurors continued to exercise their right to pose questions directly to witnesses.[148] Although little evidence of this practice remains in archival sources, depositions taken during the inquest on the newborn son of domestic cook Lucy Culley in 1869 included the jurors' questions, shedding a little light on the way in which inquest juries reached their verdict and, by extension, the knowledge that they brought to bear on the case.

The infant was found in a carpet bag removed from a corner of Culley's bedroom in Newbury, Berkshire, in September 1869; it seemed evident from her physical state and the blood about the room that the child was hers and had been killed by a deep cut to the throat. The jurors' questions focused on the obvious issues of whether the child had been born alive, what had caused his death, and whether this might have been due to unintended actions; but they also wanted to know when he was born. Thus, the housemaid who discovered Culley in distress was asked if she had heard the child cry and how much blood she thought there was. The family nurse found the afterbirth in a chamber pot under the bed; helped local GP Henry Finch, who happened to be visiting, to remove the body from the bag; looked at it closely enough to note the gash in the neck and torn umbilical cord and later handed all the physical evidence over to the borough police superintendent. The coroner asked if she had heard the child cry or suspected the pregnancy (she had not), but the jurors asked why she waited an hour to search the bag (she did not notice the blood seeping from it) and whether Culley had been given notice (no, she was leaving voluntarily to be married).[149] This evidence suggested the case might be one of concealment: there was no solid motive for murder and death might have arisen from lack of care and attention at birth. The jury needed to know more about the cut in the neck.

But Henry Finch had scarcely paid attention to the body and could not identify it as the one he found in the bag, leading to the following exchange:[150]

> I have now particularly noticed a wound on the neck but I did not sufficiently remark the body when I saw it in the bag and subsequently to be able to speak to it.
>
> By the jury: Did you remark anything particular in the formation of the hand of the body you saw in the bag? I did. Have you noticed it in the body you have now viewed and which was shown to the jury? I did not.
>
> At the request of the jury Dr Finch again went to view the body and on his return stated That he found the same malformation and in both hands.
>
> By the Coroner: Did you notice the length of the cord either on the body or to the afterbirth? No I did not.

The child had six fingers on each hand: the nurse was recalled and asked about this, to prove that the body she handed to the police was the body on which the inquest was being held. Then the jury asked her "Has there been anything to indicate that she Lucy Culley was not in her right mind?" No, she replied, "I have never noticed anything." Supt George Deane confirmed that he had received the body, afterbirth and carpet bag, and was present at the post-mortem carried out that morning by Dr John Ligertwood.

Ligertwood, another local practitioner, was asked by the coroner to conduct the post-mortem but we do not know why he was selected. He was a graduate of the University of Aberdeen who took his degree in 1859 and so had probably studied forensic medicine under Francis Ogston (1803–1887), an experienced physician and police surgeon who taught medical jurisprudence in the city for over 50 years.[151] Ligertwood provided a thorough account of the body: its size indicated viability; the umbilical cord was torn; the cut on the neck (four inches wide) had gone through to the spinal column and must have been inflicted with great force. But there was little evidence that the child had breathed fully: the lungs did not fill the chest cavity and floated only partially in water. He thought the wound had been inflicted during life but could not prove the child was born alive. He had also examined Lucy Culley's breasts and genitals, and believed she had given birth within the past five or six days. This prompted a question from the jury:

> By the Jury: Cannot a medical man say nearer than 5 or 6 days that a child has been born? I think not positively. Could the mother have inflicted the injury in the neck with some instrument with which she was endeavouring to deliver herself? She might have done so. Was the cut inflicted before the cord was separated? I cannot say.
>
> By the Coroner: Do you think from the facts that have been elicited in evidence that Lucy Culley has been delivered as long as 5 or 6 days? No but certainly within 5 or 6 days. Do you think her delivery took place as long as 3 days from the time you saw her? I did not think it had been as long as 3 days.

The purpose of the questions about when she was delivered is uncertain, since there was never any serious doubt that Culley was the mother of the dead child, albeit the bloody knife was not found until after the inquest; no one heard anything and it was difficult to say, given the child had not lived long (if at all, in the legal sense) exactly when the injuries were received and when death took place. The jurymen seem, like so many of their brethren, to have been ambivalent; ultimately, however, as was usual when there were overt signs of violence, they decided to let the assize court test Culley's defence. At her trial in December she was defended by a barrister who made a point of telling the court that this was his first appearance for the defence in such an important case; but Culley was in good hands. Indicted for murder and concealment, all the evidence pointed to the latter offence, for which she was duly convicted and sentenced to six months.[152]

Grand juries returned true bills for murder in about 86 per cent of cases of newborn child murder, endorsing the original conclusion reached by an inquest or magistrate, but under the terms of the 1828 Offences Against the Person Act they had the option of hedging their bets by indicting for both murder and concealing the birth and leaving the final decision to the petty jury. At trial, the choice was easily made: by the 1840s trials for newborn child murder followed a familiar script in which everyone from the judge to the jury knew their role. Additionally, more and more defendants had the benefit of counsel who, after 1836, could address the jury directly; their powerful pleading was frequently commended by judges and must, as intended, have influenced jurors. Thus, in the case of the unique offence of newborn child murder, medico-legal practice comprised a set of interconnected acts, questions and assumptions by doctors, laymen, coroners, police and law officers from which the purely medical evidence could never be wholly disentangled.

Conclusion

During the eighteenth and nineteenth centuries, newborn child murder was so frequent that the average medical practitioner might well have expected to encounter at least one case during his career. But the crime posed a series of potential problems to which medico-legal witnesses had to be alert if they were to avoid serious error or being made to look incompetent at an inquest or trial. By the 1730s surgeons had begun to prepare for this challenge by using the hydrostatic lung test to establish the fact of respiration, from which it was inferred that an infant had been born alive. But this was far from clear-cut: in a medical sense 'born alive' meant that the child had breathed, but in the legal sense it meant a child had breathed after it was entirely separated from the mother. The difficulty of demonstrating that an infant had had the necessary separate existence remained unresolved after the First World War, not least because standards of proof demanded by the law did not necessarily match those accepted in medicine, no matter how many tests were introduced or refined. If a child was killed immediately after birth, in the legal sense of the term, no evidence other than that of an eyewitness could prove it was born alive.[153] In the absence of such a witness, external examination alone could not hope to answer the question of live birth, so coroners and magistrates sought out the evidence provided by post-mortem examination, thereby displacing midwives as medico-legal witnesses. The data presented in this chapter suggest that their exclusion was largely complete by the end of the eighteenth century. A second type of infant murder involved the killing of a child up to one year old, but it was indicted less frequently and the medico-legal signs presented fewer complications. It was however more likely to lead to an insanity defence, particularly after a new disease associated with childbirth and lactation, puerperal insanity, was identified in the 1820s; but men also benefited from the mid-nineteenth-century acceptance of insanity as a defence to crime.[154]

The medico-legal investigation of infant murder had two key effects. Doctors adopted a language of certainty in legal settings, but the confidence they evinced with regard to infant bodies could be undermined by skilful cross-examination.

Legal historians concerned with explaining and describing the development of adversarial trial procedure in the eighteenth century have noted the important role played by the increasing presence of lawyers acting both for the prosecution and the defence. Elaborate judicial summing up developed only after lawyers began to take on more prominent roles in criminal trials at the end of the century, the 1780s being a particular turning point.[155] Defence counsel focused their efforts mainly on cross-examining prosecution witnesses, as this offered clients an effective means of undermining the case against them. The precise details of this historical development have been studied mainly in relation to the Old Bailey and need not concern us here, but few legal scholars have recognised the importance of medico-legal testimony in this process.[156] Similarly, historians of crime have not considered the significance of lawyers in trials for newborn child murder: they probed the prosecution's case by asking questions that encouraged doctors to contradict themselves or admit that they were not certain of their facts or of the inference to be drawn from them, in relation to the crucial points on which an indictment rested, live birth and independent existence. And as high rates of acquittal have consistently demonstrated, English and Welsh juries selectively interpreted medical evidence in order to offer leniency to women tried for infant murder, often under clear direction from the judge.

This direction was made to the two types of jury on which a defendant's future rested: the grand jury and the petty jury. Judges made an address to grand jurors tasked with finding indictments based on the depositions, which they had read before the court opened. Their 'charge' made clear statements about the legal complexity of the cases to be tried, to guide jurors in their assessment of the evidence presented. If grand juries were reluctant to indict women for newborn child murder, how much did this depend on the medical evidence itself and how much on what the judge had made of it? Then, despite – or rather because of the growing dominance of lawyers – judges had the last word in a trial when they summed up the case for the petty jury, making comments that, while focused on points of law, tended to single out the medical evidence on account of the unique difficulties associated with prosecuting newborn child murder. As renowned barrister William Garrow told a jury in 1784, "you will, under my Lord's direction, first enquire, whether the child was born alive, or whether it was not; and if it was, whether violent hands were laid upon it."[157] French observer Charles Cottu suggested in 1822 that judges confined themselves to "a naked statement of the affair,"[158] but in fact they appear to have told jurors, repeatedly and throughout the nineteenth century, that the medical evidence could not support a murder charge, what amounted in effect to directed verdicts. This was partly the result of the legal definition of live birth and rules of evidence, but was embedded also in the judges' personal assumptions about the accused women. The extent to which this direction influenced juries' reluctance to convict requires further study.

This chapter has demonstrated that courtroom procedures, standards of evidence and medico-legal knowledge became intertwined at precisely the period in the eighteenth century, the 1730s and the 1780s, which witnessed the rise of the adversarial criminal trial, and developed together during the nineteenth century. Under this stimulus, trials for infant murder became the main stage upon which medico-legal practitioners established and refined a distinctive contribution to the investigation of serious violent crime. No other form of medico-legal practice had such a widespread, longstanding or consistent impact on the evolution of forensic expertise or the processes of criminal justice. Infant murder should therefore be considered as more than an isolated chapter in the history of crime or a peculiar case study in the history of forensic medicine but as a principal stimulus to significant legal, academic and professional reforms of the eighteenth and nineteenth centuries.

Notes

1 Dana Rabin, "Bodies of Evidence, States of Mind: Infanticide, Emotion and Sensibility in Eighteenth-Century England," in *Infanticide: Historical Perspectives on Child Murder and Concealment, 1550–2000*, ed. Mark Jackson (Aldershot: Ashgate, 2002), pp. 73–92 and also the chapters by Hilary Marland, Cath Quinn and Jonathan Andrews in the same volume; Sheena Sommers, "Remapping Maternity in the Courtroom: Female Defenses and Medical Witnesses in Eighteenth-Century Infanticide Proceedings," in *The Body in Medical Culture*, ed. Elizabeth Klaver (Albany: State University of New York Press, 2009), pp. 37–59; Pauline M. Prior, "Psychiatry and the Fate of Women Who Killed Infants and Young Children, 1850–1900," and Clíona Rattigan, "'Half Mad at the Time': Unmarried Mothers and Infanticide in Ireland, 1922–1950," in *Cultures of Care in Irish Medical History, 1750–1970*, ed. Catherine Cox and Maria Luddy (Basingstoke: Palgrave Macmillan, 2010), pp. 92–112 and 168–190; Jade Shepherd, "'One of the Best Fathers Until He Went Out of His Mind': Paternal Child-Murder, 1864–1900," *Journal of Victorian Culture* 18 (2013), pp. 17–35.

2 Mark Jackson, *New-Born Child Murder: Women, Illegitimacy and the Courts in Eighteenth-Century England* (Manchester: Manchester University Press, 1996), chapter 4; Anne-Marie Kilday, *A History of Infanticide in Britain c. 1600 to the Present* (Basingstoke: Palgrave Macmillan, 2013), pp. 101–108; and references cited in the Introduction, notes 30, 35 and 120.

3 Mary Clayton, "Changes in Old Bailey Trials for the Murder of Newborn Babies, 1674–1803," *Continuity and Change* 24 (2009), pp. 347–351.

4 Jackson, *New-Born Child Murder*, pp. 6–7.

5 Katherine D. Watson, *Forensic Medicine in Western Society: A History* (Abingdon: Routledge, 2011), p. 106. No evidence of direct harm was required; the concealment proved the crime.

6 William Blackstone, *Commentaries on the Laws of England*, Vol. 4 (Oxford: Clarendon Press, 1769), p. 198; Jackson, *New-Born Child Murder*, pp. 87–90 links the growing awareness of the importance of medical evidence at this time to renewed interest in the inquest as a form of pre-trial inquiry.

7 Kilday, *A History of Infanticide*, pp. 121–125.

8 This question revealed the gulf between medical and legal definitions of birth: see Alfred S. Taylor, *A Manual of Medical Jurisprudence*, second edition (London: John Churchill, 1846), pp. 491–493, 496–497.

9 Regina v. Milborough Trilloe, 1842: Murder may be committed on a child still attached to the mother by the navel string. See William Moody, *Crown Cases Reserved for Consideration and Decided by the Judges of England 1837–1844*, Vol. 2 (Philadelphia: T. & J. W. Johnson, 1853), pp. 331–333.

10 Daniel J. R. Grey, "Discourses of Infanticide in England, 1880–1922," PhD thesis, Roehampton University, 2008, pp. 151–175.

11 Alfred S. Taylor, *A Manual of Medical Jurisprudence* (London: John Churchill, 1844), p. 435.

12 Ruth Ellen Homrighaus, "Wolves in Women's Clothing: Baby-Farming and the British Medical Journal, 1860–1872," *Journal of Family History* 26 (2001), p. 361.

13 A notable exception being Randolph Roth, "Child Murder in New England," *Social Science History* 25 (2001), pp. 101–147.

14 Samuel Farr, *Elements of Medical Jurisprudence* (London: T. Becket, 1788), p. 48. The first category included forced early delivery intended to cause death.

15 For example: Ann R. Higginbotham, "'Sin of the Age': Infanticide and Illegitimacy in Victorian London," in *Victorian Scandals: Representations of Gender and Class*, ed. Kristine Ottesen Garrigan (Athens, OH: Ohio University Press, 1992), pp. 259–260; Michelle Oberman, "Understanding Infanticide in Context: Mothers Who Kill, 1870–1930 and Today," *The Journal of Criminal Law and Criminology* 92 (2002), pp. 722–725; Anne-Marie Kilday, "Desperate Measures or Cruel Intentions? Infanticide in Britain since 1600," in *Histories of Crime: Britain 1600–2000*, ed. Anne-Marie Kilday and David Nash (Basingstoke: Palgrave, 2010), pp. 67, 71.

16 Jessica A. Sheetz-Nguyen, *Victorian Women, Unwed Mothers and the London Foundling Hospital* (London: Continuum, 2012), pp. 188–190 offers clues to the hurdles that unwed mothers faced, citing the "sheer desperation" that led one woman to commit infant murder. Altruistic child killing is recognised by modern psychiatrists: for a historical example, see Katherine D. Watson, "Religion, Community and the Infanticidal Mother: Evidence from 1840s Rural Wiltshire," *Family and Community History* 11 (2008), pp. 118–119, 124–128.

17 The range of explanations for newborn child murder are summarised in Kilday, *A History of Infanticide*, chapter 6.

18 William Hunter, "On the Uncertainty of the Signs of Murder, in the Case of Bastard Children," *Medical Observations and Inquiries* 6 (1784), pp. 272–277.

19 The National Library of Wales database indicates that 40% of infant murder cases (1730–1830) did not proceed to trial.

20 Hilary Marland, *Dangerous Motherhood: Insanity and Childbirth in Victorian Britain* (Basingstoke: Palgrave Macmillan, 2004).

21 Shepherd, "Paternal Child-Murder," p. 24.

22 NLW GS 4/533/3, Rex v. Mary Morgan, Radnorshire, 1804; Kilday, *A History of Infanticide*, pp. 125–131.

23 *OBP*, trials of Sarah Perry, ref. t18170219-31 and Catherine Welch, ref. t18280410-17.

24 TNA ASSI 6/2, Rex v. Mary Smith, Staffordshire, 1833.

25 Watson, "Religion, Community and the Infanticidal Mother."

26 Roth, "Child Murder in New England," p. 120.

27 TNA ASSI 65/13, Regina v. Emma Elizabeth Scott, Cheshire, 1883; *Manchester Courier and Lancashire General Advertiser*, 3 Nov 1883, p. 15. It took the police two and a half weeks to find and arrest the mother, who had left a monogrammed handkerchief in the parcel.

28 *The Liverpool Mercury*, 17 Nov 1883, p. 8.

29 Higginbotham, "'Sin of the Age'," pp. 257–258.

30 Katherine D. Watson, "Women, Violent Crime and Criminal Justice in Georgian Wales," *Continuity and Change* 28 (2013), pp. 261–262.

31 This proportion is higher than that reported in n.23 because the cases included in my database have been selected on the basis of the large amount of documentary evidence that survives, whereas the National Library of Wales database includes all cases and prosecutors' public roles have not been systematically identified.

32 Richard W. Ireland, *Land of White Gloves? A History of Crime and Punishment in Wales* (Abingdon: Routledge, 2015), pp. 69–70.

33 David J. V. Jones, *Crime in Nineteenth-Century Wales* (Cardiff: University of Wales Press, 1992), pp. 75–77.

34 Russell Grigg, "Getting Away with Murder? Infanticide in Wales, 1730–1908," *The Local Historian* 44 (2014), pp. 126, 128.

35 Ireland, *Land of White Gloves?*, pp. 60–67; R. W. Ireland, "'Perhaps My Mother Murdered Me': Child Death and the Law in Victorian Carmarthenshire," in *Communities and Courts in Britain 1150–1900*, ed. Christopher Brooks and Michael Lobban (London: The Hambledon Press, 1997), pp. 239–244. On the loss of Great Sessions, see Mark Ellis Jones, "'An Invidious Attempt to Accelerate the Extinction of our Language': The Abolition of the Court of Great Sessions and the Welsh Language," *Welsh History Review* 19 (1998), pp. 226–264. On the Rebecca 'riots' by agricultural workers in west Wales, see David Williams, *The Rebecca Riots*, reprint (Cardiff: University of Wales Press, 1978).

36 Jackson, *New-Born Child Murder*, pp. 84–109; Kilday, *A History of Infanticide*, pp. 101–108.

37 Grey, "Discourses of Infanticide," chapter 3; Tim Siddons, "Suspected New-Born Child Murder and Concealment of Pregnancy in Scotland, c.1812–c.1930," PhD thesis, University of Edinburgh, 2013, chapters 7 and 8; see pp. 217–221 for medical examination of suspected women.

38 Clíona Rattigan, *'What Else Could I Do?' Single Mothers and Infanticide, Ireland 1900–1950* (Dublin: Irish Academic Press, 2012), pp. 184–186, quotation on p. 184 (referring to the 1930s).

39 This phrase or the equivalent "something more than common" was used at least three times: TNA ASSI 6/1/2, Rex v. Ann Husband, Berkshire, 1783; NLW GS 4/906/4, Rex v. Maria Morris, Cardiganshire, 1795; *OBP*, trial of Sarah Dixon, ref. t18050710-37.

40 NLW GS 4/746/3, Rex v. Jane Thomas, Carmarthenshire, 1786.

41 Taylor, *Manual of Medical Jurisprudence*, second edition, pp. 450, 465–466; see for example *OBP*, trial of Robert Hall and Frances Douglas, ref. t18361024-2336.

42 Taylor, *Manual of Medical Jurisprudence*, second edition, pp. 484–486; *OBP*, trial of Louisa Beaumont, ref. t19030112-163.

43 Taylor, *Manual of Medical Jurisprudence*, second edition, p. 480; Alfred Swaine Taylor, *The Principles and Practice of Medical Jurisprudence* (London: John Churchill & Sons, 1865), pp. 955–956. For marks on the floor, see TNA ASSI 6/16, Regina v. Margaret Craigie, Worcestershire, 1877; for the position of a body indicating it had been pushed to the back of the vault rather than falling straight down, see TNA ASSI 72/3, Regina v. Mary Ann Osborn, Glamorgan, 1881 and n.79 below (Regina v. Sarah Varney, 1874).

44 Daniel J. R. Grey, "'What Woman Is Safe . . .?': Coerced Medical Examinations, Suspected Infanticide, and the Response of the Women's Movement in Britain, 1871–1881," *Women's History Review* 22 (2013), pp. 406–408.

45 TNA ASSI 65/1, Rex v. Ann Radley, Cheshire, 1832. Evidently at least one man had previously "concerned" her.

46 TNA ASSI 6/5, Regina v. Harriet Tarling, Gloucestershire, 1844.

47 Taylor, *Principles and Practice of Medical Jurisprudence*, p. 984; Alfred Swaine Taylor, *A Manual of Medical Jurisprudence*, ninth edition (London: J. & A. Churchill, 1874), pp. 581–584 (the topic of medical responsibility in the examination of women charged with infanticide was new to this edition, see p. iv).

48 TNA ASSI 6/5, Regina v. Jane Smith, Berkshire, 1844, evidence of Dr Silas Palmer.

49 For a detailed example, see the declaration made to the coroner by Hannah Brogden, 23 Apr 1798: TNA CHES 24/179/6, Rex v. Hannah Brogden, Cheshire, 1798.

50 TNA ASSI 6/5, Regina v. Amelia Browne, Shropshire, 1841, evidence of Richard Perkins. Textbooks of forensic medicine do not mention this, but a midwifery textbook suggests it was unlikely to be true: Graily Hewitt, *The Pathology, Diagnosis, and Treatment of Diseases of Women, Including the Diagnosis of Pregnancy*, third edition (London: Longmans, Green and Co., 1872), pp. 181–182.

51 *Morning Advertiser*, 20 Dec 1847, p. 4. This comment was made by the barrister who defended Isabella Kirk in a dock brief at the Old Bailey. None of the detail that appears in the press accounts of her trial is included in the *OBP*, ref. t18471213-386.

52 The textbooks of Farr, Male and Smith note these signs but do not mention their duration. However the first edition of Taylor's *A Manual of Medical Jurisprudence* (1844), p. 584 points out that if the examination was made eight or ten days after delivery it would be difficult if not impossible to say with certainty that delivery had taken place.

53 Joel Peter Eigen, *Mad-Doctors in the Dock: Defending the Diagnosis, 1760–1913* (Baltimore: Johns Hopkins University Press, 2016), pp. 25–27.

54 Mark Stevens, *Broadmoor Revealed: Victorian Crime and the Lunatic Asylum* (Barnsley: Pen & Sword Social History, 2013), pp. 1–6.

55 A finding suggested by Jonathan Andrews, "The Boundaries of Her Majesty's Pleasure: Discharging Child-Murderers from Broadmoor and Perth Criminal Lunatic Department, *c.*1860–1920," in *Infanticide: Historical Perspectives on Child Murder and Concealment, 1550–2000*, ed. Mark Jackson (Aldershot: Ashgate, 2002), pp. 220–221.

56 J. Stanley Hopwood, "Child Murder and Insanity," *Journal of Mental Science* 73 (1927), pp. 95–96.

57 Ibid., p. 101.

58 Dana Y. Rabin, *Identity, Crime, and Legal Responsibility in Eighteenth-Century England* (Basingstoke: Palgrave Macmillan, 2004), pp. 95–110; Marland, *Dangerous Motherhood*. For a summary of the role of mental illness in the history of infant murder, see Kilday, *A History of Infanticide*, pp. 166–179.

59 Tony Ward, "The Sad Subject of Infanticide: Law, Medicine and Child Murder, 1860–1938," *Social and Legal Studies* 8 (1999), pp. 163–180; Tony Ward, "Legislating for Human Nature: Legal Responses to Infanticide, 1860–1938," in *Infanticide*, ed. Jackson, 249–269.

60 Arlie Loughnan, *Manifest Madness: Mental Incapacity in Criminal Law* (Oxford: Oxford University Press, 2012), chapter 8; quotation on p. 203.

61 Gooch read a paper to the Royal College of Physicians in 1819 which was published in the *Transactions* in 1820. See also Robert Gooch, *An Account of Some of the Most Important Diseases Peculiar to Women* (London: John Murray, 1829), p. 108 and Hilary Marland, "At Home with Puerperal Mania: The Domestic Treatment of the Insanity of Childbirth in the Nineteenth Century," in *Outside the Walls of the Asylum: The History of Care in the Community 1750–2000*, ed. Peter Bartlett and David Wright (London: Athlone Press, 1999), pp. 45–52.

62 NLW GS 4/395/2, Rex v. Ann Jones, Breconshire, 1818.

63 NLW GS 4/521/1, Rex v. Elizabeth Price, Radnorshire, 1747.

64 TNA ASSI 6/4, Regina v. Celia Tippins, Gloucestershire, 1839. There was no medical evidence as to her state of mind at the time of the crime, though it seems likely she was insane then too.

65 *OBP*, trials of Minnie Wells, ref. t18941022-849 and Margaret Murphy, ref. t19110627-33.

66 *OBP*, trial of Ethel Harding, ref. t19081110-14.

67 *North Wales Chronicle*, 25 Jul 1885, p. 7.

68 Taylor, *Manual of Medical Jurisprudence*, second edition, p. 434.

69 Farr, *Elements of Medical Jurisprudence*, p. 14: for example, orbital sockets in the fifth month and ear bones in the seventh.

70 *OBP*, trial of Mary Lewis, ref. t17930220-38.

71 These arguments were made in trials held in 1808, 1870 and 1877.

72 *OBP*, trial of Sarah Harwood, ref. t17290416-67.

73 NLW GS 4/381/2, Rex v. Mary Harris and William Powell, Breconshire, 1755, testimony of George Williams.

74 *OBP*, trial of Mildred Cole, ref. t19040418-395.

75 *OBP*, trial of Elizabeth Parkins, ref. t17710410-35.

76 *OBP*, trial of Jane Reeves, ref. t18390204-684, testimony of Charles James Preedy.

77 *OBP*, trial of Mary Wright, ref. t18710501-383.

78 J. Dixon Mann, *Forensic Medicine and Toxicology*, third edition (London: Charles Griffin, 1902), p. 152; see also Taylor, *Principles and Practice of Medical Jurisprudence*, p. 943.

79 TNA ASSI 6/14, Regina v. Sarah Varney, Berkshire, 1874, testimony of James Hopkins Walters, magistrate's committal hearing, 24 Feb 1874.

80 TNA ASSI 6/14, Regina v. Mary Jane Brown, Gloucestershire, 1874, inquest testimony of Richard Jocelyn Swan, 25 Jun 1874. Nehemiah Philpott (d. 1914) served in the Gloucestershire Constabulary 1856–1902.

81 Ibid., marginal note at testimony of Richard Jocelyn Swan, magistrate's committal hearing, 8 Jul 1874.

82 Michael Ryan, *A Manual of Medical Jurisprudence* (London: Renshaw and Rush, 1831), p. 173; Taylor, *Manual of Medical Jurisprudence*, chapters 45 and 46. Used for the first time in the cases on which this book is based; I have no information about an earlier usage, but it is possible.

83 Taylor, *Principles and Practice of Medical Jurisprudence*, p. 938; Grey, "Discourses of Infanticide," p. 165. If meconium was forced out of a dead body by heavy pressure on the abdomen this would leave visible signs. Police surgeon Charles Graham Grant told his readers that if "with other signs you can show the presence of milk in the stomach or intestines you are in a strong position": *Practical Forensic Medicine: A Police-Surgeon's Emergency Guide*, second edition (London: H. K. Lewis, 1911), p. 62.

84 On the diagnostic presence of air in the stomach and intestines of infants, see J. Dixon Mann, *Forensic Medicine and Toxicology*, sixth edition, ed. William A. Brend (London: Charles Griffin and Company, 1922), pp. 117–118; *OBP*, testimony of Ludwig Freyberger in the trial of Louisa Lunn, ref. t19040321-332.

85 See for example TNA ASSI 65/8, Regina v. Ann Groom and George Corbett, Cheshire, 1868, inquest testimony of Dr Richard Lord.

86 The accounts given by Taylor in his textbooks of 1844 (pp. 442–443), 1865 (pp. 896–897) and 1874 (p. 522) were nearly identical, as also the edition of *Principles and Practice of Medical Jurisprudence* prepared by Thomas Stevenson in 1894, vol. 2 (pp. 332–333); Dixon Mann's text did not change between the first and third editions of 1893 and 1902.

87 Farr, *Elements of Medical Jurisprudence*, p. 65.

88 Taylor, *Principles and Practice of Medical Jurisprudence*, p. 975; Dixon Mann, *Forensic Medicine and Toxicology*, third edition, pp. 154–155.

89 TNA ASSI 6/16, Regina v. Mira Cresswell, Gloucestershire, 1878; *Cheltenham Chronicle*, 23 Apr 1878, p. 2, testimony of Henry Jessop who, according to the judge, "certainly gave his evidence in [a] clear and intelligible manner and with firmness."

90 Taylor, *Principles and Practice of Medical Jurisprudence*, pp. 633–634, 677, 698–699.

91 TNA ASSI 72/3, Regina v. Jane Badger, Glamorgan, 1883, testimony of John Evans.

92 This is set out very clearly in Dixon Mann, *Forensic Medicine and Toxicology*, third edition, p. 153. The omission of a cause of death in medical reports was a common criticism made by prosecutors in Scotland: Siddons, "Suspected New-Born Child Murder," p. 233.

93 NLW GS 4/178/2, Rex v. Jane Williams, Montgomeryshire, 1734, fols. 10, 22–23.

94 Ibid., fol. 24.

95 NLW GS 4/736/5, Rex v. Elinor Hadley, Carmarthenshire, 1739, fols. 26, 34, 42.

96 Watson, "Women, Violent Crime," pp. 258–263; www.capitalpunishmentuk.org/fem1735.html (accessed 24 Apr 2019).

97 *OBP*, trial of Ann Smith, ref. t18040704-16.

98 The case of a woman who killed her child in a fit of insanity: NLW GS 4/395/2, Rex v. Ann Jones, Breconshire, 1818. The midwife testified that on this and a previous occasion Jones "showed evident symptoms of insanity." Siddons found that midwives disappeared from the Scottish courts much later, in the 1830s: "Suspected New-Born Child Murder," p. 55. Despite on-going rivalry with male doctors, midwives continued to deliver large numbers of babies and gained professional status under the 1902 Midwives Act (2 Edw VII c.17).

99 TNA ASSI 6/1/2, Rex v. Ann Husband, Berkshire, 1783.

100 *Reading Mercury*, 8 Mar 1784, p. 3. Husband was discharged – the grand jury found no case to answer.

101 TNA ASSI 6/1/2, Rex v. Ann Husband, Berkshire, 1783.

102 *First Lines of Physiology, by the celebrated Baron Albertus Haller, MD* (Edinburgh: Charles Elliot, 1779), pp. 483–484.

103 R. J. Kellett, "Infanticide and Child Destruction: The Historical, Legal and Pathological Aspects," *Forensic Science International* 53 (1992), pp. 13–19; Chris Milroy, "Neonatal Deaths,

Infanticide, and the Hydrostatic (Floatation) Test: Historical Perspectives," *Academic Forensic Pathology International* 2 (2012), p. 344.

104 NLW GS 4/830/3, Rex v. Martha John, Pembrokeshire, 1808. The depositions do not survive.

105 Balguy, who became a stalwart of the Derbyshire legal community, was presiding over his first Great Sessions, having been appointed second justice in February 1808; Heywood had only been chief justice for a year. See William Retlaw Williams, *The History of the Great Sessions in Wales, 1542–1830: Together with the Lives of the Welsh Judges* (Brecknock: Privately Printed, 1899), pp. 187–189.

106 His abbreviations have been expanded, spelling corrected, punctuation added and page layout compressed for the sake of clarity; underlining has been represented by italics to indicate the facts that Heywood thought important, but deletions have been removed. My additions appear in square brackets.

107 Eryn M. White, "Popular Schooling and the Welsh Language 1650–1800," in *The Welsh Language before the Industrial Revolution*, ed. Geraint H. Jenkins (Cardiff: University of Wales Press, 1997), p. 327. A map shows the principal language zones in Wales c.1750: the southern half of Pembrokeshire was English-speaking, as were coastal areas of Glamorgan and the borderlands between the English and Welsh counties stretching from Monmouthshire in the south to Flintshire in the north. The rest of the country was Welsh-speaking.

108 James Oldham, "Eighteenth-Century Judges' Notes: How They Explain, Correct and Enhance the Reports," *American Journal of Legal History* 31 (1987), pp. 9–42; John H. Langbein, "Shaping the Eighteenth-Century Criminal Trial: A View from the Ryder Sources," *University of Chicago Law Review* 50 (1983), p. 18. It is clear from Old Bailey trials of the late eighteenth and early nineteenth century that sometimes more than one judge was present in court. As an example of a later judge who took careful notes, see the trial of Beatrice Elizabeth Moore at the Swansea assizes, where "Mr Justice Horridge patiently took down almost every word of the evidence in the murder case": *The South Wales Daily Post*, 17 Nov 1910, p. 5.

109 NLW MSS 196D, No. 4 Cardigan Spring 1808, pp. 40–45. © The National Library of Wales Collections.

110 *The Cambrian*, 23 Apr 1808, p. 3; *Hereford Journal*, 27 Apr 1808, p. 3.

111 Phil Handler, "Judges and the Criminal Law in England 1808–61," in *Judges and Judging in the History of the Common Law and Civil Law: From Antiquity to Modern Times*, ed. Paul Brand and Joshua Getzler (Cambridge: Cambridge University Press, 2012), pp. 145–156.

112 NLW MSS 210D, No. 19 Haverford West Spring 1814 continued to Carmarthen Spring 1814, p. 44.

113 NLW GS 4/759/3, Rex v. Margaret Francis, Carmarthenshire, 1814.

114 NLW MSS 210D, p. 47.

115 TNA ASSI 6/4, Regina v. Ann King, Worcestershire, 1839.

116 John Walliss, "The Bloody Code in Cheshire: The Chester Court of Great Sessions 1805–30," *Transactions of the Historic Society of Lancashire and Cheshire* 163 (2014), pp. 55–71.

117 David Bentley, *English Criminal Justice in the Nineteenth Century* (London: Hambledon Press, 1998), p. 131.

118 Baron Parke to grand jurors at the Monmouthshire Lent assizes: *The Hereford Times*, 1 Apr 1837, p. 2.

119 *The Worcestershire Chronicle*, 17 Jul 1839, p. 2.

120 TNA ASSI 6/22, Regina v. Sarah Ann Emma (Emily) Combes, Gloucestershire, 1889, testimony of Alfred Grace. A key piece of evidence to this effect was the fact that the placenta, umbilical cord and infant were all attached.

121 *Gloucester Citizen*, 5 Jul 1889, p. 3.

122 *Cheltenham Chronicle*, 6 Jul 1889, p. 2.

123 TNA ASSI 6/22, Regina v. Combes, testimony of Eliza Emma Combes.

124 Kilday, *A History of Infanticide*, pp. 133–137.

125 *Monmouthshire Merlin*, 17 Sep 1852, p. 6.
126 W. M. Best, *A Treatise on the Principles of Evidence*, second edition (London: S. Sweet, 1854), pp. 96–99.
127 Mr Justice Erle reported in *The Kentish Independent*, 14 Apr 1855, p. 2 during the trial of Emma Bryant, *OBP*, ref. t18550409-438.
128 *Northwich Guardian*, 11 Mar 1876, p. 5.
129 TNA ASSI 65/10, Regina v. Margaret Bracegirdle, Cheshire, 1876, testimony of James George Purcell.
130 *The Cheshire Observer*, 29 Jul 1876, p. 7.
131 *Liverpool Mercury*, 29 Jul 1876, p. 6.
132 *OBP*, trial of Leah Abrahams, ref. t19051016-748.
133 Dixon Mann, *Forensic Medicine and Toxicology*, third edition, p. 136.
134 Kilday, *A History of Infanticide*, pp. 119–124. This 'moral panic' was not new, as Kilday points out at p. 112.
135 *Berrow's Worcester Journal*, 19 Dec 1874, p. 7.
136 *OBP*, trial of Louisa Beaumont, ref. t19030112-163.
137 *Sheffield Evening Telegraph*, 22 Jul 1909, p. 7; *OBP*, trial of Nellie Betts, ref. t19090719-40.
138 Catherine Crawford, "A Scientific Profession: Medical Reform and Forensic Medicine in British Periodicals of the Early Nineteenth Century," in *British Medicine in an Age of Reform*, ed. Roger French and Andrew Wear (London and New York: Routledge, 1991), pp. 216–218.
139 Michael Ryan, *A Manual of Medical Jurisprudence* (London: Renshaw and Rush, 1831), p. 304; Andrew Amos, "Lectures on Medical Jurisprudence, Lecture II, On Medical Evidence," *The London Medical Gazette* 7 (1831), p. 614; Robert Christison, *Syllabus of the Course of Lectures on Medical Jurisprudence delivered in the University of Edinburgh* (Edinburgh: John Stark, 1831), p. 21.
140 *The Chester Chronicle*, 16 Aug 1833, p. 4.
141 TNA ASSI 65/1, Rex v. Hannah Mottram, Cheshire, 1833.
142 John Frederick Archbold, *A Summary of the Law Relative to Pleading and Evidence in Criminal Cases* (London: R. Pheney, 1822), p. 76.
143 *The Medical Register for 1859* (London: General Medical Council, 1859), p. 81. He was born circa 1786 according to the 1841 Census, available at ancestry.co.uk.
144 *The Warrington Guardian*, 12 Feb 1859, p. 1; *Pigot's National Commercial Directory for 1828–9* (London: J. Pigot, 1828–29); 1851 Census, available at ancestry.co.uk.
145 See for example Taylor, *Principles and Practice of Medical Jurisprudence*, pp. xxiv–lix; William A. Guy, *Principles of Forensic Medicine*, second edition (London: Henry Renshaw, 1861), pp. xix–xxiv.
146 Taylor, *Principles and Practice of Medical Jurisprudence*, p. 884; and see Table 3.26 in Chapter 3.
147 Carol Loar, "Medical Knowledge and the Early Modern English Coroner's Inquest," *Social History of Medicine* 23 (2010), pp. 475–491; Pamela Fisher, "Edmund Whitcombe and the Detection of Homicide in Georgian Shropshire," *Family & Community History* 14 (2011), pp. 3–23; James Sharpe and J. R. Dickinson, "Coroners' Inquests in an English County, 1600–1800: A Preliminary Survey," *Northern History* 48 (2011), pp. 253–269.
148 R. Henslowe Wellington, *The King's Coroner Being the Practice and Procedure in His Judicial and Ministerial Capacities*, Vol. 2 (London: Baillière, Tindall and Cox, 1906), p. 50.
149 TNA ASSI 6/12, Regina v. Lucy Culley, Berkshire, 1869, evidence of Jane Richards and Mrs Ann Landon.
150 Ibid., evidence of Henry Finch MRCSE.
151 *The Medical Register for 1867* (London: General Medical Council, 1867), p. 261; *Dundee Evening Telegraph*, 26 Sep 1887, p. 3.
152 *Reading Mercury*, 24 Dec 1869, p. 4; *The Berkshire Chronicle*, 1 Jan 1870, p. 6. The deliberation took longer than expected, probably because the jury considered acquitting her: the verdict was returned with a recommendation to mercy.
153 Grey, "Discourses of Infanticide," p. 173; Dixon Mann, *Forensic Medicine and Toxicology*, sixth edition, pp. 118–119.

154 There is a large literature on the history of the Victorian insanity plea. Readers are recommended in the first instance to the three books by J. P. Eigen listed in the Bibliography.

155 J. M. Beattie, *Crime and the Courts in England 1660–1800* (Princeton: Princeton University Press, 1986), p. 376.

156 The exception being Stephan Landsman, "One Hundred Years of Rectitude: Medical Witnesses at the Old Bailey, 1717–1817," *Law and History Review* 16 (1998), pp. 445–494.

157 *OBP*, trial of Elizabeth Curtis, ref. t17840915-149.

158 Charles Cottu, *On the Administration of Criminal Justice in England* (London: Richard Stevens; Charles Reader, 1822), p. 88.

5 Crime (scene) investigation

Expertise in action

> The medical man is summoned to most cases of severe illness or sudden death, and thus becomes one of the first witnesses of those simple facts, which, in criminal cases, constitute the presumptive or circumstantial evidence. He is also, in most cases, by far the best educated and most intelligent witness. Whenever, then, he is called to visit the dying or the dead, under circumstances of suspicion, he should be alive to all that is passing around him, that no object, however trifling, which may possibly throw light on the cause of death, may be overlooked.
>
> William A. Guy, *Principles of Forensic Medicine*, second edition
> (London: Henry Renshaw, 1861), pp. 203–204

This chapter examines the active role of medical practitioners in crime scene investigation, as a means of studying the evolution and bifurcation of the relationship between forensic medicine and forensic science in relation to the changing role of the expert, "one whose special knowledge or skill causes him to be regarded as an authority."[1] By the mid-eighteenth century legal officials had come to accept that medical practitioners possessed specialist knowledge important to the investigation and prosecution of serious crimes against the person, but it was in a mid-nineteenth century urban context that a group of 'experts' in the modern sense truly emerged, associated with toxicology and criminal responsibility.[2] At about the same time, rudimentary crime scene analysis was becoming a recognised task of the medical witness, as several textbook writers and university lecturers warned their readers,[3] and historians have investigated this in relation to the late Victorian origins of forensic science and the new professional identity it fashioned in the twentieth century, when policing was placed on a more recognisably scientific footing.[4] The development of 'forensics' was closely connected to detective policing, which was neither uniform in scope and standards nor even a primary duty of the numerous police forces in England and Wales before the 1930s. Thus, in the period that this chapter considers, c.1830–1914, the Metropolitan Police and large borough forces operated on an entirely different level than the majority of town and county forces:[5] the former had CID (Criminal Investigation Department) branches, but the latter made do with beat patrolling to monitor and intervene in the activities of suspect groups.[6] At some point in this parallel expansion of forensic science and scientific policing, therefore, the needs and goals of two hitherto separate groups dovetailed to create a modern, laboratory-based approach to crime investigation.

But there are two problems with this picture. The first relates to the professionalisation of detective policing, which was by no means uniform in England and Wales, and which proceeded rather slowly: significant differences in experience and practice existed between London and borough detectives, and within London, until and beyond 1914. The central squad stationed at Scotland Yard (Division A) devoted more of their time to crime investigation and dealt with serious offences as a greater proportion of their regular work, than did members of the divisional detective units set up in 1869, who adopted a mainly preventive strategy to control petty offences. These London detectives were perhaps more on a par with their provincial counterparts, who practiced a mixture of preventive and reactive tasks, and whose numbers might be temporarily augmented by uniformed officers who had adopted plainclothes for a particular occasion. Every force that employed detectives was, therefore, operating at a different standard. Furthermore, the total number of detectives in England and Wales remained small, on the order of – at most – dozens of officers per CID office, of which the branch at Scotland Yard was the largest and most clearly representative of a professional elite.[7] In the counties of Wales and the Oxford Circuit, where detective policing awaits its historian, there were no borough forces that possessed the size or experience of London or its nearest comparators, large northern cities such as Liverpool, Manchester and Birmingham. In 1899, for example, the entire Staffordshire constabulary – the largest in the counties under study – employed 687 police of all ranks (detectives were not separately enumerated), which was 13 less than Birmingham.[8]

Furthermore, the attentive reader will notice that the neat interpretation of the relationship between forensic science and scientific policing identified above leaves a significant chronological – and indeed professional – gap in the history of crime investigation. As William Guy's wordy but clear admonition to his colleagues and students suggests, and as this chapter will show, doctors were the very individuals most likely to be present at or called to the location of a sudden death; and as early as the 1840s, medico-legal texts encouraged practitioners to make careful observations at such scenes. If they did not do so, cautioned the renowned toxicologist and medico-legal writer Alfred Swaine Taylor, many facts capable of throwing important light on a case "would remain unnoticed or unknown."[9] But this attention to detail was increasingly carried out in conjunction with or in parallel to the crime scene work carried out by police officers who, as they became more ubiquitous, tended to be sent for immediately by members of the public who stumbled upon a crime scene or witnessed a violent act. Witness depositions make it clear that those who had the misfortune to find a dead body ran for a police officer and a doctor, in either order. If when he arrived a doctor was not already present, the first constable on the scene sent a colleague or a member of the public for one, and coroners who subsequently held an inquest on the victim instructed that doctor to conduct the post-mortem. Financial constraints played an important role, as coroners' fees and expenses were scrutinised by county magistrates who could, after 1856, call upon the police forces that they partly funded to undertake some of the medico-legal work that would previously have been the concern solely of the coroner. It is no coincidence that homicide investigations of the second half of the nineteenth century reveal increasingly close cooperation between coroners, magistrates, medical witnesses and the police, with the latter acting as a central point of contact and information. The business of crime investigation became more professional and systematic under the impetus of the 'new police', and doctors were an essential part of that process.

Of course the detection and investigation of felonies was not solely a feature of the period after the founding of the Metropolitan Police in 1829. J. M. Beattie and David Cox have shown that the officers attached to Bow Street Magistrates' Court, the famous Runners, played a significant detective role in both London and the provinces between their foundation in 1749 and disbandment in 1839.[10] Their involvement in homicide cases outside the capital far exceeded that within London because of the association of murder with arson and property damage and thus with complex cases initiated by the landed gentry, county magistrates or the Home Office itself.[11] The Bow Street Runners were much less likely to be engaged to solve the more usual cases of murder that appeared with monotonous regularity on assize calendars simply because there was so little mystery to them, yet these were the crimes in which local medical practitioners were always asked for their professional opinion about cause and manner of death. Questions of this nature continued to be put to medical witnesses by coroners and magistrates, as in the Georgian period, but the advent of the 'new police' changed the way in which medical evidence was obtained, by establishing professional police officers as a new link in the chain of investigation and creating a new type of witness: the police surgeon.

As was pointed out in Chapter 3, we know rather little about the formal history of police surgeons:[12] with the exception of recent work by Joel Eigen and Victoria Bates,[13] their contributions to Victorian crime investigation are not reflected in historical studies. Arthur Dixon, a Home Office civil servant who played a vital role in establishing the Forensic Science Service in the 1930s, argued for the importance of active collaboration between detectives, scientists and police surgeons from the outset of investigations.[14] In fact, cooperation of this kind actually began almost a century earlier, first in London where the role of police surgeon originated around 1805, and later spreading to the provinces. However, in contrast to the twentieth-century reliance on professional detectives and scientists, Victorian crime investigation outside London lay largely in the hands of senior officers of the uniformed branch, local surgeons and police surgeons. Victorian commentators seem to have agreed that key criteria for the successful criminal investigator included intelligence, trustworthiness, literacy, tenacity and adequate pay:[15] all characteristics shared with or aspired to by the medical profession. It is not difficult to find evidence that these ideals were applied in numerous homicide cases where local police worked with local doctors to get a suspect to court.

The first section of this chapter examines this relationship, using pictorial depictions of crime scenes as a means of identifying the issues that investigators thought most relevant. All the medical men in such investigations had expert status because of their professional education and training; and the trust placed in them by the police, who increasingly took on the burden of organising prosecutions,[16] was not misplaced.

One way to identify and evaluate expertise – its nature, who had it and how much, is to consider the content and quality of the forensic work undertaken by medical witnesses and the payment they received for it. Two trends in the history of the nineteenth-century medical profession underpinned such issues. As Anne Digby has shown in her examination of doctors' careers, the potential offered by scientific medicine was eventually to transform the practice of surgery and increase the authority of the profession, whereas the market for medicine led to a range of opportunities for surgeons to obtain salaried public and private appointments, mostly as an adjunct to private practice, which remained throughout our period the ultimate goal of the medical practitioner.[17] Michael Brown has identified a shift in medical professionalism between 1815 and the 1840s, as doctors increasingly moved away from an eighteenth-century gentlemanly culture to a more science-focused idea of what it meant to be a member of a profession with a demonstrable ability to contribute positively to the health and welfare of the nation.[18] Thus, although the rate at which scientific techniques taught to medical students may have been slow to diffuse into general practice,[19] medico-legal work is an obvious area in which to seek evidence of their application outside the classroom. This chapter will therefore examine the use of scientific aids to investigation, mainly microscopic and chemical tests on blood and semen stains. Though not common in Victorian forensic practice, they help to identify a growing distinction between forensic medicine and forensic science, and between the expert and the expert witness. Finally, professional standing, experience and connections all affected income-earning potential, and so the last section considers the fees paid to medical experts to show how and why they held a different status to lay witnesses and how a minority transformed themselves into expert witnesses to be consulted in 'special cases' considered too complicated for the average practitioner.

Examining and documenting murder scenes

As we saw in the Introduction, by the early nineteenth century the law of evidence allowed witnesses to refresh their memory from notes or texts, but they were not permitted to read their evidence. This was particularly important for medical witnesses, who had to testify to what they had seen – their direct observations of the victim and quite often the crime scene, and crucially also the conclusions they arrived at from those observations. Consequently, medical witnesses were considered to be experts because they were expected to interpret the facts they described. Tony Ward has identified three contrasting conceptions of the expert witness role in nineteenth-century case law and medico-legal literature: as observer, adviser or authority. Doctors presented facts in the observer role, not much different to the layman. In the adviser role, they drew on their experience to suggest the inferences that a jury should make from the facts, although jurors were free to accept or reject this in reaching their own decision. But in the authority role, a medical practitioner's evidence was essential: jurors could not reach any independent conclusion about the facts without the expert's support.[20] A pure observer role was untenable in a forensic setting: in recounting facts, medical practitioners also provided an opinion based on their training and prior experience. Thus, all medico-legal witnesses adopted an adviser role from the moment they examined a victim.[21] However, only some of these experts took on an authority role as well. As an example of this distinction, recall the comments made by police surgeon Charles Graham Grant (an adviser) when comparing himself to Professor A. J. Pepper (an authority), recounted in Chapter 3.

In their recent history of forensic science, Ian Burney and Neil Pemberton stress the medical and hence body-centred nature of early crime scene observation in contrast to the things-focus of forensic trace evidence and the distinctive 'CSI' method advocated by Hans Gross (1847–1915), the Austrian jurist considered the founding father of scientific policing.[22] Gross's influential *Handbuch für untersuchungsrichter als system der kriminalistik* (1893, translated as *Criminal Investigation: A Practical Handbook* in 1906) is taken as a superior and clearly different sort of work to its nearest English equivalent, Howard Vincent's *Police Code and Manual of the Criminal Law* (1881; sixteenth edition, 1924) because of the body-focused attention to crime scene management adopted by Vincent (1849–1908), the Director of Criminal Investigation at Scotland Yard from 1878 to 1884. Writing for police officers, his approach was not much different from that of earlier medico-legal writers like Taylor and Guy: the position and appearance of a dead body were of vital concern but investigators were given no formal protocols to follow at crime scenes.[23] Significantly, however, Vincent envisaged the initial crime scene investigation as a collaborative effort between the ranking police officer and a surgeon:

> As soon as the Inspector arrives (or if delay is impossible, the Sergeant or constable), he must make, in conjunction with the Surgeon, a minute and careful examination – (a) For any footmarks about the body, which should be modelled or covered over before fresh imprints are made by the Surgeon and police. (b) Of the position of the body. (c) Of the condition of its clothing. (d) Of the position of the wound, and judging by the body and clothing, in what way, and from which quarter, and with what instrument, and under what circumstances it was probably inflicted. (e) Whether the murderer has left his weapon or any trace of his identity in the vicinity of the body. (f) Whether there is in the pockets, or about the person of the deceased, any paper or article disclosing his identity, if unknown, or the name of his probable murderer, or any circumstances pointing in any particular direction.[24]

By 1912 this advice had expanded to include fingerprints and photographs but had not otherwise altered.[25] Clearly the police expected doctors, who were trained to observe, to play an important role at crime scenes and it is evident that many went beyond the immediate legal requirement to examine the victim. Medical interest naturally focused on the body but could extend beyond it to the wider physical setting, taking in indoor or outdoor details of stains, footprints, weapons, items on or near the body, the position of furniture, and even the actions or words of other witnesses.

Although it was possible for laymen to make forensic observations at crime scenes, doctors were more likely to do so, using their own initiative or in conjunction with a police officer. In many cases a medical practitioner arrived before the police: some merely examined the victim and waited for a constable, but others took more direct action. In 1841 surgeon James R. Monday happened to be passing when he heard that a man had been shot at a public house in Tockington, Gloucestershire. He went in, saw that the victim had been "dreadfully wounded" in the face and mouth, and found that after the bullet passed through the head it had struck the back of a fireplace, dislodging some mortar. He therefore searched the grate and ashes for the ball but on not finding one, concluded that the projectile had been a marble rather than a lead bullet.[26] If unlucky, the first doctor to arrive would have to calm a confused or enraged offender, as happened to Dr James Baird at Congleton in 1885 when he was attacked by a mentally disturbed man who had just murdered his mother. After a struggle, Baird wrested a bloody knife from the culprit but was then forced to retreat backward down a staircase, fending off blows from a wooden board. It was only when a member of the public came to his aid, and still well before the police had arrived, that the prisoner was subdued – at which point Baird discovered he had cut his own throat and stitched him up on the spot.[27] Other doctors put questions to witnesses or were present as magistrates or the police did so. Some even questioned suspects directly, as we saw in Chapter 4, although this practice was liable to earn a stern rebuke from a trial judge.

Crime scenes were more easily accessible than they are today, and the deference shown to doctors by the public and police, as well as their own natural inclination to size up any situation they found themselves in, led to a tendency to adopt a broader investigative role than would be expected of the modern medico-legal witness. Lecturers on forensic medicine were clearly teaching their students to be prepared to contribute more to an investigation than purely factual information, as for example when Thomas Scattergood told students at the Leeds School of Medicine that, when confronted by a dead body, "The medical man in this position, is often the most or only intelligent or self-possessed person present, he has the opportunity and ability of knowing many circumstances that others cannot, his training ought to have fitted him for minute observation, and it is quite certain that he will be severely taken to task if he does not exercise this faculty."[28] Textbooks reinforced this dual function as successive authors reiterated their belief that doctors were "by far the best educated and most intelligent witness,"[29] and so "the medical man is often the first person trained in habits of observation upon the scene, and he may accordingly be the most important witness in any enquiry which follows."[30] By the 1890s, however, this assumption appears to have been waning: the Manchester professor of forensic medicine John Dixon Mann allowed that "everything, both as regards the [dead] body and its surroundings, should be scrupulously noted," but rather than lauding doctors as ideal scene observers he focused firmly on the body, stressing the need for specialist pathologists to "make the necessary investigations on the bodies of those whose mode of death is the subject of legal enquiry."[31] Dixon Mann recognised a distinction between the 'common' medical witness and the expert witness, but admitted that an adviser role was typical: "usually, a medical witness acts both as a common and as an expert witness, his skilled or expert opinion being founded on facts that he himself has observed."[32] He had little to say about the police, however, apart from occasional reminders about the need to communicate with them. His expectations represented a different perspective on the developing relationship between the police and forensic doctors than had previously been typical, one in which the latter were not expected to act as detectives at all and where medico-legal examinations would ideally be conducted by an exclusive minority of experts acting in an authority role.

In order to relocate this discussion from the pages of textbooks to the practices used by doctors at murder scenes, pictorial examples of crime scenes and pre-trial testimony about doctors' actions there have been examined to identify exactly what they did and how they interacted with police officers. What was the nature of the expertise exhibited at the scene? Few case files now contain drawings, plans, notes or photographs and it is impossible to estimate what proportion of cases originally included evidence of this kind. However, references to sketches, plans and models in the *Proceedings of the Old Bailey* suggest that, in London, scale plans of crime scenes became common in the 1870s but had been used steadily since the 1840s and occasionally earlier; by 1900 they were a regular feature of prosecution dossiers, included in about 31 per cent of cases in the period up to 1913.[33] Examples of plans and sketches survive in small numbers among the records of the Welsh and Oxford Circuits too, showing that the practice of making formal pictorial records of crime scenes was well established by the third quarter of the nineteenth century. In London, plans were usually drawn by an officer of the Metropolitan Police, often those who had training as draftsmen, but in other counties plans were made by city surveyors at the instruction of magistrates. Most were designed to show the locality where a crime had occurred, not the immediate scene of a death, and were used to reinforce eyewitness rather than expert testimony. It was only towards the end of the century that sketches began to exhibit a more overtly forensic quality, blending police and medical interest in a crime scene, but by then a separation between the two was already developing. Despite the fact that Howard Vincent advocated the use of photographs in pursuing criminals and identifying the dead,[34] crime scene photographs remained relatively uncommon before the First World War, and those that survive focus on spaces rather than bodies, possibly because sensitive material was removed before files were archived. However, two extant references to photographs of victims also note that plans of the premises in which they died were made – the victim was photographed on site in one case, but in a mortuary in the other.[35] This suggests that photographing the victim as part of a crime scene was not yet a recognised feature of police investigative procedures,[36] which continued to rely on the ad hoc contribution of medical professionals. Fewer examples still of surgeons' notes survive, although if they had been taken at the scene and used to refresh the memory at trial they could have been entered into formal evidence.[37] However, one of the earliest forensic images still extant among the files of the Oxford Circuit was made by a surgeon who, as might be expected, focused entirely on the victim's body.

The murder of Francis Longuet, 1817

In February 1817 Francis Longuet, a Roman Catholic priest, was robbed and murdered on the road between Pangbourn and Reading in Berkshire. The coroner asked Widdows Golding (c.1768–1820), a surgeon from Reading,[38] to examine the body and at the inquest he described five separate injuries to the head and a number of stabs in the chest; "one dreadful wound" had nearly separated the head from the neck. Suggesting that "For a better or more minute description of these wounds see the drawing annexed" (Figure 5.1), he gave his opinion that the wounds had been caused by a sword or some other heavy sharp instrument.[39] Press reports reveal the weapon was assumed to be a bayonet or broad-sword and suspicion immediately fell on the nearest regiment, but since Longuet had been

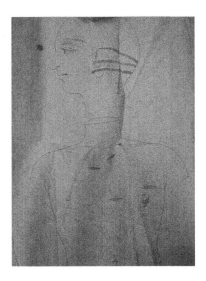

Figure 5.1 Drawing of wounds inflicted on Francis Longuet, 1817

Source: TNA ASSI 6/1/2, Rex v. Francis Sargent, Berkshire, 1817. With permission from The National Archives.

seen alive at 8 pm on the day of the murder the soldiers' whereabouts at the time could all be accounted for.[40] A week later a farmer was robbed near the spot where Longuet was found, suggesting the perpetrator was a common footpad, so the mayor of Reading offered a large reward for information, publishing details of Longuet's stolen bank notes in the hope of tracing the robber.[41] Apart from the money itself, then, Golding's evidence provided the only practical clue to the murder; when neither yielded results, the crime became unsolvable. Although at least one man was arrested, he was released for lack of evidence.

The diagram reproduced in Figure 5.1 was part of the inquest file and represents one of only three such examples found among the papers examined for this project, the others being a multi-angle depiction of head injuries in a Cheshire case of 1890 and a sketch of an umbilical cord made by a doctor in Flintshire in 1915.[42] We know, however, that medical men entered the witness box with other types of objects which were technically part of the prosecution case, particularly bullets or shot removed from victims and the tangible products of chemical tests for arsenic, but also parts of bodies. Sometimes this was more to do with their examination of the body as part of a crime scene than simply a report of post-mortem findings, as for example occurred when Edward Roe examined the scene of a murder in Islington in 1840: he found two of the victim's teeth and a police officer found a third. These, with the body's position, the way it was bound and the bloodstains around it, helped Roe to provide the court with both a grisly scene description and an interpreted sequence of events, in support of which he produced part of a stick matted with the victim's hair and blood.[43] In 1875 Metropolitan Police divisional surgeon Thomas Bond (1841–1901), who will be discussed at greater length in a later section, was testifying about a victim's scar when, after being asked if it could be produced, replied "I have it in my pocket."[44] The flesh was in a bottle, preserved in spirits. Bond had not viewed the body in situ, however, but at the mortuary; another surgeon, Frederick George Larkin, examined the body where it was found, decomposing in ten parts, and also visited the presumed crime scene. Both agreed that the probable victim's boots fit the severed feet. Bond acted as an authority, Larkin as an adviser; they worked closely with each other and with the senior investigating officer, Inspector Fox.

Improved techniques for preserving bodily tissues made evidence productions such as body parts far more practical than they had once been,[45] and such exhibits remained the responsibility of medical witnesses. Probably the most famous example of this occurred during the trial of Dr Crippen in 1910, when a contested piece of flesh marked by either a scar or a fold – depending on the perspective of the prosecution or the defence, was handed around court on a soup plate.[46] An effective partnership developed between Victorian medical witnesses and police officers, the logistics of which clearly exceeded the resources available to the magistrates tasked with solving Francis Longuet's murder. Although the relative importance of eyewitness testimony and the material evidence derived from bodies had not altered in the intervening decades, techniques for investigating murder had, and significantly so, as indicated by the changes in how and by whom the evidence needed to support a prosecution case was obtained. The police cooperated with doctors in searching crime scenes and retrieving weapons, clothing and other objects of evidential value, demonstrating an increasingly professional approach both to crime investigation and the specialist nature of medical expertise.

Medical investigator: Regina v. John Isaac Jones, 1859

On 17 May 1859 a widowed housekeeper was murdered at Ledbury in Herefordshire. This was a complex case: John Isaac Jones, a solicitor's clerk, was suspected of burglary and setting fire to the house where he worked and the victim lived; both were employed by a magistrate's clerk, in whose home the crime occurred. Burnt papers were found and later examined under a microscope by the printers to a London bank. The suspect's photograph was circulated to gaols around the country and his true identity, Robert Dibble from Somerset, was established; his two diaries revealed him to be a fantasist in want of friends and money. A London detective, Frederick Williamson, was summoned within four days of the murder to conduct inquiries "with the assistance of the local police."[47] But almost the first person on the scene had been a local surgeon, William Griffin, who contributed far more to the investigation than merely establishing the cause of Harriett Baker's death: he observed a great deal at the crime scene, which was depicted by a plan and model, neither of which survive.[48] An indication of the centrality of his observations is provided by a four-page list of the "important points" of the case together with the names of the witnesses who would prove them. Of 72 separate points to be proved by 35 witnesses cited a total of 132 times, Williamson's name appears twice and local police superintendent Tanner three times, but Griffin is cited 20 times. Table 5.1 summarises his actions, observations and conclusions.

The trial took place in early August 1859, by which time the witness list had grown to 43 people.[49] Following three days of testimony the judge's summing up was favourable to the prisoner in pointing out that the evidence against him was entirely circumstantial and, after deliberating for three hours, the jury acquitted Jones.[50] Some press accounts reported Griffin's testimony but none recognised the central role his involvement played in the way the prosecution built its case, focusing instead on the police. The murder of Harriett Baker, like that of Francis Longuet, remained unsolved, but the procedures taken to try to identify and prosecute a culprit were very different, relying substantially on the professional expertise of the police, two bank employees (who examined paper ashes) and an extensive witness list; what had not changed was the importance of the local surgeon. No expert witness could have done more than Griffin in a medico-legal capacity: the cause and manner of death revealed nothing probative about the perpetrator, and there were no stains or weapons that could be linked to Jones; only an eyewitness could have tied him (or the real killer) securely to the murder. Press reports were silent on whether recriminations followed the acquittal and consequent failure to secure justice for Mrs Baker, as

Table 5.1 Regina v. J. I. Jones, important points proved by William Griffin, 1859

Called to victim's house > Found body on floor > Conducted external examination > Discovered a mark on the right front temple and the mark of a ligature around the neck, bloody mucus issuing from mouth; found a rope near the right leg with a noose; found two lucifer [phosphorus] matches

Sent for the police

Examined the house: observations detailed and objects found (key, postage stamps); smelled and tasted the contents of a glass (gin and water)

Questioned Jones, who was present > evidence of his remarks and demeanour

Conducted the post-mortem; reviewed the external marks; once the clothes were removed he saw that the body was charred in some places and blistered in others

Cause of death definitely strangulation; no signs of sexual assault; food in stomach was there for three to four hours > time of death

Opinion: two blows were received before death but they may have been delivered afterwards

No struggle ↔ victim was small and spare ↔ Jones possessed average strength for a man of his size independently of his cork leg

Source: Adapted from TNA ASSI 6/9, Regina v. John Isaac Jones, Important points, analysis.

indeed they were on the working relationship between Detective Williamson and the Herefordshire police, who may have resented his intrusion as much as the Wiltshire police resented that of his colleague Jack Whicher the following year, when the two men investigated the murder of a child by his older half-sister, Constance Kent.[51] There may have been something of a mid-century gulf between London detectives and provincial police, but with the exception of the expertise required in cases of murder by poison, the latter did not rely extensively on outside capability; local doctors continued to serve as both observers and advisers at murder scenes.

Diagnosing murder? The Kidwelly tragedy, Carmarthenshire, 1881

In early February 1881 in the town of Kidwelly, South Wales, two young brothers named David and Benjamin Mazey, aged 12 and 10, were accused of murdering 11-year-old John Thomas by cutting and wounding him about the head. At their committal hearing the boys claimed it was an accident: the victim fell from a low roof, hit his head and died. They admitted taking money from his pocket (they spent some and hid the rest), throwing water at his bloody head and, when something white came out one of them picked it up and threw it across the path. Then they hid the body in their garden. Although the local surgeon, David Jones, was unable to state positively that brain matter discovered at the scene came from the victim, his post-mortem revealed that the skull was completely shattered and the brain gone; he thought the injuries were inflicted with a blunt instrument. Most damningly, he had a clear opinion about the nature of Thomas's wounds: "I do not think the injuries sustained by the deceased could

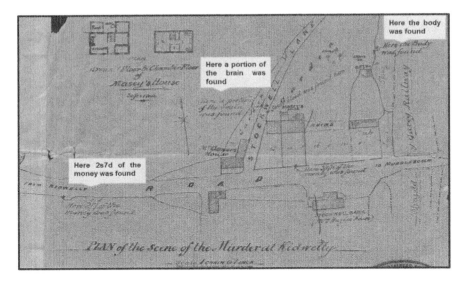

Figure 5.2 Plan of the scene of the murder at Kidwelly, 1881

Source: TNA ASSI 72/3. With permission from The National Archives.

have been produced by a fall. I think the deceased was murdered within three hours after he took his food." This is all that the committal documents reveal, but the conclusion about time of death linked the victim to the defendants, with whom he had been seen shortly after lunch.[52]

The plan in Figure 5.2 was drawn to display the spatial connection between the Mazeys' home and the victim, showing where stolen money, blood, tissue and the body were found: "Here 2*s.* 7*d.* of the money was found/Here a portion of the brain was found/Some blood was found here/Here the body was found/Here 3*s.* 9½*d.* of the money was found." The upper left corner pictures the interior floor plan of their house, but the alleged murder occurred in an adjoining garden by a ruined wall. The plan was used by the police to build a case against the two brothers and their pregnant 34-year-old mother as an accessory after the fact. Local gossip soon revealed that the brothers had been the only witnesses to the drowning of another boy just six months earlier, a deeply suspicious fact in the light of the way they behaved when John Thomas disappeared: he was missing for two days before his body was found and the boys had denied knowing his whereabouts.[53]

However, at the inquest Jones told the coroner:

> It is possible, but not probable, that two boys, aged 12 and 10, might have caused the injuries which deceased showed. I believe a blunt instrument was used. It might have been a hammer. There was a superficial wound on the left cheek which must have been caused by a sharp instrument. The nature of

the wounds to the skull would account for the body being devoid of blood. I do not think the side of a smoothing-iron could have caused the wound on the cheek. I conclude that the deceased was murdered before 5 p.m.

He also noted that decomposition had set in. His assistant similarly doubted that two children could have inflicted the injuries. The inquest brought in a verdict of murder against some persons unknown,[54] but the police had the Mazey family in their sights and sent their clothes to the county analyst, William Morgan. His evidence was actually more important than the surgeon's, since his chemical and microscopic tests revealed blood on the clothing; but he could not tell whether it was human or animal, nor how long it had been on the clothes. Despite the public feeling against them, the boys and their mother were acquitted following a day-long trial but a swift jury deliberation of only five minutes.[55]

This case demonstrates that the medical contribution to crime investigation was not solely about medicine. Rather, medicine as a system of knowledge was adapted to the needs of legal process and judged by its standards of proof and persuasive evidence, all of which formed a single narrative that jurors had to evaluate. Despite extensive investigation, the police were forced to build their case on largely circumstantial evidence and a contradictory medical foundation which the defence barrister exploited, stressing the "presumptive weakness of the boy prisoners."[56] The time of death could be established but there was no obvious weapon: a couple of tools had been examined but eliminated. The blood evidence that linked the boys to the victim was contradicted by the surgeon's doubt as to the physical probability that children could inflict such a wound; but no test of this supposition was made. Thus, if the death was murder, no firm connection to the prisoners was established and in the absence of clear evidence that they could have or actually did inflict the wounds with murderous intent, the Mazeys' tale of accidental death was accepted, if not actually believed: two months after the trial the family had been forced from their home and was suffering "pitiless persecution."[57]

A modern investigation: the Herefordshire murder, 1885

In stark contrast to the Kidwelly case, a murder investigation that took place in Herefordshire four years later showcased the contribution of a local surgeon to establishing what had happened and thus to proving the case against two suspects. At the end of September 1885 two hop pickers, Ann Dickson and Mary Ann Farrell, found themselves in the village of Weobley, where they stopped at a public house. Two local men were there, John Hill and John Williams. The latter carried a heavy stick and made the women nervous, so they allowed Hill to accompany them when they left. This proved a fatal mistake: the two men attacked them as they went through a gate, marked on a plan that accompanied the case file. Farrell was able to call for help near a shepherd's house, but Dickson was less fortunate: her dead body was found the next morning, the head beaten in.[58]

The investigation that followed was representative of a by now well developed and recognisably modern criminal inquiry, led by the police but with a significant medical contribution. W. F. Walker, a local surgeon, accompanied the police superintendent to the field where the victim's body lay. He observed two large pools of blood a few feet from the body, round marks on the ground like those of a man's knees, and later found that mud on the knees of Williams's trousers was similar to that near the body. He examined and described the victim's extensive facial injuries, which had been caused by a blunt instrument like the stick that Williams had carried. Two days later Walker went back to the field with the police and searched it, finding a piece of flesh that had been gouged from the victim's face. A plan of the murder location was made by a local surveyor on the same day, 2 October, at the request of the magistrates to whom the police reported their findings; photographs were taken by a local photographer.[59]

The victim's clothes were covered with blood, mud and faeces. Once the suspect John Hill had been arrested, Walker examined his clothes and located similar faecal stains, and some blood. He found scratches on Hill's hands and face; and on then examining under the victim's fingernails found pieces of skin "such as might have been scratched off a man's face." He also discovered mud and blood on Williams's clothes. Walker examined the surviving victim and concluded that her wound could not account for all the blood found on Williams. He noted that his careful examination of the field and the spot where Farrell was assaulted showed "that if a man had struggled and knelt on the ground at the latter spot, he could not have got on his knees such marks as were on the trousers belonging to Williams." Finally, the depositions show that Walker confirmed his conclusions about the faecal matter and blood by using the "usual tests" and a microscope, and examined the dead woman for semen (no specific details were provided) but did not find any. Not one of these tests was cited in detail in the press reports of the trial.[60]

Once the police had completed their investigation, the magistrates opened a committal hearing; it was closed on the same day, 12 October, and the two men were tried less than a month later. The surgeon's testimony helped to seal the case against them, since it provided physical evidence that linked them to the murder, and both men were convicted and executed. But despite the momentous nature of his intervention in this case, nothing is known of William Frederic Walker apart from the fact that he was a local practitioner in a small rural community, the population of which was then about 900, who was able to carry out aspects of crime investigation now associated with the police (inspection of the crime scene), as well as forensic pathology (post-mortem examination) and forensic science (examination of blood and trace evidence).[61] This appears to be the first and only time that he did so, but it is likely that there were many other surgeons like him during the second half of the nineteenth century.

"The position of Mrs Griffiths as I found her": Regina v. Thomas Henry Bevan, 1887

The first detailed depiction of a crime scene that also portrays the victims dates from 1887 when a plan was prepared for use in the case against Thomas Henry Bevan for the murder and attempted murder of his aunt and half-sister at Church Coppenhall in Cheshire.[62] An architect from Crewe drew the plan after surveying the premises in the company of a senior police officer, but he did not see the bodies: "the figures representing the woman and child are placed in the position pointed out to me by police Inspector Oldham." The plan was therefore slightly inaccurate: Dr Joseph Moody noted that the dead body of Sarah Griffiths was in about the position shown but the head was a little more to the left.[63] In a form of early blood spatter analysis, Moody also concluded that blood found on Bevan's legs came from the child's head. But there is no blood shown in the plan: either it had been cleaned away before the architect arrived or he did not see fit to include it. He did however add details that earlier plans of crime locations did not include, such as the peg (which had fresh blood on it) and potatoes seen to the right in Figure 5.3.

The senior investigating officer, Superintendent Jesse Leah, reached the murder scene within one hour of receiving information about the crime but the bodies had already been moved: the dead woman had been laid out in the front parlour and the unconscious girl had been put to bed upstairs. Both he and Moody, who arrived before the police, were present when she regained consciousness: Moody questioned her about the attack, and when she said Bevan had done it, Leah went to arrest him. Inspector Alfred Oldham had preceded Leah to the house at the request of the killer, who had tried to deflect suspicion by reporting that Griffiths had murdered the child, Mary Jones. Oldham found the dead woman on the kitchen floor, the little girl having already been taken upstairs at Moody's insistence, and took detailed and careful note of her position and other aspects of the crime scene, including pools and splashes of

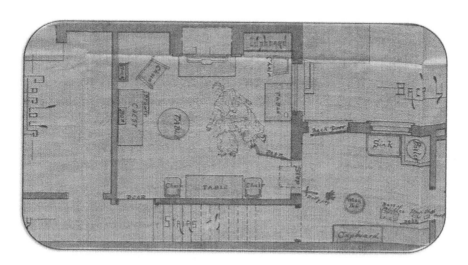

Figure 5.3 Scene of the murder at 37 Henry Street, Church Coppenhall, drawn in April 1887

Source: TNA ASSI 65/15, Regina v. Thomas Henry Bevan, Cheshire, 1887. With permission from The National Archives.

blood, before helping to carry her body into the parlour. In what might now be considered a 'rookie error', Oldham had not excluded Bevan from the scene, and so the latter helped to move the woman's body. The magistrates questioned Oldham about this, but he avowed that "I should think it was impossible for him to get the blood on his clothes in the way it was on, I did much more than the prisoner and I got none on my clothes."[64] He was not asked about this at the trial.[65]

The blood evidence was not scrutinised until three days after the murder: Leah first asked Moody to examine Bevan's clothes and then took them to the county analyst, Joseph Carter Bell, the next day. At the final committal hearing nearly a month later both Bell and Moody were asked how long they had been in practice, today a question typically used to establish expertise,[66] before presenting their respective conclusions about the blood, which was definitely mammalian though it was impossible to determine whether human or not, and the probable manner in which the wounds and bloodstains were incurred. Thus, despite the porosity of the original crime scene, which was not closed to the public nor preserved until it had been thoroughly inspected by senior officers, the investigation was on the whole handled efficiently. Medicine and science, the post-mortem and blood results, played key parts in that process. Bell, a professional chemical analyst employed by the county, had the authority of an expert witness; there was no suggestion that he might be biased as a result. Moody switched between an adviser role with respect to the blood evidence, weapon and cause of death, and an authority role concerning the manner of death, which explained that Bevan had probably jumped on the victim to cause the observed blood staining and injuries. His testimony during the trial was particularly expedient when he was asked about the star witness's memory lapses: on cross-examination he stated firmly "that considering the injuries to Mary Jones's head there was nothing unusual in the fact that she should give different versions at different times of what had previously happened."[67] Bevan, an "undersized, semi-developed youth" of 20 whose motive was robbery and who compounded his brash stupidity by confessing to a gaol inmate, was convicted and executed.[68]

Later crime scene plans seem to have reverted to the practice of leaving the body out of the picture: their purpose remained the support of a prosecution narrative based on eyewitness statements, not the representation of a unique space in which experts deployed a "highly structured way of seeing" as in the 'Grossian' regime identified by Burney and Pemberton.[69] This is at least partly because most homicides remained sad affairs of little mystery. While some murders undoubtedly spawned the need for specialist spaces of forensic activity – the Crippen case of 1910, for example – there was no need for such a construct in most investigations. However, professional boundaries were clearly becoming more demarcated: doctors confined their interest more closely to the body, leaving the scene investigation to the police. When George Stills kicked his mother to death in a drunken rage in September 1907 in a Glamorgan coal-mining town, evidence of where the blood was located in the room was given by a surgeon and a police sergeant, but the crime scene plan focused on the window and the distances from it to the outside pavement, from where eyewitnesses had seen Stills beat his mother both inside the house and in the street after he dragged her outside to die. The plan proved it was possible for the witnesses to have seen and heard all they said they had.[70]

Although there was no formal expectation in the early nineteenth century that medical men would provide evidence of anything other than the injuries suffered by a victim, in practice they regularly included judgements about the way in which wounds had been inflicted, by what weapon, in what manner and even by whom. Doctors used close visual examination of bodies, scenes and objects to establish and support a charge against a specific culprit, working increasingly closely with the police of England and Wales. Victorian medico-legal practice relied on doctors' training as observers, and as they stepped increasingly confidently into roles as partners of the police and advisers to the courts, a few individuals emerged as recognised authorities. The increasing distinction between the expert and the expert witness can be seen in the developing reliance on forensic science.

Scientific aids to investigation

A now well-developed historiography has established the role played by poisoning in the evolution of the expert witness, when two factors worked together to reveal hidden crime: the development of reliable chemical tests for and medical recognition of the characteristic symptoms of the poisons most commonly used for homicidal purposes. The 1830s marked a watershed: the rising incidence of criminal poisoning stimulated the creation of a new science, toxicology, while growing numbers of medical and scientific institutions trained professionals to use chemical experiments effectively. Some toxicologists became authority figures with regional or national reputations, serving as the first true expert witnesses.[71] But with the exception of those who wrote the textbooks and who in theory defined 'best practice', and the handful of medico-legal experts who established their status through their work on poisoning crimes, little is known about the individuals who were consulted by legal officials in criminal cases that warranted the use of some other form of scientific test, or the nature of the evidence they provided.

Murder cases investigated in London, Wales and the counties of the Oxford Circuit reveal, however, that poisonings were not alone in lending themselves to the use of scientific techniques by medico-legal witnesses; the previous section has already given an indication of the focus of such procedures. Unlike the scientific aids to investigation explored at length by the forensic scientist F. G. Tryhorn in the mid-1930s,[72] Victorian and Edwardian forensic techniques were not concerned by trace evidence in the form of dust or particles but primarily by biological samples of blood or semen, sometimes found with other forms of physical evidence such as hair. Nonetheless, there are indications that the sort of partnership between science and policing that Tryhorn wished to foster already existed in the nineteenth century, though it was unsystematic and based on individual overtures made by the police to local chemists or doctors whose professional education provided the necessary training in chemistry and microscopy.

Most forensic examinations performed on dead adults involved investigating head injuries, beating and stabbing, the most common causes of homicidal death: surgeons were asked whether blows, kicks or a particular bladed instrument could have produced the injuries, and if those injuries were the direct cause of death. If the victim had any prior disease or bodily weakness, its effects were also of concern. Occasionally it was possible to show that a suspect's shoes corresponded to bruises on the victim. In shootings, surgeons often tried to match bullets or shot retrieved from wounds to a suspected murder weapon, in a form of crude ballistic analysis, and from about the middle of the nineteenth century attempts were made to establish that stains on objects or clothing were blood, using chemical tests and microscopic examination techniques pioneered in France during the first third of the century.[73] Although A. S. Taylor discussed the tests at length in his 1843 textbook,[74] he did not mention the microscope in relation to blood until the third edition of *Medical Jurisprudence* five years later, noting the scientific progress made since that book's first appearance in 1844.[75] He was cautious in recommending the use of a microscope to examine for semen in rape cases, but did so with increasing conviction in the second half of the same decade.[76] Twenty years later, writing in the first edition of his *Principles and Practice of Medical Jurisprudence* (1865), Taylor noted that the subject had grown so extensively that it necessitated a complete revision of his *Manual of Medical Jurisprudence*, which had already been revised six times. The topics added to the new volume were resolutely medical, but scientific techniques were now clearly integral to medico-legal tasks. These included chemical and microscopic analysis of bloodstains and stains resembling them; or of semen in rape cases; the examination of bullets; confirming live birth by microscopic evidence of food in an infant's stomach; and, citing work published by Norman Chevers in India a decade earlier, the potential importance of vegetation found in or on drowned bodies. The microscopic appearance of hair and fibres, and of epithelial scales (the cells that cover all body surfaces and line body cavities), were discussed in relation to blood and other bodily fluids.[77]

Notwithstanding Taylor's increasingly confident endorsement of scientific techniques, chemical and microscopic examinations were used in relatively few homicide investigations, cited in only 89 of the 2,615 cases studied for this book.[78] Most of these involved professional analysts who were experts in the use of such techniques and who started to become more visible during the 1860s, as the number of scientific institutions and employment opportunities for chemists grew. Francis Wrightson (1817–1893), for example, completed a PhD in chemistry at the University of Marburg before taking up a professorship at Sydenham College, one of Birmingham's two medical schools;[79] eventually he went into private practice as an analytical chemist. In a Staffordshire case of 1864 he reported chemical and microscopic experiments to identify blood on clothing, emphasising his experience: "I am in the constant habit of making an analysis."[80] Chemists based in medical schools, particularly in London, were approached by the police, as occurred in the case of the Clerkenwell bombing of 1868: Dr William Odling (1829–1921), then professor of chemistry at St Bartholomew's Hospital, was asked to study secret ink and explosive residue left by the Fenian perpetrators.[81] In another case tried at the Old Bailey, James Cameron identified himself as a Fellow of the Institute of Chemistry employed in the Government Laboratory, Somerset House – the Inland Revenue Laboratory. In 1884 he studied a chisel under a powerful microscope in order to identify letters scratched on it, while a gunsmith examined three bullets to ascertain the weapon that fired them. Their evidence provided the final links in the chain that secured the conviction of the defendant for the murder of a police constable nearly two years earlier.[82]

Scientific evidence from medical doctors was less common than that by professional chemists, but in both instances the records reveal little about the rationale that made such tests a necessary support to a particular prosecution case. In 1860 a London surgeon named Samuel Gill examined a boot with a powerful magnifying glass and found three hairs which, after further study under a microscope, he believed to be human; he gave part of his sample to Henry Letheby (1816–1876), the City of London medical officer of health and public analyst, but Letheby – an expert of wide experience – did not testify. Gill also examined the ends of two pieces of tape under a microscope; as each had 33 strands, he concluded that they were "the same sort of tape." This provoked the following exchange between the prisoner's counsel, Gill, and lead counsel for the prosecution Mr Serjeant Parry (1816–1880):

MR. BEST. Q. You are not engaged in the manufacture of tape, I suppose? A. No; I have been in the habit of examining all fabrics, I examine all things that I feel an interest in, under the microscope – I am in the habit of examining cotton, silk, or anything, for my own private investigation.

MR. SERJEANT PARRY. Q. It is a very beautiful investigation sometimes, is it not, to examine fabrics? A. It is exceedingly beautiful.

This sounds very much like the view that a modern forensic scientist might adopt toward an area of specialist study, but Gill's knowledge was gained entirely informally. Moreover, it was pure chance that he became a witness in this case: summoned to the crime scene by the layman who found the victim dead, he coincidentally happened to have an interest in fibres, as did the senior investigating officer, Detective Inspector Thornton, who had once been a draper.[83] Gill made only one subsequent appearance at the Old Bailey, five years later, to testify that head wounds had caused a child's death.[84]

Samuel Gill served as an adviser, providing his opinion on objects that he found in situ, but Henry Letheby, a far more frequent witness at the Old Bailey, acted as an authority to whom the police sent samples collected by others or asked to interpret a crime scene. Between 1844 and 1871 he testified in 32 trials: 17 homicides, 1 attempted poisoning, and assorted prosecutions for breaching public health regulations. Better known to historians for his expertise in toxicology and food adulteration, he testified about blood and trace evidence on four occasions beginning in the mid-1860s. During the trial of the first railway murderer, Franz Muller, Letheby reported his blood pattern analysis of the carriage where the victim had been battered, confirming that it was human (he had measured the size of the "globules") and consistent with a head injury. In answer to the prosecuting counsel's question, "You have used a microscope, I take it for granted?" he replied "I have used chemical tests, and the microscope – the microscope is the surest."[85] In the following year, 1865, the police asked him to examine a bloody hatchet, which he found bore traces of wool and cotton fibres, paint, blood and skin. Asked whether he could distinguish "the scales of the epithelium of the human body from any other," he responded that human skin was very "marked."[86] In 1868 he examined blood, hair and three possible weapons in a case that resulted in the execution of an eighteen-year-old.[87] By 1871 he had transformed himself into an authority on blood and bloodstains, having made them "a matter of special inquiry" and, in his last appearance at the Old Bailey, testified at length about blood and hair, the latter of which he produced in court. But this was a case in which the police, who were roundly criticised by the judge, had identified a suspect and then tried to make the evidence fit a theory that the prisoner's barrister demolished with ease, not least because so little blood was found on the alleged killer's clothes that it was unreasonable to conclude he had inflicted the wounds suffered by the victim.[88]

By the 1860s the microscope had gained a position of importance in medico-legal practice. There were no chemical tests for seminal fluid until 1896, and so a microscopic examination was the only way to prove the presence of sperm in sexual assaults.[89] Among the few rape cases extant in the Welsh and Oxford Circuit records, its use by local surgeons is noted in all instances save one that occurred in 1832. In a Staffordshire murder case of 1865, a Wolverhampton surgeon examined the victim, whose throat had been cut, to see whether she had been raped:

> The uterus presented the usual and characteristic appearance of the virgin state, the secretion from various parts of the vagina was placed under the microscope and demonstrated that nothing beyond the usual appearances were noticed; no marks of violence on the vulva were perceived.[90]

Thirty years later a workhouse medical officer and his colleague examined the clothes and body of a female victim very carefully with a microscope but could not find semen, yet genital abrasions and bruises on her knees and arms all suggested that she had been raped.[91] As a consequence, three men originally charged with murder and rape were allowed to plead guilty to a lesser offence: "the medical evidence proved that death resulted from apoplexy, and the counsel for the prosecution preferred to accept their plea of guilty to indecent assault rather than offer evidence upon the graver charge, which they and the learned judge thought would not be established." The judge believed the prisoners had been very wisely advised by their counsel.[92]

Bloodstains were susceptible to chemical analysis from a much earlier date than semen, and such tests are mentioned more frequently in surviving case files, which show that chemists relied on a process of elimination before the development of the first specific test for blood in 1853; the first screening test was developed in 1863.[93] In the 1849 case of Frederick and Maria Manning, the young William Odling identified himself as a "practical chemist" who had been studying the subject for five years, and told the court that he had made experiments on part of a dress to identify some stains: "I have subjected it to the usual chemical tests, and have arrived at the conclusion that the stains are blood." The judge asked how he had done so, and received a detailed reply:

> I cut out the stained portion of the dress and cut it into several slips, which I suspended one after another in a small quantity of distilled water; they imparted their colour to the water – it was a smoky red colour, from which I afterwards obtained a precipitate indicating albumen, one of the constituents of the blood – the colouring matter was not affected by the materials I used; it was not any colouring matter with which I am acquainted – there is no direct chemical process which will identify blood stains – my chemical process included a very large number of sources of stains, but I cannot swear it was blood – I did not examine it by the microscope; it did not appear to me to be a case suitable for microscopic observation – it is stated that the globules of blood can be detected long after.[94]

In the second edition of his *Manual of Medical Jurisprudence* (1846), Taylor had cited the presence and properties of blood's "red colouring matter," haematosine (haemoglobin), as a presumptive test, advocating a sequence of three checks: ready solubility in water, lack of reaction with ammonia and the coagulation of albumen on boiling.[95] He put little credence in French research that claimed it was possible to distinguish human from animal blood by odour, an assertion that attracted few, if any, adherents outside France.[96] Medico-legal practitioners were well aware that it was impossible to differentiate human from the blood of other mammals, and did not hesitate to say so when asked; this changed only after 1901, when Paul Uhlenhuth developed the antigen–antibody precipitin test, based on the discovery that the blood of different species contains characteristic proteins.[97] But red blood cells could be clearly recognised under a microscope even after being dried for years, and the microscope could, in capable hands, differentiate mammalian blood from that of birds, reptiles and fish, particularly if stains were examined; liquid blood was less reliable because its cells tended to become misshapen in air.[98]

Most experts and local surgeons used chemical tests and the microscope to examine blood,[99] but in 1882 Augustus Pepper of St Mary's Hospital referred to "the modern tests" to confirm that the blood he examined "was undoubtedly that of a mammal."[100] This was possibly a reference to the use of blood spectra, developed by the Sheffield scientist Henry Clifton Sorby (1826–1908) in the early 1870s after he invented a spectrum microscope, but as spectra could not differentiate human from animal blood, it is more likely a reference to a technique which attempted to measure visual differences in burst red blood cells.[101] Criminal depositions tend to provide little detailed information about the tests used, and there is no direct reference to the precipitin test in the records consulted for this book. In fact, its acceptance into Anglo-Welsh practice took a decade: the first trials in which it was used occurred in 1910.[102] Charles Graham Grant's manual for police surgeons, *Practical Forensic Medicine* of 1911, did not even mention the precipitin test,[103] but it seems to have entered medico-legal practice that year. Although police surgeons may have used it,[104] it was adopted mainly by the public analysts who, due to their professional positions, held the status of authorities. In London, the senior scientific analyst to the Home Office, William Willcox (1870–1941) referred to it in two cases, prompting the judge in the earlier case, Mr Justice Darling, to note it as the "first occasion upon which, in a Court of Justice, medical evidence had gone so far as to differentiate (specifically) human blood from (generally) mammalian blood."[105] He evidently discounted, or was unaware of, the two trials of 1910 and that of Stinie Morrison in February 1911, when William Robert Smith, professor of forensic medicine and toxicology at King's College Medical School and public analyst for Woolwich and Boston, claimed to have identified human blood; however he had quickly backtracked, admitting "it might have been the blood of one of the higher apes; it is either the one or the other."[106] In July 1911, just a month after Darling's comment, the analyst for the county of Monmouth, George Rudd Thompson, stated confidently of an alleged murder weapon that "there was a minute, but well defined clot of blood, which exhibited all the characteristics of human blood."[107]

The sluggish adoption of the precipitin test and the generally ad hoc nature of the medico-legal use of scientific aids to investigation is difficult to explain until one considers just how seldom advanced forensic science seems to have been required to close murder investigations. In the vast majority of typical cases, the police had a suspect, a motive and a chain of circumstantial evidence that medico-legal witnesses needed no scientific innovations to support: many perpetrators were literally caught in the act, with bloody hands, clothes or weapons; had confessed or had been spotted by a reliable witness. The prosecution then had only to create a plausible narrative to explain the facts, against which the defence could at best argue provocation, insanity or mistaken identity. Flaws in this crime-solving methodology were revealed only when basic police work failed to identify a suspect against whom a persuasive case could be built by conventional means. In such instances, scientific evidence could go only so far before factors outside the control of the police or the experts undermined their efforts. Even fingerprints were not commonly used, despite the well-known success represented by the conviction of the Stratton brothers in 1905.[108] Case files reveal a single occasion when Scotland Yard's Fingerprint Bureau was consulted in a provincial murder investigation: in 1908 a gun used in a Shropshire killing was taken to London for examination by Chief Inspector Charles Collins, but was too dirty to yield usable prints.[109] Collins, the country's foremost fingerprint expert, testified in only one Old Bailey murder trial other than the Stratton case.[110]

Just as in the present day, the use of forensic science before the First World War was dictated by case seriousness, the availability of other evidence and cost.[111] Few cases really required specialist evidence, but those that did raised the question of who had the authority to provide and interpret it, an issue clearly related to developing investigative procedures. As the police began to take a greater hand in directing the course of investigations, they identified medical and chemical professionals to whom they could turn for scientific assistance. In matters requiring a degree of analytical skill, the public analysts were preferred: their training and formal employment equipped them for specialist medico-legal work, and their professional standing bestowed an innate confidence. In London, the members of this select group were frequently medical professionals who held hospital and teaching positions, adding an additional level of authority. In the provinces, the analysts were more chemical and less medical, a result of fewer teaching hospitals and a greater separation in the roles of public analyst and medical officer of health.[112] Local doctors in all parts of the country continued to provide post-mortem reports and to help interpret crime scenes. The use of specialist pathologists remained relatively uncommon, but police surgeons began increasingly to take on this responsibility in urban areas. It was from among the members of these three groups – the public analysts, police surgeons and hospital consultants – that the modern expert witness emerged in the third quarter of the nineteenth century, the most eminent among them being those who combined two or more official positions. Multiple office holding was however both a mark of esteem and a financial imperative.

Expertise and expert status: fees and costs

The fees and costs associated with forensic work have not been systematically studied,[113] but they are an important aspect of the history of medico-legal practice. Chapter 3 considered the financial impetus that underpinned the role of the coroner's officer, a policeman who determined whether a case merited an inquest and, by deciding in the negative, thereby helped reduce his district's fiscal expenditure. Here, attention shifts to the fees paid to medical witnesses. The coroners and police, by deciding who to consult and what to pay them, helped to define the expert witness, who, by the end of the nineteenth century was distinguished from his lesser peers by the fact that he could command a higher fee than those permitted by statute. Under the terms of the Medical Witnesses Act 1836, "any legally qualified medical practitioner" was to be paid 1 guinea to give evidence at an inquest, or 2 guineas if he had conducted a post-mortem examination; no fee was to be paid to the medical officer "whose duty it may have been to attend the deceased" in any public medical institution. The Inquest Expenses Act 1837 directed that such costs be borne by the county or borough rates.[114] The 2 guinea fee also included chemical analysis of the stomach or intestines. These financial provisions were unchanged by the Coroners' Act

1887, which gave the inquest jury the power to require the coroner to summon a second medical witness in cases where they were dissatisfied with the first; and remained in place until 1926 when the fees were raised slightly.[115] Under the terms of the 1887 Act, inquest costs were to be paid by the local authority, which could create a schedule of additional "fees, allowances, and disbursements which on the holding of an inquest may lawfully be paid and made by the coroner holding such inquest";[116] this clause was a near-verbatim reiteration of one of the original provisions of the Inquest Expenses Act (s.1). Thus, for the whole period 1836–1926, the normal expectation was that in all inquest cases a local medical practitioner would conduct a post-mortem examination, a toxicological analysis if required, and give evidence for a maximum fee of 2 guineas; no extra was payable for attendance on successive days. If the victim was taken to hospital and died there, so much the better: the house surgeon would see to the required tasks but did not have to be paid.

The most obvious potential for financial differences arose in cases of suspected poisoning, when local practitioners were not necessarily skilled enough to conduct the necessary analysis, thereby opening a window on to distinctions between the professionally competent and the truly expert. In late 1848, when poisoning crimes seemed to have reached epidemic proportions,[117] county clerks of the peace were canvassed for information "as to paying extra fees to Medical Witnesses on Coroners Inquests." In September 1848 Oxfordshire magistrates had refused to reimburse 2 guineas paid to Dr William Gull (1816–1890) of Guy's Hospital for analysing a stomach in which he discovered arsenic, prompting a furious response from the coroner, James Westell; and the circular that the clerk of the peace, John Davenport, subsequently distributed to colleagues in other English counties, noting that an analogous case had just occurred in Somerset. The 23 responses he received revealed widely differing practices.[118] In some counties, including Worcestershire and Staffordshire, the magistrates agreed to pay extra fees, recognising that the coroners would not otherwise be able to perform their duties properly; in Essex, which was experiencing a poisoning crisis,[119] they always paid but could not recover those costs from central government with other prosecution expenses. In other counties, including Hertfordshire and East Yorkshire, the magistrates always refused, while in Bedfordshire the onus lay on an inquest jury to request further medical evidence. In Herefordshire the coroner had insisted that there was "no difficulty in procuring at any time satisfactory medical assistance, young but able surgeons for the sake of practice information etc being always ready to undertake post mortem examinations for the fee allowed by the statute." Several clerks believed that the Inquest Expenses Act did not permit *any* additional payments, but a few others, more hopeful, expressed the view that magistrates had the power to allow any fees they pleased; in Warwickshire, a schedule of fees permitted a daily payment of up to 2 guineas "to a chemist, engineer, or other scientific person, at the discretion of the coroner." In the 1845 case of the notorious Buckinghamshire poisoner John Tawell, the court rather than the county magistrates had allowed the expenses of an "experimental chemist," but from Devon came the acerbic reply "I hardly see how the witness going to London and seeing another exercise his science could be able to depose satisfactorily as to results which he himself was unable to work out – it hardly appears evidence." Notwithstanding the fact that expert evidence in poisoning cases had become increasingly common, those who held the purse strings adopted a nonchalant attitude to paying for it. In Somerset, it appears that all expenses in the case in question had been allowed except those of the analyst, William Herapath (1796–1868), professor of chemistry at the Bristol Medical School "to whom the contents of the stomach were taken by the medical man."[120] Herapath had no doubt of his worth, having earlier that year charged the county of Monmouthshire 15 guineas for a series of analyses that took him three days to complete.[121]

It is uncertain whether Herapath recovered his fee in either of these cases, but the more important point concerns the fees that he thought it appropriate to charge, given his acknowledged status as a regional toxicological expert. Henry Letheby and Alfred S. Taylor had also realised that the costs they incurred in such analyses were not met by the statutory fee, and therefore charged more (for Taylor, about 2 guineas per sample) for their services.[122] A fee of 2 guineas per organic sample appears to have been fairly standard among professional analysts, who charged half that amount for inorganic samples. In April 1868, Edward Davies of the Royal Institution Laboratory in Liverpool charged the city magistrates 7 guineas in a case of suspected poisoning: 4 guineas for analysing the viscera and the vomit, plus a further 3 guineas for analysing the contents of three bottles.[123] In the same month, A. R. Arrott and Thomas Huson, analytical and consulting chemists in Liverpool, stated their fees for testing explosive or inflammable materials:

> The fee for each sample to be £1.1.0 for which we will state that the sample is inflammable or explosive (as the case may be) at a certain temperature, and under certain conditions, but no analysis either partial or detailed will be given. If such were required, an additional fee would be entailed, which would vary according to the complexity of the analysis. The fee of £1.1.0 would be exclusive of any attendance at Court, which might be required.[124]

However, we do not have to look to recognised experts in analytical chemistry or toxicology to identify a distinction in the financial arrangements that the legal system allowed for professional expertise. Prosecution costs demonstrate that doctors, in contrast to lay witnesses including police officers, had long been reimbursed for their attendance at criminal trials at a higher daily rate than other witnesses, reflecting the value of their professional status and potential loss of income. A statute of 1754 permitted the courts to reimburse the expenses incurred by poor prosecutors and witnesses on conviction of the defendant,[125] a provision that was extended in 1778 to felony cases that ended in an acquittal;[126] and Peel's Criminal Law Act of 1826 allowed financial compensation for costs, expenses and loss of time incurred by prosecutors and witnesses *before* a felony suspect was committed for trial.[127] Although these provisions were ostensibly for the support of poorer persons, bills compiled for the Welsh Court of Great Sessions and the Cost Books of the Oxford Circuit reveal that doctors were routinely paid more than others – even if, as Welsh records suggest, the court did not always allow the full sums claimed by the counties.[128]

In late eighteenth-century North Wales, surgeons received a higher per diem rate than others. Trial records for Anglesey reveal that in a case heard at the Lent Great Sessions of 1786, Dr Johnson "a witness for the prosecution for his loss of time and expenses he being absent from his own business 4 days" was paid £5 5s.;[129] in 1793 "Dr Wynn a witness for the prosecution for his attendance to give evidence before the grand jury upon the bill of indictment and upon the trial" received 10s. 6d., as he was resident in the assize town.[130] The prosecutors and witnesses were paid a significantly lower per diem: 3s. in the earlier case and 3s. 6d. in the later one. In 1827 Thomas Browning Haslam, a surgeon from Carnarvon, was paid a total of 4 guineas for attending the trial of a woman at Beaumaris, which occupied him for two days.[131] At the Carnarvonshire spring sessions of 1817 the witnesses in two different trials were paid 7s. 6d. per day, but the medical witnesses recouped significantly more: Dr Edward Carreg (the coroner discussed in Chapter 3) was paid 3 guineas for his four days' attendance, while surgeon Edward Williams claimed five days at £1 11s. 6d., for a total of £7 17s. 6d. – but in both cases these costs also included attendance at pre-trial hearings.[132] In 1820 John Roberts, a surgeon from Carnarvon, claimed the same daily rate for attendance and loss of time, £1 11s. 6d.,[133] but in the following year a surgeon named Robert Roberts claimed at the lower rate of one guinea per day.[134] In 1825 a prosecutor designated "a great invalid" was paid a total of £1 6s. for two days' attendance, including expenses and horse-hire; but the same two surgeons, Robert Roberts and John Roberts, were paid 2 and 4 guineas, respectively,[135] suggesting the recognition of some differential in their professional status. During the previous year two other surgeons in the county had been reimbursed at the rate of 2 guineas per day.[136] While the statutes stipulated that payments were to be made to those in most financial need, it is clear that members of the medical profession were consistently paid at a rate that acknowledged professional standing rather than lack of wealth. As befit their local status as experts and in stark contrast to all other witnesses, the trust and credibility vested in these surgeons by officers of the law was formally documented in higher expense claims.

Similar bills of costs for trials held in other Welsh counties do not appear to survive, but the evidence from Anglesey and Carnarvonshire shows that parish constables could expect a per diem of four or five shillings;[137] the 1826 Act enabled them to claim for all expenses incurred in the course of their duties. This is particularly interesting in the context of bills paid for assize trials held on the Oxford Circuit in the mid-1850s, which reveal a clear disparity in the costs reimbursed to witnesses. A series of 89 bills for assize trials held across the circuit's eight counties during the summer of 1856 shows that surgeons were paid a daily rate of 21s. while other witnesses, including police constables, skilled and manual workers, servants and senior police officers were paid rates ranging from 2s. 6d. to 5s.[138] In trials held during the summers of 1867 and 1868, surgeons were paid the same 21*s*., sometimes noted as "professional evidence." Surgeons who appeared for the defence were paid the same, but other witnesses received lower amounts, between one and four shillings.[139] The daily rate paid to surgeons had not changed 20 years later: in 1888 it was still 21*s*. But other witnesses seem to have been receiving even less than before, with police constables getting as little as 1*s*. 6*d*.[140] Thus it would appear that the police and lay witnesses experienced a gradual reduction in the amount they could claim in expenses from central government for attending the assizes. For medical witnesses, however, the passage of a century had not diminished their per diem rate, which remained around a generous one guinea in recognition of the professional expertise that their role in the criminal justice system presumed.

Yet by the 1880s a divide had opened between the expert and the expert witness, continuing a trend that had begun in the 1840s when the courtroom successes and failures of toxicology separated the true medico-legal authorities from those who served as advisers. The distinction was formalised in 1872 when the Home Office appointed Thomas Stevenson (1838–1908), then a chemistry lecturer at Guy's Hospital, to the post of Scientific Analyst, a position from which he dominated successive trials for criminal poisoning as a witness for the prosecution.[141] In 1881 Stevenson was promoted to Senior Scientific Analyst, an office he held until his death, and Charles Meymott Tidy (1843–1892), who had trained under and taught with Henry Letheby at the London Hospital, was appointed to the vacant junior position. After Tidy's early death from cancer, Dr Arthur P. Luff (1856–1938), lecturer in forensic medicine at St Mary's Hospital, took up the position of Scientific Analyst in June 1892. He resigned 12 years later, having delayed the decision for two years because of his friendship with Stevenson, due to his growing private practice and the pressure placed on his "scanty holidays" by the "liability to be suddenly called on for a Home Office case."[142] This is interesting for two reasons. Tidy had been forced to complain to the Home Office about the lack of work he was given; and Luff had himself complained about the costs he incurred in relation to the fees received, resulting in the decision taken in August 1899 to pay the scientific analysts an annual retainer: £150 to Stevenson and £75 to Luff, both of whom also earned extra fees by acting directly for the Director of Public Prosecutions without reference to the Home Office.[143] Part of the problem, for Luff, was the fact that he had to maintain a laboratory for which, being a practising physician and not a public analyst, he had no use except to enable him to carry out toxicological work.[144] Stevenson, meanwhile, had also complained about a financial matter, annoyed that since 1896 he had received less work than usual in relation to suicides. This prompted the Home Office to tabulate the fees that he and Luff had earned in the period 1894–1897, respectively, £755 9*s*. 1*d*. and £164 16*s*. 5*d*., noting that although Stevenson had no suicide cases from August 1896 to November 1897, since then he had had six.[145] Thus, all three of the analysts had cause to grumble about the financial arrangements under which they provided their expertise; Luff eventually realised that he could earn more in private practice. But he and Stevenson ultimately fared much better than Tidy, whose request for a greater share of the Home Office's analytical work, initially raised in March 1886, was not resolved until October 1888 when Godfrey Lushington (1832–1907), the Permanent Under-Secretary of State of the Home Office (1886–1895) decided tersely "No alteration to be made."[146]

The importance of the Home Office in defining the expert witness and deciding on the appropriate level of remuneration was strengthened by its relationship to the Metropolitan Police, the largest force in the country, because the Commissioner of Police of the Metropolis had to seek the approval of the Home Secretary for all financial decisions, including appointments and salaries.[147] The records of the negotiations between the two institutions in relation to Dr Thomas Bond reveal the decision-making process that determined the rate at which this quintessential forensic expert would be paid. Like the Home Office Analysts, Bond, the surgeon to Division A of the Metropolitan Police, was accustomed to being fairly compensated for his time and expertise and was not afraid to ask for more money. In doing so, he helped to create the terms on which medico-legal expertise was understood to be different from more routine forensic practice, and it was this definition, albeit still rather vague, that was written in to the Coroners (Amendment) Act of 1926. This law empowered coroners to ask anyone whom they considered to hold "special qualifications" to conduct a "special examination" by "analysis, test or otherwise" – for which the standard fees did not apply – to ascertain how the deceased came by their death.[148] In such cases, the Home Office would pay the fees, allowances and disbursements made by coroners where the local schedule of additional fees was insufficient.[149] Thus, for the first time, statutory provision for the recognition and adequate payment of medico-legal experts was introduced, finally placing the informal practices that had been on-going for about 80 years on a legal footing.

Sufficient charge for the services rendered

In the midst of the on-going crisis of confidence in police investigative techniques associated with the notorious killings committed by 'Jack the Ripper' in the autumn of 1888,[150] senior officials in the Metropolitan Police and in the Home Office to whom they reported began to consider the role that medical professionals might play in such difficult cases. But it was not serial murder that sparked a series of correspondence between Sir Charles Warren (1840–1927), Commissioner of the Metropolitan Police, the force's Chief Surgeon Alexander MacKellar (1845–1904) and Godfrey Lushington at the Home Office, but an angry complaint made by Thomas Bond who, in January 1888, learned he was to be "superseded in his appointment." Apart from the fact that he naturally "should feel aggrieved by such treatment," Bond estimated a consequent reduction to his salary of £100 and pressed for a satisfactory resolution to the matter.[151] The underlying rationale for the decision to transfer several hundred police officers from Bond's care and the maladroit manner in which it was communicated to him were undoubtedly examples of the famously difficult relations that existed between Warren, a career soldier who attempted to run the police service along military lines, and those with whom he worked at a senior level;[152] unsurprisingly, he adopted an intractable position, claiming that Bond had "no claim to a monopoly on medical charge of the constables at Scotland Yard."[153] The issue caused a territorial skirmish between Warren and Lushington, who noted that the Commissioner had "attempted to confer upon himself functions previously exercised either by the Chief Surgeon or the Home Secretary,"[154] and discussion stalled amid increasing frustration on both sides.

Over the course of the summer the issue of payments made to divisional surgeons re-emerged as a general question of procedure: Warren introduced practices deemed "irregular and insubordinate" by Lushington in early August, while the Home Secretary complained that the regular salaries of the divisional surgeons had still to be dealt with.[155] Within weeks the first of five Ripper murders occurred, however, and changed the focus of the debate completely, from the salaries paid to all of London's police surgeons to the fees to be paid for medico-legal work in "special cases." In early October Bond was consulted in one such special case: he conducted the post-mortem examination of a headless female torso found in Westminster near the new headquarters of Scotland Yard – the second of what became known as the Thames Mysteries of 1887–1889, a series of four unsolved murders in which female victims were dismembered.[156] On the day after the torso was discovered, 4 October 1888, Bond resigned the disputed part of his position in exchange for more lucrative employment, as MacKellar explained to Warren on 1 November:

> He has had a very large medico-legal experience, and he would naturally prefer to be referred to by the Commissioner as a medico-legal expert, than to retain charge of an extra number of men . . . which would further in many instances disqualify him from being consulted in police civil and criminal business in his higher capacity of Medical Jurist. London, unlike foreign capitals has few medical men possessed of large medico-legal knowledge and experience, and Mr Bond has both, is an exceedingly good witness, and has intimate and extensive acquaintance with the Force. I consider that it would be an advantage to the Service that he should be consulted in medico-legal difficulties.[157]

Warren passed this decision on to the Home Office, acknowledging "the many very important police medical duties which [Bond] has to perform in connection with police civil and criminal business; and he naturally prefers to be called in by the Commissioner for criminal business in which he is an expert instead of other specialists."[158] A civil servant took this for the Commissioner's agreement to give all medico-legal cases to Bond, but Lushington was keen to avoid any such assumption: "the arrangement sanctioned does not imply an undertaking that medico-legal cases shall as a matter of right be sent to Dr Bond."[159]

This at times ill-tempered correspondence represents far more than a clash of personality or power: it marks an important turning point in the history of medico-legal expertise in London, and identifies a clear moment in time when the nation's largest and most experienced police force acknowledged a doctor as an expert witness in the modern sense of the term. Over the next 13 years until his death in 1901, Thomas Bond was recognised as "the best medical witness of his day;" each time he asked the Metropolitan Police for a pay rise they forwarded his request to the Home Office with alacrity, and each request was granted. Despite, or perhaps because of the fear caused by the Ripper crimes during the autumn of terror, Lushington's attempt to keep both Bond and, more successfully, Charles Tidy from assuming an inflated importance was destined to fail.[160] By the end of the century the Home Office experts had a national reputation for excellence, and had become the exceptions that proved the rule: only a few medico-legal witnesses had the experience, status and authority to take on especially challenging cases with confidence.

Bond was one of dozens of divisional surgeons in London, but was one of the longest serving, having been appointed in 1867. He was perhaps lucky in that he worked in A Division, where the Detective Branch was located, giving him easier and more regular access to complex cases and to his superiors, who were headquartered at Scotland Yard. Despite the size of the metropolis, however, murder was uncommon and difficult cases were atypical: statistics compiled in the 1880s indicate that apart from cases of newborn child murder, most killers were caught and punished. In the whole of England and Wales only 145 murders were reported in 1880, and 152 in 1886.[161] Medico-legal expertise was therefore more typically required for cases heard in the coroner's court rather than the criminal courts, but this raised a financial problem of its own: the Coroners Act of 1887 expected that any post-mortem examination or analysis would be done by the main medical witness in the particular case, but if their expertise was inadequate coroners had to pay someone else and might not always be able to recoup the cost from the local authority. During the 1890s this led to a lack of adequate medical testimony at inquests, and on his appointment to the position of coroner for the South-Western District by the London County Council in 1902, John Troutbeck (c.1853–1912) developed a solution for this predicament: he asked Dr Ludwig Freyberger (1865–1934) of the Great Northern Central Hospital to perform all his post-mortem examinations, choosing his name from a list of about a dozen skilled pathologists compiled by the LCC.[162] This raised a key criticism by doctors, related to a wider argument about income and status: although Freyberger claimed to be a specialist, he was willing to accept an ordinary fee of 2 guineas to conduct a post-mortem.[163] But their collaboration continued until Troutbeck's death, which devastated Freyberger's finances.[164] The question of the level at which expertise should be recompensed, and who should pay, had also arisen in regard to toxicological analyses. In the late 1890s the Home Office recognised the problem caused by the fact that their analysts could act only when coroners had grounds to suspect foul play; other cases were normally entrusted to the county analyst, but if he had no medical training an additional set of problems might ensue.[165] Officials were perhaps less than helpful in suggesting that it would be "very difficult to suggest any table of fees which would fully meet all the various circumstances that may arise – in one case a fee of £1 1s. 0d. might be ample, in another a fee of twenty times that amount might be insufficient."[166] In response, the Coroners' Society proposed a minimum fee for an analysis of £5 5s., as was the case in London and Surrey (but not elsewhere), but this was not instituted. In 1909 the Buckinghamshire County Council reiterated "the absence of any provision in the Coroners Acts for employing and paying an Expert Analyst."[167] Although section 25 of the 1887 Act gave local authorities the power to incur further expenses for the purpose of obtaining expert evidence, it did not seem to be working.

Medico-legal work was not generally well paid, and there was a tension between the need to cut costs yet identify and punish crime. In 1889 in the wake of the Ripper murders, the Metropolitan Police instructed divisional surgeons to send a report of their post-mortem examination and conclusions in all cases of murder or manslaughter to the Commissioner, to which Dr James Adams of V Division (attached to Barnes station, in Surrey) immediately retorted "but no mention is made of remuneration for time and trouble."[168] This prompted MacKellar to consider the terms of a sliding scale of fees, in the process of which he defined the "special case" as one of mysterious murder, or rape:

> I certainly am of opinion that the demand of a fee is both reasonable and fair. I would strongly advise that these fees be treated as 'special fees', each case to be considered according to its merits and importance. A careful microscopical examination of blood or seminal stains on clothing or the investigation of a 'Whitechapel murder' would naturally require a much higher rate of remuneration than a report expressing the opinion that a child was still-born (this latter case would probably in many instances be well remunerated by a fee of 10s. 6d.). These cases do not so frequently occur as to necessitate the adoption of a tariff or scale of fees. I consider that to remunerate these cases by Special Fees, according to their degree of importance, would be found more economical and infinitely more satisfactory in practice.[169]

James Monro (1838–1920), who served as Commissioner of Police of the Metropolis from November 1888 until June 1890, supported this suggestion and put it to the Home Office, which agreed that the fee for each special report should vary according to the circumstances, but instructed that the maximum payable without the permission of the Home Secretary would be 3 guineas.[170] This did not meet the Commissioner's original request, as only special cases, not all cases of murder, would be notified to him, but he was forced to abandon his initial plan because of Home Office resistance to the potential cost. MacKellar was annoyed: "As requested by [the] Commissioner I withdrew the Circular letter of Sept 19th 1889 . . . although I regret the necessity for so doing, as I consider that the expenditure would have been trifling in amount and the advantage to Police very great."[171] In the face of Home Office scrutiny of the accounts, and suspicion that doctors might be claiming from the Police Fund fees properly payable by the LCC, in the spring of 1897 the Commissioner, then Sir Edward Bradford (1836–1911), was asked by the Home Secretary to explain why the special fees paid during 1896–1897 to divisional surgeons had risen: "The amount involved is not large in itself, but is much larger than has been incurred in any previous year, and having regard to the items, Sir Matthew Ridley [the Home Secretary] would be glad to have an explanation of the manner in which advantage is taken of this authority." The query was raised in relation to six claims totalling £27 1*s.*, of which two claims by Bond amounted to 17 guineas.[172] Following research into the circumstances of the cases, which established that Bond had been asked to act at the request of the Assistant Commissioner, Robert Anderson, and that all the cases were justified, Bradford crafted a careful reply:

> In forwarding this report, in which the details of each special case are fully set forth, I may mention that murder is practically the most serious crime with which the police have to deal; and, as far as I am aware, there is no kind of crime in relation to which the police are so badly served. In many cases, the law and practice as regards the coroner's powers and duties, and medical examination of bodies, could not be more embarrassing to police work if they were specially designed to thwart it, and, in order to avert or modify the evils of this system ^it is in many important cases desirable that extra and special medical skill should be called in[.] ~~and the expenses in this connection are more likely to increase rather than decrease~~ I feel that it is unlikely that any material economy can be effected in connection with such cases.[173]

The Home Office acknowledged receipt of his letter, and there the matter appears to have rested. But it is obvious that the Metropolitan Police were forced to keep a tight rein on their expenditure for medico-legal work, a restriction that had already caused an outburst from Dr Adams, a divisional surgeon of extensive experience who had testified at the trial of Kate Webster in 1879:[174] he became so concerned about pecuniary matters that he eventually took a stand against the police. In 1897 he refused to provide the result of his post-mortem on the body of a woman found in the River Thames unless he was paid for the information. Unsurprisingly, the officers involved in this unseemly contretemps complained to their superiors, who were aware that there had been "difficulties in getting medical reports promptly and satisfactorily in murder cases" but thought this was the worst instance by far. Adams narrowly avoided being forced to resign: he apologised and promised never to repeat his behaviour, following a favourable intervention by MacKellar.[175]

This sort of financial evidence reveals regional disparities in the fees paid for medico-legal work, but also shows that there was a growing national recognition that certain experts held a superior status and could thus command higher fees. London led the way, with the tacit support of the Home Office. In 1893 Arthur Luff wrote to enquire what his fee for court attendance as Official Analyst should be, noting that he was accustomed to charging a per diem of 10 guineas for "country cases," those that required travel outside London. Thomas Stevenson and Dr August Dupré (1835–1907), public analyst to the City of Westminster (1873–1901) and a consultant to the Local Government Board, were each allowed a fee of 10 guineas per day for country cases "in consideration of the position they hold in their profession," but it was unclear whether Luff's status was sufficiently high to merit the same.[176] Even were this fee to be agreed, he would not have been able to earn it very often: by 1899 Dupré's fees were lower than Stevenson's, but he did "a great deal of business" while Stevenson had very few cases.[177] Luff would have had even fewer, of course, because Stevenson was always the first choice and they generally only took on murder cases for the Home Office. But toxicological work was a little more lucrative than chemical analyses. Thus, Dupré charged 3 guineas to analyse organic compounds, 2 guineas for explosives and 15s. for partial analyses. Stevenson charged £10 for an analysis of human viscera, 2 guineas for the contents of bottles, and 5 guineas per day for attending court in London.[178]

Meanwhile, secure in his formally acknowledged expert status, Thomas Bond began to agitate for more adequate financial compensation. In 1893 he expressed anxiety that the "old scale of prices is certainly not a sufficient charge for the services rendered" because "my position now as a forensic expert is quite different from my position when the scale of fees was arranged."[179] By June the Home Secretary had sanctioned a table of fees personal to Bond, covering everything from post-mortems conducted within the London district (3 guineas) to writing reports on the results of microscopical examinations (1 guinea).[180] Clearly Bond was in a special category, but these costs were soon to prove too low for in the summer of 1895 he was faced with the deaths of Mrs Scott Campbell and Rose English, respectively a case of abortion and suicide, though each mysterious at the outset. Bond conducted post-mortem examinations at the request of the coroners, Dr Clifford Luxmore Drew (for the western district of London) and Dr George Danford Thomas (for the central district), and on 1 July 1896 he submitted his account to the Home Office, amounting to 18 guineas for the abortion case alone; for the Metropolitan Police the total sum was £25 4s., an amount met with consternation. Months of wrangling followed as to how the bill should be divided between the Home Office, Treasury, coroners and the police, but there does not seem to have been any serious doubt that Bond deserved the fees that he asked for. Alexander MacKellar supported him:

> I recommend that he be allowed the special fee in the case of Mrs Scott Campbell for his reports and also five guineas a day for his attendances at the inquest. The reports I am informed were very long and important, involving an attendance all day at the inquest to the neglect of everything else. The report could only be made after reading all the evidence of many witnesses and written opinions, involving considerable work and responsibility, a very tedious and arduous post-mortem on a septic and very decomposed body, another long report and attendance.[181]

The debate was still on-going in May 1897 when a police memo revealed that, in the case of Rose English, Bond had been called in at their request but the coroner could not pay him because he had the power to pay only one expert whom he had instructed himself, Professor Augustus Pepper, and as Bond had been called by the police the county council would not pay him.[182] By the end of the month the Home Secretary had acquiesced, agreeing to pay Bond 18 guineas for his work on the Scott Campbell case but noting that the scale of fees agreed in June 1893 should be "strictly adhered to in future," and that fees that exceeded the scale "should not be charged without the previous sanction of the Commissioner or Assistant Commissioner, or unless an explanation of such a nature as to justify an exception is furnished."[183]

This system functioned smoothly until, weighed down by illness and worry, Thomas Bond committed suicide in June 1901.[184] By the following spring the Metropolitan Police had begun to discuss the importance of asking the Home Office to appoint a successor, noting that the table of fees agreed with Bond would have to be revisited "whenever a vacancy occurred," and that Pepper would be a suitable replacement.[185] The impetus came from the highest level: the new Commissioner, Edward Henry (1850–1931), and his Assistant Commissioner (Crime), Melville Macnaghten (1853–1921). Within weeks of taking up their new posts in March 1903 Macnaghten had approached Pepper, who agreed to replace Bond (the two men had "a frank discussion of the question of fees") and Henry reported on this to the Home Office, noting his wish to secure the services of "a medical jurist of the first rank." The agreed fees were significantly higher than Bond had earned, including 5 guineas for "visiting and inspecting scene of criminal occurrence," 5 guineas per day for attending the Central Criminal Court, and 10 guineas and upwards for a post-mortem.[186] In several complex murder cases that followed, Pepper proved himself well worth the money paid by the police and Home Office.[187]

Conclusion

By the end of the nineteenth century the notion of the medico-scientific expert had permeated the halls of government. It was inherent in an 1893 select committee report on death certification, closely associated with the practices of French "pathological experts."[188] When the government committee appointed to enquire into the law relating to coroners and their inquests published its initial findings in 1909, it revealed an even clearer recognition of the distinction between expert and other medical witnesses: the former were closely associated with toxicology and pathology and provided an opinion, while the latter testified to facts.[189] By contrast, the word 'expert' was never used in the equivalent report of 1860.[190] The position and status of the expert witness had been acknowledged but not yet secured on a nationally consistent basis, however: coroners in London and large provincial towns could easily obtain expert medical advice, but when a difficult case arose elsewhere, "the country coroner usually has to obtain his expert advice from some distant big town or do without it."[191] The committee recommended that coroners should be allowed to request an expert analysis, toxicology or pathology, under the terms of Home Office regulations according to the Costs in Criminal Cases Act 1908, the fifth section of which had given the Home Secretary power to fix the rates of and conditions for costs payable from local funds. This suggestion, it was noted, would still leave the Home Secretary free to direct a special analysis "by an expert named by him in special cases."[192] Special murder cases were relatively few in number, however: Augustus Pepper testified in eight trials at the Central Criminal Court between 1900 and 1913, and travelled once to the hinterlands of Staffordshire in 1911.[193] In the vast majority of murder investigations, local police, coroners and magistrates made do with local talent, police surgeons and general practitioners who were able to provide the necessary attention to detail and certainty of interpretation needed to identify and get a suspect to court and, more often than not, secure a conviction. But further work will be required to ascertain the proportion and geographical range of cases which, similar to those of Mrs Scott Campbell and Rose English, did not lead to a murder charge but involved a contribution from a recognised expert during the investigation.

The collaboration of medical practitioners, the police and coroners combined to transform the investigation of murder during the course of the nineteenth century, from a process managed largely by amateurs to one dominated by professionals. These groups were relatively slow to engage with forensic science, constrained by the impact of financial concerns at the local and national level, but recognised the growing divide between forensic medicine and forensic science. The main point of overlap between the two lay in the field of toxicology, and the expert witness emerged in the mid-nineteenth century as an individual who had experience, if not formal training, in both medicine and chemistry, and was likely to be employed by an academic institution – Herapath, Letheby, Scattergood, Taylor and Wrightson being among the most able. In the 1870s the public analysts (many of whom held medical qualifications) and police surgeons joined the national roster of experts on the basis of their training and experience and the financial savings they offered to coroners and magistrates. By the turn of the twentieth century a small number of individuals based in urban academic institutions, particularly in London, had acquired the status of an expert witness. They were paid more than other medico-legal witnesses, reviewed and critiqued the work of others and contributed to murder investigations both at the crime scene and in the laboratory or mortuary. The market for such experts remained limited and geographically variable, however, because murder was both uncommon and frequently uncomplicated.

Historians of twentieth-century forensic science have noted the relative rarity of murder as a key factor in the formal separation of forensic science from forensic medicine, marked by the creation of the Forensic Science Service by the Home Office in the mid-1930s: a network of regional laboratories was established, located near university towns in the expectation that academic expertise would be forthcoming when needed. Government focus had shifted in the direction to which crime statistics pointed, the main purpose of the new service being to bring science to bear on everyday criminality, mainly property offences. Since violent crimes against the person comprised merely 2.5 per cent of reported indictable offences, of which sexual assaults outnumbered homicides by more than 50 per cent, forensic pathology was seen as exclusive to a very limited number of cases. Forensic medicine was consequently left to languish on the fringes of medical research, with no institutional focus.[194] In a further reflection of the interwar drive to specialisation, the offices of public analyst and medical officer of health also became quite separate, though usually the two officials worked together.[195] Unlike these and other studies of forensic science, however, this chapter has examined the forensic expert in action at *nineteenth-century* crime scenes, to explain how expert status was determined and attributed, the importance of location (temporal and spatial) to the production and enactment of different forms of forensic knowledge, financial and practical constraints on investigation, and the role of the developing police service on investigative practices.[196] Modern crime scene investigation may owe more to twentieth-century than Victorian developments,[197] but this chapter demonstrates that its origins cannot be understood in isolation from the logistics of Victorian forensic supply and demand. The expert witness and the crime scene emerged in tandem as local police worked with an increasingly select group of medical practitioners to investigate murder.

Notes

1 "Expert, n." *OED Online*. Oxford University Press, January 2018, www.oed.com. oxfordbrookes.idm.oclc.org/view/Entry/66551?rskey=wfSbd6&result=1 (accessed 14 Feb 2018). This definition cites sources dated 1825–1890 and reflects the historiographical interpretation of the development of the term as discussed in Katherine D. Watson, *Forensic Medicine in Western Society: A History* (Abingdon: Routledge, 2011), pp. 46–50.

2 Tony Ward, "Law, Common Sense and the Authority of Science: Expert Witnesses and Criminal Insanity in England, ca. 1840–1940," *Social & Legal Studies* 6 (1997), pp. 343–362; Katherine D. Watson, "Medical and Chemical Expertise in English Trials for Criminal Poisoning, 1750–1914," *Medical History* 50 (2006), pp. 373–390.

3 Alfred S. Taylor, *Medical Jurisprudence*, fourth edition (London: John Churchill, 1852), pp. 228–238; Johann Ludwig Casper, *A Handbook of the Practice of Forensic Medicine*, Vol. 1, trans. George William Balfour (London: New Sydenham Society, 1861), pp. 87–88. For Guy, see the chapter epigraph.

4 Alison Adam, *A History of Forensic Science: British Beginnings in the Twentieth Century* (Abingdon: Routledge, 2016); Ian Burney and Neil Pemberton, *Murder and the Making of English CSI* (Baltimore: Johns Hopkins University Press, 2016); Haia Shpayer-Makov, "Detectives and Forensic Science: The Professionalization of Police Detection," in *The Oxford Handbook of the History of Crime and Criminal Justice*, ed. Paul Knepper and Anja Johansen (Oxford: Oxford University Press, 2016), pp. 474–496. Burney and Pemberton note the lack of interest in crime scenes displayed by Casper: see *Murder and the Making of English CSI*, p. 30.

5 Haia Shpayer-Makov, *The Ascent of the Detective: Police Sleuths in Victorian and Edwardian England* (Oxford: Oxford University Press, 2011), pp. 13–61; Keith Laybourn and David Taylor, *Policing in England and Wales, 1918–39: The Fed, Flying Squads and Forensics* (Basingstoke: Palgrave, 2011), pp. 81–104.

6 Clive Emsley, *The Great British Bobby: A History of British Policing from the 18th Century to the Present* (London: Quercus, 2010), pp. 125–126, 148–153.

7   This paragraph is based on information supplied by Haia Shpayer-Makov, whom I would like to thank for her insights. See also *Ascent of the Detective*, pp. 40, 42–46.

8   See Appendix 3 and *Reports of the Inspectors of Constabulary, for the Year Ended 29th September 1899, Made to Her Majesty's Principal Secretary of State, under the Provisions of the Statute 19 & 20 Vict c.69* (London: HMSO, 1900), p. 8 for Birmingham.

9   Alfred S. Taylor, *Elements of Medical Jurisprudence* (London: Deacon, 1843), p. 367. See also, writing for a Scottish audience but available in London, Alexander Watson, *Medico-legal Treatise on Homicide by External Violence*, second edition (Edinburgh: MacLachlan, Stewart & Co., 1842), pp. 373–374. The London publisher was Simpkin, Marshall & Co. Carol Jones identified the growing collaboration between the police and 'medical detectives' as an important turning point in the evolution of the expert witness, citing London experts of the later nineteenth and early twentieth centuries but ignoring the rank and file: Carol A. G. Jones, *Expert Witnesses: Science, Medicine, and the Practice of Law* (Oxford: Clarendon Press, 1994), pp. 80–95.

10 J. M. Beattie, "Early Detection: The Bow Street Runners in Late Eighteenth-Century London," in *Police Detectives in History, 1750–1950*, ed. Clive Emsley and Haia Shpayer-Makov (Aldershot: Ashgate, 2006), pp. 15–32; J. M. Beattie, *The First English Detectives: The Bow Street Runners and the Policing of London, 1750–1840* (Oxford: Oxford University Press, 2012); David J. Cox, *A Certain Share of Low Cunning: A History of the Bow Street Runners, 1792–1839* (Abingdon: Routledge, 2010).

11 Beattie, *The First English Detectives*, pp. 182–183 (citing Cox, *A Certain Share of Low Cunning*), gives absolute numbers of 99 provincial and 6 London cases in the period 1792–1839.

12 R. D. Summers, "History of the Police Surgeon," *The Practitioner* 221 (1978), pp. 383–387. Later histories tend to cite Summers: Yvonne Bradshaw, Stephen P. Savage, Graham Moon and Kathleen Kelly, "A Different Sort of Doctor: The Police Surgeon in England and Wales," *Social Policy & Administration* 29 (1995), pp. 122–134; Michael Knight, "Changes to the Police Surgeon Service in Recent Years," *Medico-Legal Journal* 70 (2002), pp. 95–107; Martin Ernest Barrett, "Historical Development and Contemporary Dilemmas of a Police Surgeon," LL.M. thesis, University of Central Lancashire, 2012, pp. 9–11, 31–34.

13 Both scholars highlight the work of London-based police surgeons: Victoria Bates, "'So Far as I Can Define without a Microscopical Examination': Venereal Disease Diagnosis in English Courts, 1850–1914," *Social History of Medicine* 26 (2012), pp. 42–44; Joel Peter Eigen, *Mad-Doctors in the Dock: Defending the Diagnosis, 1760–1913* (Baltimore: Johns Hopkins University Press, 2016), pp. 65–66.

14 Nicholas Duvall, "Forensic Medicine in Scotland, 1914–39," PhD thesis, University of Manchester, 2013, p. 235.

15 R. M. Morris, "'Crime Does Not Pay': Thinking Again about Detectives in the First Century of the Metropolitan Police," in *Police Detectives in History*, ed. Emsley and Shpayer-Makov, pp. 89–90; Shpayer-Makov, *Ascent of the Detective*, pp. 107–126.

16 Clive Emsley has noted the paucity of research on the role played by the new police as prosecutors: see *Crime and Society in England, 1750–1900*, fourth edition (Harlow: Pearson Education, 2010), pp. 200–202.

17 Anne Digby, *Making a Medical Living: Doctors and Patients in the English Market for Medicine, 1720–1911* (Cambridge: Cambridge University Press, 1994), pp. 90–103, 108–127.

18 Michael Brown, *Performing Medicine: Medical Culture and Identity in Provincial England, c. 1760–1850* (Manchester: Manchester University Press, 2011), pp. 193–222.

19 Digby, *Making a Medical Living*, pp. 100–103; Bates, "Venereal Disease Diagnosis," pp. 42–44.

20 Tony Ward, "Observers, Advisers, or Authorities? Experts, Juries and Criminal Responsibility in Historical Perspective," *The Journal of Forensic Psychiatry* 12 (2001), pp. 105–122.

21 William A. Guy, *Principles of Forensic Medicine*, second edition (London: Henry Renshaw, 1861), p. 202 makes essentially this point: "In almost all medico-legal cases, but especially

in those referring to persons found dead, the two functions of a *common* and of a *skilled* witness, are combined." Italics as in the original.

22 Burney and Pemberton, *Murder and the Making of English CSI*, pp. 41–48.

23 Ibid., pp. 39–41; Ian Burney and Neil Pemberton, "Making Space for Criminalistics: Hans Gross and Fin-de-siècle CSI," *Studies in History and Philosophy of Biological and Biomedical Sciences* 44 (2013), pp. 16–25.

24 Howard Vincent, *The Police Code and General Manual of the Criminal Law*, eighth edition (London: Francis Edwards, 1893), p. 109.

25 Howard Vincent, *The Police Code and General Manual of the Criminal Law*, fifteenth edition (London: Butterworth, 1912), p. 160.

26 TNA ASSI 6/5, Regina v. William Weyman, Gloucestershire, 1841.

27 TNA ASSI 65/14, Regina v. James Horrabin, Cheshire, 1885.

28 Brotherton Library, University of Leeds, Notes for Lectures on Forensic Medicine c.1860s–c.1890s, MS 534/4, p. 6r.

29 Guy, *Principles of Forensic Medicine*, p. 203.

30 William A. Brend, *A Handbook of Medical Jurisprudence and Toxicology* (London: Charles Griffin, 1906), p. 2.

31 J. Dixon Mann, *Forensic Medicine and Toxicology* (London: Charles Griffin, 1893), pp. 4, 15.

32 Ibid., p. 8.

33 Numbers were compiled by searching Old Bailey trials for 'plan', 'diagram', 'model' and 'sketch', yielding a total of 315 cases: 1800–1829 (1); 1830–1839 (8); 1840–1849 (17); 1860–1869 (22); 1870–1875 (20); 1880–1885 (28); 1890–1895 (51); 1900–1913 (168 of 535 trials for murder and manslaughter).

34 Vincent, *Police Code* (1893), p. 120.

35 A deposition taken at Newcastle-under-Lyme in July 1902 refers to a photograph of the victim's body taken at the scene; the plan, which excludes the body, is included in the file but the photograph is not: TNA ASSI 6/37/7, Rex v. Patrick McDonald, Staffordshire, 1902. In the other case, the victim was photographed at the doctor's request, but the plan was made at the request of a detective inspector of police: TNA ASSI 72/32, Rex v. William Mitchell, Glamorgan, 1906.

36 Amy Bell, "Crime Scene Photography in England, 1895–1960," *Journal of British Studies* 57 (2018), pp. 53–78.

37 Taylor, *Elements of Medical Jurisprudence*, p. 16.

38 *Reading Mercury*, 20 Oct 1800, p. 3: Golding (qualified MRCS) was a surgeon, apothecary and man-midwife who moved to Reading from Wallingford at the end of 1800.

39 TNA ASSI 6/1/2, Rex v. Francis Sargent, Berkshire, 1817.

40 *Windsor and Eton Express*, 16 Feb 1817, p. 4.

41 *Bell's Weekly Messenger*, 23 Feb 1817, p. 6; *Jackson's Oxford Journal*, 1 Mar 1817, p. 3.

42 TNA ASSI 65/15, Regina v. Richard Davies and George Davies, Cheshire, 1890; TNA ASSI 65/20, Rex v. Amelia Pickering, Flintshire, 1915 (technically this case lies outside the period covered in this book).

43 *OBP*, trial of Richard Gould, ref. t18400406-1281; *Leicester Herald*, 18 Apr 1840, p. 6.

44 H. B. Irving, ed., *Trial of the Wainwrights* (Edinburgh and London: William Hodge, 1920), p. 124.

45 Erich Brenner, "Human Body Preservation: Old and New Techniques," *Journal of Anatomy* 224 (2014), pp. 316–344.

46 Filson Young, ed., *The Trial of Hawley Harvey Crippen* (Edinburgh and London: William Hodge, 1920), pp. xxxii, 137.

47 *Hereford Journal*, 25 May 1859, p. 8. For more on Williamson, who became the head of the newly founded Irish Branch at Scotland Yard in 1883, see Shpayer-Makov, *Ascent of the Detective*.

48 TNA ASSI 6/9, Regina v. John Isaac Jones, Herefordshire, 1859; the victim was strangled. The model was mentioned in press reports of the trial: *Wrexham and Denbighshire Weekly Advertiser*, 6 Aug 1859, p. 4; *Bath Chronicle and Weekly Gazette*, 11 Aug 1859, p. 3.

49 *Cardiff and Merthyr Guardian*, 23 Jul 1859, p. 6.

50 "The Ledbury Murder," *Cardiff and Merthyr Guardian*, 6 Aug 1859, p. 5; *Aberystwyth Observer*, 13 Aug 1859, p. 4; *Bath Chronicle and Weekly Gazette*, 11 Aug 1859, p. 3; *Commercial Journal*, 13 Aug 1859, p. 2.

51 Kate Summerscale, *The Suspicions of Mr Whicher, or the Murder at Road Hill House* (London: Bloomsbury, 2008), pp. 142, 177, 179.

52 TNA ASSI 72/3, Regina v. Jane Mazey, David Mazey and Benjamin Mazey, Carmarthenshire, 1881; *County Observer and Monmouth Central Advertiser*, 19 Feb 1881, p. 5.

53 *West Somerset Free Press*, 19 Feb 1881, p. 3.

54 *Cambrian News*, 11 Feb 1881, p. 7.

55 *South Wales Daily News*, 14 May 1881, p. 3.

56 Ibid.

57 *Western Mail*, 18 Jul 1881, p. 4.

58 TNA ASSI 6/19, Rex v. John Hill and John Williams, Herefordshire, 1885.

59 The plan survives in the case file, but the photographs (number unknown) do not.

60 TNA ASSI 6/19, Rex v. John Hill and John Williams; *South Wales Daily News*, 5 Nov 1885, p. 3; *South Wales Echo*, 5 Nov 1885, p. 4; *Cardiff Times*, 7 Nov 1885, p. 3; *Gloucester Citizen*, 4 Nov 1885, p. 4 and 5 Nov 1885, pp. 3–4.

61 Walker qualified LSA in 1880 and obtained the licentiate of the Royal College of Surgeons of Edinburgh in 1883, suggesting that he may have studied forensic medicine under Henry Littlejohn. Clearly, he was able to use his student learning effectively: *The Medical Register for 1887* (London: General Medical Council, 1887), p. 1057.

62 A similar plan was prepared in August 1885 but the two figures are crudely drawn, objects and bloodstains mentioned by witnesses are not included, and the depositions do not refer to it: TNA ASSI 6/19, Regina v. John Willoughby, Berkshire, 1885.

63 TNA ASSI 65/15, Regina v. Thomas Henry Bevan, Cheshire, 1887, committal depositions, p. 2.

64 Ibid., pp. 15–16.

65 *Liverpool Mercury*, 29 Jul 1887, p. 7.

66 D. J. Gee and J. K. Mason, *The Courts and the Doctor* (Oxford: Oxford University Press, 1990), p. 107. Both had been in practice about twenty years.

67 *Liverpool Mercury*, 29 Jul 1887, p. 7.

68 *Birmingham Daily Post*, 29 Jul 1887, p. 5. Strangely, Bevan told this prisoner that he preferred to be hanged than transported, but since transportation ceased in 1868 this was perhaps evidence of his lack of intellectual development.

69 Burney and Pemberton, *Murder and the Making of English CSI*, p. 17. That is, founded on the principles expounded by Hans Gross.

70 TNA ASSI 72/33, Rex v. George Stills, Glamorgan, 1907; *Nottingham Evening Post*, 11 Sep 1907, p. 6; *Glamorgan Gazette*, 22 Nov 1907, p. 8.

71 Watson, "Medical and Chemical Expertise."

72 Tryhorn wrote a series of 11 articles for *The Police Journal* in 1936–1938, covering everything from arson to poison by way of blood, dust, marks, searching for and packing trace evidence.

73 José Ramón Bertomeu-Sánchez, "Chemistry, Microscopy and Smell: Bloodstains and Nineteenth-Century Legal Medicine," *Annals of Science* 72 (2015), pp. 490–516.

74 Taylor, *Elements of Medical Jurisprudence*, pp. 376–389.

75 Alfred S. Taylor, *Medical Jurisprudence*, second American edition (Philadelphia: Lea and Blanchard, 1850), pp. iii–iv.

76 Ibid., pp. 521–523; Alfred S. Taylor, *A Manual of Medical Jurisprudence*, second edition (London: John Churchill, 1846), pp. 559–560.

77 Alfred S. Taylor, *The Principles and Practice of Medical Jurisprudence* (London: John Churchill, 1865), p. v, and respectively chapters 36, 77–78, 35, 72, 50, 35.

78 See Tables 3.23 and 3.24 in Chapter 3 above.

79 W. H. Brock, "Bunsen's British Students," *Ambix* 60 (2013), p. 233.

80 TNA ASSI 6/10, Regina v. Richard Hale, Staffordshire, 1864.

81 *OBP*, trial of William Desmond, Timothy Desmond, Nicholas English, John O'Keefe, Michael Barrett and Anne Justice, ref. t18680406-412. Only Barrett was convicted, and became the last person hanged in public in England.

82 *OBP*, trial of Thomas Henry Orrock, ref. t18840915-890. He was convicted and executed.

83 *OBP*, trial of James Mullins, ref. t18601022-874.

84 *OBP*, trial of William Amos, ref. t18650508-535.

85 *OBP*, trial of Franz Muller, ref. t18641024-920. See also Kate Colquhoun, *Mr Briggs' Hat: A Sensational Account of Britain's First Railway Murder* (London: Little, Brown, 2011).

86 *OBP*, trial of Ferdinand Edward Karl Kohl, ref. t18650111-142.

87 *OBP*, trial of Alexander Arthur MacKay, ref. t18680817-699.

88 *OBP*, trial of Edmund Walter Pook, ref. t18710710-561; *Nottinghamshire Guardian*, 21 Jul 1871, p. 12.

89 Taylor, *Principles and Practice of Medical Jurisprudence*, pp. 1011–1012; J. Dixon Mann, *Forensic Medicine and Toxicology*, second edition (London: Charles Griffin, 1898), p. 114.

90 TNA ASSI 6/10, Regina v. Charles Christopher Robinson, Staffordshire, 1865, inquest testimony of Llewellyn John Summers, 28 Aug 1865.

91 TNA ASSI 6/29, Regina v. George Hassall, George Winfield and Frederick Holford, Staffordshire, 1894.

92 *Birmingham Daily Post*, 30 Jul 1894, p. 3.

93 Suzanne Bell, *Crime and Circumstance: Investigating the History of Forensic Science* (Westport, CN and London: Praeger, 2008), pp. 158–159.

94 *OBP*, trial of Frederick George Manning and Maria Manning, ref. t18491029-1890.

95 Taylor, *Manual of Medical Jurisprudence* (1846), pp. 332–333.

96 Ibid., p. 337; Theodric Romeyn Beck and John R. Beck, *Elements of Medical Jurisprudence*, fifth edition (London: Longman et al, 1836), pp. 547–548.

97 Bell, *Crime and Circumstance*, pp. 160–161.

98 Alfred S. Taylor, *Medical Jurisprudence*, third American edition (Philadelphia: Blanchard and Lea, 1853), pp. 223–224.

99 For an example of a provincial police force seeking advice from a London expert, see Alan Moss and Keith Skinner, *The Scotland Yard Files: Milestones in Crime Detection* (Kew: The National Archives, 2006), pp. 44–48. In January 1866 the Shropshire police sent clothing to A. S. Taylor to examine for blood, but the case against the suspect was too weak and he was not committed for trial. The original file does not survive in the records of the Oxford Circuit, but Taylor's report is in TNA MEPO 3/80.

100 *OBP*, trial of John Baker, ref. t18820501-515.

101 Charles Meymott Tidy, *Legal Medicine*, Vol. 1 (New York: William Wood, 1882), pp. 192–193.

102 According to Alistair R. Brownlie, "Blood and the Blood Groups: A Developing Field for Expert Evidence," *Journal of the Forensic Science Society* 5 (1965), p. 126, the test was first used in cases tried at Aylesbury and Chester in 1910. As part of the Midland Circuit, Buckinghamshire is not part of the research on which this book is based; the Cheshire case occurred in November 1909 but no depositions survive for the North Wales Circuit for the period 1892–1909. See *The London Daily News*, 29 Nov 1910, p. 1 for the verdict of not guilty in the five-day trial of Mark Wilde for the murder of George Harry Storrs at Gorse Hall, Stalybridge; the case remains unsolved.

103 C. Graham Grant, *Practical Forensic Medicine: A Police-Surgeon's Emergency Guide*, second edition (London: H. K. Lewis, 1911). In a 1907 trial for wounding, Grant made a tentative claim that a stain was human blood: *OBP*, trial of Anthony Beinavitish, ref. t19070108-53.

104 A reference to "fresh stains of human blood" by divisional surgeon Hugh Davis may indicate use of the precipitin test: *OBP*, trial of Frederick Henry Thomas, ref. t19111010-42.

105 Willcox could not use the precipitin test in the case of Carlos Godinho, *OBP* ref. t19110905-10, as the sample was too small, but did use it in the case of George Baron Pateman, *OBP* ref. t19110627-48, eliciting the comment by Mr Justice Darling.

106 *OBP*, trial of Stinie Morrison, ref. t19110228-43.

107 TNA ASSI 6/46/8, Rex v. James Wise, Monmouthshire, 1911.

108 *OBP*, trial of Alfred Stratton and Albert Ernest Stratton, ref. t19050502-415; Moss and Skinner, *Scotland Yard Files*, pp. 113–116; Cyril John Polson, "Finger Prints and Finger Printing: An Historical Study," *Journal of Criminal Law and Criminology* 41 (1950–1951), pp. 690–704.

109 TNA ASSI 6/43/6, Rex v. Alfred Scott, Shropshire, 1908, testimony of Inspector Thomas Jones.

110 *OBP*, trial of Zurka Dubof, Jacob Peters, John Rosen and Nina Vassileva, ref. t19110425-75.

111 Mike Redmayne, *Expert Evidence and Criminal Justice* (Oxford: Oxford University Press, 2001), p. 20.

112 Medical Officers of Health held permanent positions in London under the terms of the 1891 Public Health (London) Act, but not in the provinces where many contracts were issued annually: "Medical Officers of Health," *BMJ*, 16 Mar 1895, pp. 609–610. By contrast, public analysts could only be removed from their posts subject to the agreement of the Local Government Board: Sale of Food and Drugs Act 1875, 38 & 39 Vict c.63 s.10. The rationale for combining the roles was purely financial, but this became increasingly difficult as the analytical role demanded ever greater proficiency in chemistry.

113 For an overview of late nineteenth-century London debates about financial arrangements between doctors and coroners see D. Zuck, "Mr Troutbeck as the Surgeon's Friend: The Coroner and the Doctors: An Edwardian Comedy," *Medical History* 39 (1995), pp. 259–287.

114 See Appendix 1. The relevant sections of the 1836 Act were ss. 3 and 5; of the 1837 Act, s.3.

115 An Act to Amend the Law relating to Coroners, 16 & 17 Geo V c.59 s.23. The new fees were as follows: 1½ guineas per day to attend an inquest; 2 guineas to conduct a post-mortem examination; 3 guineas to make a post-mortem examination and attend an inquest to give evidence plus 1½ guineas for each subsequent day of attendance.

116 Coroners Act 1887, 50 & 51 Vict c.71 s.25.

117 Katherine D. Watson, "Criminal Poisoning in England and the Origins of the Marsh Test for Arsenic," in *Chemistry, Medicine and Crime: Mateu J. B. Orfila (1787–1853) and His Times*, ed. J. R. Bertomeu-Sánchez and A. Nieto-Galan (Sagamore Beach, MA: Science History Publications, 2006), p. 187.

118 Oxfordshire History Centre, COR VII/5, Circular to Clerks of the Peace as to paying extra fees to Medical Witnesses on Coroners Inquests, 24 Oct 1848; prepared by J. M. Davenport, clerk of the peace, Oxfordshire.

119 Victoria M. Nagy, "Narratives in the Courtroom: Female Poisoners in Mid-Nineteenth Century England," *European Journal of Criminology* 11 (2014), pp. 213–227.

120 OHC COR VII/5, Circular. All quotations are from the replies sent to Davenport.

121 TNA ASSI 6/5, Regina v. Mary Howells and James Price, Monmouthshire, 1848. Local surgeon Richard Steel sought 25 guineas for two weeks' work and multiple chemical analyses, while prosecuting counsel was paid a mere £13 9s. 6d. for this case.

122 Watson, "Medical and Chemical Expertise," p. 387.

123 Liverpool Record Office, 352 POL 2/5, Reports of the Head Constable to the Watch Committee, 6 Apr 1868, p. 71.

124 Ibid., 20 Apr 1868, p. 77. I thank Angela Buckley for these references.

125 27 Geo II c.3 s.3.

126 18 Geo III c.19 ss.7–8.

127 7 Geo IV c.64 s.28.

128 The Cost Books, TNA ASSI 4, cover the period 1856–1888. The Welsh bills are included with the Gaol Files, National Library of Wales (hereafter NLW), Great Sessions 4, and survive haphazardly from the 1760s until 1830. For more on Welsh bills see Glyn Parry, *A Guide to the Records of Great Sessions in Wales* (Aberystwyth: National Library of Wales,

1995), p. lxxvii. All bills have been annotated as to the sums allowed by the court. For this project, financial records were sampled, not studied systematically.

129 NLW GS 4/255/1, Rex v. Margaret Roberts, Anglesey, 1785, fol. 54.

130 NLW GS 4/255/4, Rex v. Elizabeth Owen, Anglesey, 1791, fol. 58.

131 NLW GS 4/260/5, Rex v. Catherine Williams, Anglesey, 1827, fols., pp. 14–15.

132 NLW GS 4/280/2, Carnarvonshire: Rex v. Mary Williams, 1817, fol. 63; Rex v. Griffith Roberts, 1816, fol. 1.

133 NLW GS 4/281/3, Rex v. Thomas Williams, Carnarvonshire, 1820, fol. 7.

134 NLW GS 4/281/3, Rex v. Hugh Evans, Henry Jones, John Jones and John Prichard, Carnarvonshire, 1820, fol. 10.

135 NLW GS 4/282/4, Rex v. John Roberts, Carnarvonshire, 1825, fol. 3.

136 NLW GS 4/282/1, Carnarvonshire: Rex v. John Foulkes, 1824, fol. 1; Rex v. Thomas Boardman, 1824, fol. 2.

137 NLW GS 4/279/3, Rex v. Jane Hughes, Carnarvonshire, 1811, fols. 29–30; GS 4/26/3, Rex v. Evan Roberts, Anglesey, 1824, fol. 3.

138 TNA ASSI 4/32, Oxford Circuit Costs 1856–57. All trials in this sample were for crimes against the person, including murder, manslaughter, concealment of birth, wounding and rape.

139 TNA ASSI 4/40, Oxford Circuit Costs 1867–68. Records of 70 trials were examined.

140 TNA ASSI 4/45, Oxford Circuit Costs 1885–88. Records of 81 trials held in 1888 were examined.

141 Watson, "Medical and Chemical Expertise," p. 389.

142 TNA HO 45/10258/X67417, Memo by M. D. Chalmers, Assistant Secretary of State, Home Office, 28 Apr 1904 (X67417/11).

143 TNA HO 45/10258/X67417, Memorandum 6 Oct 1899 (X67417/9); for Tidy's complaint, see his letters to Stevenson, 4 Mar 1886, and to the Home Office, 20 Mar 1886 (A15734/11) in which he noted that since his appointment on 1 May 1882 he had lost both money and interesting work because only Stevenson was given cases by the Home Office.

144 Memorandum 6 Oct 1899 (X67417/9).

145 TNA HO 45/10258/X67417, Home Office Memo, 12 May 1898.

146 TNA HO 45/9620/A15734, Memo to Godfrey Lushington, 24 Oct 1888, annotated at the bottom and dated 25 Oct 1888.

147 10 Geo IV c.44 s.12.

148 16 & 17 Geo V c.59 s.22.1.b.

149 16 & 17 Geo V c.59 s.29.2.b.

150 Drew D. Gray, *London's Shadows: The Dark Side of the Victorian City* (London: Continuum, 2010), pp. 221–228; Shpayer-Makov, *Ascent of the Detective*, pp. 209–212.

151 TNA HO 45/9685/A48384, Thomas Bond to Sir Charles Warren, 2 Jan 1888 (copy).

152 Jill Pellew, *The Home Office, 1848–1914: From Clerks to Bureaucrats* (East Brunswick, NJ: Associated University Presses, 1982), pp. 47–50.

153 TNA HO 45/9685/A48384, Letter, Sir Charles Warren to Godfrey Lushington, 18 Feb 1888.

154 TNA HO 45/9685/A48384, Godfrey Lushington, Surgeons' rights to have charge of any given number of men or in any prescribed area, 3 Apr 1888. In the same file see also Financial Regulations, note of 6 Apr 1888 in which Lushington claimed that Warren had assumed a power that did not belong to him and exercised it in a high-handed manner.

155 TNA HO 45/16016, Note by Godfrey Lushington, 4 Aug 1888.

156 M. J. Trow, *The Thames Torso Murders* (Barnsley: Wharncliffe Books, 2011).

157 TNA HO 45/9685/A48384, Letter, Alexander O. MacKellar to Sir Charles Warren, 1 Nov 1888.

158 TNA HO 45/9685/A48384, Letter, Sir Charles Warren to Godfrey Lushington, 2 Nov 1888.

159 TNA HO 45/9685/A48384, 2 Nov 1888: Commissioner submits resignation of Dr Bond to the portion of A Division attached to Commissioner's office and recommends that they be attached to Dr Farr.

160 Tidy was prevented from testifying for the defence in the trial of Adelaide Bartlett (1886), but did so in the trial of Florence Maybrick (1889), when Stevenson was the main scientific witness for the prosecution.

161 House of Commons Papers, *Return of Cases in England, Wales and Ireland in which Verdict of Wilful Murder Has Been Returned by Coroner's Jury; and in Scotland When Procurator Fiscal Has Reported Murder, 1880 and 1886*, Vol. 82, Paper Number 441, Page 417, 1888.

162 Zuck, "Mr Troutbeck as the Surgeon's Friend," p. 264.

163 Ibid., p. 267.

164 Ibid., p. 286. For more on the controversy surrounding Troutbeck, see Ian A. Burney, *Bodies of Evidence: Medicine and the Politics of the English Inquest, 1830–1926* (Baltimore: Johns Hopkins University Press, 2000), pp. 122–135.

165 TNA HO 45/10459/B22443, Coroners circular from the Home Office, 28 Oct 1896.

166 TNA HO 45/10459/B22443, Letter to A. Braxton Hicks, Honorary Secretary to the Coroners' Society, 12 Apr 1899.

167 TNA HO 45/10459/B22443, Letter of 12 Aug 1909.

168 TNA MEPO 2/229, Letter, J. Adams to A. MacKellar, 20 Sep 1889.

169 TNA MEPO 2/229, Minutes, A. O. MacKellar, 4 Jan 1890.

170 TNA HO 45/9711/A51187, Note by Godfrey Lushington, 18 Feb 1890; reiterated in TNA MEPO 2/229, Home Office A51.187, 25 Mar 1890.

171 TNA MEPO 2/229, Minutes, A. O. MacKellar, 5 Jun 1890.

172 TNA MEPO 2/229, Letter, Kenelm E. Digby to Sir Edward Bradford, 13 May 1897; Return of fees paid to divisional surgeons for post-mortem examinations and special reports thereon during the year ended 31 Mar 1897.

173 TNA MEPO 2/229, Draft letter from Sir Edward Bradford to the Under Secretary of State, 13 Jul 1897. Insertion [^] and deletion as in the original.

174 *OBP*, trial of Catherine Webster, ref. t18790630-653.

175 TNA MEPO 2/229, Special Report, Metropolitan Police, Barnes Station, V Division, 27 Feb 1897. The sequence of documents relating to this incident ends with a note by the Commissioner, 28 Feb 1898.

176 TNA HO 45/9847/B12197, Dr A. P. Luff: His fees as Official Analyst to HO, 4 Sep 1893.

177 TNA HO 45/10459/B22443, Minute, 27 Mar 1899.

178 Ibid.

179 TNA MEPO 2/314, Letter, Thomas Bond to Robert Anderson, 3 Mar 1893.

180 TNA MEPO 2/314, Letter, Godfrey Lushington to Edward Henry, 19 Jun 1893.

181 TNA MEPO 2/314, Memo from Alexander O. MacKellar, 19 Nov 1896.

182 TNA MEPO 2/314, Memo from Inspector A. Hare and Superintendent Donald Swanson, 12 May 1897.

183 TNA MEPO 2/314, Letter, Kenelm E. Digby to the Commissioner of the Metropolitan Police, 29 May 1897.

184 *London Evening Standard*, 7 Jun 1901, p. 2.

185 TNA MEPO 2/314, Letter from [signature illegible] to Edward Henry, 20 Mar 1902.

186 TNA MEPO 2/314, Letter, Melville Macnaghten to Edward Henry, 23 Mar 1903; draft letter from Edward Henry to the Home Office, 24 Mar 1903.

187 "Augustus Joseph Pepper, FRCS," *BMJ*, 28 Dec 1935, p. 1285; Royal College of Surgeons, *Plarr's Lives of the Fellows*: Pepper, Augustus Joseph (1849–1935), ref. RCS: E004458.

188 *Select Committee on Death Certification: First and Second Reports, Proceedings, Evidence, Appendix, Index*, House of Commons Papers, 1893–94, Vol. 11, Paper Number 373.402, Page 195.

189 *First Report of the Departmental Committee Appointed to Inquire into the Law Relating to Coroners and Coroners' Inquests, and the Practice in Coroners' Courts: Part II. Evidence and Appendices (Coroners)*, Cd. 4782, Vol. 15, Page 389 (1909), p. 534.

190 *Select Committee on Office of Coroner: Report, Proceedings, Minutes of Evidence*, House of Commons Papers, 1860, Vol. 22, Paper Number 193, Page 257.

191 *Coroners' Committee: Second Report of the Departmental Committee Appointed to Inquire into the Law Relating to Coroners and Coroners' Inquests, and into the Practice in Coroners' Courts, Part I. Report*, Cd. 5004, Vol. 21, Page 561, pp. 11–12.
192 Ibid., p. 16.
193 TNA ASSI 6/46/3, Rex v. Thomas Mason, Staffordshire, 1911. The eight Old Bailey cases were downloaded from www.oldbaileyonline.org. These figures exclude cases that occurred outside the counties studied for this project.
194 Norman Ambage and Michael Clark, "Unbuilt Bloomsbury: Medico-Legal Institutes and Forensic Science Laboratories in England Between the Wars," in *Legal Medicine in History*, ed. Michael Clark and Catherine Crawford (Cambridge: Cambridge University Press, 1994), 293–313.
195 C. Ainsworth Mitchell, *Forensic Chemistry in the Criminal Courts* (London: Institute of Chemistry, 1938), p. 14.
196 Several of these points were identified in the concluding remarks made by Chris Hamlin at a conference on the history of forensic science and medicine in the nineteenth and twentieth centuries: Locating Forensic Science and Medicine, London, 24–25 July 2015, https://reilly.nd.edu/news-and-events/conferences/locating-forensic-science-and-medicine/.
197 Adam, *History of Forensic Science*, pp. 64–65; Burney and Pemberton, *Murder and the Making of English CSI*, pp. 41–53. See also Norman V. Ambage, "The Origins and Development of the Home Office Forensic Science Service, 1931–1967," PhD thesis, University of Lancaster, 1987, pp. 6–7, who stresses that the establishment and initial development of the Forensic Science Service "was an inseparable part of the development of the police in England and Wales," shaped by the organising principles of the Police Act 1919 and the *Report* of the Departmental Committee on Detective Work and Procedure (1938–1939).

6 Conclusion

Medicine and justice

The duties of a medical jurist are distinct from those of a physician or surgeon: the latter looks only to the treatment of disease or accident, and the saving of life; but the object of the former, in a large proportion of cases, is, whether in reference to the living or dead, to aid the law in fixing on the perpetrator of a crime, or to rescue an innocent person from a falsely imputed crime.

Alfred S. Taylor, *The Principles and Practice of Medical Jurisprudence*
(London: John Churchill, 1865), p. xix

On a March morning in 1842, two errant surgeons slunk into a courtroom in Stafford to receive a stinging judicial rebuke for their non-appearance the previous evening. In defence, both cited a duty of care to their patients, explaining that they had hurried home when it appeared the trial they were to testify in would not be heard until the next day. Suitably appeased, the judge backed down from the threat of financial sanctions, but the reason for his anger illuminates the central message of this book: the medical contribution to the process of criminal justice was both a duty and a responsibility that, when disregarded, risked the failure of "public justice."[1] In presenting the most detailed and extensive historical study of medico-legal practice in England and Wales to date, this volume has revealed the important role played by medicine and medical practitioners in the investigation and prosecution of the most serious offences against the person, homicide and rape. It has, as a consequence, situated doctors in their rightful place as partners in the effective administration of criminal justice, alongside coroners, judges, jurors, lawyers, magistrates and the police. Furthermore, in its focus on Wales and central England in conjunction with London, this analysis offers a much-needed regional rebalancing and comparison in medical, legal and policing history.

The project has engaged with familiar sources, particularly criminal depositions, Old Bailey trial proceedings and newspaper crime reportage, in new ways. It has sought full accounts of what precisely medical witnesses said in pre-trial (inquests and committal hearings) and trial proceedings, together with evidence of lawyers', judges' and jurors' reactions to their testimony. It has identified personal information about the medical witnesses: who they were, where they came from, what their qualifications were, and how they became involved in criminal cases. For some, the route into the courtroom was entirely unplanned: they simply happened to be the nearest medical practitioner when someone was seriously injured or killed. The element of chance could even lead, on occasion, to a doctor's participation in a criminal trial on the grounds that he happened to have seen the body or witnessed the post-mortem examination.[2] But such accidental encounters were rare: coroners, magistrates and the police became increasingly systematic in seeking medical opinions in criminal cases. As the knowledge and skill that medical professionals could contribute to the investigation of crime developed, so too did criminal justice procedures evolve to acknowledge and incorporate doctors. It is therefore unsurprising that key turning points in legal and police history have proved important in the history of medico-legal practice and expertise, and to the emergence of the associated academic discipline of forensic medicine.

Legal historians have recognised the 1730s, 1780s and 1830s as key decades in the evolution of the criminal trial. This is the lawyerisation argument, which explains how adversarial trial procedure was established as a contest between prosecution and defence: lawyers began to enter the courtroom in the 1730s; by the 1780s their presence had begun to change judicial practice, stimulating new rules of evidence; and in the 1830s defence counsel gained the right to address the jury. The 1830s were also a turning point in the history of medicine, as new statutes and educational ideals formalised and strengthened the place of medical evidence at inquests. At the same time, uniformed policing began to develop in earnest, encouraged by permissive legislation and the new professionalism exemplified by the efficiency and expertise of the Metropolitan Police.[3] These important changes were joined by a fourth ground-breaking development of the 1830s, the drastic reduction in the number of capital statutes.[4] Thereafter, the criminal trial, rather than judicial punishment, emerged as the central symbol of 'justice' and, since murder was the most common of the remaining capital offences,[5] its careful investigation became all the more crucial.[6] This book has demonstrated that doctors were an integral part of this process, following a parallel, and then increasingly overlapping, path to lawyers. The relationship may not always have been a collegial one, but the ultimate impact on the criminal trial is undeniable: over time, both groups of professionals became more adept – expert – so that pre-trial investigations were more detailed and trials became longer, hearing testimony from more witnesses (including expert witnesses).[7] The criminal trial became a more just means of resolving accusations against defendants, utilising and relying on ever-greater accuracy in the presentation and assessment of information. The lawyerisation argument has dominated consideration of this evolution, but as the evidence presented in this book has shown, medical professionals played an equal part in the process.[8]

The medical influence on the development of the adversarial criminal trial contributes to a wider argument about the impact of medico-legal practice on the process of criminal justice, whereas the careful attention to the everyday aspects of forensic work provides answers to the five questions set out in the Introduction. Together, these show how and why eighteenth- and nineteenth-century medical practitioners became a key component in the investigation of violent crime. Homicide and rape may not have been the most numerous violent offences notified to the authorities, but they were the most serious, and led most directly and consistently to the application of medico-legal principles. Infanticide, in particular, proved to be a critical stimulus to the development of forensic expertise, because of the importance of the hydrostatic lung test. Chapter 4 showed that medical witnesses were probably more likely to encounter newborn child murder than any other form of homicide, but it posed unique forensic challenges caused by the distinction between the legal and medical definitions of live birth. The need to address these difficulties created a professional platform for doctors at inquests and trials: they had little choice but to conduct a thorough post-mortem examination in preparation for the detailed questioning that such legal enquiries urged. The lung test and its refinements were the profession's means of ensuring the medical reliability and legal pertinence of conclusions drawn from fragile infant bodies. As a consequence, infanticide provided a footing for the emergence of the academic subject of forensic medicine. The lecture courses and textbooks surveyed in Chapter 2 revealed that the nineteenth-century discipline focused disproportionately on infanticide and poisoning, even though adult victims of homicide tended to die from head injuries or stab wounds.

But this is not to say that opportunities for knowledge exchange between doctors, lawyers and the police existed only in relation to infant murder or poisoning. Chapter 3 demonstrated the growing importance of professional assessments of defendants' sanity and the emergence of a number of roles that combined or developed elements from different professions, chief among them the police surgeon and medical coroner, but also prison medical officers and coroner's officers – posts that contributed to the medicalisation of the courtroom.[9] The use of the post-mortem examination was part of this wider evolution of expertise. Moreover, Chapter 5 showed how the police and coroners collaborated with doctors to develop the modern murder investigation, including the recognition of what we now call the 'crime scene', invoking forensic science and expert witnesses when needed. As a result of these confluences, the process of professionalisation that began in the eighteenth century reached its culmination before the First World War: the trust placed in local GPs as de facto experts was met by their improved qualifications, knowledge and experience (an internal push), while expert witnesses gained a central standing in the most complex murder cases, satisfying the needs of the police and central government (an external pull). The role played by doctors increased in tandem with the growing authority of lawyers and the police, creating the modern system of criminal justice.

Regional differences existed, of course. In the rural locales that characterised so much of the area under study, the low number of serious cases and small population centres militated against the development of the experience-driven expertise that some Londoners and practitioners in other large English cities developed. But local communities were, in the main, well served by local practitioners. There was no regular use of English expertise in Wales, for example, though the option was there and was used when necessary; in all other instances, Welsh surgeons provided the necessary medico-legal knowledge. Alun Withey has pointed out that the early modern Welsh "had strong links beyond their borders and assimilated information from elsewhere,"[10] and this was, evidently, equally true of later centuries. Peripheral locations did not necessarily mean reduced ability, energy or awareness.

As befits a study that has embraced three areas of history – medicine, law and criminal justice, this project suggests several new pathways for research. Many arise from the fact that legal records and newspaper trial reportage contain a vast amount of local detail about doctors, lawyers, policemen and the ways in which they conducted their professional business.[11] Such information permits a more integrated approach to the professional history of the eighteenth and nineteenth centuries, as well as a firmer attention to provincial contexts. Some of the areas of research that could usefully be addressed include the use of the title 'Doctor' by those who lacked university degrees,[12] the work of solicitors in building prosecution cases,[13] and the role of the police as prosecutors.[14] The use of a historical geographic information system to map locations could connect professional development to expanding road and rail networks; or identify spatial patterns in criminality.[15] A survey of medico-legal practice in a wider range of non-fatal violent confrontations would reveal an additional set of forensic activities and witnesses, including (possibly) female medical practitioners, and would identify legal responses to assault. Lastly, there is still much to be learned about what it was like to experience crime and the criminal justice system, and legal records and newspapers can provide a basis for such a study.[16]

One final point should be noted. This book integrates doctors into the historiography of eighteenth- and nineteenth-century criminal justice in a manner not previously attempted, and in so doing lends strength to a comment which underpins the rationale for our system of law enforcement: "A legal system works effectively only when its operations have a firm basis in public consent."[17] The public role in the history of medico-legal practice extends beyond that of victim or witness, because local people had an active role at the start of most investigations. When a member of the public came across a crime scene, they had to decide what to do. In the eighteenth century the inevitable response was to call for the local surgeon and the coroner. By the late nineteenth century, the local doctor was still the first to be summoned: as one horrified witness exclaimed on coming across a murder scene in Worcestershire in 1894, "there wants a doctor and a policeman here."[18]

Notes

1   *The Staffordshire Advertiser*, 19 Mar 1842, p. 2.
2   *OBP*, trial of Godfrey Walker, ref. t17380628-16 (a surgeon happened to go into a public house during an inquest; the jury were about to return a verdict of death from natural causes until he demanded to see the body and identified a skull fracture); *OBP*, trial of

Owen Sullivan, ref. t18320705-108 (the second doctor in the case entered the dead-house accidentally during the post-mortem and decided to stay).

3 While not without their (at times, strident) critics, the Metropolitan Police proved particularly important in relation to the development of detective policing and murder investigations: Haia Shpayer-Makov, "From Menace to Celebrity: The English Police Detective and the Press, c.1842–1914," *Historical Research* 83 (2010), pp. 672–692; G. R. Rubin, "Calling in the Met: Serious Crime Investigation Involving Scotland Yard and Provincial Police Forces in England and Wales, 1906–1939," *Legal Studies* 31 (2011), pp. 411–441.

4 Brian P. Block and John Hostettler, *Hanging in the Balance: A History of the Abolition of Capital Punishment in Britain* (Hook, Hampshire: Waterside Press, 1997), chapters 3 and 4.

5 In 1861 the number of capital offences was reduced to five (murder, treason, espionage, arson in royal dockyards and piracy with violence); the last execution for any crime other than murder or treason occurred in 1861 (see Appendix 1).

6 Lindsay Farmer, "'With All the Impressiveness and Substantial Value of Truth': Notable Trials and Criminal Justice, 1750–1930," *Law and Humanities* 1 (2007), pp. 57–78; Lindsay Farmer, "Criminal Responsibility and the Proof of Guilt," in *Modern Histories of Crime and Punishment*, ed. Markus D. Dubber and Lindsay Farmer (Stanford: Stanford University Press, 2007), pp. 46–47.

7 Farmer makes this point in relation to the growing emphasis on prisoners' mental states in "Criminal Responsibility and the Proof of Guilt," pp. 49–53.

8 I am grateful to Anne-Marie Kilday for this insight.

9 In the first half of the twentieth century, PMOs played an important role in determining whether prisoners were fit to plead to the charge: Janet Weston, "Sexual Crimes, Medical Cures: The Development of a Therapeutic Approach Toward Sexual Offenders in English Prisons, c.1900–1950," *Canadian Journal of History* 49 (2014), pp. 404–405, 410.

10 Alun Withey, "Unhealthy Neglect? The Medicine and Medical Historiography of Early Modern Wales," *Social History of Medicine* 21 (2008), p. 171.

11 On the importance of legal records as a source of information about medical practice, albeit in a different era, see Hannes Kleineke, "The Records of the Common Law as a Source for the Medieval Medical History of England," *Social History of Medicine* 30 (2017), pp. 483–499.

12 Penelope J. Corfield, "From Poison Peddlers to Civic Worthies: The Reputation of the Apothecaries in Georgian England," *Social History of Medicine* 22 (2009), p. 2; Alun Withey, *Physick and the Family: Health, Medicine and Care in Wales, 1600–1750* (Manchester: Manchester University Press, 2011), pp. 151–162.

13 John H. Langbein, "The Prosecutorial Origins of Defence Counsel in the Eighteenth Century: The Appearance of Solicitors," *The Cambridge Law Journal* 58 (1999), pp. 314–365.

14 Barry Godfrey, "Changing Prosecution Practices and Their Impact on Crime Figures, 1857–1940," *British Journal of Criminology* 48 (2008), pp. 171–189.

15 Kallum Dhillon, "Locating Crime and Criminality in Edwardian London," PhD thesis, University College London, 2015, chapter 4. Louise Roy is undertaking a similar study at Oxford Brookes University: "Mapping Murder: A Socio-Legal Investigation of Homicide in Lancashire, c.1816–1914."

16 Kim Stevenson, "'She Got Past Knowing Herself and Didn't Know How Many There Were': Uncovering the Gendered Brutality of Gang Rapes in Victorian London," *Nottingham Law Journal* 18 (2009), pp. 1–17 uses newspaper reports qualitatively to highlight and reflect legal practices and victim experiences (p. 5). To gain deeper insights into individual experiences, one would also need to consult letters, diaries and memoires.

17 Judith Rowbotham and Kim Stevenson, "'For Today in This Arena . . .': Legal Performativity and Dramatic Convention in the Victorian Criminal Justice System," *Journal of Criminal Justice and Popular Culture* 14 (2007), p. 121.

18 TNA ASSI 6/29, Regina v. Patrick Groarke and James Groarke, Worcestershire, 1894, testimony of Mary Bell.

Appendix 1

Chronology of events and statutes affecting medical and legal practice

Statutes are presented in the format: regnal year and chapter number, *full title* (short title, date of royal assent).

Year	Events and Statutes
1194	The office of Coroner was created by chapter 20 of the articles of the eyre (circuit court) held in September, which provided that the knights and freeholders of each county were to elect three knights and a clerk as keepers of the pleas of the crown. The amount of the freehold estate was never defined, unlike that for parliamentary elections.
1276	4 Edw I st.2, *Of what things a Coroner shall inquire*, established cases of sudden death as one of many things that a coroner was required to investigate.
1340	14 Edw III st.1 c.8 required coroners to have "lands in fee sufficient to answer to all manner of people," a condition that remained in effect until 1926.
1354	28 Edw III c.6, *Who shall be Coroners, and by whom, and where they shall be chosen*, effectively abolished the knighthood qualification by failing to mention knightly status as a requirement for the office of coroner.
1361	34 Edw III c.1, *What sort of persons shall be Justices of Peace; and what Authority they shall have*, provided for the appointment of Justices of the Peace (JPs) in every English county to be responsible for maintaining law and order.
1487	3 Hen VII c.1, *A Coroner's Duty after a Murder committed*, established homicide investigation as the coroner's chief function, by authorising a payment of 13s. 4d. from the goods and chattels of the killer when it was otherwise illegal for coroners to accept money for inquiring into deaths.
1509	1 Hen VIII c.7, *For Coroners*, reiterated the illegality of a coroner accepting money to hold an inquest on a person who died from misadventure, instituted a fine of 40s. for so doing, and granted county justices the "authority and power to enquire thereof" [s.2] – thereby giving the JPs jurisdiction over coroners.
1518	The College of Physicians was founded by royal charter; in 1523 Parliament extended its powers to regulate the medical profession from London to the whole of England.
1535	27 Hen VIII c.26, *Concerning the Laws in Wales*, required the laws of England to be used in Wales, integrated the medieval Marcher lands into the thirteen Welsh counties, and forbade [s.20] use of the Welsh language in any legal context and by any office holder.
1540	The Company of Barber-Surgeons was established.

(Continued)

(Continued)

Year	Events and Statutes
1541	33 Hen VIII c.13, *Certain Lordships translated from the County of Denbigh to the County of Flint*, limited Cheshire to two coroners [s.1].
1542	34 & 35 Hen VIII c.26, *An Act for certain Ordinances in the King's Dominion and Principality of Wales*, divided Wales into 12 counties with Monmouthshire placed in England and the three counties of north Wales (Denbighshire, Flintshire, Montgomeryshire) linked formally to Cheshire for the purposes of the legal system; established the Court of Great Sessions to hold assizes in Wales twice each year; grouped the Welsh counties into four legal entities (assize circuits though not so called in the statute) to which judges were to be appointed [ss.6–9]; specified the election of two coroners in every Welsh county [s.68]; and required Welsh jurors to hold property worth 40s. per year [s.107].
1548	2 & 3 Edw VI c.24, *An Act for Trial of Murders and Felonies committed in several Counties*, eased the trial of cases that crossed county boundaries, when a victim was wounded in one county but died in another [s.2].
1554	1 & 2 Phil & Mary c.13, *An Act touching Bailment of Persons*, required coroners and JPs to take written depositions in all cases of murder or manslaughter, and to bind prosecution witnesses to appear in court for trial; coroners could enquire into accessories before but not after the fact [ss.4–5].
1555	2 & 3 Phil & Mary c.10, *An Act to take Examination of Prisoners suspected of any Manslaughter or Felony*, required JPs to conduct a pre-trial examination of felony suspects and the witnesses against them, to record the evidence in writing and send it to the trial court to be used against the accused, and to bind prosecution witnesses to appear in court for trial [s.2].
1576	18 Eliz I c.7, *An Act to take away Clergy from the Offenders in Rape or Burglary, and an Order for the Delivery of Clerks convict without Purgation* (Benefit of Clergy Act, effective 1 June 1576), made rape a felony without benefit of clergy, as also [s.4] "the unlawful and carnal knowledge" of any female under the age of 10 (in common law the age of consent for girls was 12).
1601	43 Eliz I c.2, *An Act for the Relief of the Poor* (Elizabethan or Old Poor Law, effective Easter 1602) formed the basis of poor relief in England and Wales for the next two centuries, placing the relief of the poor, including responsibility for their medical care, in the hands of parish churchwardens and overseers of the poor appointed annually by local JPs.
1624	21 Jac I c.27, *An Act to prevent the Destroying and Murthering of Bastard Children* (Infanticide Act, 27 May) stiffened the capital offence of newborn child murder by assuming that a woman who concealed the death of her illegitimate child had murdered it, unless she could produce at least one witness to prove the child was born dead. Prosecutors had to prove that the death had been deliberately concealed; but not the pregnancy, birth or dead body – cases where the usual presumptions about murder applied. This statute was repealed in 1803 by 43 Geo III c.58.
1692	4 Will & Mary c.24, *An Act for reviving, continuing, and explaining several laws therein mentioned, which are expired and near expiring*, introduced a property qualification of £10 rateable freehold land for trial or inquest jury membership in England, and £6 in Wales [s.15]; effective 1 May 1693.
1695	7 & 8 Will III c.3, *An Act for regulating of Trials in Cases of Treason and Misprision of Treason* (Treason Act) allowed individuals accused of treason to have access to a copy of the indictment against them five days before trial and to be defended by counsel; it also enabled the judge to appoint defence counsel and permitted defence witnesses to testify under oath [s.1]; effective 25 March 1696.

Year	Events and Statutes
1702	1 Anne st.2 c.9, *An Act for punishing of Accessories to Felonies, and Receivers of stolen Goods, and to prevent the wilful burning and destroying of Ships*, extended the right of defence witnesses to testify under oath to all felony trials [s.3]; effective 12 February 1702.
1717	4 Geo I c.11, *An Act for the further preventing of Robbery, Burglary, and other Felonies, and for the more effectual Transportation of Felons, and unlawful Exporters of Wool; and for declaring the Law upon some Points relating to Pirates* (Transportation Act), permitted the courts to reprieve those convicted of capital offences and sentence them instead to be transported to America for 14 years or any other specified term [s.1]; effective 20 January 1718. Returning before the expiration of the term became a capital offence [s.2].
1730	3 Geo II c.25, *An Act for the better Regulation of Juries*, enacted that from 1 September 1730 poor law and land tax returns be used to compile lists of local men qualified to serve as jurors [s.1].
1731	4 Geo II c.26, *An Act that all Proceedings in Courts of Justice within that Part of Great Britain called England, and in the Court of Exchequer in Scotland, shall be in the English Language*, made English the language of legal proceedings in England and Scotland from 25 March 1733 [s.1] but did not include the Court of Admiralty, where Latin was retained [s.3]. This Act was extended to Wales in 1733 by 6 Geo II c.14.
1733	6 Geo II c.14, *An Act for the more effectual preventing frivolous and vexatious Arrests, and for the more easy recovery of Debts and Damages in the Courts of Great Sessions in the Principality of Wales, and in the Court of Assize in the County Palatine of Chester, and for the obviating a Doubt which has arisen upon an Act made in the Fourth Year of his present Majesty's Reign, intituled . . . so far as the same Act doth or may relate to the Courts of Justice holden within the said Principality, and for explaining and amending the said Act.* This amending Act clarified that the provisions of the 1731 Act relating to the use of English in law courts also applied to Wales [s.3], and levied fines on those who spoke any other language in the courts [s.4]. The Welsh language was not specified but clearly fell within the remit of this statute.
1745	The Company of Surgeons was established as an independent entity, becoming the Royal College of Surgeons in London by royal charter in 1800, and the Royal College of Surgeons of England in 1843. Membership of the Company/Royal College of Surgeons (MCS/MRCS) was based on examination and became a key professional qualification for GPs.
1748	Henry Fielding was appointed a Westminster magistrate in October and to the Middlesex bench of magistrates in January 1749, and set about making his house at 4 Bow Street, Covent Garden, a centre for crime fighting. The Bow Street police office, funded by a government subsidy, employed men known as Runners who worked both to prevent and detect crime. This early police force was disbanded in August 1839.
1752	25 Geo II c.29, *An Act for giving a proper reward to coroners for the due execution of their office; and for the amoval of coroners upon a lawful conviction for certain misdemeanours* (Coroners Act,[1] effective 24 June 1752) authorised coroners to receive a fee of 20s. per inquest "duly taken" in England (and Wales) plus 9d. per mile travelled from their usual residence, payable from the county rates on the order of the JPs [s.1]; if the death occurred in gaol or prison the maximum payment was 20s. [s.2]; the homicide fee of 13s. 4d. was still payable where relevant [s.3].
1752	25 Geo II c.36, *An Act for the better preventing thefts and robberies, and for regulating places of publick entertainment, and punishing persons keeping disorderly houses*, permitted the courts to order reimbursement of the costs, including a "reasonable allowance" for time and trouble, incurred by prosecutors in felony cases resulting in conviction; payments were to be made from county funds [s.11].

(Continued)

(Continued)

Year	Events and Statutes
1752	25 Geo II c.37, *An act for better preventing the horrid crime of murder* (Murder Act, effective 31 March 1752) stipulated that convicted murderers be executed within three days of sentencing [s.1], and their bodies delivered to surgeons for anatomisation [s.2]; sentence was to be passed immediately after conviction [s.3], changing the normal practice of the assize courts.
1753	Bow Street Police Office, under the leadership of the chief magistrate for Westminster – who already received a personal stipend of £400 from the government – was awarded an annual subsidy to support the detection and arrest of offenders.
1754	27 Geo II c.3, *An Act for the better securing to constables and others the expences of conveying offenders to gaol; and for allowing the charges of poor persons bound to give evidence against felons*, effective 24 June 1754, allowed the courts to reimburse poorer individuals for their time, trouble and expense when bound over to give evidence for the prosecution [s.3].
1761	A ruling in King's Bench encouraged a grand jury comprising 23 members.[2]
1778	18 Geo III c.19, *An Act for the payment of costs to parties, on Complaints determined before justices of the peace out of sessions; for the payment of the charges of constables in certain cases; and for the more effectual payment of charges to witnesses and prosecutors of any larceny, or other felony* (Expenses for Prosecutions Act) extended payments of expenses to all prosecutors and witnesses, whether poor or not and regardless of whether the accused was convicted; payments were to cover costs incurred, as well as trouble and loss of time "in case the said person shall appear to the court to be in poor circumstances" [ss.7–8].
1782	Home Office established, to oversee domestic affairs including crime; by the mid-1830s it was staffed by only 29 permanent officials.
1784	24 Geo III c.6, *An Act to enable such officers, mariners, and soldiers, as have been in the land or sea service, or in the marines, or in the militia, or any corps of fencible men, since the second year of his present Majesty's reign, to exercise trades* gave all personnel employed by the military since 1 April 1763 the right to practice their trade without the permission of any corporate body. This statute was designed for retirees who had not completed an apprenticeship and so applied to surgeons, who could therefore practice without the permission of the Company of Surgeons, but not to physicians. In the 1790s the Scottish courts ruled that the Act was purely retrospective and did not apply to men who entered the service after it was passed in 1784.[3] It was superseded by 6 Geo IV c.133 and repealed in 1871.
1788	Samuel Farr's *Elements of Medical Jurisprudence* becomes the first textbook of forensic medicine published in English.
1792	32 Geo III c.53, *An Act for the more effectual administration of the office of a justice of the peace in such parts of the counties of Middlesex and Surrey as lie in and near the metropolis, and for the more effectual prevention of felonies* (Middlesex Justices Act, effective 1 June 1792) created seven new police offices in London each staffed by three stipendiary magistrates [ss.1, 8] and up to six paid constables [ss.15–16]. The scheme, which appears to have been modelled on the Bow Street Police Office, was originally intended to lapse in June 1795.
1798	The Thames River Police was set up as a privately funded initiative in July, under the supervision of magistrate Patrick Colquhoun; the government transformed it into a public police agency under the terms of the Marine Police Act on 28 July 1800 (40 Geo III c.87, *An Act for the more effectual prevention of depredations on the river Thames, and in its vicinity; and to amend an act, made in the second year of the reign of his present Majesty, to prevent the committing of thefts and frauds by persons navigating bum boats and other boats upon the river Thames*).

Year	Events and Statutes

1800 40 Geo III c.94, *An Act for the safe Custody of insane Persons charged with Offences* (Criminal Lunatics Act, 28 July). A direct reaction to the trial of James Hadfield, this statute created a new verdict, not guilty on the grounds of insanity [s.1]; and ordered anyone so acquitted, or found to be unfit to plead to an indictment for felony, to be kept in "strict custody" indefinitely [s.2].

1803 43 Geo III c.58, *An Act for the further prevention of malicious shooting, and attempting to discharge loaded fire-arms, stabbing, cutting, wounding, poisoning, and the malicious using of means to procure the miscarriage of women; and also the malicious setting fire to buildings; and also for repealing a certain act, made in England in the twenty-first year of the late King James the First, intituled, An act to prevent the destroying and murthering of bastard children; and also an act made in Ireland in the sixth year of the reign of the late Queen Anne, also intituled, An act to prevent the destroying and murthering of bastard children; and for making other provisions in lieu thereof* (Lord Ellenborough's Act, 24 June). The lengthy title of this statute, which came into effect on 1 July 1803, explains its rationale: attempted murder, abortion, and arson with intent to defraud became capital offences, and the Infanticide Act was repealed. Trials of unmarried women charged with murdering their infant were henceforth to proceed as for other types of murder [s.3]; but a defendant acquitted on the murder charge could be convicted of concealing the birth of her child (even if it had been stillborn), for which the maximum penalty was two years in gaol [s.4].

1808 48 Geo III c.96, *An Act for the better Care and Maintenance of Lunatics, being Paupers or Criminals in England* (County Asylums or Wynn's Act, 23 June), permitted JPs to establish publically funded asylums for the mentally ill in the counties of England and Wales; stipulated that in counties where an asylum had been established "any lunatic, insane person or dangerous idiot" should be kept there [s.17]; and required JPs to organise payment of the maintenance costs of individuals detained as criminal lunatics under the Act of 1800 [s.27].

1815 55 Geo III c.194, *An Act for better regulating the Practice of Apothecaries throughout England and Wales* (Apothecaries Act, 12 July), introduced qualifying examinations administered by The Society of Apothecaries, from 1 August [ss.14–15]. After an apprenticeship of five years, attendance at lectures on anatomy, botany, chemistry, materia medica and physic, and six months' practical hospital experience over the course of up to seven years, men aged 21 or older were examined at Apothecaries' Hall in London; successful completion conferred a recognised medical qualification, the Licentiate of The Society of Apothecaries (LSA), the first examination designed for aspiring GPs.

1818 58 Geo III c.95, *An Act to regulate the Election of Coroners for Counties* (10 June). Noting the absence of "sufficient regulations" for the election of county coroners, this statute introduced a formal procedure for England and Wales whereby coroners were to be elected by view or poll of the eligible freeholders, the costs to be borne by the candidates in equal proportion [s.3].

1823 4 Geo IV c.48, *An Act for enabling Courts to abstain from pronouncing Sentence of Death in certain Capital Felonies* (Judgment of Death Act, 4 July). Passed at a time when there were over 200 offences which carried a mandatory death sentence (the Bloody Code), this statute allowed judges to record a formal death sentence against an individual convicted of any felony except murder; this had the effect of a reprieve [s.2], subject to imprisonment or transportation.

1825 6 Geo IV c.50, *An Act for consolidating and amending the Laws relative to Jurors and Juries* (County Juries Act, 22 June) sustained a Welsh property qualification three fifths that in England [s.1]. This discrepancy was eliminated in 1870.

(Continued)

(Continued)

Year	Events and Statutes
1825	6 Geo IV c.133, *An Act to amend and explain an Act of the Fifty fifth Year of His late Majesty, for better regulating the Practice of Apothecaries throughout England and Wales* (6 July) entitled anyone formerly or currently employed as a surgeon in the army, navy or East India Company to practice as an apothecary in England and Wales without the Society of Apothecaries qualification [s.4]; this exemption, together with the entire Act, expired on 1 August 1826.
1826	7 Geo IV c.64, *An Act for improving the Administration of Criminal Justice in England* (Peel's Criminal Law Act, 26 May) required coroners to take written evidence in all cases in which an individual was indicted for murder or manslaughter, and authorised them to bind witnesses to prosecute or give evidence [s.4]; s.22 allowed financial compensation for costs, expenses and loss of time incurred by witnesses and prosecutors in all cases of felony, even when no bill of indictment was preferred. The Act also prevented the quashing of indictments on technical grounds [s.20], and the Marian statutes relating to committal and bail were extended, requiring JPs to take in writing as much evidence "as shall be material" to the facts and circumstances of a case [s.2].
1828	9 Geo IV c.31, *An Act for consolidating and amending the Statutes in England relative to Offences against the Person* (Offences Against the Person Act, 27 June) repealed Lord Ellenborough's Act and made concealment of birth by any woman, not just unmarried mothers, a misdemeanour offence subject to imprisonment for up to two years; it also allowed juries to convict on this charge when a murder indictment could not be proved [s.14]. Concealing the birth and child's body were the key issues of evidence rather than whether the child had died before, at or after birth, making concealment a lesser but more readily provable offence. This statute also introduced an important amendment in the law relating to rape: the crime was deemed complete upon proof of penetration only, eliminating the former need to demonstrate ejaculation [s.18].
1829	10 Geo IV c.44, *An Act for improving the Police in and near the Metropolis* (Metropolitan Police Act, 19 June) created the nation's first uniformed police force for a new Metropolitan Police District covering the City of Westminster, and parts of Middlesex, Kent and Surrey in a 12-mile radius from Charing Cross; the first officers went out on patrol at 6 pm on 29 September. Officers had the authority of constables throughout Middlesex, Essex, Hertfordshire, Kent and Surrey [s.4]. The District was divided into 17 divisions: the role of divisional police surgeon was established to look after the health and welfare of members of the force and (Sir) John Fisher was appointed as Chief Surgeon to the Metropolitan Police at a salary of £350 per year, having previously served as surgeon to the Bow Street patrol, 1821–1829.[4]
1829	10 Geo IV c.97, *An Act to enable the Magistrates of the County Palatine of Chester to appoint Special High Constables for the several Hundreds or Divisions, and Assistant Petty Constables for the several Townships of that County* (Cheshire Constabulary Act, 1 June), enabled the county magistrates to appoint constables, thereby establishing the first county constabulary in the earliest police reform in provincial England. This constabulary was disbanded in the wake of the 1856 County and Borough Police Act.
1830	11 Geo IV & 1 Will IV c.70, *An Act for the more effectual Administration of Justice in England and Wales* (Law Terms Act, 23 July): effective 12 October 1830, this statute abolished the Welsh Court of Great Sessions and the independent jurisdiction of the courts of the County Palatine of Chester [s.14] and replaced them with two new assize circuits, North and South Wales [s.20]; the three common law courts gained a puisne judge each to bring the total number of common law judges to 15 [s.1].
1831	From 1 January the Society of Apothecaries medical qualification required formal training in forensic medicine.[5]

Year	Events and Statutes

1831 The new lecturer in medical jurisprudence at Guy's Hospital, Alfred Swaine Taylor, began teaching on 20 January.

1832 The Provincial Medical and Surgical Association, forerunner of the British Medical Association, was founded in Worcester by (Sir) Charles Hastings on 19 July.

1832 2 & 3 Will IV c.75, *An Act for regulating Schools of Anatomy* (The Anatomy Act, 1 August), opened the legal supply of bodies for medical teaching by giving licensed instructors and students access to corpses unclaimed after death, particularly corpses of those who had died in hospital, prison or a workhouse.

1834 4 & 5 Will IV c.36, *An Act for establishing a New Court for the Trial of Offences committed in the Metropolis and Parts adjoining* (Central Criminal Court Act, 25 July) established the Old Bailey, renamed the Central Criminal Court, as the assize court for London, Middlesex and parts of Essex, Kent and Surrey. It also authorised this court to try offences committed on the high seas [s.22].

1834 4 & 5 Will IV c.76, *An Act for the Amendment and better Administration of the Laws relating to the Poor in England and Wales* (Poor Law Amendment Act, 14 August): among its many provisions, this law permitted magistrates to order medical attendance in an emergency [s.54]; enabled the appointment of district medical officers for poor law unions that were geographically larger than parishes [s.46]; and repealed laws that allowed a woman or local officials to charge a man with fathering a bastard and force him to pay maintenance costs [s.69], deliberately shifting the financial burden to the unmarried mother [s.71]. MOs were – for the first time – explicitly included among the positions required for the relief of the poor [s.109].[6]

1835 5 & 6 Will IV c.76, *An Act to provide for the Regulation of Municipal Corporations in England and Wales* (Municipal Corporations Act, 9 September) required each of the 178 corporate boroughs in England and Wales possessing its own court of quarter sessions to appoint a coroner, and extended the system of payment of inquest and travel fees for county coroners to boroughs [s.62]. Inquests in boroughs without a court of quarter sessions were to be held by the district or county coroner [s.64]. This statute enabled boroughs to set up a police force under the supervision of a Watch Committee consisting of members of the elected town council [ss.76–77]; and provided for the creation of borough justices and police magistrates [ss.98–101]. While not without serious defects, this Act was a major stepping stone in the history of policing.[7]

1836 6 & 7 Will IV c.30, *An Act to repeal so much of Two Acts of the Ninth and Tenth Years of King George the Fourth as directs the Period of the Execution and the Prison Discipline of Persons convicted of the Crime of Murder* (14 July) abolished the requirement for convicted murderers to be executed within three days of sentencing.

1836 6 & 7 Will IV c.86, *An Act for registering Births, Deaths, and Marriages in England* (Births and Deaths Registration Act, 17 August) and its clarifying partner, *An Act to explain and amend Two Acts passed in the last Session of Parliament, for Marriages, and for registering Births, Deaths, and Marriages, in England* (1 Vict c.22, 30 June 1837) ordered the civil registration of births, marriages and deaths in England and Wales from 1 July 1837, putting pressure on coroners to record more precise causes of death.

1836 6 & 7 Will IV c.89, *An Act to provide for the Attendance and Remuneration of Medical Witnesses at Coroners Inquests* (Medical Witnesses Act, 17 August) stipulated a payment to medical witnesses of 1 guinea to give evidence at an inquest or 2 guineas if they conducted a post-mortem examination; the larger fee was also to cover any toxicological analysis of the stomach and intestines. Costs were to be reimbursed from local poor relief funds [s.3]; but were not payable if the deceased died in any public medical institution such as a hospital, infirmary or asylum, as the institutional medical officer was expected to conduct the examination [s.5].

(Continued)

(Continued)

Year	Events and Statutes
1836	6 & 7 Will IV c.105, *An Act for the better Administration of Justice in certain Boroughs* (20 August) permitted borough coroners to appoint a deputy when ill or unavoidably absent [s.6].
1836	6 & 7 Will IV c.114, *An Act for enabling Persons indicted of Felony to make their Defence by Counsel or Attorney* (Prisoners' Counsel Act, 20 August): individuals tried for felony were allowed to have their entire defence conducted by legal counsel from 1 October 1836 [s.1]; this included a closing speech to the jury, previously possible only when the charge was treason. In addition, defendants were permitted to have "for a reasonable sum" copies of the depositions against them [s.3] before the assizes began, or free of cost at the time of their trial [s.4]. This important statute inaugurated a new phase in the development of the adversarial criminal trial: defence barristers could construct an alternative hypothesis for the facts presented in evidence and present it directly to the jury.[8]
1836	The last execution for rape in Britain occurred on 30 March when Richard Smith was hanged at Nottingham.
1836	In April the Royal College of Physicians reorganised the way they granted medical licences, by instituting a five- + three-year programme of education that included forensic medicine.[9]
1836	The Marsh Test for arsenic was published in the *Edinburgh New Philosophical Journal*, vol. 21 (April–October 1836), pp. 229–236.
1837	7 Will IV & 1 Vict c.68, *An Act to provide for Payment of the Expences of holding Coroners Inquests* (Inquest Expenses Act, 15 July), compensated coroners for the reasonable expenses of inquests and paid them an extra 6s. 8d. per inquest (an increase of one third to £1 6s. 8d.) if the county justices of the peace or town council were satisfied by the accounts. This was necessary because the Poor Law Commission decided in 1836 that local poor rates could not meet inquest costs.
1839	2 & 3 Vict c.93, *An Act for the Establishment of County and District Constables by the Authority of Justices of the Peace* (County Police Act, 27 August): permissive legislation that allowed county magistrates to create and fund rural police forces, for which the Home Secretary was empowered to make rules and regulations [s.3]; each force was to have a chief constable [s.4] who would be responsible for appointing the men under his command [s.6], a power that the borough chief constables did not gain until 1964.[10]
1839	2 & 3 Vict c.94, *An Act for regulating the Police in the City of London* (City of London Police Act, 17 August) created an independent police force for the Square Mile (the City Day Police and Night Watch having merged in 1838), under the authority of a Commissioner.
1840	The Metropolitan Police District was enlarged under the terms of the Metropolitan Police Act 1839 (2 & 3 Vict c.47, *An Act for further improving the Police in and near the Metropolis*, 17 August 1839), by an Order in Council issued on 3 January 1840. The enlargement included the entire county of Middlesex and parts of Essex, Kent, Surrey and Hertfordshire within a 15-mile radius from Charing Cross. The River Police became the Thames Division of the Metropolitan Police [s.5], and the Bow Street patrol was disbanded [s.4].

Year	Events and Statutes
1840	3 & 4 Vict c.54, *An Act for making further Provision for the Confinement and Maintenance of Insane Prisoners* (Insane Prisoners Act, 4 August) allowed two JPs, with the aid of two doctors, to transfer serving prisoners found to be insane to an asylum, upon certification; it also extended the process of custodial detention to prisoners acquitted of misdemeanours on the grounds of insanity [s.3].
1842	The General Rule issued by the Poor Law Commissioners on 12 March required poor law MOs to have both medical and surgical training, specified four types of professional qualification, and restricted the size of the districts they served to 15,000 residents or 15,000 acres. In Wales the geography and "small number of resident medical practitioners" made it necessary to permit larger districts; MOs had to live within 7 miles of any part of any parish included within a Welsh district.[11] The medical qualifications required, which were basically those held by GPs, were reiterated in the Consolidated General Order issued by the Commissioners in July 1847.[12]
1842	A Detective Branch was established by the Metropolitan Police in August, based at the force headquarters in Scotland Yard (A Division, Whitehall).
1843	Acting under the influence of a mental illness, probably paranoid schizophrenia, Daniel McNaughtan murdered the prime minister's private secretary in January, believing him to be Sir Robert Peel. McNaughtan was tried and acquitted on the grounds of insanity; the government then sought the opinion of five judges on the law concerning insane people who committed crimes. The judges' reply constituted the McNaughtan Rules, a test of criminal responsibility which stated that a defence on grounds of insanity was established if the accused, due to mental disease, did not know the nature of the act or did not know that it was wrong. The Rules survived as a legal defence for murder defendants until the 1957 Homicide Act brought in the concept of diminished responsibility.
1843	6 & 7 Vict c.83, *An Act to amend the Law respecting the Duties of Coroners* (22 August), allowed county coroners to appoint a deputy when ill or unavoidably absent [s.1] and prevented the quashing of inquisitions on technical grounds [s.2].
1843	The Fellowship of the Royal College of Surgeons (FRCS) was introduced as a higher professional qualification than the MRCS.
1844	7 & 8 Vict c.92, *An Act to amend the Law respecting the Office of County Coroner* (Coroners Act, 9 August) forbade coroners from acting as attorneys in any trial that resulted from an inquest they had held [s.18] and allowed reimbursement of coroners' travel expenses even if they had decided an inquest was unnecessary [s.21].
1845	8 & 9 Vict c.100, *An Act for the Regulation of the Care and Treatment of Lunatics* (Lunatics Act, 4 August) and 8 & 9 Vict c.126, *An Act to amend the Laws for the Provision and Regulation of Lunatic Asylums for Counties and Boroughs, and for the Maintenance and Care of Pauper Lunatics, in England* (County Asylums Act, 8 August): these acts passed through Parliament simultaneously. The former established the Lunacy Commission, to monitor conditions in asylums and the treatment of patients; the latter mandated the creation of a network of public asylums for every county and borough that did not already have one, either singly or in a joint agreement with other counties and/or boroughs [s.3]. Each asylum was to have a resident medical officer [s.42].
1846	The Coroners' Society of England and Wales, the representative body for coroners, held its inaugural meeting on 4 February.

(Continued)

(Continued)

Year	Events and Statutes
1848	11 & 12 Vict c.42, *An Act to facilitate the Performance of the Duties of Justices of the Peace out of Sessions within England and Wales with respect to Persons charged with indictable Offences* (Indictable Offences Act, 14 August) required magistrates to take written, signed depositions against individuals charged with an indictable offence, and permitted that person, or their counsel, to put questions to the witnesses [s.17]; magistrates were then to advise the accused that they did not have to answer any questions but if they did, the answers would be taken down (usually on a form printed specifically for the purpose) and might be used in evidence against them at trial [s.18]. The accused was allowed a copy of the depositions against them for a "reasonable sum" [s.27]; and could be remanded to gaol for up to eight days during the investigation, for "any reasonable cause" [s.21]. An attached schedule set out the form of wording for the necessary paperwork, stipulated that all statements must be taken down "as nearly as possible" in the exact words of the deponents or accused, and inaugurated the modern police caution. This statute was one of three Jervis Acts, named for the Attorney-General, (Sir) John Jervis, and created the modern form of magistrates' judicial enquiry (known as a committal hearing in the Victorian era) when it came into effect on 2 October 1848.
1848	11 & 12 Vict c. 63, *An Act for promoting the Public Health* (Public Health Act, 31 August) set up local Boards of Health outside London, enabled them to appoint a medically qualified Officer of Health [s.40], and allowed them to provide public mortuaries for the short-term storage of the dead [s.81]. This was the first official recognition that such a need existed.[13]
1848	11 & 12 Vict c.78, *An Act for the further Amendment of the Administration of the Criminal Law* (Crown Cases Act, 31 August) created the Court for Crown Cases Reserved, which had the power to quash convictions on points of law; it remained the highest judicial forum for deciding questions of criminal law until superseded by the Court of Criminal Appeal in 1908.
1851	14 & 15 Vict c.13, *An Act to regulate the Sale of Arsenic* (The Arsenic Act, 5 June) attempted to control the sale of a dangerous substance by requiring purchasers to sign a poison register [ss.1–2]; arsenic sold in quantities under ten pounds in weight had to be coloured with soot or indigo [s.3].
1851	14 & 15 Vict c.55, *An Act to amend the Law relating to the Expenses of Prosecutions, and to make further Provision for the Apprehension and Trial of Offenders, in certain Cases* (Criminal Justice Administration Act, 1 August) enabled the Home Secretary to provide a schedule of payments for costs, compensations and expenses awarded to prosecution witnesses [s.5] and permitted the court to change the awards allowed by county magistrates [s.6]. This gave more leeway for the payment of higher fees to expert witnesses.
1851	14 & 15 Vict c.100, *An Act for further improving the Administration of Criminal Justice* (Criminal Procedure Act, 7 August) gave judges the power to amend an indictment at the trial, to avoid acquittals based on technicalities. In indictments for murder and manslaughter, the means by which the fatal injury was inflicted no longer had to be specified [s.4]; effective 1 September 1851.
1852	15 & 16 Vict c.85, *An Act to amend the Laws concerning the Burial of the Dead in the Metropolis* (Metropolitan Burials Act, 1 July) enabled London parishes to provide mortuaries for the reception and care of bodies prior to interment [s.42].
1853	Ludwig Teichmann developed the first specific test for blood, based on the formation of distinctive haematin crystals that could be viewed under a microscope.

Year	Events and Statutes

1855   In November the Council of the Provincial Medical and Surgical Association resolved to change its name to the British Medical Association[14] to represent the interests of the national medical profession. Its weekly journal became the *British Medical Journal* on 3 January 1857.

1856   19 & 20 Vict c.16, *An Act to empower the Court of Queen's Bench to order certain Offenders to be tried at the Central Criminal Court* (Central Criminal Court Act, 11 April), originally known as the Trial of Offences Act and popularly known as Palmer's Act, was passed to allow a crime committed outside London to be tried at the Central Criminal Court (Old Bailey), to avoid local prejudice in the case of the Staffordshire poisoner William Palmer. Those convicted could be sentenced to be punished either in the county where the offence was committed or within the jurisdiction of the Central Criminal Court [s.19].

1856   19 & 20 Vict c.69, *An Act to render more effectual the Police in Counties and Boroughs in England and Wales* (County and Borough Police Act, 21 July): from 1 December 1856 it became compulsory for an efficient police force to be established in any county which had not already formed a constabulary, one quarter of the cost of constables' pay and clothing to be met by the Treasury [s.16]. Boroughs with a population of 5,000 or less received no financial support, to encourage smaller forces to consolidate with the county police [s.17]. The existing Cheshire Constabulary was brought under the terms of the new Act [ss.25–29].

1858   21 & 22 Vict c.90, *An Act to regulate the Qualifications of Practitioners in Medicine and Surgery* (The Medical Act, 2 August), introduced compulsory registration to practice medicine, surgery or both [ss.15, 31]; set up the General Medical Council as a watchdog over medical education [ss. 18–20], required the annual publication of a *Medical Register* to list qualified members of the profession [s.27], and introduced the term 'legally (or duly) qualified medical practitioner' [s. 34] by which medical professionals were to style themselves from 1 January 1859. Under s.36 it became illegal for unregistered persons to hold official institutional appointments.

1860   23 & 24 Vict c.75, *An Act to make better Provision for the Custody and Care of Criminal Lunatics* (Criminal Lunatic Asylums Act, 6 August) authorised the Home Secretary to direct that individuals found to be unfit to plead to an indictment, acquitted on the grounds of insanity, or who became insane in prison be removed to any suitable asylum under a formal warrant [s.2]; persons so confined had to be accompanied by a certificate that provided information about their status as a criminal lunatic. They could be discharged or removed from the asylum by the Home Secretary upon the advice of the asylum's medical superintendent and two members of its Council of Supervision [ss.7–8].

1860   23 & 24 Vict c.116, *An Act to amend the Law relating to the Election, Duties, and Payment of County Coroners* (County Coroners Act, 28 August) replaced the fees and mileage allowances paid to coroners with an annual salary paid from the county rate and agreed with magistrates, who retained control over inquest expenses [s.4]. Effective from 1 January 1861.

1861   24 & 25 Vict c.100, *An Act to consolidate and amend the Statute Law of England and Ireland relating to Offences against the Person* (Offences Against the Person Act, 6 August): a charge of concealment of birth could now be made against anyone, not just the mother, and it did not matter if the child was born dead or alive; a trial jury could use concealment as an alternative verdict to a murder charge [s.60].

1861   The last execution in Britain for any crime other than murder or treason occurred on 27 August when Martin Doyle was hanged at Chester for attempted murder.

(Continued)

(Continued)

Year	Events and Statutes
1863	The first screening test for blood was developed by Christian Schönbein; the reaction it relied on was catalysed by an enzyme found in many substances, so the test was not unique to blood.
1863	Broadmoor Criminal Lunatic Asylum admitted its first patient, a woman convicted of newborn child murder, on 27 May.
1865	28 & 29 Vict c.126, *An Act to consolidate and amend the Law relating to Prisons* (The Prison Act, 6 July) required every prison to have a surgeon [s.10]; the schedule of regulations inaugurated medical exams for prisoners who appeared in ill health and required the prison governor to report insane prisoners to the magistrates who had administrative oversight of each prison.
1867	30 & 31 Vict c.12, *An Act to amend the Law relating to Criminal Lunatics* (Criminal Lunatics Act, 12 April) defined a criminal lunatic as follows: any person ordered to be detained during Her Majesty's pleasure, or any person authorized by the Home Secretary to be removed to an asylum under the terms of any law, or any person sentenced to penal servitude but found to be unfit due to "imbecility of mind" [s.3]; it also gave the Home Secretary the power to discharge absolutely or conditionally any criminal lunatic from custody [s.5]; those who had not recovered their sanity when their sentence expired were to be removed to a county asylum as a pauper lunatic [s.6].
1867	30 & 31 Vict c.35, *An Act to remove some Defects in the Administration of the Criminal Law* (Criminal Law Amendment Act, 20 June) required JPs presiding over committal hearings to ask the accused if they wished to call defence witnesses, who could then be examined and cross-examined under oath [s.3]; enabled JPs to take the deposition of a witness who was believed to be dangerously ill, and for the deposition to be read in evidence for the defence or prosecution at trial if the deponent had died [s.6]; and gave the defendant the right to be present when the statement was made (in order to cross-examine the witness) [s.7]. Effective 1 October 1867.
1870	33 & 34 Vict c.77, *An Act to amend the Laws relating to the qualifications, summoning, attendance, and remuneration of Special and Common Juries* (Juries Act, 9 August) imposed uniform property qualifications for all jurors in England and Wales [s.7].
1871	34 & 35 Vict c.70, *An Act for constituting a Local Government Board, and vesting therein certain functions of the Secretary of State and Privy Council concerning the Public Health and Local Government, together with the powers and duties of the Poor Law Board* (Local Government Board Act, 14 August) created the Local Government Board (LGB) which took over responsibility for all public health, local government and Poor Law functions until 1919.
1872	35 & 36 Vict c.38, *An Act for the better Protection of Infant Life* (Infant Life Protection Act, 25 July) attempted to eliminate baby farming by requiring houses where two or more children under the age of one were cared for by paid nurses to be registered with local authorities and keep records of the infants; the district coroner was to be notified of all deaths [s.8] and failure to do so became an offence punishable by a fine or imprisonment [s.9]. Effective 1 November 1872.
1872	35 & 36 Vict c.74, *An Act to amend the Law for the prevention of Adulteration of Food and Drink and of Drugs* (Adulteration of Food and Drugs Act, 10 August) permitted the appointment of public analysts "possessing competent medical, chemical, and microscopical knowledge" [s.5], but made no provision for ensuring appropriate qualifications or pay; repealed by the Sale of Food and Drugs Act 1875.
1872	Dr Thomas Stevenson (Guy's Hospital) was appointed Scientific Analyst to the Home Office; in May 1882 he became Senior Scientific Analyst when a second Home Office analyst was appointed.[15]

Year	Events and Statutes

1874   37 & 38 Vict c.58, *An Act to make further provision respecting the contribution out of moneys provided by Parliament towards the expenses of the Police Force in the Metropolitan Police District, and elsewhere in Great Britain* (Police (Expenses) Act, 7 August) increased the government grant for pay and clothing from 25% to 50%, allowing the state to exert more influence over the county police forces that it funded. This legislation inaugurated fifteen years of professionalising police reforms.[16]

1874   37 & 38 Vict c.88, *An Act to amend the Law relating to the Registration of Births and Deaths in England, and to consolidate the Law respecting the Registration of Births and Deaths at Sea* (Births and Deaths Registration Act, 7 August), made death registration compulsory [s.9] and required the certifying practitioner to be registered (under the terms of the Medical Act 1858) [s.20].

1875   38 & 39 Vict c.55, *An Act for consolidating and amending the Acts relating to Public Health in England* (Public Health Act, 11 August) gave local authorities the power to provide mortuaries, making doing so mandatory if required by the LGB [s.141]; also to provide a place other than at a workhouse or mortuary for the reception of dead bodies during the time required to conduct any post-mortem examination ordered by a coroner or other legal authority [s.143]. Rural authorities were required to appoint medical officers of health [s.190].

1875   38 & 39 Vict c.63, *An Act to repeal the Adulteration of Food Acts, and to make better provision for the Sale of Food and Drugs in a pure state* (Sale of Food and Drugs Act, 11 August) required all local authorities to appoint public analysts "possessing competent knowledge, skill, and experience," subject to the approval of the LGB [s.10]; costs were to be paid from the county or borough rates [s.29]. This Act repealed the Adulteration of Food and Drugs Act 1872 and came into effect on 1 October 1875.

1875   38 & 39 Vict c.94, *An Act to amend the Law relating to Offences against the Person* (Offences against the Person Act, 13 August) raised the age of consent from 12 to 13 years for girls [s.4].

1876   39 & 40 Vict c.18, *An Act to incorporate the Solicitor for the affairs of Her Majesty's Treasury, and make further provision respecting the grant of the administration of the Estates of deceased persons for the use of Her Majesty* (Treasury Solicitor Act, 27 June) established the office of Treasury Solicitor as a government corporation with perpetual succession [s.1].

1876   39 & 40 Vict c.57, *An Act to amend the Law respecting the holding of Winter Assizes* (Winter Assizes Act, 11 August) made provision for prisoners awaiting trial in counties in which winter assizes were not held to be tried in the sessions of neighbouring counties where they were, under the terms of Orders in Council made to that effect [s.2]. The jurisdiction of the Central Criminal Court could be extended to neighbouring counties in the months of November to January [s.5].

The provisions of this Act were extended to September and October under 40 & 41 Vict c.46, *An Act to extend the provisions of the Winter Assizes Act, 1876* (Winter Assizes Act, 10 August, **1877**). Followed up by the Spring Assizes Act 1879.

These acts affected prisoners in smaller counties such as those of north Wales: in shortening the period between committal and trial, it meant that Welsh defendants might be tried in an English county such as Cheshire.

1877   40 & 41 Vict c.21, *An Act to amend the Law relating to Prisons in England* (Prison Act, 12 July) centralised prison bureaucracy under a new Board of Prison Commissioners.

(Continued)

(Continued)

Year	Events and Statutes
1878	In March the Metropolitan Police created the Criminal Investigation Department, a detective force based at Scotland Yard, under the leadership of soldier-turned-barrister Howard Vincent, its aim being to prevent crime by offering certainty of detection.
1879	42 & 43 Vict c.1, *An Act to amend the Law respecting the holding of Assizes* (Spring Assizes Act, 14 March) extended the provisions of the Winter Assize Act 1876 to the months of March, April and May [s.2].
1879	42 & 43 Vict c.22, *An Act for more effectually providing for the Prosecution of Offences in England; and for other purposes* (Prosecution of Offences Act, 3 July), initiated the appointment of a Director of Public Prosecutions (DPP) who had the power to take important or difficult cases to court [s.2] and authorise specific costs (including for medical evidence or counsel's fees) [s.3]; effective 1 January 1880. The DPP was concerned merely with cases submitted to him for advice or investigation by government departments and local police authorities and courts. Once the decision to prosecute had been made, the handling of the prosecution was taken over by the Treasury Solicitor; the two offices were combined in 1884. Responsibility for most prosecutions rested with the police until 1986.[17]
1883	46 & 47 Vict c.38, *An Act to amend the Law respecting the Trial and Custody of Insane Persons charged with offences* (Trial of Lunatics Act, 25 August) created a new special verdict of guilty but insane (in place of acquittal on the grounds of insanity); such offenders were to be kept in strict custody indefinitely ("till Her Majesty's pleasure shall be known") [s.2].
1884	In a statement to the House of Commons on 17 March, the Attorney General confirmed that he had ordered the Treasury Solicitor to conduct all capital prosecutions, and that in cases where the accused was allegedly insane, the Treasury Solicitor should facilitate a full enquiry into their sanity.[18]
1884	47 & 48 Vict c.58, *An Act for amending the Prosecution of Offences Act, 1879* (Prosecution of Offences Act, 4 August) combined the posts of Treasury Solicitor and Director of Public Prosecutions [s.2].
1884	47 & 48 Vict c.64, *An Act to consolidate and amend the Law relating to Criminal Lunatics* (Criminal Lunatics Act, 14 August) required two legally qualified medical practitioners to certify the insanity of any prisoner or capital convict suspected to be insane [s.2]; criminal lunatics were then detained in prison or an asylum and subject to periodic (3-yearly) review [s.4].
1885	48 & 49 Vict c.69, *An Act to make further provision for the Protection of Women and Girls, the suppression of brothels, and other purposes* (Criminal Law Amendment Act, 14 August) made sex with a girl under 13 a felony [s.4] and raised the age of consent from 13 to 16 years [s.5]; it also criminalised all forms of sexual activity between males [s.11].
1886	49 & 50 Vict c.48, *An Act to amend the Medical Acts* (Medical Act, 25 June), established a common set of training proficiencies in the essential branches of medical practice – medicine, surgery and midwifery [s.2]; and extended the power of the General Medical Council to audit the examinations set by the medical corporations and university medical faculties but did not displace them [s.3], thus failing to establish a common curriculum.[19]
1886	Regulations of 11 June relating to carrying out the Prosecution of Offences Acts 1879 and 1884, confirmed the requirement for the DPP to prosecute all capital cases, a duty inherited when the post was combined with that of Treasury Solicitor.[20]

Year	Events and Statutes
1887	50 & 51 Vict c.71, *An Act to consolidate the Law relating to Coroners* (Coroners Act, 16 September) established the coroners' dominion over all sudden deaths of which the cause was unknown, violent, unnatural and deaths in prison [s.3], giving them the discretion to decide not to hold an inquest and which remained the legal basis of their jurisdiction until the 1980s. The sole qualification for the role was financial [s.12]. The Act set the terms under which medical evidence was to be sought from any legally qualified doctor in practice "in or near the place where the death happened." It did not change the fees set in 1836, but refused remuneration to practitioners who had attended the deceased in any medical institution [ss. 21–22] – that is, house surgeons, workhouse or asylum MOs, who were expected to carry out medico-legal examinations for free.
1887	The Metropolitan Police Surgeons' Association was founded in November and by January 1888 it was fully operational, with 156 out of 190 police surgeons as members.
1887	In December a Home Office circular instructed that in cases of open verdict which afterwards became subject to prosecution, coroners were to send the depositions to the clerk of assize.
1888	51 & 52 Vict c.41, *An Act to amend the Laws relating to Local Government in England and Wales, and for other purposes connected therewith* (Local Government Act, 13 August) created county councils as the unit of local administration [s.1]; established an administrative County of London which included the City of London and for which the local authority was the London County Council (LCC) [ss.40–41]; and replaced the election of coroners by appointments made by the councils of counties or county boroughs [ss.5, 34]. Boroughs with populations of less than 10,000 lost the ability to appoint coroners and public analysts [s.38]. The serving coroners of Middlesex, Surrey and Kent kept their posts, but coroner's districts split between a county and the LCC were to be altered in due course [s.114].
1897	60 & 61 Vict c.57, *An Act to amend the Law for the better Protection of Infant Life* (Infant Life Protection Act, 6 August) came into force on 1 January 1898, requiring suspicious infant deaths to be notified to the district coroner so that an inquest to establish cause of death could be carried out [s.8]. It increased the age of the children it protected to 5 years, and repealed the 1872 Act.
1898	61 & 62 Vict c.36, *An Act to Amend the Law of Evidence* (Criminal Evidence Act, 12 August): for the first time, defendants and their spouses were allowed to testify on oath for the defence at every stage of criminal proceedings, subject to cross-examination.
1900	Prison Standing Orders issued in 1900 and 1902 required Prison Medical Officers to provide pre-trial reports to the court on all remand prisoners of doubtful sanity; and to attend court in all cases where questions about the prisoner's mental state might arise, whether they were subpoenaed or not.[21]
1903	A Home Office Circular of 7 January advised coroners who required an analysis of viscera and other substances in cases of poisoning that raised suspicions to apply to the Home Secretary to authorise one of the Home Office analysts to undertake a special analysis. The application was to include a full and precise statement of the "reasonable" grounds for suspicion, the reasons for thinking an analysis likely to "promote the ends of justice," and a list of the substances or items to be analysed.[22]
1904	In an Order of 14 June the Home Secretary set a scale of expenses for witnesses attending to give evidence at the assizes.

(Continued)

(Continued)

Year	Events and Statutes

1907   7 Edw VII c.23, *An Act to establish a Court of Criminal Appeal and to amend the Law relating to Appeals in Criminal Cases* (Criminal Appeal Act, 28 August) established the Court of Criminal Appeal, superseding the Court for Crown Cases Reserved. The new court began sitting in May 1908 to hear appeals against conviction and sentence: it had the power to uphold or quash a conviction (including on the grounds of insanity, s.5.4) but not to order a re-trial. Significantly for medico-legal practice, the court could appoint "any person with special expert knowledge to act as assessor to the court" [s.9e], their expenses to be paid at the rates set for felony cases tried at assizes [s.13(2)].

1908   In an Order of 27 March issued under s.13(2) of the Criminal Appeal Act, the Home Secretary set a maximum fee of 10 guineas per day for persons appointed as assessors to the Court,[23] in essence capping the daily maximum rate for expert witnesses.

1908   8 Edw VII c.3, *An Act to amend the Prosecution of Offences Acts, 1879 and 1884* (Prosecution of Offences Act, 1 August) separated the roles of Treasury Solicitor and DPP, and, under the Rules of 11 June 1886, made the latter responsible for prosecuting any case which carried the death penalty.

1908   8 Edw VII c.15, *An Act to consolidate and amend the Law relating to the Payment of Costs in Criminal Cases* (Costs in Criminal Cases Act, 1 August), empowered the Home Secretary to make regulations determining the rates or scales of costs, and the conditions under which costs could be allowed, in the criminal courts [s.5].

1922   12 & 13 Geo V c.18, *An Act to provide that a woman who wilfully causes the death of her newly-born child may, under certain conditions, be convicted of infanticide* (Infanticide Act, 20 July), created a new offence equivalent to manslaughter. It applied to any woman found to have deliberately killed her newborn child while the balance of her mind was disturbed because of giving birth. The Act brought the law into line with what had become "the usual practice";[24] it was repealed by s.2(3) of the Infanticide Act 1938.

1926   16 & 17 Geo V c.59, *An Act to Amend the Law relating to Coroners* (Coroners (Amendment) Act, 15 December) instituted professional qualifications for coroners, who henceforth had to be doctors or lawyers of at least 5 years' standing [s.1], abolished franchise coronerships [s.4] and the requirement for inquest juries to view the body [s.14], and allowed coroners to order post-mortem examinations without holding an inquest [s.21]. The Act also set the daily fees payable to medical witnesses [s.23]. Committing a named individual for trial on an inquisition remained possible [s.25], but coroners were now to adjourn an inquest if the suspect had already been committed for trial by magistrates [s.20].[25] Effective 1 May 1927.

1938   1 & 2 Geo VI c.36, *An Act to repeal and re-enact with modifications the provisions of the Infanticide Act, 1922* (Infanticide Act, 23 June) created the current legal definition of the crime. Jurors were enabled to return a verdict of infanticide, equivalent to manslaughter, in the trial of a woman for the murder of her own infant aged under 12 months, if they believed that she caused the child's death by any wilful act or omission when "the balance of her mind was disturbed." The statute lists two causes: "not having fully recovered from the effect of giving birth to the child or by reason of the effect of lactation consequent upon the birth of the child."

Notes

1 Amoval is an obsolete term for 'removal' or 'putting away', according to the *Oxford English Dictionary*.
2 J. M. Beattie, *Crime and the Courts in England 1660–1800* (Princeton: Princeton University Press, 1986), p. 26.
3 Cecil Wall, *The History of the Surgeons' Company 1745–1800* (London: Hutchinson's Scientific & Technical Publications, 1937), p. 152.
4 TNA HO 45/1896, Letter from J. W. Fisher to S. M. Phillipps, 25 Jan 1847.
5 *The Lancet* 1 (1830–31), p. 6.
6 For an introduction to the Poor Laws, see www.workhouses.org.uk/poorlaws/.
7 Richard Cowley, *A History of the British Police: From Its Earliest Beginnings to the Present Day* (Stroud: The History Press, 2011), pp. 36–46.
8 David J. A. Cairns, *Advocacy and the Making of the Adversarial Criminal Trial 1800–1865* (Oxford: Clarendon Press, 1998), pp. 67–125; John H. Langbein, *The Origins of Adversary Criminal Trial* (Oxford: Oxford University Press, 2003), pp. 291–306; Cerian Charlotte Griffiths, "The Prisoners' Counsel Act 1836: Doctrine, Advocacy and the Criminal Trial," *Law, Crime and History* 2 (2014), pp. 28–47.
9 Anon., "Important Changes in the College of Physicians," *London Medical Gazette* 18 (1836), pp. 146–149.
10 Cowley, *History of the British Police*, pp. 54, 60–70.
11 John Frederick Archbold, *The New Poor Law Amendment Act, and the Recent Rules and Orders of the Poor Law Commissioners; with a Practical Introduction, Notes, and Forms* (London: John Richards and Co., 1842), pp. 57–61. The four qualifications were as follows: in medicine and surgery; as an apothecary and surgeon; certification as having been in practise as an apothecary in August 1815; an army, navy or East India Company commission as a surgeon prior to August 1826.
12 Consolidated General Order, 26 July 1847, www.workhouses.org.uk/gco/gco1847.shtml (accessed 31 Dec 2018).
13 Pam Fisher, "Houses for the Dead: The Provision of Mortuaries in London, 1843–1889," *The London Journal* 34 (2009), pp. 1–15.
14 For a short account of the meeting at which the decision was adopted, see *Sheffield Daily Telegraph*, 24 Nov 1855, p. 3.
15 TNA HO 45/9620/A15734, Appointment of Analysts, 1882–1888.
16 Cowley, *History of the British Police*, pp. 105–106.
17 TNA, Records of the Director of Public Prosecutions, http://discovery.nationalarchives.gov.uk/details/r/C87 (accessed 3 Jan 2019).
18 HC Deb 17 March 1884 vol. 286 cc40-1, http://hansard.millbanksystems.com/commons/1884/mar/17/law-and-justice-the-director-of-public (accessed 17 Aug 2017).
19 M. J. D. Roberts, "The Politics of Professionalization: MPs, Medical Men, and the 1858 Medical Act," *Medical History* 53 (2009), p. 53.
20 *Return of Working of Regulations for Carrying Out Prosecution of Offences Acts, June–December 1886*, House of Commons Papers, Paper Number 119, Vol. 67, p. 143 (1887).
21 *Report of the Commissioners of Prisons and the Directors of Convict Prisons, 1899–1900, with appendices*, Cd. 380, Vol. 41 (1900), p. 118; *Report of the Commissioners of Prisons and the Directors of Convict Prisons, with Appendices*, Cd. 1278, Vol. 46 (1902), p. 155. See also Tony Ward, "Law, Common Sense and the Authority of Science: Expert Witnesses and Criminal Insanity in England, ca. 1840–1940," *Social & Legal Studies* 6 (1997), p. 351.
22 R. Henslowe Wellington, *The King's Coroner Being the Practice and Procedure in His Judicial and Ministerial Capacities*, Vol. 2 (London: Baillière, Tindall and Cox, 1906), p. 26.
23 Herman Cohen, *The Criminal Appeal Act, 1907: And the Rules, Forms and Rates and Scales of Payment Thereunder, with Notes* (London: Jordan & Sons, 1908), p. 82.
24 *The Woman's Leader*, 18 Aug 1922, p. 227.
25 This provision recognised that the principal responsibility for investigating and prosecuting homicide now lay with the police: Peter J. Dean, "Changes in the Coroner's Jurisdiction," LL.M. thesis, University of Wales, 1992, pp. 57–58, 87.

Appendix 2

Medical practitioners in Wales, 1783

Adapted from *The Medical Register for the Year 1783* (London: Joseph Johnson, 1783), pp. 124–126. All individuals are styled surgeons and apothecaries unless noted as a physician, here indicated by the title Dr. Spellings have been modernised. Although the Register includes Monmouthshire, it has been omitted here because there are no extant depositions for the county in the late eighteenth century. Names in bold are not listed in the *Medical Register* but have been identified from the records of Great Sessions.

County	Town	Name
Anglesey	Beaumaris	Mr Wynne, Mr Hughes
	Holyhead	Mr Johnston[1]
	Llanerchymedd	Mr Williams
	Amlwch	Mr Jones
Breconshire	Brecon	Mr C. Pritchard; Samuel Price; John Williams; Mr W. Gunter; Thomas Williams
	Builth Wells	David Moythen; Mr Powell; John Morgan
	Hay	James Lyde; John Jones; James Bevan
Cardiganshire	Aberystwyth	David William Hopkins
	Cardigan	David Davies; John Bower
	Lampeter	David Edwards
	Llanilar	David Lloyd Newnam
	Tregaron	Joseph Rees
Carmarthenshire	Carmarthen	Dr Charles Brown; William Price; Edward Dalton; Mark Roch; Richard Rees; Mr Pryce; William Thomas
	Llandeilo	David Edwards; William Prothero[2]
	Llangadog	**Thomas Williams**[3]
	Laugharne	Mr Eliott
	Llandovery	David Davis
		William Price; James Lloyd;[4]**John Jones**[5]
	Newcastle Emlyn	Mr Edwards
Carnarvonshire	Bangor	Mr Ellis

(Continued)

(Continued)

County	Town	Name
	Carnarvon	Mr Edwards; Mr Roberts; Mr Jones **Evan Morris, apothecary**[6]
Denbighshire	Denbigh	Mr Jones; Mr Evans; Mr Roberts
	Llanwrst? or Llanrhydd?	Mr Titley; Mr Roberts
	Ruthin	Mr Nichols; Mr Jones; Mr Conway
	Wrexham	Dr Richard Worthington;[7] Messrs Lloyd and Massey; Mr Crew; Mr Prosser; **Thomas Griffiths**[8]
Flintshire	Hawarden	Mr Thomas
	Holywell	Mr Thoresby; Mr Blunt; Mr Ingleby; Mr Speed
	Mold	Messrs Parry and Davis
	St Asaph	Mr Rogers
Glamorgan	Bridgend	Thomas Smith; Mr Sydney; Mr Williams
	Cardiff	Bloom Williams
	Cowbridge	John Walton; Edward Bates
	Llandaf	John Mergam
	Llantrisant	Mr Lloyd; **William Prichard**[9]
	Margam	Dr Andrew Paterson[10]
	Merthyr Tydfil	**Thomas Williams**[11]
	Neath	Richard Bevan;[12] William Jones; David Lloyd; Lewis Jenkins; Walter Morris; Alexander Davis[13]
	Swansea	Charles Collins; Mr Silvester;[14] David Evans; Mr Hancorn; **Thomas Williams, surgeon-apothecary**[15]
Merionethshire	Dolgellau	Mr Owen; Mr Roberts
Montgomeryshire	Llanfyllin	Mr Lloyd
	Machynlleth	Mr Pugh
	Newtown	Mr Poole
	Welshpool	Three unnamed apothecaries
Pembrokeshire	Fishguard	Evan Lloyd
	Haverfordwest	Dr George Phillips; Dr John Jones;[16] Francis Edwards; Messrs Essex Devereux Jones and W. Thomas; Nathaniel Davies; Henry Davies
	Hubberston	Nathaniel Stokes
	Narberth	Morgan Gwynne
	Pembroke	Joshua Allen; William Mansell; David Davies
	Tenby	Gabriel Kringle; Mr Middleton
Radnorshire	Presteigne	George Pyfinch; Richard Ayres
	Knighton	William Russell; Richard Ayres

Notes

1 Robert Johnson committed suicide in June 1794; coroner Hugh Wynne held an inquest on him at Holyhead, when he was declared a lunatic (NLW GS 4/256/1).
2 NLW GS 4/746/3: a witness in the case against David Jones at Llangathen, Nov 1785.
3 NLW GS 4/744/3: "Thomas Williams of the parish of Llangadock in the county of Carmarthen chirurgeon comes before me this 24th day of December 1781" to report having been stabbed.
4 NLW GS 4/746/3: two surgeons entered into recognizances in the case of Jane Thomas for infanticide at Llanfair-ar-y-bryn, April 1786.
5 NLW GS 4/744/3: a document relating to a civil suit regarding the will of John Jones late of the county of Carmarthen doctor in physic, involving a Lady Stepney and property in Market Street, Carmarthen; he is described as a surgeon of Llandovery in February 1782, fol. 47.
6 He was a witness at an inquest held 28 Mar 1783 by coroner John Morris at Llanbeblig (NLW GS 4/276/2).
7 Worthington took his MD at Edinburgh in 1778.
8 A witness in the case of Stephen Tailor, see NLW GS 4/59/7, February 1781. It is possible that he died before the *Medical Register* was compiled.
9 A witness in the case of William David at Llantrisant, see NLW GS 4/624/1, March 1778. It is possible that he died before the *Medical Register* was compiled.
10 Paterson took his MD at St Andrews in 1756.
11 A witness in the case of William Owen at Merthyr Tydfil, see NLW GS 4/626/5, April 1787. Judging by the signature, this is clearly a different individual from the Thomas Williams in n.15.
12 "Formerly a Navy Surgeon."
13 Davis moved to Neath from Margam.
14 Thomas Sylvester, see NLW GS 4/626/5, April 1787. He and Charles Collins were asked to conduct a post-mortem in a case that occurred at Llanrhidian, about 11 miles away.
15 See NLW GS 4/626/5: he was called in on 5 Apr 1787 to visit the victim in the case noted in n.11.
16 George Phillips and John Jones were both Oxford graduates in medicine in 1745, respectively from Jesus College and Trinity College.

Appendix 3

Introduction of the new police into London, Wales and the counties of the Oxford Circuit

Adapted from Richard Cowley, *A History of the British Police: From its Earliest Beginnings to the Present Day* (Stroud: The History Press, 2011), pp. 38–43, 62–63, 77–78. See also Richard W. Ireland, *Land of White Gloves? A History of Crime and Punishment in Wales* (Abingdon: Routledge, 2015), pp. 111–113; and Martin Stallion and David S. Wall, *The British Police: Police Forces and Chief Officers 1829–2000* (Hook: Police History Society, 1999).

Forces for which no end date is provided survived as independent institutions until after 1914.

Early police forces

Metropolitan Police: 29 Sep 1829.
Town/Borough Police: Birkenhead (10 Jun 1833); Brecon (1829–1889); Carmarthen (1831); Cheltenham (1831–1839); Haverfordwest (1835–1889); Kidderminster (1835); Newbury (1835–1875); Newcastle-under-Lyme (1 Nov 1834); Walsall (6 Jul 1832); Wantage (1828–1856); Worcester (18 Jan 1833).

Voluntary borough forces created in accordance with the Municipal Corporations Act, 1835

Abingdon (1836–1889); Banbury (March 1836); Beaumaris (1836–1860); Bridgnorth (1836–1850); Bristol (22 Jun 1836); Cardiff (Jan 1836); Chester (1 Jan 1836); Chipping Norton (1836–1856); Congleton (Feb 1836); Droitwich (1836–1881); Evesham (1836–1850); Gloucester (1836–1859); Hereford (1 Jan 1836); Leominster (1836–1889); Ludlow (1836–1889); Macclesfield (19 Jan 1836); Maidenhead (1836–1889); Monmouth (1836–1881); Neath (1836); Newport (1 Feb 1836); Oxford (1 Jan 1869); Pembroke (1856–1858); Pwllheli (1857–1879); Reading (21 Feb 1836); Shrewsbury (5 Feb 1836); Stafford (1840–1858); Stockport (23 Mar 1870); Swansea (4 Apr 1836); Tamworth (1840–1857); Tenby (c.1840–1889); Tewkesbury (1836–1854); Wallingford (1836–1856); Windsor (5 Mar 1836).

Voluntary town forces: Wolverhampton (3 Aug 1837); City of London (Nov 1839); Henley-on-Thames (1838–1856).

Voluntary forces created in accordance with the County Police Act, 1839

Gloucestershire: 18 Nov 1839.

Worcestershire: 13 Dec 1839.

Shropshire: Dec 1839.

Denbighshire: May 1840.

Montgomeryshire: 25 Jul 1840.

Staffordshire: unknown date in 1840 (covered south of county only until extended in Oct 1842).

Glamorgan: unknown date in 1841.

Carmarthenshire: 25 Jul 1843.

Cardiganshire: 2 Jan 1844.

Berkshire: 9 Feb 1856.

Forces created in accordance with the County and Borough Police Act, 1856

Flintshire: Nov 1856.

Breconshire: 6 Jan 1857.

Radnorshire: 8 Jan 1857.

Herefordshire: 19 Jan 1857.

Monmouthshire: 23 Mar 1857.

Oxfordshire: 25 Mar 1857.

Carnarvonshire: 9 Apr 1857.

Anglesey: 20 Apr 1857.

Cheshire: 20 Apr 1857.

Pembrokeshire: 9 Jun 1857.

Merionethshire: 30 Sep 1857.

Other local police forces

Hanley, Staffordshire (1870–1910); Hyde, Cheshire (1899–1947); Lichfield, Staffordshire (1856–1889); Merthyr Tydfil, Glamorgan (1908–1969); Stalybridge, Cheshire (1857–1947); Stoke-on-Trent, Staffordshire (1910–1968); Trevethin, Monmouthshire (c.1840–1860).

Rural policing, 1855

County	Date of Appointment	Total Strength	Annual Cost, 1855
ENGLAND			
Berkshire	14 Jan 1856		
Cheshire	N/A – refer to the Cheshire Constabulary Act, 1852		
Gloucestershire	Nov 1839	254	£16,334 4s. 3¼d.
Herefordshire	None		
Oxfordshire	None		
Shropshire	Dec 1839	58	£3,517 10s. 7d. excluding the cost of lock-up houses
Staffordshire	Jan 1843	278 across 3 districts: Mining – 91 Pottery – 82 Rural – 105 + 1 chief constable	£16,861 12s. 8d. £5,858 8s. 7d. £5,428 0s. 3d. £5,575 3s. 10d.
Worcestershire	1839, increased in 1845 and 1855	116	£7,305
WALES			
Anglesey	No return		
Breconshire	None		
Cardiganshire	5 Mar 1844	26	£1,619 5s. 9½d.
Carmarthenshire	Oct 1843	35	£2,444 13s. 10¼d.
Carnarvonshire	None		
Denbighshire	1840	33	£1,827 9s. 3d.
Flintshire	None		
Glamorgan	8 Jul 1841	70	£4,569 8s. ½d. excluding reimbursed costs for attending inquests and transporting prisoners
Merionethshire	None		
Monmouthshire	No return		
Montgomeryshire	23 Jul 1840	19	£1,444 6s. 5½d.
Pembrokeshire	None		
Radnorshire	No return		

Data taken from *Return of the Number of Rural Police in each County in England and Wales, appointed under Acts 2 & 3 Vict c. 93, and 3 & 4 Vict c. 88* (London: House of Commons, 1856).

Police strength, Counties and Boroughs, 1899

Force	Total Strength	Vacancies	Augmentation during the Year	Population per Constable	Population per Constable in 1881
Anglesey	30			1,670	1,820
Berkshire	173			952	1,112
– Reading	75			800	1,051
Breconshire	44			1,168	1,436
Cardiganshire	40			1,586	1,801
Carmarthenshire	90		7	1,336	2,006
Carnarvonshire	81		1	1,467	1,702
Cheshire	439			983	1,211
– Birkenhead	145			688	757
– Chester	50			742	876
– Stockport	84			836	1,123
Denbighshire	82		1	1,473	1,378
Flintshire	58	1	4	1,349	1,575
Glamorgan	415		14	1,100	1,740
– Cardiff	239		20	539	862
– Swansea	104			868	911
Gloucestershire	353		10	1,026	1,296
– Bristol	499			563	553
Herefordshire	79			1,216	1,358
– Hereford	33			614	661
London – Met	13,574			412	
London – City	1,001			38	
Merionethshire	35			1,406	1,543
Monmouthshire	164			1,240	1,558
– Newport	91		6	601	720
Montgomeryshire	36			1,611	1,993
Oxfordshire	111			1,180	1,363
– Banbury	12			1,064	720
– Oxford	62	1		738	915
Pembrokeshire	69		3	1,279	1,613
Radnorshire	18			1,210	1,384
Shropshire	165	4	2	1,272	1,537
– Shrewsbury	37			729	1,059
Staffordshire	687	2	2	1,249	1,443
– Hanley	58		2	947	1,179
– Walsall	78	1		920	1,200
– Wolverhampton	93			889	1,037
Worcestershire	345	13	37	863	1,301
– Worcester	47			913	1,028

Figures for London are the average daily strength; population per constable based on 1891 census.

Data taken from *Reports of the Inspectors of Constabulary, for the Year ended 29th September 1899, made to Her Majesty's Principal Secretary of State, under the Provisions of the Statute 19 & 20 Vict c.69* (London: HMSO, 1900).

Appendix 4

Coroners trained as surgeons or physicians

Physicians are styled as Dr; all others are surgeons. Organised by county and then in date order.

County	Name	Details
Anglesey	Hugh Wynne (c.1759–1841)	Served 1792–1841.
Breconshire	Benjamin Williams	Gave up practice 1823; resigned coronership 1828, new election 6 Feb 1828.
Breconshire	Clement Ekins (d.1832)	Elected Feb 1828, resigned June 1831 on appointment as assistant surgeon, 93d Highland Regiment; died in Barbados.
Breconshire	Lewis Watkins	Elected 11 Jul 1831.[1]
Cardiganshire	Dr Richard Williams	Active c.1845–1855 (son of William Williams, surgeon, Aberystwyth, d. Dec 1847).
Cardiganshire	Dr Evan Rowland	Circa late 1888; his deputy was Mr W. Hughes Jones.
Carmarthenshire	James Rowlands	Liberty of Kidwelly, 1879; lived in Carmarthen.
Carmarthenshire	John Hughes, FRCS	Borough of Carmarthen, 1884; also a police surgeon.
Carnarvonshire	Edward Carreg	Elected 15 Oct 1816, resigned 1832; he had given up medical practice by 1823.
Carnarvonshire	Thomas Hughes	Elected 29 May 1833, for the upper division of the county; lived at Pwllheli, succeeded by his son.
Carnarvonshire	Dr Hugh Hunter Hughes (c.1807–1880)	Served c.1840–1880, South Carnarvonshire; succeeded by his son, who had served as his deputy for many years;[2] lived at Pwllheli.
Carnarvonshire	Dr Thomas Hunter Hughes (c.1837–1904)	Served 1880–1904, South Carnarvonshire; at his death the coronership had been in his family for three generations.[3]
Cheshire	Henry Churton (c.1813–1897)	Elected late December 1841, West Cheshire; resigned 1897 but remained coroner for the borough of Birkenhead until his death in Dec 1897 (he was then the oldest coroner in England).

(*Continued*)

(Continued)

County	Name	Details
Denbighshire	Dr Evan Pierce (1808–1895)	Served 1848–1895, West Denbighshire; in his later years he had a deputy, Dr James Caithness.
Flintshire	Robert Davies	Active 1790s to c.1806.
Flintshire	Peter Parry (1792–1874)	Elected 4 Jan 1816 and was Britain's oldest coroner at the time of his death; succeeded by his nephew Peter Parry (c.1839–1879), who had acted as his deputy and was also a medical professional; in the 1840s his deputy was surgeon Robert Parry (possibly another relative).[4]
Glamorgan	Dr John Charles Collins	Active 1805–1824, Gower and Kilvey.
Gloucestershire	William Trigg (d.1831)	Active 1810s.
Gloucestershire	Dr James Teague (c.1822–1867)	Served 1856–1867, Dean Forest District.
Gloucestershire	Dr Edward Mills Grace (1841–1911)	Served 1875–1911, Western Division; he was also a famous cricketer, brother of the even more celebrated Dr W. G. Grace.
Herefordshire	Thomas Cotes (c.1759–1821)	Served 1790–1808; replaced after he was convicted of giving an improper charge to the jury in an inquest on a suspected murder victim.
Middlesex	Thomas Wakley (1795–1862)	Served 1839–1862, West Middlesex. Founded *The Lancet* and also served as an MP.
Middlesex	Dr Edwin Lankester (1814–1874)	Served 1862–1874, Central Middlesex.
Middlesex	Dr Thomas Bramah Diplock (1830–1892)	Served 1868–1892, Western Division of London and Middlesex.
Middlesex	Dr William Hardwicke (c.1817–1881)	Served 1874–1881, Central Middlesex, having previously acted as Lankester's deputy for 12 years.
Middlesex	Dr George Danford Thomas (1846–1910)	Appointed deputy to Hardwicke in the mid-1870s, succeeding him in 1881; at his death he served the Central District, County of London.
Monmouthshire	William Brewer, MRCS (c.1773–1863)	Elected May 1808 and served for 51 years; also a JP; succeeded by his son W. H. Brewer, surgeon.
Monmouthshire	William Henry Brewer (c.1813–1883)	Served as deputy coroner c.1852–1859.
Monmouthshire	Dr W. W. Morgan	Appointed deputy to W. H. Brewer, 1869; he was also a borough magistrate in Newport.[5]
Monmouthshire	Benjamin Meredith Bradford, junior	Manor of Chepstow c.1834–35; moved to Gloucester in 1865.

County	Name	Details
Montgomeryshire	Dr Edward Johnes	Elected c.1805 following the death of Ambrose Gethyn; also a JP; served until c.1818.
Montgomeryshire	William Slyman, FRCS (1807–1869)	Served 1845–1869, Newtown (South) Division.
Oxfordshire	Dr Augustine Batt (c.1829–1883)	Deputy county coroner, Western District, c. 1872–1883; succeeded by his son Dr Charles Dorrington Batt.
Oxfordshire	Edward Law Hussey, FRCS (1816–1899)	Served 1877–1894, City of Oxford.[6]
Radnorshire	Hector Applebury Cooksey (c.1752–1809)	Served 1794–1809; also surgeon to the gaol at Presteigne.
Shropshire	Dr Robert Temple Wright, FRCS (1843–1902)	Served Oct 1877 – May 1879, Bradford North District; removed from office for absence due to appointment to the Indian Medical Service.
Shropshire	Dr William Alma Aylmer Lewis (c.1855–1930)	Served 1881–1930, Oswestry Division; the first of three generations of medical coroners from this family.

Notes

1 *Monmouthshire Merlin*, 16 Jul 1831, p. 3. Due to Ekins' resignation and the death of the other county coroner, two replacements were elected from among three candidates, two of whom were surgeons and the other a solicitor; the second successful candidate was the solicitor.
2 *The North Wales Express*, 20 Aug 1880, p. 1.
3 *Carnarvon and Denbigh Herald and North and South Wales Independent*, 18 Mar 1904, p. 8.
4 *The North Wales Chronicle and Advertiser for the Principality*, 17 Feb 1846, p. 3.
5 *The County Observer and Monmouthshire Central Advertiser*, 7 Aug 1869, p. 4.
6 Elizabeth T. Hurren, "Remaking the Medico-Legal Scene: A Social History of the Late-Victorian Coroner in Oxford," *Journal of the History of Medicine and Allied Sciences* 65 (2009), pp. 207–252.

Appendix 5
Glossary of medical and legal terms

Abdominal cavity   The cavity within the abdomen containing crucial organs including those of the digestive system; specifically, the lower part of the oesophagus, stomach, small intestine, liver, gallbladder, pancreas, spleen and kidneys. It lies between the thoracic and pelvic cavities and is the largest of the four body cavities.

Adipocere   a greyish waxy substance formed on dead bodies by the bacterial decomposition of soft tissue in the presence of moisture. The process is known as saponification.

Asphyxia   lack of respiration. In the nineteenth century this term encompassed death by suffocation, strangulation and drowning.

Baby farming   the lodging and care of (typically unwanted) babies for profit in the form of a lump sum or weekly payment from the parent(s).

Bruise   typically occurs when an injury, such as a fall or a knock, causes blood from damaged blood vessels to leak into the skin.

Burke   to murder in a manner that leaves no or few marks of violence, as by suffocation; from the series of murders committed in Edinburgh by William Burke and William Hare (1828), who sold the bodies for anatomical dissection.

Churchwarden   a parochial official nominated annually from among householders of middling rank to be responsible for the upkeep of the local church; under the terms of the Old Poor Law, they served also as overseers of the poor.

Clerk of the peace   a legally trained adviser to justices of the peace, responsible for administering the courts of quarter session.

Committal hearing   an investigative hearing held by magistrates to determine whether a suspect had a case to answer; if the evidence supported an indictment, the suspect was committed for trial at the assizes.

Congestion   an abnormal or excessive accumulation of a body fluid; in forensic practice, this term was usually used in relation to an accumulation of blood in internal organs or veins.

Contusion   a severe bruise or injury caused by external violence.

Coroner   an elected county or borough official whose main duty was to investigate any sudden or unnatural death to which he was alerted by a member of the public. Two other types of coroners existed but were rarely involved in criminal cases: coroners by virtue of their office, such as judges; and franchise coroners appointed by the crown or by lords holding a charter from the crown.

Cranial bones   the eight bones of the cranium include the two frontal, parietal, occipital, two temporal, sphenoid and ethmoid bones.

Cranial cavity   the smallest body cavity, containing the brain.

Cranium   the skull, especially the part enclosing the brain.

Crepitation   the slight crackling noise caused by pressing a part of the body when air is collected in the cellular tissue. An equivalent term is crepitus.

Cruentation   the supposed spontaneous bleeding of the wounds of a murder victim in the presence of the killer.

Decomposition   the natural process of organic decay in dead bodies; also known as putrefaction or putrescence.

Delirium tremens   a violent delirium with tremors induced by excessive and prolonged consumption of alcohol.

Ductus arteriosus   a blood vessel unique to the foetus, it allows blood to flow between the heart and the pulmonary artery, bypassing the non-functioning lungs.

Dura mater   the tough outermost membrane covering the brain, located just beneath the cranium.

Ecchymosis   a discolouration of the skin caused when blood leaks from a broken capillary into an area of surrounding tissue. Typically, but not always caused by bruising. Because the blood has to travel through tissue to settle, ecchymosis provides evidence that, at the time of receiving an injury, blood was circulating, indicating the victim was alive.

Effusion   the escape of a fluid such as blood from its vessels into a body cavity.

Erysipelas   an acute disease caused by a streptococcal infection; it produces fever and local inflammation of the skin and subcutaneous tissues.

Excoriation   a slight wound which removes only the skin.

Extravasation   the leakage of blood or other fluid from an internal vessel into the tissue around it.

Fauces   the name given to the back part of the mouth and start of the gullet and windpipe.

Felony   a serious crime punishable by death, transportation or imprisonment; included all forms of homicide and rape.

Frontal bone   a bowl-shaped bone located in the forehead region of the human skull.

Funis   the umbilical cord or navel string.

Grand jury   a jury of inquiry made up of county gentry and magistrates who assembled at the assizes to hear the charges that were to be brought against each prisoner and determine whether they should go to trial before a judge and petty jury. By the 1760s the ideal number of grand jurors was 23.

Haemorrhage   an escape or flow of blood from a ruptured blood vessel.

House surgeon   a surgeon resident in or attached to a hospital.

Indictment   the formal written accusation of a crime upon which an individual could be tried. The details included in it had to be correct or the document was not legally valid.

Inquisition   the formal written record of the findings of a coroner's inquest; it could be used as the basis for an indictment or as a document upon which an accused individual could be tried.

Inquest   the legal proceedings by which a coroner, with a jury, investigated sudden or unnatural deaths.

Justice of the peace   an unpaid magistrate, usually a member of the county gentry without formal legal qualifications commissioned by the monarch to administer justice locally; abbreviated to JP.

Leucorrhoea   a white or coloured discharge from the vagina; usually associated with young or pubescent girls.

Lividity   an unnatural colour of the skin resulting from bruising (usually bluish-purple), carbon monoxide poisoning (cherry red), hypothermia (bright pink) or livor mortis.

Livor mortis   purplish-red discolouration of the skin surfaces of a dead body, resulting from blood draining downward as a result of gravity and pooling within blood vessels; also known as hypostasis.

Lochia   a vaginal discharge following childbirth, different in colour and odour from menstrual blood.

Magistrate   a civil officer charged with local administration of the law, associated first with boroughs but by the nineteenth century the countryside also; used interchangeably with JP.

Materia medica   the study of the origin and properties of substances used in the practice of medicine, particularly drugs. The term can therefore be understood as a synonym for the science now known as pharmacology.

Meconium   the dark green substance forming the first faeces of a newborn infant.

Misdemeanour   an offence subject to a penalty short of death, generally a fine or gaol sentence of up to two years.

Monomania   in nineteenth-century psychiatry, a kind of partial insanity in which the patient was irrational on one subject only but otherwise mentally sound. In the form of homicidal monomania, it was believed to be a disease responsible for sudden fits of violence.

Occipital bone   the bone which forms the back and base of the human skull and encircles the spinal cord.

Overseer of the poor   under the terms of the Old Poor Law, an official appointed annually by local JPs from among substantial householders in each parish of England and Wales; responsible for the financial administration of poor relief at a local level, including contracting for medical services.

Parietal bones   two bones that form the roof and sides of the human skull.

Parish surgeon   a surgeon contracted by overseers of the poor to provide medical services to the poor inhabitants of a parish.

Pelvic cavity   located below the abdominal cavity, this body cavity contains the reproductive organs, bladder, colon and rectum.

Pericardium   the membrane enclosing the heart, consisting of an outer fibrous layer and an inner double layer filled with pericardial fluid.

Perimortem   taking place at or around the time of death.

Peritoneum   the membrane that lines the inside of the abdominal cavity and encloses the abdominal organs.

Petty jury   trial jury.

Petty treason   the murder of a person by a legal subordinate such as a servant or wife.

Physic   a now obsolete word for medicines.

Pia mater   the delicate innermost membrane of the brain, which covers it and contains the cerebrospinal fluid that cushions the brain and spine.

Police court   a court of summary jurisdiction for the trial or investigation of charges brought by the police; a magistrates' court.

Police office   a term first associated with the Bow Street magistrates in London, denoting an office with regular hours where members of the public could go to lay a complaint before a magistrate. Equivalents were created in the metropolis by the Middlesex Justices Act of 1792, each staffed by three stipendiary magistrates, two clerks and six constables; known as police courts by the 1830s.

Poor Law union   under the terms of the Poor Law Amendment Act of 1834, parishes in England and Wales were grouped into unions, responsible for the administration of poor relief in their areas and each governed by a board of guardians. There were 635 unions (47 in Wales) and each was required to have a workhouse.

Post-mortem   an examination of a dead body performed to determine the cause of death; an autopsy.

Puerperal   of or belonging to, or consequent on, childbearing.

Puisne   any judge other than the most senior in the higher courts of law.

Pyaemia   blood poisoning (septicaemia) caused by the spread in the bloodstream of pus-forming bacteria; usually associated with abscesses in the body.

Recognizance   a legal bond or obligation issued by a coroner or magistrate obliging a person to observe some condition, such as to appear to prosecute or give evidence at the assizes. Usually linked to a sum of money pledged as a surety and forfeited by failure to fulfil the obligation.

Rigor mortis   stiffening of the joints and muscles of a body which typically begins a few hours after death and usually lasts from one to four days; also known as post-mortem rigidity. It is caused by chemical reactions that cause muscle to contract, is affected by ambient temperature and persists until decomposition begins.

Saponification   see adipocere.

Skull   the bony structure of the head, which supports the face and protects the brain; it is composed of two parts, the cranium and the mandible.

Spectrum The pattern of absorption or emission of light (or other electromagnetic radiation) by a substance over any range of wavelengths; appears as bands of colour. The plural is spectra.

Stipendiary magistrate a salaried official exercising judicial functions similar to those exercised by the unpaid justices of the peace; associated with police offices.

Syncope sudden but temporary loss of consciousness from a drop in blood pressure, which causes oxygen deprivation in the brain.

Temporal bones two bones that form the sides and base of the skull.

Thoracic cavity the part of the body cavity above the diaphragm containing the heart, lungs and oesophagus. Also called the chest cavity, it is the second largest of the four body cavities.

Viscera the soft contents of the principal cavities of the body; the internal organs.

Bibliography

Primary sources

Manuscript sources

The National Archives, Kew

ASSI 4: Oxford Circuit, Miscellaneous Books, Costs Books, 1856–1888.

ASSI 6: Assizes, Oxford Circuit, Criminal Depositions and Case Papers, 1719–1914.

ASSI 65: Assizes, North Wales Circuit, Criminal Depositions, 1831–1914.

ASSI 72: Assizes, South Wales Circuit, Criminal Depositions, 1837–1914.

CHES 24: Palatinate of Chester, Court of Great Sessions of Chester, Files, 1754–1824.

HO 45/1896: Police: Chief Surgeon, Increase of Salary, 1847–1848.

HO 45/4320: Police: Salary of Surgeon in Chief Raised from £600 to £800, 1852.

HO 45/9620/A15734: Home Office (Staff and Office Questions): Appointment of Analysts, 1882–1888.

HO 45/9685/A48384: Metropolitan Police: Appointment of Divisional Surgeons, 1888.

HO 45/9711/A51187: Metropolitan Police: Fees for Special Medical Reports of Divisional Surgeon, 1890.

HO 45/9847/B12197: Official Analyst: 1. Appointment 2. Scale of Fees, 1892–1893.

HO 45/10258/X67417: Home Office (Staff and Office Questions): Analysts: Duties and Remuneration, 1898–1904.

HO 45/10459/B22443: Coroners and Inquests: Payments to Analysts Out of Local Funds, 1896–1914.

HO 45/16016: Police: Divisional Surgeons: Remuneration, 1888–1912.

MEPO 2/229: Metropolitan Police: Divisional Surgeons: Post-Mortem Examinations Fees, 1889–1900.

MEPO 2/314: Metropolitan Police: Medical Fees in Special Cases: Murder, Rape, etc, 1893–1907.

MEPO 2/321: Medical: Divisional Surgeons Salaries, 1893–1895.

The National Library of Wales, Aberystwyth

Great Sessions 4: Court of Great Sessions, Gaol Files, 1730–1830.

L3542: Letter from Coroner Daniel Price to John Jones, 6 Apr 1825.

NLW MSS 193D-224D: Notebooks of Samuel Heywood, J., Carmarthen Circuit, Spring 1807 to Autumn 1820.

Oxfordshire History Centre

COR VII/5: J. W. Westell, Coroner, Medical Extra Fees, Sep 1848.
COR VII/5: Circular to Clerks of the Peace as to paying extra fees to Medical Witnesses on Coroners Inquests, 24 Oct 1848.
COR VIII/3: As to Coroners Summoning Juries and Witnesses etc Through Medium of County Police, 1857.
Coroner/City/1901: Inquest Depositions, City of Oxford, 1901.

The Signet Library, Edinburgh

L61: Notes on Lectures on Medical Jurisprudence and Forensic Medicine, Sir Henry Little-john, 1900.

Brotherton Library, University of Leeds: Thomas Scattergood collection

MS 534/4: Thomas Scattergood, Notes for Lectures on Forensic Medicine, c.1860s–c.1890s.

Online printed primary sources

The British Newspaper Archive, www.britishnewspaperarchive.co.uk/.
Hansard 1803–2005, https://api.parliament.uk/historic-hansard/index.html.
The Proceedings of the Old Bailey, 1674–1913, www.oldbaileyonline.org/ [version 8.0].
UK Parliamentary Papers, https://parlipapers.proquest.com/parlipapers.
A Vision of Britain Through Time, www.visionofbritain.org.uk/.
Welsh Newspapers Online, The National Library of Wales, https://newspapers.library.wales/home.

Statutes

See Appendix 1.

Contemporary printed works

Medical

Amos, Andrew. "Lectures on Medical Jurisprudence, Lecture II, on Medical Evidence." *The London Medical Gazette* 7 (1831), pp. 609–616.
Anon. "Important Changes in the College of Physicians." *London Medical Gazette* 18 (1836), pp. 146–149.
Anon. *British and Foreign Medical Review* 17 (1844), pp. 228–232.
Anon. "Augustus Joseph Pepper, FRCS." *BMJ* (28 Dec 1935): 1285.
Beck, Theodric Romeyn. *Elements of Medical Jurisprudence*, second edition, ed. William Dunlop. London: John Anderson, 1825.
Beck, Theodric Romeyn and John R. Beck. *Elements of Medical Jurisprudence*, fifth edition. London: Longman et al., 1836.
Brend, William A. *A Handbook of Medical Jurisprudence and Toxicology for the Use of Students and Practitioners*. London: Charles Griffin & Co., 1906.

Brend, William A. *A Handbook of Medical Jurisprudence and Toxicology for the Use of Students and Practitioners*, sixth edition. London: Charles Griffin & Co., 1928.

Casper, Johann Ludwig. *A Handbook of the Practice of Forensic Medicine*, vol. 1, trans. George William Balfour. London: New Sydenham Society, 1861.

Christison, Robert. *Syllabus of the Course of Lectures on Medical Jurisprudence delivered in the University of Edinburgh*. Edinburgh: John Stark, 1831.

Clarke, J. F. *Autobiographical Recollections of the Medical Profession*. London: J. & A. Churchill, 1874.

Cummin, William. *The Proofs of Infanticide Considered*. London: Longman, Rees, Orme, Brown, Green and Longman, 1836.

Cummin, William. "Lectures on Forensic Medicine." *The London Medical Gazette* 19 (1837), pp. 1–12, 33–41, 65–73, 97–104, 129–138, 161–169, 209–217, 257–264, 289–295, 321–328, 353–360, 385–392, 433–440, 481–488, 513–520, 561–568, 593–600, 641–648, 673–680, 721–727, 753–762, 801–808, 881–888, 913–921.

Dease, William. *Remarks on Medical Jurisprudence: Intended for the General Information of Juries and Young Surgeons*. Dublin: James Reilly, 1793.

Devaux, Jean. *L'art de faire les raports en chirurgie*. Paris: Laurent d'Houry, 1703.

Dixon Mann, J. *Forensic Medicine and Toxicology*. London: Charles Griffin, 1893.

Dixon Mann, J. *Forensic Medicine and Toxicology*, second edition. London: Charles Griffin, 1898.

Dixon Mann, J. *Forensic Medicine and Toxicology*, third edition. London: Charles Griffin, 1902.

Dixon Mann, J. *Forensic Medicine and Toxicology*, fourth edition. London: Charles Griffin, 1908.

Dixon Mann, J. *Forensic Medicine and Toxicology*, sixth edition, ed. William A. Brend. London: Charles Griffin and Company, 1922.

Duncan, Andrew. *Heads of Lectures on Medical Jurisprudence*. Edinburgh: Neill & Co., 1792.

Farr, Samuel. *Elements of Medical Jurisprudence*. London: T. Becket, 1788.

Faselius, Johann Friedrich. *Elementa Medicinae Forensis*, ed. Christian Rickmann. Jena: Wilhelm Hartung, 1767.

Glaister, John. "The Law of Infanticide: A Plea for its Revision." *Edinburgh Medical Journal* 41 (1895), pp. 1–18.

Glaister, John. *A Textbook of Medical Jurisprudence, Toxicology and Public Health*. Edinburgh: E. & S. Livingstone, 1902.

Gooch, Robert. *An Account of Some of the Most Important Diseases Peculiar to Women*. London: John Murray, 1829.

Grant, C. Graham. *Practical Forensic Medicine: A Police-Surgeon's Emergency Guide*, second edition. London: H. K. Lewis, 1911.

Grant, C. Graham. *The Diary of a Police Surgeon*. London: C. Arthur Pearson Ltd., 1920.

Guy, William A. *Principles of Forensic Medicine*, second edition. London: Henry Renshaw, 1861.

Guy, William A. and David Ferrier. *Principles of Forensic Medicine*, sixth edition. London: Henry Renshaw, 1888.

Haller, Albrecht von. *First Lines of Physiology, by the celebrated Baron Albertus Haller, MD*. Edinburgh: Charles Elliot, 1779.

Hewitt, Graily. *The Pathology, Diagnosis, and Treatment of Diseases of Women, Including the Diagnosis of Pregnancy*, third edition. London: Longmans, Green and Co., 1872.

Hopwood, J. Stanley. "Child Murder and Insanity." *Journal of Mental Science* 73 (1927), pp. 95–108.

Hunter, William. "On the Uncertainty of the Signs of Murder, in the Case of Bastard Children." *Medical Observations and Inquiries* 6 (1784), pp. 266–290.

Husband, H. Aubrey. *The Student's Handbook of Forensic Medicine and Medical Police*. Edinburgh: E. & S. Livingstone, 1874.

Husband, H. Aubrey. *The Student's Handbook of Forensic Medicine and Public Health*, sixth edition. Edinburgh: E. & S. Livingstone, 1895.

Littlejohn, Harvey. "Respiration and the Proof of Live Birth." *Transactions of the Medico-Legal Society* 16 (1922), pp. 86–113.

Littlejohn, Henry D. "How to Perform a Post-mortem Examination: The Experience of a Lifetime, and Its Practical Teaching." *The Hospital* (5 Oct 1907), pp. 5–8 and (12 Oct 1907), pp. 31–33.

Male, George Edward. *An Epitome of Juridical or Forensic Medicine: For the Use of Medical Men, Coroners and Barristers*. London: T. & G. Underwood, 1816.

Mayne, R. G. *An Expository Lexicon of the Terms, Ancient and Modern, in Medical and General Science: Including a Complete Medico-Legal Vocabulary*. London: John Churchill, 1860.

"Medical Officers of Health." *BMJ* (16 Mar 1895), pp. 609–610.

The Medical Register for the Year 1783. London: Joseph Johnson, 1783.

The Medical Register for 1859. London: General Medical Council, 1859.

The Medical Register for 1867. London: General Medical Council, 1867.

The Medical Register for 1887. London: General Medical Council, 1887.

The Medical Register for 1891. London: General Medical Council, 1891.

The Medical Register for 1895. London: General Medical Council, 1895.

The Medical Register for 1907. London: General Medical Council, 1907.

Newman, Sir George. *Some Notes on Medical Education in England*. London: HMSO, 1918.

"Obituary: Alfred Swaine Taylor, MD, FRS." *BMJ* (12 June 1880), pp. 905–906.

Paris, J. A. and J. S. M. Fonblanque. *Medical Jurisprudence*, 3 vols. London: W. Phillips, 1823.

Ploucquet, Wilhelm Gottfried. *Commentarius medicus in processus criminales super homicidio, infanticidio, et embryoctonia*. Strasbourg: A. Koenig, 1787.

Ryan, Michael. *A Manual of Medical Jurisprudence*. London: Renshaw and Rush, 1831.

Simpson, James Y. "Memoir on the Sex of the Child as a Cause of Difficulty and Danger in Human Parturition." *Edinburgh Medical and Surgical Journal* 62 (1844), pp. 387–439.

Smith, John Gordon. *The Principles of Forensic Medicine, Systematically Arranged, and Applied to British Practice*. London: T. and G. Underwood, 1821.

A Statement by the Society of Apothecaries, on the Subject of Their Administration of the Apothecaries' Act, with Reference to Some Supposed Features of Sir James Graham's Promised Measure of Medical Reform. London: Samuel Highley, 1844.

Struthers, John. *The Royal Colleges of Physicians and Surgeons under the Medical Act*. Edinburgh: Maclachlan and Stewart, 1861.

Taylor, Alfred Swaine. *Elements of Medical Jurisprudence*, vol. 1. London: Deacon, 1836.

Taylor, Alfred Swaine. *Elements of Medical Jurisprudence*. London: Deacon, 1843.

Taylor, Alfred Swaine. *A Manual of Medical Jurisprudence*. London: John Churchill, 1844.

Taylor, Alfred Swaine. *A Manual of Medical Jurisprudence*, second edition. London: John Churchill, 1846.

Taylor, Alfred Swaine. *A Manual of Medical Jurisprudence*, ninth edition. London: J. & A. Churchill, 1874.

Taylor, Alfred Swaine. *Medical Jurisprudence*, second American edition. Philadelphia: Lea and Blanchard, 1850.

Taylor, Alfred Swaine. *Medical Jurisprudence*, fourth edition. London: John Churchill, 1852.

Taylor, Alfred Swaine. *Medical Jurisprudence*, third American edition. Philadelphia: Blanchard and Lea, 1853.

Taylor, Alfred Swaine. *The Principles and Practice of Medical Jurisprudence*. London: John Churchill & Sons, 1865.

Taylor, Alfred Swaine. *The Principles and Practice of Medical Jurisprudence*, fourth edition, ed. Thomas Stevenson. London: J. & A. Churchill, 1894.

"Thomas Scattergood, M.R.C.S., L.S.A." *BMJ* (3 Mar 1900), pp. 547.

"Thomas Scattergood, M.R.C.S. Eng., L.S.A." *The Lancet* (10 Mar 1900), pp. 737–738.

Thomson, Anthony Todd and Andrew Amos. *Syllabus of Lectures on Medical Jurisprudence in the University of London*. London: Joseph Mallett, 1830.

Tidy, Charles Meymott. *Legal Medicine*, 3 vols. New York: William Wood, 1882–1884.

Virchow, Rudolph. *A Description and Explanation of the Method of Performing Post-Mortem Examinations in the Dead-House of the Berlin Charité Hospital, with Especial Reference to Medico-Legal Practice*, trans. T. P. Smith. London: J. and A. Churchill, 1876.

Watson, Alexander. *Medico-Legal Treatise on Homicide by External Violence*, second edition. Edinburgh: MacLachlan, Stewart & Co., 1842.

Wethered, Frank J. *Medical Microscopy: A Guide to the Use of the Microscope in Medical Practice*. London: H. K. Lewis, 1892.

"William Cummin, MD." *The Gentleman's Magazine*, new series 8 (1837), pp. 95.

Legal

Archbold, John Frederick. *A Summary of the Law Relative to Pleading and Evidence in Criminal Cases*. London: R. Pheney, 1822.

Archbold, John Frederick. *The New Poor Law Amendment Act, and the Recent Rules and Orders of the Poor Law Commissioners, with a Practical Introduction, Notes, and Forms*. London: John Richards and Co., 1842.

Best, W. M. *A Treatise on the Principles of Evidence and Practice as to Proofs in Courts of Common Law*, second edition. London: S. Sweet, 1854.

Blackstone, William. *Commentaries on the Laws of England*, vol. 4. Oxford: Clarendon Press, 1769.

Burn, Richard. *The Justice of the Peace and Parish Officer*, third edition. London: Henry Lintot, 1756.

Cohen, Herman. *The Criminal Appeal Act, 1907: And the Rules, Forms and Rates and Scales of Payment Thereunder, with Notes*. London: Jordan & Sons, 1908.

Cottu, Charles. *On the Administration of Criminal Justice in England, and the Spirit of the English Government*. London: Richard Stevens and Charles Reader, 1822.

Evans, Sir William David, Anthony Hammond and Thomas Colpitts Granger. *A Collection of Statutes Connected with the General Administration of the Law*, third edition, vols. 5 and 6. London: Thomas Blenkarn, Edward Lumley and W. H. Bond, 1836.

Lofft, Capel, ed. *The Law of Evidence by Lord Chief Baron Gilbert*, vol. 1. London: J. F. & C. Rivington, T. Longman, C. Dilly, W. Clarke & Son and W. Otridge, 1791.

Moody, William. *Crown Cases Reserved for Consideration and Decided by the Judges of England: From the Year 1837 to the Year 1844, with Notes Referring to American Decisions, by Hon. George Sharswood*, vol. 2. Philadelphia: T. & J. W. Johnson, 1853.

Oldnall, William Russell. *The Practice of the Court of Great Sessions on the Carmarthen Circuit: Much of Which Is Common to All the Courts of Great Sessions in Wales*. London: J. Butterworth, 1814.

Pratt, John Tidd. *A Collection of the Late Statutes, Passed for the Administration of Criminal Justice in England*. London: W. Benning, 1827.

Roome, Henry Delacombe and Robert Ernest Ross, eds. *Archbold's Pleading, Evidence and Practice in Criminal Cases, by Sir John Jervis*, twenty-sixth edition. London: Sweet and Maxwell, 1922.

Umfreville, Edward. *Lex Coronatoria: Or, the Office and Duty of Coroners*, vols. 1 and 2. London: R. Griffiths and T. Becket, 1761.

Vincent, Howard. *The Police Code and General Manual of the Criminal Law*, eighth edition. London: Francis Edwards, 1893.

Vincent, Howard. *The Police Code and General Manual of the Criminal Law*, fifteenth edition. London: Butterworth, 1912.

Wellington, R. Henslowe. *The King's Coroner being the Practice and Procedure in His Judicial and Ministerial Capacities*, vol. 2. London: Baillière, Tindall and Cox, 1906.

Wills, William. *An Essay on the Rationale of Circumstantial Evidence*. London: Longman, Orme, Brown, Green and Longmans, 1838.

Trial pamphlets

The Evidence on the Trial of John Thornhill, for the Murder of Sarah Statham, at Lymm, in Cheshire, for Which He Was Executed, at Chester, on Monday the Twenty-Third of April, 1798. Chester: W. Minshull, 1798.

The Genuine Trial of Charles Drew, for the Murder of His Own Father, at the Assizes Held at Bury St Edmund's, second edition. London: C. Corbett, 1740.

The Suffolk Parricide: Being the Trial, Life, Transactions, and Last Dying Words, of Charles Drew, of Long-Melford, in the County of Suffolk. London: J. Standen, 1740.

Parliamentary papers

1881 Census of England and Wales, www.visionofbritain.org.uk/census/.

Coroners' Committee. *First Report of the Departmental Committee Appointed to Inquire Into the Law Relating to Coroners and Coroners' Inquests, and the Practice in Coroners' Courts: Part II: Evidence and Appendices (Coroners)*, Cd. 4782, Vol. 15 (1909).

Coroners' Committee. *Second Report of the Departmental Committee Appointed to Inquire Into the Law Relating to Coroners and Coroners' Inquests, and Into the Practice in Coroners' Courts*. Part I. Report, Cd. 5004, Vol. 21, p. 561 (1910).

Judicial Statistics 1881, England and Wales. London: HMSO, 1882.

Metropolitan Police. 1880–81. *Accounts Showing the Sums Received and Expended for the Purposes of the Metropolitan Police, Police Superannuation Fund, and Police Courts, between the 1st April 1880 and 31st March 1881*. Paper No. 197, Vol. 76, p. 573 (1881).

Report of the Commissioners of Prisons and the Directors of Convict Prisons, 1899–1900, with Appendices, Cd. 380, Vol. 41 (1900).

Report of the Commissioners of Prisons and the Directors of Convict Prisons, with Appendices, Cd. 1278, Vol. 46 (1902).

Reports of the Inspectors of Constabulary, for the Year Ended 29th September 1899, Made to Her Majesty's Principal Secretary of State, under the Provisions of the Statute 19 & 20 Vict c.69 (London: HMSO, 1900).

Return of Cases in England, Wales and Ireland in Which Verdict of Wilful Murder Has Been Returned by Coroner's Jury, and in Scotland When Procurator Fiscal Has Reported Murder, 1880 and 1886, House of Commons Papers, Vol. 82, Paper Number 441, p. 417 (1888).

Return of Working of Regulations for Carrying Out Prosecution of Offences Acts, June–December 1886, House of Commons Papers, Paper Number 119, Vol. 67, p. 143 (1887).

Select Committee on Death Certification: First and Second Reports, Proceedings, Evidence, Appendix, Index, House of Commons Papers, Vol. 11, Paper Number 373.402, p. 195 (1893–94).

Select Committee on Office of Coroner: Report, Proceedings, Minutes of Evidence, House of Commons Papers, Vol. 22, Paper Number 193, p. 257 (1860).

Directories

The Universal British Directory of Trade, Commerce and Manufacture, 5 Vols. London: The Patentees, 1793–1798.

Newspapers, journals and periodicals

The Aberdeen Daily Journal.
Aberystwyth Observer.
Bath Chronicle and Weekly Gazette.
Bell's Weekly Messenger.
The Berkshire Chronicle.
Berrow's Worcester Journal.
The Birmingham Daily Post.
The Bolton Chronicle.
Bradford Observer.
Bristol Mercury.
British Medical Journal.
Cambrian News.
Cardiff and Merthyr Guardian.
Cardiff Times.
Carmarthen Journal and South Wales Weekly Advertiser.
The Carmarthen Weekly Reporter.
Carnarvon and Denbigh Herald and North and South Wales Independent.
Cheltenham Chronicle.
The Cheshire Observer.
The Chester Chronicle.
Commercial Journal.
The County Observer and Monmouthshire Central Advertiser.
The Dover Express.
Dundee Evening Telegraph.
The Edinburgh Evening Courant.
Glamorgan Gazette.
Gloucester Citizen.
Gloucestershire Chronicle.
Hereford Journal.
The Hereford Times.
The Huddersfield Daily Chronicle.
The Hull Packet.
Jackson's Oxford Journal.
The Lakes Chronicle.
The Lancet.
Leicester Herald.
Liverpool Daily Post.
The Liverpool Mail.
Liverpool Mercury.
The London Daily News.
London Evening Standard.
London Medical Gazette.

Manchester Courier and Lancashire General Advertiser.
Manchester Evening News.
Monmouthshire Merlin.
Morning Advertiser.
The Morning Post.
The Norfolk Chronicle and Norwich Gazette.
The North Wales Chronicle and Advertiser for the Principality.
The North Wales Express.
Northwich Guardian.
Nottingham Evening Post.
Nottingham Journal.
Nottinghamshire Guardian.
Public Ledger and Daily Advertiser.
Reading Mercury.
Sheffield Daily Telegraph.
Sheffield Evening Telegraph.
South Wales Daily News.
The South Wales Daily Post.
South Wales Echo.
The Staffordshire Advertiser
The Staffordshire Sentinel.
The Warwick and Warwickshire Advertiser.
Western Mail.
The Western Times.
West Somerset Free Press.
Wigan Observer and District Advertiser.
Windsor and Eton Express.
The Woman's Leader.
The Worcestershire Chronicle.
Wrexham and Denbighshire Weekly Advertiser.

Secondary sources

Books

Adam, Alison. *A History of Forensic Science: British Beginnings in the Twentieth Century.* Abingdon: Routledge, 2016.

Alyagon Darr, Orna. *Marks of an Absolute Witch: Evidentiary Dilemmas in Early Modern England.* Farnham: Ashgate, 2011.

Anderson, Olive. *Suicide in Victorian and Edwardian England.* Oxford: Clarendon Press, 1987.

Bailey, Victor. *This Rash Act': Suicide Across the Life Cycle in the Victorian City.* Stanford: Stanford University Press, 1998.

Baker, J. H. *An Introduction to English Legal History*, fourth edition. London: Butterworths, 2002.

Bates, Victoria. *Sexual Forensics in Victorian and Edwardian England: Age, Crime and Consent in the Courts.* Basingstoke: Palgrave Macmillan, 2016.

Beattie, J. M. *Crime and the Courts in England 1660–1800.* Princeton: Princeton University Press, 1986.

Beattie, J. M. *The First English Detectives: The Bow Street Runners and the Policing of London, 1750–1840.* Oxford: Oxford University Press, 2012.

Bell, Amy Helen. *Murder Capital: Suspicious Deaths in London, 1933–53*. Manchester: Manchester University Press, 2015.

Bell, Suzanne. *Crime and Circumstance: Investigating the History of Forensic Science*. Westport, CN and London: Praeger, 2008.

Bentley, David. *English Criminal Justice in the Nineteenth Century*. London: Hambledon Press, 1998.

Block, Brian P. and John Hostettler. *Hanging in the Balance: A History of the Abolition of Capital Punishment in Britain*. Hook, Hampshire: Waterside Press, 1997.

Bonner, Thomas Neville. *Becoming a Physician: Medical Education in Britain, France, Germany, and the United States, 1750–1945*. Baltimore and London: Johns Hopkins University Press, 1995.

Borsay, Anne, ed. *Medicine in Wales c. 1800–2000: Public Service or Private Commodity*. Cardiff: University of Wales Press, 2003.

Bourke, Joanna. *Rape: A History from 1860 to the Present*. London: Virago Press, 2007.

Brown, Michael. *Performing Medicine: Medical Culture and Identity in Provincial England, c. 1760–1850*. Manchester: Manchester University Press, 2011.

Burney, Ian A. *Bodies of Evidence: Medicine and the Politics of the English Inquest, 1830–1926*. Baltimore: The Johns Hopkins University Press, 2000.

Burney, Ian A. *Poison, Detection, and the Victorian Imagination*. Manchester: Manchester University Press, 2006.

Burney, Ian A. and Neil Pemberton. *Murder and the Making of English CSI*. Baltimore: Johns Hopkins University Press, 2016.

Butler, Sara M. *Forensic Medicine and Death Investigation in Medieval England*. New York: Routledge, 2015.

Cairns, David J. A. *Advocacy and the Making of the Adversarial Criminal Trial 1800–1865*. Oxford: Clarendon Press, 1998.

Clark, Anna. *Women's Silence, Men's Violence: Sexual Assault in England 1770–1845*. London: Pandora, 1987.

Clark, Michael and Catherine Crawford, eds. *Legal Medicine in History*. Cambridge: Cambridge University Press, 1994.

Colquhoun, Kate. *Mr Briggs' Hat: A Sensational Account of Britain's First Railway Murder*. London: Little, Brown, 2011.

Cornish, William, J. Stuart Anderson, Ray Cocks, Michael Lobban, Patrick Polden and Keith Smith. *The Oxford History of the Laws of England*, vol. 11, The Legal System 1820–1914. Oxford: Oxford University Press, 2010.

Cowley, Richard. *A History of the British Police: From Its Earliest Beginnings to the Present Day*. Stroud: The History Press, 2011.

Cox, David J. *A Certain Share of Low Cunning: A History of the Bow Street Runners, 1792–1839*. Abingdon: Routledge, 2010.

Crowther, M. Anne and Marguerite W. Dupree. *Medical Lives in the Age of Surgical Revolution*. Cambridge: Cambridge University Press, 2007.

Crowther, M. Anne and Brenda White. *On Soul and Conscience: The Medical Expert and Crime: 150 Years of Forensic Medicine in Glasgow*. Aberdeen: Aberdeen University Press, 1988.

D'Cruze, Shani. *Crimes of Outrage: Sex, Violence and Victorian Working Women*. London: UCL Press, 1998.

D'Cruze, Shani and Louise A. Jackson. *Women, Crime and Justice in England since 1600*. Basingstoke: Palgrave, 2009.

Digby, Anne. *Making a Medical Living: Doctors and Patients in the English Market for Medicine, 1720–1911*. Cambridge: Cambridge University Press, 1994.

Digby, Anne. *The Evolution of British General Practice 1850–1948.* Oxford: Oxford University Press, 1999.

Duman, Daniel. *The Judicial Bench in England 1727–1875: The Reshaping of a Professional Elite.* London: Royal Historical Society, 1982.

Eigen, Joel Peter. *Witnessing Insanity: Madness and Mad-Doctors in the English Court.* New Haven: Yale University Press, 1995.

Eigen, Joel Peter. *Unconscious Crime: Mental Absence and Criminal Responsibility in Victorian London.* Baltimore: Johns Hopkins University Press, 2003.

Eigen, Joel Peter. *Mad-Doctors in the Dock: Defending the Diagnosis, 1760–1913.* Baltimore: Johns Hopkins University Press, 2016.

Emsley, Clive. *Crime and Society in England 1750–1900,* fourth edition. Harlow: Pearson, 2010.

Emsley, Clive. *The Great British Bobby: A History of British Policing from the 18th Century to the Present.* London: Quercus, 2010.

Farrell, Elaine. *'A Most Diabolical Deed': Infanticide and Irish Society, 1850–1900.* Manchester: Manchester University Press, 2013.

Fielding, Steve. *The Hangman's Record, Volume One 1868–1899.* Beckenham: Chancery House Press, 1994.

Fisher, Pam. *An Object of Ambition? The Office and Role of the Coroner in Two Midland Counties, 1751–1888.* Leicester: Friends of the Centre for English Local History, 2003.

Forbes, Thomas Rogers. *Surgeons at the Bailey: English Forensic Medicine to 1878.* New Haven: Yale University Press, 1985.

Gee, D. J. and J. K. Mason. *The Courts and the Doctor.* Oxford: Oxford University Press, 1990.

Golan, Tal. *Laws of Men and Laws of Nature: The History of Scientific Expert Testimony in England and America.* Cambridge, MA: Harvard University Press, 2004.

Gray, Drew D. *London's Shadows: The Dark Side of the Victorian City.* London: Continuum, 2010.

Green, David R. *Pauper Capital: London and the Poor Law, 1790–1870.* Farnham: Ashgate, 2010.

Harris, Andrew T. *Policing the City: Crime and Legal Authority in London, 1780–1840.* Columbus: Ohio State University Press, 2004.

Havard, J. D. J. *The Detection of Secret Homicide: A Study of the Medico-Legal System of Investigation of Sudden and Unexplained Deaths.* London: Macmillan, 1960.

Hunnisett, R. F. *The Medieval Coroner.* Cambridge: Cambridge University Press, 1961.

Hunnisett, R. F., ed. *Wiltshire Coroners' Bills 1752–1796.* Devizes: Wiltshire Record Society, 1981.

Ireland, Richard W. *Land of White Gloves? A History of Crime and Punishment in Wales.* Abingdon: Routledge, 2015.

Irving, H. B., ed. *Trial of the Wainwrights.* Edinburgh and London: William Hodge, 1920.

Jackson, Louise A. *Child Sexual Abuse in Victorian England.* London and New York: Routledge, 2000.

Jackson, Mark. *New-Born Child Murder: Women, Illegitimacy and the Courts in Eighteenth-Century England.* Manchester: Manchester University Press, 1996.

Jones, Carol A. G. *Expert Witnesses: Science, Medicine, and the Practice of Law.* Oxford: Clarendon Press, 1994.

Jones, David J. V. *Crime in Nineteenth-Century Wales.* Cardiff: University of Wales Press, 1992.

Jones, G. E. *Modern Wales: A Concise History,* second edition. Cambridge: Cambridge University Press, 1994.

Jones, Rachael. *Crime, Courts and Community in Mid-Victorian Wales: Montgomeryshire, People and Places.* Cardiff: University of Wales Press, 2018.

Kilday, Anne-Marie. *A History of Infanticide in Britain c. 1600 to the Present.* Basingstoke: Palgrave Macmillan, 2013.

King, Peter. *Crime, Justice and Discretion in England 1740–1820.* Oxford: Oxford University Press, 2000.

King, Peter. *Crime and Law in England, 1750–1840: Remaking Justice from the Margins.* Cambridge: Cambridge University Press, 2006.

Langbein, John H. *The Origins of Adversary Criminal Trial.* Oxford: Oxford University Press, 2003.

Laybourn, Keith and David Taylor. *Policing in England and Wales, 1918–39: The Fed, Flying Squads and Forensics.* Basingstoke: Palgrave Macmillan, 2011.

Lemmings, David. *Professors of the Law: Barristers and English Legal Culture in the Eighteenth Century.* Oxford: Oxford University Press, 2000.

Lockwood, Matthew. *The Conquest of Death: Violence and the Birth of the Modern English State.* New Haven: Yale University Press, 2017.

Loughnan, Arlie. *Manifest Madness: Mental Incapacity in Criminal Law.* Oxford: Oxford University Press, 2012.

Manchester, A. H. *A Modern Legal History of England and Wales.* London: Butterworths, 1980.

Marland, Hilary. *Dangerous Motherhood: Insanity and Childbirth in Victorian Britain.* Basingstoke: Palgrave Macmillan, 2004.

Michael, Pamela. *Care and Treatment of the Mentally Ill in North Wales, 1800–2000.* Cardiff: University of Wales Press, 2003.

Michael, Pamela and Charles Webster, eds. *Health and Society in Twentieth-Century Wales.* Cardiff: University of Wales Press, 2006.

Mitchell, C. Ainsworth. *Forensic Chemistry in the Criminal Courts.* London: Institute of Chemistry, 1938.

Moss, Alan and Keith Skinner. *The Scotland Yard Files: Milestones in Crime Detection.* Kew: The National Archives, 2006.

Mussell, James. *The Nineteenth-Century Press in the Digital Age.* Basingstoke: Palgrave Macmillan, 2012.

Parry, Glyn. *A Guide to the Records of Great Sessions in Wales.* Aberystwyth: National Library of Wales, 1995.

Pellew, Jill. *The Home Office, 1848–1914: From Clerks to Bureaucrats.* East Brunswick, NJ: Associated University Presses, 1982.

Rabin, Dana. *Identity, Crime and Legal Responsibility in Eighteenth-Century England.* Basingstoke: Palgrave Macmillan, 2004.

Rattigan, Clíona. *'What else could I do?' Single Mothers and Infanticide, Ireland 1900–1950.* Dublin: Irish Academic Press, 2012.

Redmayne, Mike. *Expert Evidence and Criminal Justice.* Oxford: Oxford University Press, 2001.

Rowbotham, Judith, Kim Stevenson and Samantha Pegg. *Crime News in Modern Britain: Press Reporting and Responsibility, 1820–2010.* Basingstoke: Palgrave, 2013.

Sheetz-Nguyen, Jessica A. *Victorian Women, Unwed Mothers and the London Foundling Hospital.* London: Continuum, 2012.

Shoemaker, Robert B. *The London Mob: Violence and Disorder in Eighteenth-Century England.* London: Hambledon and London, 2004.

Shpayer-Makov, Haia. *The Ascent of the Detective: Police Sleuths in Victorian and Edwardian England.* Oxford: Oxford University Press, 2011.

Smith, Roger. *Trial by Medicine: Insanity and Responsibility in Victorian Trials.* Edinburgh: Edinburgh University Press, 1981.

Spence, Craig. *Accidents and Violent Death in Early Modern London 1650–1750*. Woodbridge: The Boydell Press, 2016.

Stallion, Martin and David S. Wall. *The British Police: Police Forces and Chief Officers 1829–2000*. Hook: Police History Society, 1999.

Stevens, Mark. *Broadmoor Revealed: Victorian Crime and the Lunatic Asylum*. Barnsley: Pen & Sword Social History, 2013.

Summers, Ralph D. *History of the Police Surgeon*. London: Association of Police Surgeons of Great Britain, 1988.

Summerscale, Kate. *The Suspicions of Mr Whicher, or the Murder at Road Hill House*. London: Bloomsbury, 2008.

Taylor, David. *The New Police in Nineteenth-Century England: Crime, Conflict and Control*. Manchester: Manchester University Press, 1997.

Taylor, David. *Crime, Policing and Punishment in England, 1750–1914*. Basingstoke: Macmillan, 1998.

Trow, M. J. *The Thames Torso Murders*. Barnsley: Wharncliffe Books, 2011.

Waddington, Keir. *An Introduction to the Social History of Medicine: Europe since 1500*. Basingstoke: Palgrave, 2011.

Wall, Cecil. *The History of the Surgeons' Company 1745–1800*. London: Hutchinson's Scientific & Technical Publications, 1937.

Watkin, Thomas Glyn. *The Legal History of Wales*. Cardiff: University of Wales Press, 2007.

Watson, Katherine D. *Poisoned Lives: English Poisoners and Their Victims*. London: Hambledon and London, 2004.

Watson, Katherine D. *Forensic Medicine in Western Society: A History*. Abingdon: Routledge, 2011.

Wiener, Martin J. *Men of Blood: Violence, Manliness and Criminal Justice in Victorian England*. Cambridge: Cambridge University Press, 2004.

Williams, David. *The Rebecca Riots*, reprint. Cardiff: University of Wales Press, 1978.

Williams, William Retlaw. *The History of the Great Sessions in Wales, 1542–1830: Together with the Lives of the Welsh Judges, and Annotated Lists of the Chamberlains and Chancellors, Attorney Generals, and Prothonotaries of the Four Circuits of Chester and Wales: The Lord Presidents of Wales, and the Attorney Generals and Solicitor Generals of the Marches*. Brecknock: Privately Printed, 1899.

Withey, Alun. *Physick and the Family: Health, Medicine and Care in Wales, 1600–1750*. Manchester: Manchester University Press, 2011.

Wood, J. Carter. *Violence and Crime in Nineteenth-Century England: The Shadow of Our Refinement*. London: Routledge, 2004.

Woods, Robert and Chris Galley. *Mrs Stone & Dr Smellie: Eighteenth-Century Midwives and Their Patients*. Liverpool: Liverpool University Press, 2014.

Young, Filson, ed. *The Trial of Hawley Harvey Crippen*. Edinburgh and London: William Hodge, 1920.

Chapters in edited collections

Ambage, Norman and Michael Clark. "Unbuilt Bloomsbury: Medico-Legal Institutes and Forensic Science Laboratories in England between the Wars." In *Legal Medicine in History*, ed. Michael Clark and Catherine Crawford, pp. 293–313. Cambridge: Cambridge University Press, 1994.

Andrews, Jonathan. "The Boundaries of Her Majesty's Pleasure: Discharging Child-Murderers from Broadmoor and Perth Criminal Lunatic Department, c. 1860–1920." In *Infanticide: Historical Perspectives on Child Murder and Concealment, 1550–2000*, ed. Mark Jackson, pp. 216–248. Aldershot: Ashgate, 2002.

Beattie, J. M. "Early Detection: The Bow Street Runners in Late Eighteenth-Century London." In *Police Detectives in History, 1750–1950*, ed. Clive Emsley and Haia Shpayer-Makov, pp. 15–32. Aldershot: Ashgate, 2006.

Brody, Howard, Zahra Meghani and Kimberley Greenwald. "Michael Ryan: A Biographical Summary." In *Michael Ryan's Writings on Medical Ethics*, ed. Howard Brody, Zahra Meghani and Kimberley Greenwald, pp. 17–34. London and New York: Springer, 2009.

Burney, Ian A. "Bones of Contention: Mateu Orfila, Normal Arsenic and British Toxicology." In *Chemistry, Medicine and Crime: Mateu J.B. Orfila (1787–1853) and His Times*, ed. José Ramón Bertomeu-Sánchez and Agustí Nieto-Galan, pp. 243–259. Sagamore Beach, MA: Watson Publishing International, 2006.

Crawford, Catherine. "A Scientific Profession: Medical Reform and Forensic Medicine in British Periodicals of the Early Nineteenth Century." In *British Medicine in an Age of Reform*, ed. Roger French and Andrew Wear, pp. 203–230. London and New York: Routledge, 1991.

Crawford, Catherine. "Legalizing Medicine: Early Modern Legal Systems and the Growth of Medico-Legal Knowledge." In *Legal Medicine in History*, ed. Michael Clark and Catherine Crawford, pp. 89–116. Cambridge: Cambridge University Press, 1994.

Crowther, Anne. "The Toxicology of Robert Christison: European Influences and British Practice in the Early Nineteenth Century." In *Chemistry, Medicine and Crime: Mateu J.B. Orfila (1787–1853) and His Times*, ed. José Ramón Bertomeu-Sánchez and Agustí Nieto-Galan, pp. 125–152. Sagamore Beach, MA: Watson Publishing International, 2006.

Dickinson, J. R. and J. A. Sharpe. "Infanticide in Early Modern England: The Court of Great Sessions at Chester, 1650–1800." In *Infanticide: Historical Perspectives on Child Murder and Concealment, 1550–2000*, ed. Mark Jackson, pp. 35–51. Aldershot: Ashgate, 2002.

Farmer, Lindsay. "Criminal Responsibility and the Proof of Guilt." In *Modern Histories of Crime and Punishment*, ed. Markus D. Dubber and Lindsay Farmer, pp. 42–65. Stanford: Stanford University Press, 2007.

Handler, Phil. "Judges and the Criminal Law in England 1808–61." In *Judges and Judging in the History of the Common Law and Civil Law: From Antiquity to Modern Times*, ed. Paul Brand and Joshua Getzler, pp. 138–156. Cambridge: Cambridge University Press, 2012.

Harley, David. "The Scope of Legal Medicine in Lancashire and Cheshire, 1660–1760." In *Legal Medicine in History*, ed. Michael Clark and Catherine Crawford, pp. 45–63. Cambridge: Cambridge University Press, 1994.

Higginbotham, Ann R. "'Sin of the Age': Infanticide and Illegitimacy in Victorian London." In *Victorian Scandals: Representations of Gender and Class*, ed. Kristine Ottesen Garrigan, pp. 257–288. Athens, OH: Ohio University Press, 1992.

Hunnisett, R. F. "The Importance of Eighteenth-Century Coroners' Bills." In *Law, Litigants and the Legal Profession*, ed. E. W. Ives and A. H. Manchester, pp. 126–139. London: Royal Historical Society, 1983.

Ireland, R. W. "'Perhaps My Mother Murdered Me': Child Death and the Law in Victorian Carmarthenshire." In *Communities and Courts in Britain 1150–1900*, ed. Christopher Brooks and Michael Lobban, pp. 229–244. London: The Hambledon Press, 1997.

Jackson, Mark. "Suspicious Infant Deaths: The Statute of 1624 and Medical Evidence at Coroners' Inquests." In *Legal Medicine in History*, ed. Michael Clark and Catherine Crawford, pp. 64–86. Cambridge: Cambridge University Press, 1994.

Jenkins, Geraint H., Richard Suggett and Eryn M. White. "The Welsh Language in Early Modern Wales." In *The Welsh Language before the Industrial Revolution*, ed. Geraint H. Jenkins, pp. 45–122. Cardiff: University of Wales Press, 1997.

Jenner, Mark S. R. and Patrick Wallis. "The Medical Marketplace." In *Medicine and the Market in England and Its Colonies, c. 1450–1850*, ed. Mark S. R. Jenner and Patrick Wallis, pp. 1–23. Basingstoke: Palgrave, 2007.

Kilday, Anne-Marie. "Desperate Measures or Cruel Intentions? Infanticide in Britain since 1600." In *Histories of Crime: Britain 1600–2000*, ed. Anne-Marie Kilday and David Nash, pp. 60–79. Basingstoke: Palgrave, 2010.

Madea, Burkhard. "History of Forensic Medicine: A Brief Introduction." In *History of Forensic Medicine*, ed. Burkhard Madea, pp. 13–37. Berlin: Lehmanns Media, 2017.

Marland, Hilary. "At Home with Puerperal Mania: The Domestic Treatment of the Insanity of Childbirth in the Nineteenth Century." In *Outside the Walls of the Asylum: The History of Care in the Community 1750–2000*, ed. Peter Bartlett and David Wright, pp. 45–65, 280–285. London: Athlone Press, 1999.

Morris, R. M. "'Crime Does Not Pay': Thinking again about Detectives in the First Century of the Metropolitan Police." In *Police Detectives in History*, ed. Clive Emsley and Haia Shpayer-Makov, pp. 79–102. Aldershot: Ashgate, 2006.

Paley, Ruth. "Dragging the Law Into Disrepute." In *Law in the City: Proceedings of the Seventeenth British Legal History Conference 2005*, ed. Andrew Lewis, Paul Brand and Paul Mitchell, pp. 283–304. Dublin: Four Courts Press, 2007.

Prior, Pauline M. "Psychiatry and the Fate of Women Who Killed Infants and Young Children, 1850–1900." In *Cultures of Care in Irish Medical History, 1750–1970*, ed. Catherine Cox and Maria Luddy, pp. 92–112. Basingstoke: Palgrave Macmillan, 2010.

Rabin, Dana. "Bodies of Evidence, States of Mind: Infanticide, Emotion and Sensibility in Eighteenth-Century England." In *Infanticide: Historical Perspectives on Child Murder and Concealment, 1550–2000*, ed. Mark Jackson, pp. 73–92. Aldershot: Ashgate, 2002.

Rattigan, Clíona. "'Half Mad at the Time': Unmarried Mothers and Infanticide in Ireland, 1922–1950." In *Cultures of Care in Irish Medical History, 1750–1970*, ed. Catherine Cox and Maria Luddy, pp. 168–190. Basingstoke: Palgrave Macmillan, 2010.

Shpayer-Makov, Haia. "Detectives and Forensic Science: The Professionalization of Police Detection." In *The Oxford Handbook of the History of Crime and Criminal Justice*, ed. Paul Knepper and Anja Johansen, pp. 474–496. Oxford: Oxford University Press, 2016.

Siena, Kevin. "Contagion, Exclusion, and the Unique Medical World of the Eighteenth-Century Workhouse: London Infirmaries in Their Widest Relief." In *Medicine and the Workhouse*, ed. Jonathan Reinarz and Leonard Schwarz, pp. 19–39. Rochester and Woodbridge: University of Rochester Press, 2013.

Sommers, Sheena. "Remapping Maternity in the Courtroom: Female Defenses and Medical Witnesses in Eighteenth-Century Infanticide Proceedings." In *The Body in Medical Culture*, ed. Elizabeth Klaver, pp. 37–59. Albany: State University of New York Press, 2009.

Stephen, James Fitzjames. "On Trial by Jury, and the Evidence of Experts." In *Papers Read before the Juridical Society, Vol. 2, 1858–1863*, pp. 236–249. London: William Maxwell, 1863.

Stevenson, Kim. "'Most Intimate Violations': Contextualising the Crime of Rape." In *Histories of Crime: Britain 1600–2000*, ed. Anne-Marie Kilday and David Nash, pp. 80–99. Basingstoke: Palgrave, 2010.

Suggett, Richard. "The Welsh Language and the Court of Great Sessions." In *The Welsh Language before the Industrial Revolution*, ed. Geraint H. Jenkins, pp. 153–180. Cardiff: University of Wales Press, 1997.

Ward, Tony. "Legislating for Human Nature: Legal Responses to Infanticide, 1860–1938." In *Infanticide: Historical Perspectives on Child Murder and Concealment, 1550–2000*, ed. Mark Jackson, pp. 249–269. Aldershot: Ashgate, 2002.

Ward, Tony. "A Mania for Suspicion: Poisoning, Science, and the Law." In *Criminal Conversations: Victorian Crimes, Social Panic, and Moral Outrage*, ed. Judith Rowbotham and Kim Stevenson, pp. 40–56. Columbus: Ohio State University Press, 2005.

Watson, Katherine D. "Criminal Poisoning in England and the Origins of the Marsh Test for Arsenic." In *Chemistry, Medicine and Crime: Mateu J.B. Orfila (1787–1853) and His Times*, ed. José Ramón Bertomeu-Sánchez and Agustí Nieto-Galan, pp. 183–206. Sagamore Beach, MA: Science History Publications, 2006.

Watson, Katherine D. "Is a Burn a Wound? Vitriol-Throwing in Medico-Legal Context, 1800–1900." In *Lawyers' Medicine: The Legislature, the Courts and Medical Practice, 1760–2000*, ed. Imogen Goold and Catherine Kelly, pp. 61–78. Oxford: Hart Publishing, 2009.

White, Eryn M. "Popular Schooling and the Welsh Language 1650–1800." In *The Welsh Language before the Industrial Revolution*, ed. Geraint H. Jenkins, pp. 317–341. Cardiff: University of Wales Press, 1997.

Wilson, Adrian. "Midwifery in the 'Medical Marketplace'." In *Medicine and the Market in England and Its Colonies, c. 1450–1850*, ed. Mark S. R. Jenner and Patrick Wallis, pp. 153–174. Basingstoke: Palgrave, 2007.

Articles

Aylett, Philip. "A Profession in the Marketplace: The Distribution of Attorneys in England and Wales 1730–1800." *Law and History Review* 5 (1987), pp. 1–30.

Bates, Victoria. "'So Far as I Can Define without a Microscopical Examination': Venereal Disease Diagnosis in English Courts, 1850–1914." *Social History of Medicine* 26 (2012), pp. 38–55.

Beattie, J. M. "Sir John Fielding and Public Justice: The Bow Street Magistrates' Court, 1754–1780." *Law and History Review* 25 (2007), pp. 61–100.

Behlmer, G. K. "Deadly Motherhood: Infanticide and Medical Opinion in Mid-Victorian England." *Journal of the History of Medicine and Allied Sciences* 34 (1979), pp. 403–427.

Bell, Amy. "Crime Scene Photography in England, 1895–1960." *Journal of British Studies* 57 (2018), pp. 53–78.

Bertelsen, Lance. "Committed by Justice Fielding: Judicial and Journalistic Representation in the Bow Street Magistrate's Office January 3–November 24, 1752." *Eighteenth-Century Studies* 30 (1997), pp. 337–363.

Bertomeu-Sánchez, José Ramón. "Chemistry, Microscopy and Smell: Bloodstains and Nineteenth-Century Legal Medicine." *Annals of Science* 72 (2015), pp. 490–516.

Bradshaw, Yvonne, Stephen P. Savage, Graham Moon and Kathleen Kelly. "A Different Sort of Doctor: The Police Surgeon in England and Wales." *Social Policy & Administration* 29 (1995), pp. 122–134.

Brenner, Erich. "Human Body Preservation: Old and New Techniques." *Journal of Anatomy* 224 (2014), pp. 316–344.

Brock, W. H. "Bunsen's British Students." *Ambix* 60 (2013), pp. 203–233.

Brownlie, Alistair R. "Blood and the Blood Groups: A Developing Field for Expert Evidence." *Journal of the Forensic Science Society* 5 (1965), pp. 124–174.

Burney, Ian A. "A Poisoning of No Substance: The Trials of Medico-Legal Proof in Mid-Victorian England." *Journal of British Studies* 38 (1999), pp. 59–92.

Burney, Ian A. "Testing Testimony: Toxicology and the Law of Evidence in Early Nineteenth-Century England." *Studies in History and Philosophy of Science* 33 (2002), pp. 289–314.

Burney, Ian and Neil Pemberton. "Bruised Witness: Bernard Spilsbury and the Performance of Early Twentieth-Century English Forensic Pathology." *Medical History* 55 (2011), pp. 41–60.

Burney, Ian and Neil Pemberton. "Making Space for Criminalistics: Hans Gross and fin-de-siècle CSI." *Studies in History and Philosophy of Biological and Biomedical Sciences* 44 (2013), pp. 16–25.

Clayton, Mary. "Changes in Old Bailey Trials for the Murder of Newborn Babies, 1674–1803." *Continuity and Change* 24 (2009), pp. 347–351.

Cockburn, J. S. "Patterns of Violence in English Society: Homicide in Kent 1560–1985." *Past & Present* 130 (1991), pp. 70–106.

Corfield, Penelope J. "From Poison Peddlers to Civic Worthies: The Reputation of the Apothecaries in Georgian England." *Social History of Medicine* 22 (2009), pp. 1–21.

Crowther, M. A. and Brenda M. White. "Medicine, Property and the Law in Britain 1800–1914." *The Historical Journal* 31 (1988), pp. 853–870.

Crozier, Ivan and Gethin Rees. "Making a Space for Medical Expertise: Medical Knowledge of Sexual Assault and the Construction of Boundaries between Forensic Medicine and the Law in Late Nineteenth-Century England." *Law, Culture and the Humanities* 8 (2012), pp. 285–304.

Cullen, Lynsey T. "Post-mortem in the Victorian Asylum: Practice, Purpose and Findings at the Littlemore County Lunatic Asylum, 1886–7." *History of Psychiatry* 28 (2017), pp. 280–296.

Davidson, Roger. "'This Pernicious Delusion': Law, Medicine, and Child Sexual Abuse in Early-Twentieth-Century Scotland." *Journal of the History of Sexuality* 10 (2001), pp. 62–77.

Davies, T. G. "Judging the Sanity of an Individual: Some South Wales Civil Legal Actions of Psychiatric Interest." *The National Library of Wales Journal* 29 (1996), pp. 455–467.

Davis, B. T. "George Edward Male MD: The Father of English Medical Jurisprudence." *Proceedings of the Royal Society of Medicine* 67 (1974), pp. 117–120.

Dwyer, Déirdre M. "Expert Evidence in the English Civil Courts, 1550–1880." *The Journal of Legal History* 28 (2007), pp. 93–118.

Eigen, Joel Peter. "Diagnosing Homicidal Mania: Forensic Psychiatry and the Purposeless Murder." *Medical History* 54 (2010), pp. 433–456.

Ellis Jones, Mark. "'An Invidious Attempt to Accelerate the Extinction of Our Language': The Abolition of the Court of Great Sessions and the Welsh Language." *Welsh History Review* 19 (1998), pp. 226–264.

Emmerichs, Mary Beth. "Getting Away with Murder? Homicide and the Coroners in Nineteenth-Century London." *Social Science History* 25 (2001), pp. 93–100.

Evans, Megan and Peter Jones. "'A Stubborn, Intractable Body': Resistance to the Workhouse in Wales, 1834–1877." *Family & Community History* 17 (2014), pp. 101–121.

Farmer, Lindsay. "'With All the Impressiveness and Substantial Value of Truth': Notable Trials and Criminal Justice, 1750–1930." *Law and Humanities* 1 (2007), pp. 57–78.

Fisher, Pamela. "Houses for the Dead: The Provision of Mortuaries in London, 1843–1889." *The London Journal* 34 (2009), pp. 1–15.

Fisher, Pamela. "Edmund Whitcombe and the Detection of Homicide in Georgian Shropshire." *Family & Community History* 14 (2011), pp. 3–23.

Forbes, Thomas Rogers. "Inquests Into London and Middlesex Homicides, 1673–1782." *Yale Journal of Biology and Medicine* 50 (1977), pp. 207–220.

Forbes, Thomas Rogers. "Crowner's Quest." *Transactions of the American Philosophical Society* 68 (1978), pp. 5–52.

Forbes, Thomas Rogers. "Early Forensic Medicine in England: The Angus Murder Trial." *Journal of the History of Medicine and Allied Sciences* 36 (1981), pp. 296–309.

Forbes, Thomas Rogers. "Coroners' Inquisitions from London Parishes of the Duchy of Lancaster: The Strand, Clapham, Enfield, and Edmonton, 1831–1883." *Journal of the History of Medicine and Allied Sciences* 43 (1988), pp. 191–203.

Gallanis, T. P. "The Rise of Modern Evidence Law." *Iowa Law Review* 84 (1999), pp. 499–560.

Gallanis, T. P. "The Mystery of Old Bailey Counsel." *Cambridge Law Journal* 65 (2006), pp. 159–173.

Gaskill, Malcolm. "The Displacement of Providence: Policing and Prosecution in Seventeenth- and Eighteenth-Century England." *Continuity and Change* 11 (1996), pp. 341–374.

Glasgow, Gordon H. H. "The Election of County Coroners in England and Wales Circa 1800–1888." *Legal History* 20 (1999), pp. 75–108.

Glasgow, Gordon H. H. "The Campaign for Medical Coroners in Nineteenth-Century England and Its Aftermath: A Lancashire Focus on Failure (Part I) (Published in Two Parts)." *Mortality* 9 (2004), pp. 150–167.

Glasgow, Gordon H. H. "The Campaign for Medical Coroners in Nineteenth-Century England and Its Aftermath: A Lancashire Focus on Failure (Part II)." *Mortality* 9 (2004), pp. 223–234.

Godfrey, Barry. "Changing Prosecution Practices and Their Impact on Crime Figures, 1857–1940." *British Journal of Criminology* 48 (2008), pp. 171–189.

Green, M. A. "Dr Scattergood's Case Books: A 19th Century Medico-Legal Record." *The Practitioner* 211 (1973), pp. 679–684.

Greenwald, Gary I. and Maria White Greenwald. "Medicolegal Progress in Inquests of Felonious Deaths: Westminster, 1761–1866." *Journal of Legal Medicine* 2 (1981), pp. 193–264.

Grey, Daniel J. R. "'What Woman Is Safe . . .?': Coerced Medical Examinations, Suspected Infanticide, and the Response of the Women's Movement in Britain, 1871–1881." *Women's History Review* 22 (2013), pp. 403–421.

Griffiths, Cerian Charlotte. "The Prisoners' Counsel Act 1836: Doctrine, Advocacy and the Criminal Trial." *Law, Crime and History* 2 (2014), pp. 28–47.

Grigg, Russell. "Getting Away with Murder? Infanticide in Wales, 1730–1908." *The Local Historian* 44 (2014), pp. 115–133.

Harley, David. "Political Post-Mortems and Morbid Anatomy in Seventeenth-Century England." *Social History of Medicine* 7 (1994), pp. 1–28.

Hitchcock, Tim. "Confronting the Digital: Or How Academic History Writing Lost the Plot." *Social and Cultural History* 10 (2013), pp. 9–23.

Hitchcock, Tim and Robert Shoemaker. "Making History Online: The Colin Matthews Lecture for the Public Understanding of History." *Transactions of the Royal Historical Society*, 6th series 25 (2015), pp. 75–93.

Hobbs, Andrew. "When the Provincial Press Was the National Press (c. 1836–c. 1900)." *International Journal of Regional and Local History* 5 (2009), pp. 16–43.

Homrighaus, Ruth Ellen. "Wolves in Women's Clothing: Baby-Farming and the British Medical Journal, 1860–1872." *Journal of Family History* 26 (2001), pp. 350–372.

Hurren, Elizabeth T. "Remaking the Medico-Legal Scene: A Social History of the Late-Victorian Coroner in Oxford." *Journal of the History of Medicine and Allied Sciences* 65 (2009), pp. 207–252.

Ireland, R. W. "Eugene Buckley and the Diagnosis of Insanity in the Early Victorian Prison." *Llafur* 6 (1993), pp. 5–17.

Kaufman, Matthew H. "Origin and History of the Regius Chair of Medical Jurisprudence and Medical Police Established in the University of Edinburgh in 1807." *Journal of Forensic and Legal Medicine* 14 (2007), pp. 121–130.

Kellett, R. J. "Infanticide and Child Destruction: The Historical, Legal and Pathological Aspects." *Forensic Science International* 53 (1992), pp. 1–28.

King, Peter. "The Impact of Urbanization on Murder Rates and on the Geography of England and Wales, 1780–1850." *Historical Journal* 53 (2010), pp. 671–698.

King, Peter and Richard Ward. "Rethinking the Bloody Code in Eighteenth-Century Britain: Capital Punishment at the Centre and on the Periphery." *Past & Present* 228 (2015), pp. 159–205.

Kleineke, Hannes. "The Records of the Common Law as a Source for the Medieval Medical History of England." *Social History of Medicine* 30 (2017), pp. 483–499.

Knight, Michael. "Changes to the Police Surgeon Service in Recent Years." *Medico-Legal Journal* 70 (2002), pp. 95–107.

Landsman, Stephan. "The Rise of the Contentious Spirit: Adversary Procedure in Eighteenth Century England." *Cornell Law Review* 75 (1990), pp. 497–609.

Landsman, Stephan. "Of Witches, Madmen, and Products Liability: An Historical Survey of the Use of Expert Testimony." *Behavioral Sciences and the Law* 13 (1995), pp. 131–157.

Landsman, Stephan. "One Hundred Years of Rectitude: Medical Witnesses at the Old Bailey, 1717–1817." *Law and History Review* 16 (1998), pp. 445–494.

Lane, Joan. "The Medical Practitioners of Provincial England in 1783." *Medical History* 28 (1984), pp. 353–371.

Lane, Joan. "A Provincial Surgeon and His Obstetric Practice: Thomas W. Jones of Henley-in-Arden, 1764–1846." *Medical History* 31 (1987), pp. 333–348.

Langbein, John H. "The Criminal Trial before the Lawyers." *University of Chicago Law Review* 45 (1978), pp. 263–316.

Langbein, John H. "Shaping the Eighteenth-Century Criminal Trial: A View from the Ryder Sources." *University of Chicago Law Review* 50 (1983), pp. 1–136.

Langbein, John H. "The Historical Origins of the Privilege Against Self-Incrimination at Common Law." *Michigan Law Review* 92 (1994), pp. 1047–1085.

Langbein, John H. "Historical Foundations of the Law of Evidence: A View from the Ryder Sources." *Columbia Law Review* 96 (1996), pp. 1168–1202.

Langbein, John H. "The Prosecutorial Origins of Defence Counsel in the Eighteenth Century: The Appearance of Solicitors." *The Cambridge Law Journal* 58 (1999), pp. 314–365.

Lawrence, Susan C. "Entrepreneurs and Private Enterprise: The Development of Medical Lecturing in London, 1775–1820." *Bulletin of the History of Medicine* 62 (1988), pp. 171–192.

Lemmings, David. "Criminal Trial Procedure in Eighteenth-Century England: The Impact of Lawyers." *The Journal of Legal History* 26 (2005), pp. 73–82.

Levack, Brian P. "Review of Marks of an Absolute Witch: Evidentiary Dilemmas in Early Modern England, by Orna Alyagon Darr." *Law and History Review* 30 (2012), pp. 937–938.

Loar, Carol. "Medical Knowledge and the Early Modern English Coroner's Inquest." *Social History of Medicine* 23 (2010), pp. 475–491.

Loughnan, Arlie and Tony Ward. "Emergent Authority and Expert Knowledge: Psychiatry and Criminal Responsibility in the UK." *International Journal of Law and Psychiatry* 37 (2014), pp. 25–36.

Lyons, J. B. "Sir William Wilde's Medico-legal Observations." *Medical History* 42 (1997), pp. 437–454.

May, Allyson. "Advocates and Truth-Seeking in the Old Bailey Courtroom." *Journal of Legal History* 26 (2005), pp. 83–90.

McMahon, Vanessa. "Reading the Body: Dissection and the 'Murder' of Sarah Stout, Hertfordshire, 1699." *Social History of Medicine* 19 (2006), pp. 19–35.

Milroy, Christopher M. "Neonatal Deaths, Infanticide, and the Hydrostatic (Floatation) Test: Historical Perspectives." *Academic Forensic Pathology International* 2 (2012), pp. 338–345.

Milroy, Christopher M. "A Brief History of 'Asphyxia'." *Academic Forensic Pathology International* 5 (2015), pp. 254–265.

Minkes, John. "Wales and the 'Bloody Code': The Brecon Circuit of the Court of Great Sessions in the 1750s." *Welsh History Review* 22 (2005), pp. 673–704.

Nagy, Victoria M. "Narratives in the Courtroom: Female Poisoners in Mid-Nineteenth Century England." *European Journal of Criminology* 11 (2014), pp. 213–227.

Newsom Kerr, Matthew L. "'Perambulating Fever Nests of Our London Streets': Cabs, Omnibuses, Ambulances, and Other 'Pest-Vehicles' in the Victorian Metropolis." *Journal of British Studies* 49 (2010), pp. 283–310.

Ober, W. B. "Infanticide in Eighteenth-Century England: William Hunter's Contribution to the Forensic Problem." *Pathology Annual* 21 (1986), pp. 311–319.

Oberman, Michelle. "Understanding Infanticide in Context: Mothers Who Kill, 1870–1930 and Today." *The Journal of Criminal Law and Criminology* 92 (2002), pp. 707–738.

Oldham, James. "Eighteenth-Century Judges' Notes: How They Explain, Correct and Enhance the Reports." *American Journal of Legal History* 31 (1987), pp. 9–42.

Oldham, James. "The Jury of Matrons." *Georgetown Law* (Fall/Winter 2006), pp. 50–55.

Parris, Patricia. "Mary Morgan: Contemporary Sources." *The Radnorshire Society Transactions* 53 (1983), pp. 57–64.

Polson, Cyril John. "Finger Prints and Finger Printing: An Historical Study." *Journal of Criminal Law and Criminology* 41 (1950–1951), pp. 690–704.

Roberts, M. J. D. "The Politics of Professionalization: MPs, Medical Men, and the 1858 Medical Act." *Medical History* 53 (2009), pp. 37–56.

Roberts, Stephen. "'Necessary Precautions': Public Health in Wrexham 1830–1848." *Transactions of the Denbighshire Historical Society* 45 (1996), pp. 59–88.

Robinson, Daniel J. "Crime, Police and the Provincial Press: A Study of Victorian Cardiff." *Welsh History Review* 25 (2011), pp. 551–575.

Roth, Randolph. "Child Murder in New England." *Social Science History* 25 (2001), pp. 101–147.

Rowbotham, Judith and Kim Stevenson. "'For Today in This Arena . . .': Legal Performativity and Dramatic Convention in the Victorian Criminal Justice System." *Journal of Criminal Justice and Popular Culture* 14 (2007), pp. 113–141.

Rubin, G. R. "Calling in the Met: Serious Crime Investigation Involving Scotland Yard and Provincial Police Forces in England and Wales, 1906–1939." *Legal Studies* 31 (2011), pp. 411–441.

Rudolph, Julia. "Gender and the Development of Forensic Science: A Case Study." *English Historical Review* 123 (2008), pp. 924–946.

Sacco, Lynn. "Sanitized for Your Protection: Medical Discourse and the Denial of Incest in the United States, 1890–1940." *Journal of Women's History* 14 (2002), pp. 80–104.

Shapiro, Barbara J. "The Beyond Reasonable Doubt Doctrine: 'Moral Comfort' or Standard of Proof?" *Law and Humanities* 2 (2008), pp. 149–173.

Shapiro, Barbara J. "Oaths, Credibility and the Legal Process in Early Modern England: Part Two." *Law and Humanities* 7 (2013), pp. 19–54.

Sharpe, James A. "Domestic Homicide in Early Modern England." *The Historical Journal* 24 (1981), pp. 29–48.

Sharpe, James A. and J. R. Dickinson. "Coroners' Inquests in an English County, 1600–1800: A Preliminary Survey." *Northern History* 48 (2011), pp. 253–269.

Sharpe, James A. and J. R. Dickinson. "Homicide in Eighteenth-Century Cheshire." *Social History* 41 (2016), pp. 192–209.

Shepherd, Jade. "'One of the Best Fathers Until He Went Out of His Mind': Paternal Child-Murder, 1864–1900." *Journal of Victorian Culture* 18 (2013), pp. 17–35.

Shpayer-Makov, Haia. "From Menace to Celebrity: The English Police Detective and the Press, c. 1842–1914." *Historical Research* 83 (2010), pp. 672–692.

Sindall, R. S. "The Criminal Statistics of Nineteenth-Century Cities: A New Approach." *Urban History* 13 (1986), pp. 28–36.

Smith, Bruce P. "English Criminal Justice Administration, 1650–1850: A Historiographic Essay." *Law and History Review* 25 (2007), pp. 593–634.

Smith, Greg T. "Recent Themes in English Criminal Justice History." *Manitoba Law Journal* 35 (2011–2012), pp. 285–292.

Steed, Michael. "The Core–Periphery Dimension of British Politics." *Political Geography Quarterly* 5 (1986), pp. s91–s103.

Stevenson, Kim. "'She Got Past Knowing Herself and Didn't Know How Many There Were': Uncovering the Gendered Brutality of Gang Rapes in Victorian London." *Nottingham Law Journal* 18 (2009), pp. 1–17.

Summers, R. D. "History of the Police Surgeon." *The Practitioner* 221 (1978), pp. 383–387.

Swift, Roger. "The English Urban Magistracy and the Administration of Justice during the Early Nineteenth Century: Wolverhampton 1815–1860." *Midland History* 17 (1992), pp. 75–92.

Taylor, Howard. "Rationing Crime: The Political Economy of Criminal Statistics since the 1850s." *Economic History Review* 51 (1998), pp. 569–590.

Valier, Claire. "True Crime Stories: Scientific Methods of Criminal Investigation, Criminology and Historiography." *British Journal of Criminology* 38 (1998), pp. 88–105.

Walker, Garthine. "Rape, Acquittal and Culpability in Popular Crime Reports in England, c. 1670–c. 1750." *Past & Present* 220 (2013), pp. 115–142.

Walliss, John. "The Bloody Code in Cheshire: The Chester Court of Great Sessions 1805–30." *Transactions of the Historic Society of Lancashire and Cheshire* 163 (2014), pp. 55–71.

Walliss, John. "Wales and the 'Bloody Code': The Courts of Great Sessions, 1805–30." *Welsh History Review* 27 (2014), pp. 28–52.

Walliss, John. "Crime and Justice in Georgian Cheshire: The Chester Court of Great Sessions, 1760–1830." *Journal on European History of Law* 6 (2015), pp. 38–55.

Ward, Tony. "Law, Common Sense and the Authority of Science: Expert Witnesses and Criminal Insanity in England, ca. 1840–1940." *Social & Legal Studies* 6 (1997), pp. 343–362.

Ward, Tony. "The Sad Subject of Infanticide: Law, Medicine and Child Murder, 1860–1938." *Social and Legal Studies* 8 (1999), pp. 163–180.

Ward, Tony. "Observers, Advisers, or Authorities? Experts, Juries and Criminal Responsibility in Historical Perspective." *The Journal of Forensic Psychiatry* 12 (2001), pp. 105–122.

Watson, Katherine D. "Medical and Chemical Expertise in English Trials for Criminal Poisoning, 1750–1914." *Medical History* 50 (2006), pp. 373–390.

Watson, Katherine D. "Religion, Community and the Infanticidal Mother: Evidence from 1840s Rural Wiltshire." *Family and Community History* 11 (2008), pp. 116–133.

Watson, Katherine D. "Women, Violent Crime and Criminal Justice in Georgian Wales." *Continuity and Change* 28 (2013), pp. 245–272.

Weston, Janet. "Sexual Crimes, Medical Cures: The Development of a Therapeutic Approach Toward Sexual Offenders in English Prisons, c. 1900–1950." *Canadian Journal of History* 49 (2014), pp. 395–422.

Williams, W. Llewelyn. "The King's Court of Great Sessions in Wales." *Y Cymmrodor* 26 (1916), pp. 1–87.

Withey, Alun. "Unhealthy Neglect? The Medicine and Medical Historiography of Early Modern Wales." *Social History of Medicine* 21 (2008), pp. 163–174.

Wood, J. Carter. "A Useful Savagery: The Invention of Violence in Nineteenth-Century England." *Journal of Victorian Culture* 9 (2004), pp. 22–42.

Wrightson, Keith. "Infanticide in Earlier Seventeenth-Century England." *Local Population Studies* 15 (1975), pp. 10–22.

Zuck, D. "Mr Troutbeck as the Surgeon's Friend: The Coroner and the Doctors: An Edwardian Comedy." *Medical History* 39 (1995), pp. 259–287.

Unpublished theses

Ambage, Norman V. "The Origins and Development of the Home Office Forensic Science Service, 1931–1967." PhD thesis, University of Lancaster, 1987.

Barrett, Martin Ernest. "Historical Development and Contemporary Dilemmas of a Police Surgeon." LLM thesis, University of Central Lancashire, 2012.

Bates, Victoria L. "'Not an Exact Science': Medical Approaches to Age and Sexual Offences in England, 1850–1914." PhD thesis, University of Exeter, 2012.

Crawford, Catherine. "The Emergence of English Forensic Medicine: Medical Evidence in Common-Law Courts, 1730–1830." DPhil thesis, University of Oxford, 1987.

Dean, Peter J. "Changes in the Coroner's Jurisdiction." LLM thesis, University of Wales, 1992.

Dhillon, Kallum. "Locating Crime and Criminality in Edwardian London." PhD thesis, University College London, 2015.

Duvall, Nicholas. "Forensic Medicine in Scotland, 1914–39." PhD thesis, University of Manchester, 2013.

Easton, Holly. "Communities and Interactions in Nineteenth-Century Scottish and English Toxicology." MA thesis, University of Canterbury, 2017.

Fisher, Pamela Jane. "The Politics of Sudden Death: The Office and Role of the Coroner in England and Wales, 1726–1888." PhD thesis, University of Leicester, 2007.

Grey, Daniel J. R. "Discourses of Infanticide in England, 1880–1922." PhD thesis, Roehampton University, 2008.

Jones, M. S. "Murder in Wales 1730–1830." MA thesis, University of Wales, 2005.

Loar, Carol A. "'Go and Seek the Crowner': Coroners' Inquests and the Pursuit of Justice in Early Modern England." PhD thesis, Northwestern University, 1998.

Merry, Karen Jane. "Murder by Poison in Scotland during the Nineteenth and Early Twentieth Centuries." PhD thesis, University of Glasgow, 2010.

Newell, Desmond J. "Masculinity and the Plebeian Honour Fight: Dispute Resolution in Georgian England." PhD thesis, Oxford Brookes University, 2016.

Siddons, Tim. "Suspected New-Born Child Murder and Concealment of Pregnancy in Scotland, c. 1812–c. 1930." PhD thesis, University of Edinburgh, 2013.

Ward, Jennifer. "Origins and Development of Forensic Medicine and Forensic Science in England 1823–1946." PhD thesis, Open University, 1993.

Online publications

Goldsborough, Gordon. "Memorable Manitobans: Henry Aubrey Husband (1844–1933)." *Manitoba Historical Society*, 2014, www.mhs.mb.ca/docs/people/husband_ha.shtml.

Hutton, Peter. "A Review of Forensic Pathology in England and Wales: Submitted to the Minister of State for Crime Prevention, March 2015." *Home Office*, 16 Nov 2015, www.gov.uk/government/publications/review-of-forensic-pathology-in-england-and-wales.

Watson, Cassie. "Death's Gatekeepers: The Victorian Coroner's Officer." *Legal History Miscellany*, 30 July 2016, https://legalhistorymiscellany.com/2016/07/30/deaths-gatekeepers-the-victorian-coroners-officer.

Watson, Cassie and Laura Sellers. "Thomas Scattergood: Forensic Toxicology in Victorian Yorkshire." *Legal History Miscellany*, 19 Dec 2017, https://legalhistorymiscellany.com/2017/12/19/thomas-scattergood-forensic-toxicology-in-victorian-yorkshire.

Reference texts

Black's Law Dictionary, eighth edition, 2004, www.republicsg.info/Dictionaries/2004_
   Black%27s-Law-Dictionary-Edition-8.pdf.
Oxford Dictionary of National Biography Online, www.oxforddnb.com/.
Royal College of Surgeons, *Plarr's Lives of the Fellows*, https://livesonline.rcseng.ac.uk/client/
   en_GB/lives.
UK Medical Registers, 1859–1959, www.ancestry.co.uk/.

Websites

A Brief History of Victorian Wolverhampton, www.historywebsite.co.uk/articles/Victorian
   Wolves/victorianwolves.htm.
National Library of Wales, *Crime and Punishment*, https://crimeandpunishment.library.wales.
The Poor Laws, www.workhouses.org.uk/poorlaws/.
Public Executions 1837–1868, www.capitalpunishmentuk.org/1837.html.
Wolverhampton in the 19th Century, http://historywebsite.co.uk/articles/VictorianBuildin
   gs/19thCentWolves.htm.

Index

Acts of Parliament 249–264; Apothecaries (1815) 35, 253; County and Borough Police (1856) 83, 254, 259, 272; Infanticide (1624) 11, 21, 107, 144, 145, 151, 173, 250, 253; Inquest Expenses (1837) 83, 221, 222, 256; Lord Ellenborough's (1803) 144, 151, 179, 253, 254; Medical Witnesses (1836) 36, 65n20, 83, 90, 94, 221, 255; Offences Against the Person (1861) 53, 247n5, 259
Adams, Dr James 139n108, 229, 230
Alderson, Sir Edward 181
Apothecaries, Society of 5, 35, 42, 102, 183, 253, 254
assault 11, 28n81, 55, 100, 246; sexual 209, 218
assizes 12, 15, 16, 17, 163, 250, 255, 261, 262, 279, 280, 282; circuits 15; process at 9, 18, 93, 134, 180, 252, 256; trials 102, 110, 123, 153, 154, 181, 182, 183–184, 187, 224; witness expenses 224–225, 263, 264; see also grand jury; judges; jurors; North Wales Circuit; Oxford Circuit; South Wales Circuit

Baggallay, Sir Richard 153
Balguy, John 175–176, 179, 180, 195n105
barristers 1, 93, 167, 187, 192n51, 211
Bates, Victoria 7, 201
Berkshire 12, 13, 83, 84, 104, 167, 174, 186, 206–207, 272, 273, 274
Birmingham 34, 38, 200; medico-legal expertise 21, 98, 127; police surgeons 102
blood: forensic tests 37, 48, 49, 60, 129, 202, 214, 215, 218–220, 258, 260; and infanticide 40, 44, 45, 46, 143, 155, 157, 158, 168, 169, 178, 182, 186, 281; spatter 213; see also microscope
Bond, Dr Thomas 207, 226–228, 230–232

Bow Street: magistrates' court 8, 201, 282; Runners 100, 201, 251
Broadmoor Criminal Lunatic Asylum 260
Buckinghamshire 13, 229, 238n102
Buist, Dr James Joseph 96, 97, 102

Cardiff 38, 75, 77, 91–92, 96, 97, 99, 171, 268, 271, 274
case studies: Bevan, Thomas Henry 212–214; Culley, Lucy 186–187; Hill, John 211–212; Husband, Ann 174–175; John, Martha 175–180; Jones, John Isaac 208–209; Longuet, Francis 206–208; Mazey, Benjamin 209–211; Mazey, David 209–211; Mottram, Hannah 183–185; Stills, George 214–215; Williams, Jane 173; Williams, John 211–212
cause of death 111–118; newborn infants 114–115; see also head injuries; poisoning; wounds
Central Criminal Court see Old Bailey
Cheshire 12, 13, 15, 25n30, 75, 92, 98, 109, 127, 129, 130, 132, 136n38, 151, 153, 182, 183–185, 207, 213–214, 238n102, 250, 254, 259, 261, 272, 273, 274, 275; medical profession 91, 121; see also Great Sessions courts of
child sexual abuse 5, 7, 25n34, 61, 78, 80, 115, 126
Christison, Robert 42, 47, 70n126
coroners 255, 257, 263; medical 103–106, 133, 245, 275–277; office 7, 249; pre-trial investigation 8–9, 17, 19, 39, 78, 90, 158, 201, 246; as prosecutors 9, 81; salaries 105; Troutbeck, John 228; Wakley, Thomas 35, 104, 276; see also case studies; expenses; inquests; London
coroner's officer 81, 83–85, 221
costs see expenses; fees

Cottu, Charles 9, 189
counsel: defence 10, 11, 15, 18, 85, 126, 132, 160, 164, 170, 180, 183, 188, 189, 217, 218, 244, 250, 256, 258; prosecution 11, 85, 132, 164, 168, 179, 180, 182, 189, 217, 218, 239n121; *see also* barristers; solicitors
Crawford, Catherine 3, 33
crime scenes 155, 157–158, 202–215; exhibits 207; plans of 205–206, 208, 210, 211, 212–213, 214–215, 236n35
criminal justice: history 1–2, 7; procedure 4, 7–11, 13, 18; professionalisation 7
criminal trials 4, 9–11; adversarial 2, 5, 11, 132, 189, 190, 244, 256; for infanticide 175–188; law of evidence 2, 10–11, 202; lawyerisation 7, 85, 244; medical evidence in 3, 10–11, 12, 19, 202, 211, 243–244; newspaper reports 16–17, 78, 179, 180, 182, 183–184, 192n51, 208, 212, 243, 246; prosecution 2, 9, 12, 22, 81–82, 125, 153, 202, 205, 264, 265n25; *see also* barristers; counsel; expertise; expert witnesses; solicitors
Cummin, William 20, 38, 42–47, 56, 67n60, 70n141, 73, 74, 90, 158

'dark figure' of unreported crime 17, 30n99, 130
Darling, Sir Charles 220
Dease, William *see* textbooks (forensic medicine)
Denman, George 153
depositions 13, 15–16, 109, 243; evidence from 1, 18, 40, 78, 85, 91, 94, 99, 102, 105–106, 139n112, 158, 169, 173, 200, 212, 220; pre-trial process 9, 17, 83–84, 104, 109, 179, 180, 186, 189, 236n35, 250, 256, 258, 260, 263
Digby, Anne 36, 130, 202
Dixon Mann, John 37, 66n27, 74, 167, 205
Dublin 1, 42; Apothecaries' Hall in 139n107; Royal College of Surgeons of 36
Duncan, Andrew junior 42
Duncan, Andrew senior 34, 38, 39, 41–42

education *see* medical education
Eigen, Joel 120–121, 201
Ellenborough, Edward Law, Lord 179, 180
Erle, Sir William 196n127
expenses: coroners 83, 201, 228, 232, 233, 257, 259; experts 229, 264; medical witnesses 102–103, 224–225, 230;

prosecution 222–23, 252, 254, 258, 263; *see also* fees; police
expertise 62, 108, 133, 190, 244, 245; fees 202, 221–234; historiography 3, 5, 34, 215; police surgeons 100, 101; relation to locality 13, 18–19, 20–21, 97–98, 121, 130, 134, 246; *see also* crime scenes; expert witnesses; forensic science; forensic toxicology
expert witnesses 5–6, 18–19, 20, 22, 23n13, 37, 84, 97, 101, 111, 121–123, 126–127, 199, 202–203, 221, 228, 233–234, 235n9, 244, 245, 258, 264; adviser or authority role 203, 205, 207, 209, 214, 217; fees 226–232; and poisoning 98, 132, 134, 215, 222–223, 225–226, 233, 263; *see also* Bond, Dr Thomas; Letheby, Henry; Littlejohn, Sir Henry; Pepper, Augustus; Scattergood, Thomas; Stevenson, Dr Thomas; Taylor, Alfred Swaine; Wrightson, Dr Francis

Farr, Samuel *see* textbooks (forensic medicine)
Farrell, Elaine 7, 21
fees: experts 223, 225–234, 258; in London 101, 230–231; medical education 38, 42; medical witnesses 5, 36, 221–223, 262, 263, 264; translation 30n109; *see also* expenses
Fisher, Pamela 7, 17, 99, 104, 106
Fisher, Sir John 100–101, 254
forensic medicine: academic discipline 4, 47, 73, 90, 244, 245; education 20, 33–71; *see also* infanticide; medical education; textbooks (forensic medicine)
forensic science 6, 12, 22, 129, 199–200, 202, 203–204, 215–221, 233–234, 245; *see also* blood; expertise; expert witnesses; forensic tests; microscope
Forensic Science Service 201, 233, 242n197
forensic tests 127–129
forensic toxicology 5, 6, 26n40, 127, 215; in education 37, 38, 48, 56; experts 95, 199, 218, 220, 223, 225, 232–233; in textbooks 40, 47, 64
Freyberger, Dr Ludwig 96, 97, 228

Gallanis, T. P. 10, 11
Glaister, John 37, 66n27
Glamorgan 18, 19, 75, 99, 123, 129, 130, 132, 135n9, 153, 195n107, 214, 272, 273, 274, 276

grand jury 8, 9, 16, 52, 78, 110, 224, 252, 280; and infanticide 150, 151, 180–183, 184, 187–188, 189, 194n100

Grant, Charles Graham 101, 182, 194n83, 203, 220

Great Sessions courts of: Cheshire 15, 91, 92, 93, 122, 136n47, 254; Wales 15, 18, 21, 30n109, 91–92, 153, 154, 179, 224, 250, 251, 254

Grey, Daniel 7, 31n126, 144, 154

head injuries 78; forensic examination 40, 41, 54, 64, 78, 93, 115, 134, 206–207, 209–210, 216, 218, 245; and infanticide 46, 106, 158, 164, 174, 182, 183; major cause of death 6, 20, 64, 111, 245

Herefordshire 104, 133, 208–209, 211–212, 222, 272, 273, 274, 276

Heywood, Samuel 21, 175–176, 180, 195n105

Higgs, Thomas Frederic 103, 136n54

Home Office 100, 121, 132, 201, 226, 233, 252, 263; analysts 127, 220, 225–226, 260; pathologists 127, 134n4; support for forensic science 233–234; support for medical experts 226–232

Horridge, Sir Thomas 195n108

hospital(s) 67, 83; Great Northern Central 228; Guy's 5, 37, 222, 225, 255, 260; Haywood 110; London 91, 225; Middlesex 71n162; ship 91; St Bartholomew's 217; St Mary's 101, 127, 219, 225; St Thomas's 35

Hunter, William 41, 43, 44, 58, 64, 146

Husband, H. Aubrey *see* textbooks (forensic medicine)

hydrostatic lung test *see* newborn infants

indictments 9, 13, 67n62, 79, 92, 189, 224, 250, 254, 258, 281; grand jury 181, 189; in homicide cases 104, 108, 111, 151, 153, 173, 175–176, 258; insanity defence 121, 162, 253, 259

infanticide 2, 5, 6, 7, 19, 20, 21, 78, 91, 104–105, 106, 109, 143–197; case characteristics 145–154; concealment of birth 15, 43, 46, 58, 67n62, 78, 129, 132, 144, 146, 153, 154, 160, 161, 162, 164, 174, 179–181, 182, 183, 186–187, 190n5, 254, 259; crime scenes 155, 157–158; forensic characteristics 154–173; in forensic education 40–41, 43–46, 56–60, 64; forensic examination

of suspected mother 158–160, 173, 174; forensic examination of victim 155–156, 163–173, 175, 184–185, 187, 188; infants up to one year 145, 151, 162; moral panic 182, 183; trials 144, 153, 164, 170, 175–190; in Wales 153–154, 162, 173, 175–180; *see also* Acts of Parliament; judges; midwives; newborn infants; puerperal insanity

inquests 249, 263, 264; expenses and fees 221–222, 231, 251, 255, 256, 259; forensic evidence at 48, 97, 103, 110, 159, 174–175, 184; historiography 3, 7; location 99; medical witnesses 8–9, 103, 200, 246n2; numbers of 49, 104, 132; pre-trial investigation 9, 17, 21, 78, 181, 185; publicity 35; *see also* case studies; coroners; coroner's officer; jurors

inquisitions 9, 24n22, 28n62, 79, 110, 150, 162, 264, 281

insanity 6; assessment of 4, 120–123; in forensic education 46–47, 62; *see also* puerperal insanity

Ireland 7, 157, 253, 259; medical education 36, 90; *see also* Dublin

Jackson, Mark 21, 65n6, 143, 154

Jelf, Sir Arthur 182

Jennette, Matthew 96, 102

judges 7; charges to grand jury 16, 180–182, 189; and evidence in criminal trials 10–11, 133, 218, 220; and infanticide 153, 175–183, 184, 188; relationship with trial jury 21, 85; summing up 9, 16, 182, 189, 208; taking notes in court 9, 176; Welsh 93; *see also* Alderson, Sir Edward; Baggallay, Sir Richard; Balguy, John; Darling, Sir Charles; Denman, George; Ellenborough, Edward Law, Lord; Erle, Sir William; Heywood, Samuel; Horridge, Sir Thomas; Jelf, Sir Arthur; Kelly, Sir Fitzroy; Lawrence, Sir Soulden; Parke, James, Baron Wensleydale; Pollock, Sir Charles

jurors 2, 251; and infanticide 144, 160, 170–171, 183, 188, 189, 264; inquest 83, 99, 105, 185–187, 222; views on insanity 120–121, 163; trial 7, 52, 133, 188, 203, 211, 243; *see also* grand jury; Wales

Kelly, Sir Fitzroy 182

Kilday, Anne-Marie 104, 146, 154, 182

King, Peter 6–7, 75

Lane, Joan 67n39, 97, 99
Langbein, John 10, 11, 85, 92
Lawrence, Sir Soulden 180
lay witnesses 118–121
Letheby, Henry 217–218, 223, 225, 233
Littlejohn, Sir Henry 20, 39, 43, 54–63, 237n61
Liverpool 38, 153, 200; medico-legal expertise 21, 98, 127, 223; police surgeons 102
London 6, 7, 10, 12, 13, 16, 131, 136n39, 243, 258; coroners 104, 239n113, 276; coroner's officer 84; crime 75, 76, 77, 96, 132; crime scenes 205; County Council 228, 229, 232, 263; experts 18, 127, 134, 216–217, 220, 221, 225, 227–228, 229, 232–233, 235n9, 238n99; forensic tests 129–130, 164, 215, 216–218, 220, 223; hospitals 71n162, 127, 225, 255; infanticide 151, 153, 163–167; insanity defence 121, 122, 123; medical coroners 276; medical education 20, 33, 34–35, 38, 42–47, 98, 109, 251; medical profession 66n30, 71n162, 91, 96, 109, 136n41, 249; medico-legal practice 92, 93, 99, 103, 130; police offices 252; police surgeons 63, 98, 100–101, 102, 103, 109, 137n77, 138n79, 228, 235n13; *see also* Bond, Dr Thomas; Bow Street; fees; Home Office; London City of; Medical Officers of Health; Metropolitan Police; Old Bailey
London City of 15, 256; police 274
Lushington, Godfrey 226–227, 228, 240n154

MacKellar, Alexander 226, 227, 229, 230, 231
magistrates: crime scenes 157, 205; disputes with coroners 83, 222; and experts 127, 223; medical evidence 74, 81, 174, 188; pre-trial investigation 4, 12, 19, 122, 126, 185, 243–244, 258, 264, 279; stipendiary 18; *see also* case studies; murder investigation
Male, Dr George Edward *see* textbooks (forensic medicine)
McNaughton, Daniel 257
medical defences 120–6
medical education 35–38, 98; Cardiff 38, 97; Edinburgh 20, 34, 36, 38, 39, 41–42, 47, 54–63; Leeds 20, 38–39, 47–54, 204; London 33, 35, 38, 42–47
medical jurisprudence *see* forensic medicine
medical market 4, 130, 137n64, 202; and medico-legal practice 4, 34, 37, 73–74, 108, 233
Medical Officers of Health 258; in London 239n112

medical witnesses 6, 94–99; female 106–110, 142n189; *see also* expert witnesses; medico-legal practice; midwives; prison medical officers
medico-legal practice 20, 91–93, 244; geographical distribution 74–78, 93, 97, 130–132, 184; historiography 5–7; by midwives 91, 94; offences 78–81; post-mortem examination 4, 19, 85–91, 93–94, 98–99, 122, 245; *see also* cause of death; expert witnesses; insanity; lay witnesses; medical witnesses; midwives; mortuaries; Scotland
Metropolitan Police 18, 244, 254, 271, 274; A Division 200, 228; crime scenes 205; detectives 199–200, 201, 208–209, 257, 262; and Jack the Ripper case 226, 227, 228, 229; police surgeons 100, 103, 109, 139n108, 207, 254, 263; relationship with Home Office 226–232; V Division 229; *see also* Scotland Yard
Metropolitan Police Commissioners: Bradford, Sir Edward 101, 230; Henry, Edward 232; Monro, James 229; Warren, Sir Charles 226–227, 240n154
Metropolitan Police District 131, 142n187, 254, 256
microscope 129, 208, 217–219; blood analysis 211–212, 216, 229; semen analysis 43, 61–62, 129, 202, 218, 229
Middlesex 9, 13, 15, 16, 35, 74, 131, 132, 251, 252, 254, 255, 256, 263, 276, 282
midwives 19, 106–109, 120, 126, 133, 163, 164, 169, 171, 174, 188, 194n98
Monmouthshire 13, 15, 75, 105, 135n9, 136n38, 168, 195n107, 223, 250, 272, 273, 274, 276
mortuaries 99, 106, 132, 140n149, 206, 207, 233, 258, 261; Edinburgh medical education 39, 54–55, 56, 58
murder investigation 8, 132–134, 199–242, 245; as collaborative effort 7, 201–202, 203–204, 207–208, 211–215, 220–221, 233–234, 245–246; cross-border 13, 20, 98, 134, 246; doctors' contributions 190, 199, 204, 216; *see also* coroners, expert witnesses; forensic science; infanticide; magistrates; police; police surgeons

newborn child murder *see* infanticide
newborn infants: cause of death 169–172, 175; hydrostatic lung test 44, 56–57, 59, 64, 129, 134, 145, 156, 164–169, 170, 171, 175, 179, 180, 185, 188, 245;

viability 43, 58, 59, 154, 156, 163, 179, 180, 182, 187
North Wales Circuit 15, 30n109, 92, 121, 129, 153, 238n102, 254

Odling, William 217, 219
Old Bailey 6, 15, 189, 255, 259; midwives 106–107, 169; *Proceedings* 16, 78, 205, 243; testimony 101, 102, 118, 121, 125–126, 164, 167, 182, 217–218, 221; trials 13, 15–16, 75, 81, 85, 91, 93, 94, 98, 115, 174, 192n51, 195n108
Oxford Circuit 15, 75, 92, 98, 109, 121, 122, 123, 127, 129, 200, 206, 215, 218, 224

Paine, Dr Henry J. 91
parish surgeons 9, 81, 95, 97, 109, 281
Parke, James, Baron Wensleydale 195n118
pathology 98, 127, 167; experts 205, 221, 232–233; forensic 74, 212, 234; at inquests 106; *see also* Freyberger, Dr Ludwig
Pepper, Augustus 101, 127, 141n178, 203, 219, 232, 233
peripheral regions 91, 92, 246; periphery 13
poisoning 5, 11, 118, 127, 217, 222, 253, 281; blood 49, 52, 282; in forensic education 37, 40, 41, 46, 47, 48, 50, 56, 57, 60, 64, 68n83, 245; *see also* forensic toxicology
police: called with a doctor by the public 8, 103, 134, 200, 246; caution 258; at crime scenes 145, 157, 207–208; detectives 199–200; expenses 223–225; and expert witnesses 18, 111, 217–218, 221, 235n9, 238n99; and forensic science 215, 220–221; helping victims 91; infanticide investigations 21, 158, 167–168, 182, 186–187, 188, 191n27; and local medical witnesses 37, 74, 81, 98, 103, 114, 132, 201, 216, 233; in London 252; murder investigations 4, 8–9, 103, 105, 126, 133, 201, 203, 206, 208–215, 234, 244–245; as murder victims 78, 129, 217; 'new' 8, 28n56, 93, 201, 254, 255, 256, 259, 261, 271–272; numbers of 130–133, 200, 273–274; as prosecutors 82, 202, 246, 262, 265n25; stations 99; as translators 30n109; *see also* Bow Street; coroner's officer; Forensic Science Service; Metropolitan Police; murder investigation; police surgeons
police surgeons 6, 16, 19, 20, 39, 63, 74, 91, 95–98, 100–103, 109, 133, 137n77, 142n189, 153, 187, 201, 220, 221, 227,

233, 245, 254, 263, 275; salaries 100, 102; *see also* Adams, Dr James; Grant, Charles Graham; Higgs, Thomas Frederic; Jennette, Matthew; Paine, Dr Henry J.; Ross, Daniel; Shore, Dr Harry
Pollock, Sir Charles 181
post-mortem examination: in forensic education 49–53, 55, 64; in homicide investigations 200, 205, 206–214; *see also* infanticide; medico-legal practice
prison medical officers 20, 91, 96, 110, 121, 123, 133, 162, 163, 245, 263
public analysts 37, 98, 217, 220, 221, 233, 234, 239n112, 260, 261, 263; Dupré, Dr August 231; Thompson, George Rudd 220; *see also* Home Office
puerperal insanity 62, 146, 151, 160–163, 188

Radnorshire 104, 106, 133, 140n137, 151, 272, 273, 274, 277
railways 84, 153
rape 2, 12, 13, 15–16, 19, 78, 79, 80, 86, 91, 106, 112, 124, 229, 243, 245; execution for 30n100, 256; in forensic education 39–40, 41, 43, 47, 55, 56, 60–62, 68n83; forensic examination 80, 81, 86, 87, 94, 100, 107, 108, 119, 216, 218; law 10, 81, 250, 254, 280; *see also* assault; child sexual abuse; microscope
recognizances 9, 13, 269, 282
reprieves 121, 180, 253
Ross, Daniel 98, 101
Rudolph, Julia 3, 108
Ryan, Dr Michael *see* textbooks (forensic medicine)

Scattergood, Thomas 20, 38–39, 43, 47–54, 55, 60, 63, 69n90, 94, 204, 233
Scotland 56, 71n153, 251; infanticide 58–59; medical education 36, 54–63, 90; medico-legal practice 6, 7, 34, 49, 194n92, 194n98; Ogston, Dr Francis 187
Scotland Yard 200, 203, 227, 228, 236n47, 257, 262; Fingerprint Bureau 220
sentencing 2, 144, 254, 259, 260; execution 30n100, 151, 173, 218, 238n81, 247n5, 255, 256, 259; imprisonment 105, 139n106, 170, 180, 183, 184, 187; transportation 10, 151, 237n68, 251, 253, 280; *see also* reprieves
Shoemaker, Robert 96
Shore, Dr Harry 139n111
Shropshire 13, 21, 104, 220, 238n99, 272, 273, 274, 277

Siddons, Tim 7, 21, 154, 194n98
Smith, Dr John Gordon 42; textbooks 35, 90, 192n52
solicitors 9, 10, 84, 106, 110, 186, 246, 277; Treasury Solicitor 82, 261, 262, 264
South Wales Circuit 15, 92, 121, 129, 153, 254
Staffordshire 13, 21, 31, 75, 90, 98, 110, 130, 132, 200, 216, 218, 222, 233, 259, 272, 273, 274
Stevenson, Dr Thomas 225, 231, 241n160, 260
suicide 3, 5, 17, 30n101, 53, 55, 83, 84, 94, 225, 231, 232, 269; attempted 110; murder-suicide 80, 81
Surrey 13, 15, 29n89, 142n187, 229, 254, 255, 256, 263
Swansea 31, 75, 77, 84, 129, 195n108, 268, 271, 274

Taylor, Alfred Swaine 5, 25n32, 44, 51, 57, 68n66, 200, 255; as expert 48, 54, 63, 223, 233, 238n99; textbooks 37, 47, 63, 69n98, 69n105, 90, 203, 216, 219, 243
textbooks (forensic medicine) 4, 5, 34–35, 37, 48, 59, 63–64, 66n39; Dease, William 1, 2, 22n1, 38, 39, 40–41, 65n12, 67n44; Farr, Samuel 1, 20, 34, 38, 39–41, 85, 145, 169, 175, 192n52, 252; Guy, William A. 199, 200, 235n21; Husband, H. Aubrey 48, 49, 69n89; Male, Dr George Edward 34, 90, 143, 145, 192n52; Ryan, Dr Michael 33, 63, 168; *see also* Dixon Mann, John; Smith, Dr John Gordon; Taylor, Alfred Swaine
Tidy, Charles Meymott 225, 228, 241n160
toxicology *see* forensic toxicology

Umfreville, Edward 9, 97, 104, 139n118
universities: Aberdeen 187; Cambridge 38; Edinburgh 38; Glasgow 38; London 37, 38, 47; Oxford 38

Vincent, Howard 203, 205, 262

Wales 6, 13, 20, 134, 136n38, 243, 261, 282; asylums 121, 122–123, 253; crime in 75, 81, 135n9, 209–211; detectives 200; forensic tests 129, 142n179, 164; infanticide 153–154, 162; jurors 250, 253, 260; language 18, 30n108, 30n109, 30n110, 195n107, 249, 251; lawyers 92–93; medical coroners 104–105, 275–277; medical education 38, 97; medical profession 66n34, 91, 109, 246, 257, 267–269; police surgeons 102; workhouses 98; *see also* Glamorgan; Great Sessions courts of; Monmouthshire; Radnorshire
Walsall 133, 139n111, 271, 274
Wapping 77, 98, 101
Ward, Jennifer 3, 35, 100
Ward, Tony 120–121, 161, 202–203
Wethered, Dr Frank 62, 71n162
Willcox, Dr William 220, 238n105
witnesses *see* expert witnesses; lay witnesses; medical witnesses
Wolverhampton 75, 77, 133–134, 218, 272, 274
women *see* infanticide; medical witnesses; midwives; rape
Worcestershire 93, 99, 114, 181, 222, 246, 272, 273, 274
workhouses 146, 255, 261, 282; infirmaries 98, 99, 115, 136n41; medical officer 19, 96, 97, 98, 137n65, 218, 263
wounds 40, 41, 47, 54, 70n128; forensic examination 46, 50–53, 55, 115, 118, 169, 206, 209, 211, 214, 215, 218; gunshot 48, 49, 51, 53, 69n98, 90, 216; and infanticide 169, 175, 180; stab 20, 91, 93, 109, 111, 115, 118, 245
Wrightson, Dr Francis 31n120, 216, 233